Music's Immanent Future

The conversations generated by the chapters in *Music's Immanent Future* grapple with some of music's paradoxes: that music of the Western art canon is viewed as timeless and universal while other kinds of music are seen as transitory and ephemeral; that in order to make sense of music we need descriptive language; that to open up the new in music we need to revisit the old; that to arrive at a figuration of music itself we need to posit its starting point in noise; that in order to justify our creative compositional works as research, we need to find critical languages and theoretical frameworks with which to discuss them; or that despite being an auditory system, we are compelled to resort to the visual metaphor as a way of thinking about musical sounds. Drawn to musical sound as a powerful form of non-verbal communication, the authors include musicologists, philosophers, music theorists, ethnomusicologists and composers. The chapters in this volume investigate and ask fundamental questions about how we think, converse, write about, compose, listen to and analyse music. The work is informed by the philosophy primarily of Gilles Deleuze and Félix Guattari, and secondarily of Michel Foucault, Julia Kristeva and Jean-Luc Nancy. The chapters cover a wide range of topics focused on twentieth and twenty-first century musics, covering popular musics, art music, acousmatic music and electro-acoustic musics, and including music analysis, music's ontology, the noise/music dichotomy, intertextuality and music, listening, ethnography and the current state of music studies. The authors discuss their philosophical perspectives and methodologies of practice-led research, including their own creative work as a form of research. *Music's Immanent Future* brings together empirical, cultural, philosophical and creative approaches that will be of interest to musicologists, composers, music analysts and music philosophers.

Sally Macarthur is a musicologist whose work focuses on recent musical practices in Australia with a particular emphasis on music of the western classical tradition and women's music. She is Associate Professor and Director of Academic Program (Music) in the School of Humanities and Communication Arts at Western Sydney University, Australia.

Judy Lochhead is a theorist and musicologist whose work focuses on the most recent musical practices in North America and Europe, with particular emphasis on music of the western classical tradition. She is Professor of Music at Stony Brook University, USA.

Jennifer Shaw is a musicologist whose work focuses on the Second Viennese School, music copyright and on creative practice as research. She is Professor and Executive Dean of the Faculty of Arts at the University of Adelaide, Australia.

Music's Immanent Future
The Deleuzian Turn in Music Studies

Edited by
Sally Macarthur
Judy Lochhead
and
Jennifer Shaw

LONDON AND NEW YORK

First published 2016
by Routledge
2 Park Square, Milton Park, Abingdon, Oxon OX14 4RN

and by Routledge
711 Third Avenue, New York, NY 10017

Routledge is an imprint of the Taylor & Francis Group, an informa business

© 2016 selection and editorial matter, Sally Macarthur, Judy Lochhead and Jennifer Shaw;
individual chapters, the contributors

The right of the editors to be identified as the authors of the editorial material, and
of the authors for their individual chapters, has been asserted in accordance with
sections 77 and 78 of the Copyright, Designs and Patents Act 1988.

All rights reserved. No part of this book may be reprinted or reproduced or utilised in any
form or by any electronic, mechanical, or other means, now known or hereafter invented,
including photocopying and recording, or in any information storage or retrieval
system, without permission in writing from the publishers.

Trademark notice: Product or corporate names may be trademarks or registered trademarks, and are
used only for identification and explanation without intent to infringe.

British Library Cataloguing in Publication Data
A catalogue record for this book is available from the British Library

Library of Congress Cataloging in Publication Data
Music's immanent future: the deleuzian turn in music studies / edited by Sally Macarthur,
Judy Lochhead and Jennifer Shaw.
     pages cm
Includes bibliographical references and index.
ISBN 9781472460219 (hardcover: alk. paper) — ISBN 9781315597027 (ebook)
1. Music—Philosophy and aesthetics. I. Macarthur, Sally, editor. II. Lochhead, Judith Irene, editor.
III. Shaw, Jennifer Robin, editor.
ML3800.M892 2016
781.1—dc23
                                                                                    2015029920

ISBN: 9781472460219 (hardcover: alk. paper)
ISBN: 9781315597027 (ebook)

Bach musicological font developed by © Yo Tomita

Typeset in Baskerville
by codeMantra

Contents

List of figures	ix
List of tables	xi
List of music examples	xiii
Notes on contributors	xv
Acknowledgements	xix

Introduction   1

SALLY MACARTHUR AND JUDY LOCHHEAD

PART I
The academic music machine

1   **The academic music machine**   17

SALLY MACARTHUR

2   **From the universal and timeless to the here and now: Rethinking music studies**   25

SUSAN McCLARY

3   **Music and the intertextualities of listening, performing and teaching**   36

JENNIFER SHAW

4   **An immanent approach to theory and practice in creative arts research**   46

JOSEPH WILLIAMS

vi *Contents*

PART II
Deleuzian encounters

5 **Intra-active soundings: Becoming-woman,
becoming-minor**   59
SALLY MACARTHUR AND JUDY LOCHHEAD

6 **Chaotic mappings: On the ground with music**   72
JUDY LOCHHEAD

7 **Meeting the composer halfway: Which Anne Boyd?**   90
SALLY MACARTHUR

8 **Schaeffer's sound effects**   102
IAN STEVENSON

PART III
Materialities of sounding

9 **Applied aesthetics**   117
JUDY LOCHHEAD

10 *Living colours*: **An Asian-Pacific conceptual frame
for composition**   125
BRUCE CROSSMAN

11 *Kawaii* **aesthetics and the exchange between anime
and music**   139
PAUL SMITH

12 **A musical portmanteau: Rock viscerality,
juxtaposition and modernist textures
in** *Frumious*   149
HOLLY HARRISON

PART IV
Immanent listening

13 **Immanent listening**   171
SALLY MACARTHUR

Contents vii

14 Seeing the sense: Imagining a new approach to acousmatic music and listening 179
MICHELLE STEAD

15 Listening to ethnographic Holocaust musical testimony through the 'ears' of Jean-Luc Nancy 188
JOSEPH TOLTZ

PART V
Deleuzian ontologies

16 Musical becomings 201
JUDY LOCHHEAD

17 Material music: Speculations on non-human agency in music 207
GREG HAINGE

Bibliography 219
Index 235

Figures

4.1	A model of creative arts and research processes: Smith and Dean's iterative cyclic web of practice-led research and research-led practice.	50
6.1	Map of Saariaho's, *Prés*, Movement 1, timings based on a performance by Ansi Karttunen.	77
6.2	*Prés*, Movement 1, six simultaneous strands and types within each strand.	78
6.3	Map of converging processes and surges, *Prés*, Movement 1.	81
6.4	Map of Garrop, Third String Quartet, three moments of the Gaia motive's becoming.	82
6.5	Third String Quartet, iterations of the gaia motive and chain of intervallic transformation, bars 1–12.	85
6.6	Third String Quartet, interacting systems and emergent expressions.	87
12.1	*Frumious* global stylistic block map.	162

Tables

8.1	Four quadrants of Schaeffer's listening model	109
8.2	Key concept pairs in Schaeffer's lexicon	112
12.1	Dichotomies as an oppositional music aesthetic	151
12.2	Changing metres of *Frumious*, bars 22–117	155
12.3	*Frumious* – Groove variegated timbre accents	159
12.4	*Frumious* tempo map	163

Music examples

6.1	*Prés*, Movement 1, instances of Noise events, Rising Gestures and Glisses, bars 33–46.	79
6.2	*Prés*, Pitch Areas 1 and 2 and Transitions 1 and 2.	80
6.3	Third String Quartet, four iterations of the Gaia motive: Intervallic arrangements, bars 1–12.	83
6.4	Third String Quartet, bars 187–212: Parallel major chords, bars 197–211.	86
6.5	Third String Quartet, bars 264–283, Ekstasis and the Transcendence of Opposition during bars 266–282.	88
10.1	Crossman, *In Gentleness and Suddenness* (*shakuhachi*), inside-the-note, bars 1–12.	130
10.2	Philippine *Kulintang* (Atherton and Western Sydney University gong-sets) – pentatonic and whole-tone materials.	131
10.3	Crossman, *Not Broken Bruised Reed*, resonance reduction diagram, bars 95–100.	132
10.4	Crossman, *Not Broken Bruised Reed*, altered resonances, bars 1–6.	132
10.5	Crossman, *Gentleness–Suddenness*, 'Spirit', intense confluence, bars 127–131.	134
11.1	Smith, *Kawaii Suite*, 'Mokona', bars 38–41.	144
11.2	Smith, *Kawaii Suite*, 'Mokona', bars 18–21.	144
12.1	*Frumious*, changing time signatures, bars 174–184.	153
12.2	Michael Torke, *Adjustable Wrench* layers, John Roeder analysis, bars 1–24.	156
12.3	*Frumious*, groove reduction, bars 124–129 (second part of L).	157

xiv *Music examples*

12.4a–c *Frumious*, interval stacking: Atonal stacks and 'hidden chords'.   160
   a. Chord reduction, bar 1
   b. Atonal stacks, bars 22–23
   c. 'Hidden chords', bars 22–23
12.5 *Frumious*, rhythmic textures and slap pizzicato, bars 145–150.   161
12.6 *Frumious*, dense slabs vs. pointillistic scattering, bars 134–144.   164

Contributors

Bruce Crossman has studied with Ross Edwards and David Blake and holds a Doctor of Creative Arts degree from the University of Wollongong. He also holds a Master of Philosophy from York University and Master of Music (Distinction) from Otago University. Crossman was a Composition Fellow at the Pacific Music Festival, Sapporo and his music has featured at festivals throughout the Pacific Rim. These festivals include the Tongyeong International Music Festival, Asian Music Festival in Tokyo, and the ISCM World New Music Days. The Korean Symphony, Kanagawa Philharmonic, New Zealand Symphony and Queensland Philharmonic orchestras have performed his work. His music has been featured on radio in Australia on ABC Classic FM. Crossman has won several awards, including a Finalist Nomination (Vocal or Choral Work of the Year) at the Australian Classical Music Awards 2007. Crossman is an Associate Professor and Coordinator of Composition at Western Sydney University.

Greg Hainge is Reader in French at the University of Queensland. He is the author of *Noise Matters: Towards an Ontology of Noise* (Bloomsbury Academic, 2013), a monograph on Louis-Ferdinand Céline and numerous articles on film, music, literature and philosophy. He serves on the editorial boards of *Culture, Theory and Critique, Studies in French Cinema, Contemporary French Civilization, Études Céliniennes* and *Corps: Revue interdisciplinaire*. He is also the co-editor of a new Bloomsbury Academic series entitled 'ex:centrics' that examines people, practices and movements related to the field of music and sound studies, broadly defined, that are neither mainstream nor underground. He is currently working on a monograph to appear in this series in 2016 on the French multimedia artist, Philippe Grandrieux.

Holly Harrison is a young Australian composer from the Blue Mountains in the Greater Western Sydney region. A recipient of an Australian Postgraduate award, she recently completed a Doctor of Creative Arts at Western Sydney University. Harrison's music has been performed in Australia, Asia, Europe and the USA by the Melbourne Symphony Orchestra, Orkest de Ereprijs, Alarm Will Sound, The Riot Ensemble, Cabrillo Festival Orchestra, Minot Symphony Orchestra, Hwaum Chamber Orchestra, National Taiwan Normal University Orchestra, Jason Noble and Antonietta Loffredo. Harrison's awards include First Prize at the 2014 Young Composers Meeting in Apeldoorn, The Netherlands, and first place at the inaugural 2013 Pyeongchon Arts Hall International Chamber Music Composition Competition, South Korea. Harrison is currently working on commissions for the Sydney Youth Orchestra, Ensemble Offspring, and the Orchestra of the 21st Century, a combined ensemble of het gelders Orkest and Orkets de Ereprijs. She also plays the drum kit in an experimental rock duo, Tabua-Harrison.

Judy Lochhead is a theorist and musicologist whose work focuses on the most recent musical practices in North America and Europe, with particular emphasis on music of the Western classical tradition. Lochhead has articles appearing in such journals as *Music Theory Spectrum*, the *Journal of the American Musicological Society*, *Music Theory Online*, *Theory and Practice*, *In Theory Only* and in various edited collections. With Joseph Auner, Lochhead co-edited *Postmodern Music/Postmodern Thought* (Routledge, 2001). In 2015, Routledge published her monograph *Reconceiving Structure in Contemporary Music: New Tools in Theory and Analysis*. More details on Lochhead's work may be accessed at: www.judylochhead.com.

Sally Macarthur is Director of Academic Program (Bachelor of Music and Master of Creative Music Therapy), and Associate Professor of Musicology at Western Sydney University. Her work focuses on recent musical practices in Australia with a particular emphasis on music of the Western classical tradition and women's music. Her recent monograph, *Towards a Twenty-First-Century Feminist Politics of Music* (Ashgate, 2010), applies feminist theory and the philosophy Deleuze and Guattari to the analysis of music. Other books include *Feminist Aesthetics in Music* (Greenwood Press, 2002), with co-editors, Bruce Crossman and Ronaldo Morelos, *Intercultural Music: Creation and Interpretation* (AMC, 2006) and, with co-editor Cate Poynton, *Musics and Feminisms* (AMC, 1999). She has published in a number of scholarly journals such as *Australian Feminist Studies*, *Radical Musicology*, *Cultural Studies Review* and *Musicology Australia*.

Susan McClary (PhD, Harvard) is Professor of Music at Case Western Reserve University; she has also taught at the University of Minnesota, McGill University, UC Berkeley, University of Oslo, and UCLA. Her research focuses on the cultural analysis of music, both the European canon and contemporary popular genres. Best known for her book *Feminine Endings: Music, Gender, and Sexuality*, she is also author of *Georges Bizet:* Carmen; *Conventional Wisdom: The Content of Musical Form*, *Modal Subjectivities: Renaissance Self-Fashioning in the Italian Madrigal*, *Reading Music: Selected Essays by Susan McClary*, *Desire and Pleasure in Seventeenth-Century Music* and *Structures of Feeling in Seventeenth-Century Expressive Culture*. Her work has been translated into at least 20 languages. McClary received a MacArthur Foundation Fellowship in 1995.

Jennifer Shaw is Professor and Executive Dean of the Faculty of Arts at the University of Adelaide, a role that oversees the Elder Conservatorium of Music, the Schools of Education, Humanities and Social Sciences, seven research centres, plus a node of the Australian Research Council's Centre of Excellence in the History of Emotions. Jennie holds qualifications in music and law from the University of Sydney and an MA and PhD from Stony Brook University. A musicologist and oboist, her research and teaching interests cross the arts and humanities broadly, with a particular focus on the Second Viennese School, music copyright and on creative practice as research. Publications include *The Cambridge Companion to Schoenberg* (2010), co-edited with Joseph Auner. Jennie is Deputy Chair of the Australian Music Examinations Board, Reviews Editor for *Musicology Australia* and on the Management Committee of the J. M. Coetzee Centre for Creative Practice.

Paul Smith is a composer and director based in Sydney. He holds a Doctorate of Creative Arts from Western Sydney University where he works as a sessional lecturer in musicology. He has also worked as a music theory lecturer and research supervisor for the University of New England. His compositions have been recorded and performed in Australia, New Zealand and Italy. His most recent collaboration has been with the Sydney-based Blush Opera in which he composed a two-person cabaret opera entitled *Fancy Me Dead*. This work premiered in Hobart and Sydney in 2015. Future projects return him to his interest in Japanese art aesthetics with a commissioned chamber opera based on an original story entitled *The Spider Maiden and the Runaway Plum Blossom* being planned for a performance in Singapore in 2016.

Michelle Stead is a PhD candidate at Western Sydney University where she also teaches musicology. She was awarded first class honours and was the recipient of the University medal for outstanding scholarship. Her PhD considers the creative role of discourse in relation to the development of knowledge surrounding listening to electroacoustic music. She is particularly interested in how knowledge moves from simply being discursive to how it is physically taken up as a listening practice.

Ian Stevenson is a lecturer in Sound Technologies in the School of Humanities and Communication Arts at Western Sydney University. He recently completed a PhD at the University of Sydney in 'radical sound design'. His research interests are in sound studies, the philosophy of sound, sonic communication and sound design. In recent years he has produced and engineered a number of CDs of contemporary chamber music, produced gallery installation works and completed a series of collaborative projects with the performer Tess De Quincey and the author/academic Jane Goodall. Prior to joining Western Sydney University in 2004, he held a variety of positions in product and information management for leading Australian technology companies and worked in theatre sound design and system engineering in Australia and the UK. He has worked as an artist, engineer, sound designer and production supervisor in galleries, theatre, live music, broadcast and post-production in Australia and Europe.

xviii *Contributors*

Joseph Toltz, PhD, is Research Fellow at the Sydney Conservatorium of Music, and Early Career Researcher for 'Performing the Jewish Archive', a three-year Arts and Humanities Research Council (AHRC) project spanning four continents. A former Fellow at the United States Holocaust Memorial Museum, he has spoken at 23 international conferences and institutions over the past three years. Currently completing his research on the musical recordings from the 1946 interviews conducted by David Boder in Displaced Persons' homes and camps in Europe, he is also documenting David Bloch's oral history archive of Terezín survivors, and working on the first published Holocaust songbook (1945). Joseph continues work as a professional singer, composer and arranger. In August 2014 at the Angel Place Recital Hall, he staged the first Sydney performances of the children's opera *Brundibár*, the most popular and beloved work performed in the Terezín Ghetto.

Joseph Williams is a guitarist and a PhD candidate in musicology at Western Sydney University. His doctoral research aims to evaluate the influence of Deleuzian philosophy in the field of musicology, and to extend it by employing a Deleuzian process of concept creation that is plugged into the specific problems of musical performance. He is also following his tangential academic interests in practice-led research and in the musical philosophy of busking.

Acknowledgements

This edited collection would not have been possible without the encouragement of the Philosophy Initiative (research group) and its Director, Dimitris Vardoulakis, School of Humanities and Communication Arts, Western Sydney University. This group very generously supported two symposia leading to the publication of this book: An Immanent Future: Music Beyond Past and Present with keynote addresses by Judy Lochhead, Jennie Shaw and Greg Hainge (August 2012); and An Immanent Future: Music and Philosophy Sydney Seminar, which included a distinguished panel of speakers, Professors Susan McClary (Case Western Reserve University), Robert Walser (Case Western Reserve University), Kate Stevens (MARCS Institute, Western Sydney University) and Roger Dean (MARCS Institute, Western Sydney University) (June 2013).

Sally Macarthur is grateful to the Dean, Professor Peter Hutchings, School of Humanities and Communication Arts, Western Sydney University, for his support both of the Philosophy Initiative projects and also of the Crossing Boundaries in Music Postgraduate Conference which featured keynote addresses by Professors Susan McClary and Robert Walser (June 2013).

Sally Macarthur also recognises the generous support of Deputy Dean, Professor Lynette Sheridan Burns, School of Humanities and Communication Arts, Western Sydney University. She also thanks her colleagues in Music and the many postgraduate students in Music who participated in the lively discussions of the two symposia and the postgraduate conference.

Thanks are also extended to the very hard-working administrative staff in the School of Humanities and Communication Arts, Western Sydney University, who assisted with the travel and accommodation arrangements of the distinguished guest speakers, Greg Hainge, Judy Lochhead, Susan McClary, Jennie Shaw and Robert Walser. Notable mention for their tireless work is made to Jenny Purcell, School Manager, and Robyn Mercer, administrative assistant.

Judy Lochhead recognises the assistance of the Department of Music at Stony Brook University under the leadership of Perry Goldstein, who made available the editorial assistance of two PhD students in the preparation of the manuscript for publication. Thanks to Hayley Roud and Michael Boerner for their expert editorial work. Judy also recognises the assistance of the Dean of the College of Arts xx *Acknowledgements*

and Sciences, Sacha Kopp, for granting her the additional semester of research leave during the Spring of 2015.

Finally, Heidi Bishop, commissioning editor at Ashgate, offered very helpful advice throughout the period of the book's gestation and publication process. Thanks are also extended to Michael Bourne, Editorial Administrator for Humanities at Ashgate for his helpful advice on a number of editorial and logistical matters. Our thanks to all at Routledge and Ashgate who had a hand in assisting with the production of this book.

Sally Macarthur
Judy Lochhead
Jennifer Shaw
March 2016

Introduction

Sally Macarthur and Judy Lochhead

Music's Immanent Future addresses music from multiple perspectives and from a cross-section of scholars. Drawn to musical sound as a powerful form of non-verbal communication, the authors include musicologists, philosophers, music theorists, ethnomusicologists and composers. The chapters assembled in this collection point to the diversity of musical practices and of thinking about those practices in the twenty-first century. The immanent philosophy of Gilles Deleuze, and that of Deleuze in collaboration with Félix Guattari, is mobilised throughout the pages of this book for considering a series of questions about music.[1] The chapters of this collection ask who we are as musicians and how we might encounter music in the rapidly changing world of the twenty-first century. We ponder the ways in which we might reconcile old ways of thinking and writing about music with new ways of thinking that are opened up by Deleuzian philosophy. While not all of the authors in this volume are directly inspired by Deleuzian philosophy, this book as a whole maps out a Deleuzian generative network of relations. In juxtaposing these chapters we intend to demonstrate how their differences can serve a generative function for music scholarship and in particular how they embody a Deleuzian turn in music studies. Our goal in this collection is to demonstrate how Deleuzian thought illuminates the productive potential of these differences for music.

The diversity of perspectives brought together in this collection points to musical immanence. Rather than proposing a single, over-arching concept or theory that might establish an identifying thread through the chapters, we instead foster the diversity of practices and perspectives, allowing their interactions to generate the potentials for new, emergent modes of musical thinking. The immanent philosophy of Deleuze provides profoundly insightful and productive concepts for engaging this diversity.[2] His philosophy does not impose a counter-order but revitalises thinking itself, and especially outmoded thinking within the academy. Such a renewal of the sheer project of thinking brings a fresh, dynamic perspective to the research domain. The project of Deleuzian philosophy is the creation of concepts, diverging from the conventional propositional thinking of philosophy 'proper'. Within music studies, Deleuzian thought has inspired a number of recent researchers, yet his philosophy is not always well-received in this discipline. Many find the philosophical terms difficult, and do not always see the point in its futural orientation or to the virtual plane which resists the striated and segmented

2 Sally Macarthur and Judy Lochhead

ways of thinking. These aspects of Deleuze's thought are sometimes unsettling, leading some of the most erudite and forward thinkers in music to regard it with suspicion.[3] One of our goals in *Music's Immanent Future* is to exemplify the productive potentials of Deleuzian thought, to demonstrate how the Deleuzian turn promotes thinking about the issues and problems of the twenty-first century.

Some of the chapters in *Music's Immanent Future* engage Deleuzian concepts directly; some are located in the thought of other poststructuralist philosophers, such as Michel Foucault, Julia Kristeva and Jean-Luc Nancy; and some unfold a personal philosophy arising from the sensations and embodied knowing of music making. Each contributor investigates a different problem from a different perspective. To demonstrate how Deleuzian thought illuminates the productive potential of these differences, we have incorporated five 'folding chapters' with generative potentials. These chapters preface each of the five parts of the book and fold, following Deleuze's idea of the 'fold', the conceptual and practical implications of the other chapters in this collection. Deleuze develops the concept of the 'fold' in his work on Foucault and Leibniz.[1] He advances the idea that there are not two kinds of being — a subject and an object, or inert matter and a representing subject — but rather that life is an infinity of folds. Following Colebrook, the idea of the infinite fold produces 'one virtual whole of being that is then given or actualised through an infinity of perceptions'.[5]

Deleuze's concept of the virtual breathes life into *Music's Immanent Future*. Referring to the real potentialities that are actualised in the world, the virtual allows the collected chapters to exceed a set of single ideas as presented by a set of single authors. To view the book as such a set limits its potential and leads to privileging the identity of the author. The identity-of-the-author perspective gives the illusion of representing a single world-view of music as dictated by an authorising voice. Deleuze's concept of the 'fold' opens up another level that enables us to work against the idea of representing a single point of view. The virtual makes possible an infinite array of experiences in which an infinity of perceptions are folded into the book from the outside. Connecting and reconnecting the multiple strands of the authored chapters, the first or "folding" chapters in each part, together with the multitude of ideas from the readership, create origami-like movements within and beyond the chapters of the collection and show their generative potential for music scholarship. The fold becomes both the critique of typical accounts of music, which assumes music to have an essence, surface and depth, and a multiplicity, in which the writing about music moves through multiple sites into the minds, bodies and hearts of readers and listeners, each of whom engage with the book in entirely different ways. In this sense, there is no boundary between the book and the human subject, or between the authors and readers of this book. To draw on O'Sullivan, the organic (human) and inorganic (book) is 'folded into the other in a continuous texturology'.[6] We argue, then, that even when some of the authors of the book seem to be located in older paradigms, such as those who are consciously representing their musical worlds, their thoughts are folded with our thoughts.

It is well known that Deleuze wrote a series of works on important figures in philosophy (Hume, Bergson, Nietzsche, Kant and Spinoza) with the aim of uncovering the assumptions that lead to the privileging of identity over difference. His whole project aimed to pursue a fully immanent critique. Since, as Deleuze argues, philosophy is the production of concepts, his own often idiosyncratic readings of historical figures have as their goal the production of new thought, of new concepts. For Deleuze, philosophy is never fixed: there is always room for other images of thought. In a similar vein, we engage with the images of thought presented by the authors in this volume to open up, through our own styles of conceptual thought, other images of thought.[7] Forces of the outside fold to the inside. Folds from the outside disturb and challenge the territorial spaces of the inside.

Mapping the Deleuzian terrain

We have grouped the chapters of *Music's Immanent Future* into five thematic parts. The five opening chapters of these parts fold the conceptual and practical implications that emerge from the interaction of the parts' chapters and they elaborate on specific Deleuzian concepts. The next section of the introduction maps out these concepts, providing a taste of the terms and ideas that flow through and interact within the several chapters. While presented here according to the sequence of parts, the concepts apply across the several chapters. The five parts are: 'The Academic Music Machine', 'Deleuzian Encounters', 'Materialities of Sounding', 'Immanent Listening' and 'Deleuzian Ontologies'.

The academic music machine

In the first chapter, 'The Academic Music Machine', the concepts of 'machine', 'assemblage' and 'machinic assemblage' introduce a Deleuzian approach to thinking about the entity of the tertiary music institution. The *Oxford Dictionary* defines assemblage as 'the fitting together of a number of components'.[8] It implies that the various components pre-exist the assemblage. In their coming together, they create a whole in the manner of the pieces of a jig-saw puzzle being assembled. Deleuze and Guattari eschew the idea of the whole pre-existing its connections. Instead, they conceive of the assemblage as dynamic and emergent, constituted as a becoming. Becomings arise from the processes involved in their emergence, and from thought, or the virtual world, that gives rise to these becomings. Livesey says that the Deleuzian assemblage derives from the French concept of *agencement* (arrangement), which captures the idea of 'the processes of arranging, organising, and fitting together'.[9] The emphasis in a Deleuzian conception, then, is that the assemblage is continuously evolving and constantly under construction and/or deconstruction and/or reconstruction. Deleuze and Guattari suggests that the assemblage is driven by an abstract machine. It is this aspect of the assemblage that makes it operational, such as when bodies connect with other bodies, and when bodies connect with other components involved in the processes that form the assemblage. For example, a piano assemblage might consist of a body, fingers, keys, and musical sounds. The various components would be assembled to produce a piano-machinic-assemblage.

The piano-machine would be thus formed from the processes that give rise to the assemblage, and the body connecting with the inert object of the piano would make it operational.

The idea that the assemblage is a fluid, malleable and ever-changing entity is sometimes resisted in higher education music institutions. Many such institutions are divided into rigidly defined camps. These camps, which we might also call 'assemblages', are sometimes determined by the nature of their activities and sometimes by the activities underpinning the disciplinary expertise of a particular group within an assemblage.[10] Often these activities will create assemblages that resemble territorial spaces such as happens with the various sub-disciplines within music. These sub-disciplines are often conceived in terms of oppositional relationships. For example Western musicology is viewed as distinct from ethnomusicology. Classical music is seen as distinct from popular music. Practice-led research is understood to oppose research-led practice. Theory is viewed as the antithesis of practice. And music analysis, with its focus on musical scores, is considered the converse of music history, with its focus on composers and musical epochs. These various disciplinary assemblages are identified by their particular labels and, over a period of time, they establish distinct territories which are difficult to dislodge. The potential multiple entry points into these assemblages are often denied to bodies that belong in opposing assemblages.

The formation of territorial assemblages arises from the particular habits and repetitive behaviours of the assemblage memberships. For example, a music analysis assemblage might establish a particular way of working with music, creating theoretical templates   such as Schenker or Set Theory   for analysing music. The Schenkerian and Set Theory assemblages emerge as intra-assemblages of the music analysis assemblage and they arise from the habitual activities of the participants: like-minded scholars working in particular ways in these fields, regardless of where they are in the world, reproduce and perpetuate the codes of behaviour and working practices of the assemblage. The habitual activities of the bodies connected with the assemblages shore up their territorial sides. Territorial assemblages in music institutions, however, lead to a compartmentalised way of thinking, reducing the institution to a monologic structure with a functional order.

In this scenario, the music institution is composed of what Deleuze refers to as molar lines. Molar lines are founded on hierarchical relationships which divide the space into rigid, over-coded segments, producing a negative structure. Within this negative structure, one assemblage is deemed to be better than another. The institution becomes characterised by a value system that produces a pecking order: in a conservatorium, for example, practice might be privileged over theory; or in a university music department, theory might be privileged over practice; and in the wider university science might be privileged over practice-led work in the creative arts. Molar lines territorialise the music institution, creating territorial assemblages that produce the music institution as a static, highly differentiated, unchanging entity.

This conception of the institution as a static entity, however, ignores the possibilities that are opened up by what Deleuze refers to as minoritarian tendencies.

These are tendencies that diverge from the majority-view. Such tendencies have a deterritorialising effect on the institution, making it less stable. And, in the three chapters that follow on from 'The Academic Music Machine', concrete examples are presented, demonstrating the ways in which these music assemblages are deterritorialised. Susan McClary uses the concept of 'musicking', borrowed from Christopher Small,[11] to intercede into the majoritarian practices associated with the teaching of Western art music in the conservatorium. Jennifer Shaw uses the concept of 'intertextuality', which she conceives as a set of processes, to break down the view of music as a static, autonomous system. Joseph Williams takes up the Deleuzian concept of 'assemblage' to address the divisions that have emerged between practice and theory, and between the various practice-driven approaches themselves. These minoritarian tendencies of the authors in this part of the book, then, open a space for challenging the majoritarian power structures in the music institution.

Deleuzian encounters

Music's Immanent Future engages with one of the most difficult ideas for composers and performers in music, namely, identity. Identity matters a great deal to music and continues to be pivotal in the Western traditions of music creation. In Deleuzian philosophy, however, identity is strongly opposed because of its falsifying power in representational thought. James Williams comments that 'the commitment to identity in representation furthers an illusion that leads us to repress [the] processes of becoming at work in our own existence[s]'.[12] On the one hand, traditional approaches to music assert the importance of identity, suggesting that musical identities and musical works must be represented in order to be recognised and identified. On the other hand, a Deleuzian approach is advocating the idea of identity as emergent, where the identity is not so much a fixed entity as it is an active becoming. How do we reconcile these two positions? How do we negotiate the reality that we all have identities while at the same time recognising that our identities can never be pinned down to stable essences? How do we account for the idea that all of life is a plane of becoming? How do we discuss the particular musical identities with which we are concerned when they are always in flux or process? As Colebrook says, 'the perception of fixed beings – such as man – is an effect of becoming'.[13] Deleuze and Guattari understand that identity categories – such as gender, sexuality, ethnicity and class – is one way to organise and make sense of the world. However, they also suggest that these are limiting given that, as Hickey-Moody and Malins put it, 'they reduce the body to particular modes of being and interacting; affecting not only how the body is understood but its potentiality; its future capacity to affect and be affected'.[14]

The first chapter of Part II, 'Deleuzian Encounters', and those that follow in this part of the book take up the challenge of encountering identity, drawing on Deleuzian modes of thought. Sally Macarthur employs the concept of the 'dividual' in her section of the first chapter, demonstrating how her personal narrative (recalled from memory) intersects with some of the contemporaneous feminist

6 *Sally Macarthur and Judy Lochhead*

narratives of the time. The idea of the 'dividual' allows her to consider her story from the perspective of a fundamentally divided rather than unified individual. She goes on in her other chapter in this part, on the Australian composer Anne Boyd, to examine how the collective assemblage of enunciation constructs particular images of the living composer and she argues that a Deleuzian understanding challenges these fixed images. Judy Lochhead suggests that her path to writing about women composers is an akin to an intra-active becoming. Rhizomatic in conception, Lochhead's life is shown to intra-act with events, circumstances, music, and women composers to produce a non-linear, dynamic cartography of music. She focuses on two living women composers, Stacey Garrop and Kaja Saariaho. The identity of Pierre Schaeffer, with which Ian Stevenson is engaged, is posited as minoritarian, thus working against a majoritarian perspective of the composer-identity and his music.

These three chapters reveal the difficulties of working with identity and Deleuzian thought simultaneously. In their critiques, they note that the processes of becoming tend to be repressed in most music research and that this research is dominated by representational modes of thought. Even while recognising that not everything can be represented, representational modes of thinking tend to assume that it is enough to focus only on those aspects of identity that can be represented. The chapters in this book, then, attempt to talk about those unknowable aspects of identity in ways that acknowledge its complexity and that it is always emergent and multiple. In other words, we suggest that the two aspects of identity — the knowable and the unknowable — cannot be separated and that they are mutually implicated through their dependence on each other.

According to Deleuze, as summarised by James Williams, 'identity is opposed to multiplicity in that multiplicity is both uncountable and not open to a reductive logical or mathematical analysis'.[15] When identity is defined as a series of identifiable predicates or properties, it presents a false image of reality. For Davies, while an individualised subject's specificity 'is ontologically real; and it observably works to accomplish a sense of itself as coherent, knowable, continuous and predictable ... that orderly predictability itself can be the foundation of its own limitations and vulnerability to institutional coercion and control, its lack of agency'.[16] Furthermore, such a view assumes that identity has a stable essence and, in music, it leads to some of the scholarship having a pre-occupation with the value system used to judge music and its composer or performer identities. Such research tends to be peppered with questions such as: 'is it good music?'; or 'has it stood, or will it stand, the test of time?'; or 'what makes this music and/or composer and/or performer distinctive and/or unique?' Davies says that these kinds of questions are driven from the assumption that an individual *has* an identity which is fixed and static, rather than from the idea that identity is constantly under construction. Identity as a process of becoming is ignored in traditional approaches, especially when scholars are defending their composers or musicians for their uniqueness and distinctiveness, or when they are judging them and their work to be found wanting.

Instead of judging an individual against a pre-determined ideal and finding it wanting, a Deleuzian approach to thinking about identity suggests, to draw

Introduction   7

on Davies, that 'there are other intensities of forces working on us and through us'.[17] We, as researchers, are co-implicated in our research, 'diffracting with it'.[18] In the chapter, 'Intra-active Soundings: Becoming-Woman, Becoming-Minor', Lochhead and Macarthur introduce the Deleuzian concepts of 'becoming', 'becoming-woman', 'becoming-imperceptible', 'becoming-minoritarian' and the 'dividual' to consider the identities of the woman composer, ourselves as researchers, and the male creator, Schaeffer, who was considered an 'outsider' in his own time.

Materialities of sounding

Deleuzian immanent philosophy engages the materials of the world, ascribing causal force not only to humans but also to matter and other living creatures. This engagement with the complex interactions between human and non-human beings follows from Deleuze's concern for how the new is produced. Rather than representing how 'things are' through the constructivist actions of a transcendental subject, Deleuze's philosophy draws attention to the complex relations between human and non-human beings. The human subject is not the unitary, constituting figure of reason; instead the subject is a multiplicity itself produced by the complex and differential interactions of forces of human and non-human beings. As Daniel W. Smith notes, this entails a change from the 'monadic subject … to the nomadic subject' or, in other words, to a 'process of subjectivation' that is 'variable and extraordinarily diverse'.[19] This re-orientation to how the new is produced and the de–centering of the constituting function of the subject has focused renewed attention on non-human beings and their roles in this production.

The recognition of the forces of non-human beings and their roles in the production of the new in Deleuze's philosophy of immanence entails a related rethinking of the nature of sensation and the body. The nature of the reciprocity between human and non-human in the production of the new is characterised by the concepts of affects and force. The reciprocal relation between humans or between humans and non-humans is enacted through forces which produce affects. It is through the sensations of the body that humans feel the forces of things and people. As Bogue points out (quoting Deleuze), these sensations have a special kind of function: 'sensation "is in the body" … but it is traversed by something that surpasses the lived body, by "a Power … that is deeper and almost surpasses the lived body"'.[20] Deleuze notoriously names this force of sensation the 'body without organs'.[21] This concept refers not to an actual lack of organs but rather to a 'body of sensations': as Bogue writes, the body of sensations 'is without organization'. It is not 'a coordinated, unified, regulated whole, with senses that operate together in their reports of the outside world …'.[22] The body without organs, in Daniel Smith's terms, is the 'intensive reality of the body, an intensity that is "beneath" or "adjacent to" the organism and continuity in the process of constructing itself'.[23] The forces of the world then are manifest in the body through sensation. This notion of bodily sensation not tied to specific senses or to habituated forms of 'hearing' is crucial for thinking about music. Rather than

8 *Sally Macarthur and Judy Lochhead*

construing the ear and hearing as the primary access to musical sounding, we may enlist the full sensory capacities of the body in our engagements with the vibratory forces of music.

The emphasis on matter and non-human beings in their reciprocal relation with human in Deleuze's philosophy of immanence motivates a turn in music studies to the embodied sensations of listening, to the matter of instruments, to vibratory forces of sound, and the feelings that arise with sound — to name just a few potential pathways toward producing new thought about music.

Immanent listening

The nature of 'sonorous material' and its relationship to — and in — listening is explored in the first chapter, 'Immanent Listening'. In the spirit of Deleuze and Guattari, this chapter presents a cartography in which some of the representational (or transcendental) modes of listening are critiqued while exploring the concept of 'immanent listening'. As Colebrook remarks, immanence is one of the key terms and aims of Deleuzian philosophy.[24] As such, it draws a distinction between immanence and transcendence, a distinction that arises from the way that each – the transcendent and the immanent planes — deal with the relationships between things and beings in the world. According to James Williams, if the relationship is 'to' something, then it is transcendence. If the relationship is 'in' something, then it is immanence.[25]

Listening appeals to both the formal elements of transcendence and to the flux of experience, producing a pure multiplicity, as in immanent listening. Deleuze and Guattari contrast the plane of transcendence with the plane of consistency or composition, the latter also characterised as the plane of immanence. On the one hand, transcendence is, as they write:

> a plan(e) of analogy, either because it assigns the eminent term of a development or because it establishes the proportional relations of a structure. It may be in the mind of a god, or in the unconscious of life, of the soul, or of language: it is always concluded from its own effects. It is always inferred ... The tree is given in the seed, but as a function of a plane that is not given. The same applies to music. The developmental or organisational principle does not appear in itself, in a direct relation with that which develops or is organised: There is a transcendent compositional principle that is not the nature of sound, that is not 'audible' by itself or for itself ... Life plan(e), music plan(e), writing plan(e), it's all the same: a plan(e) that cannot be given as such, that can only be inferred from the forms it develops and the subjects it forms, since it is for these forms and these subjects.[26]

On the other hand, as they continue:

> there are no longer forms or developments of forms: nor are there subjects or the formation of subjects ... There are only haecceities, affects,

> subjectless individuations that constitute collective assemblages … We call this plane … the plane of consistency or composition (as opposed to the plan(e) of organization and development). It is necessarily a plane of immanence and univocality.[27]

Transcendent thinking separates thought from life, establishing the illusion that there is a unified ground for experience by making thought immanent to something outside of experience. As Carfoot writes, 'Deleuze's philosophical project relies on a marked distinction between the terms "transcendence" and "transcendental"',[28] pointing out that the former refers to that which exists outside our experience – that which we perceive as external and unreachable in our everyday worlds – and the latter to a style of philosophical thought that, as Carfoot puts it, 'offers no ultimate grounds through which we might supposedly pinpoint "reality"'.[29] As he continues, 'in Western thought, illusions of transcendence take a number of forms, including Truth, God and Being'.[30] If we believe, then – to apply the idea to listening – that the starting point of the listening experience is the listener him- or herself, we have created an instance of transcendence. To paraphrase Carfoot, in this view, the listener is conceived as a stable being who is set apart from the world listening experience and whose experience of the sonorous material as a listener is deemed knowable and identifiable. If, however, the listener is understood as a process of becoming, along with the sonorous material to which she or he is listening, then we have created an instance of immanent listening. In this view, listening is both within the sonorous material, and the sonorous material is within the listening experience. These two ideas are inseparable.

The difficulty with the concept of immanence for listening, and especially for those practices of listening that predominantly defer to transcendence, is how to think about the listening experience as immanent to nothing outside itself while maintaining the sense of what constitutes an actual listening experience. How can we think of listening in terms that do not rely on pre-established ideas about the sound object, or that want to separate the listener from the sound object? It is important to note that for Deleuze, transcendence is not opposed to immanence. Rather, these are two interdependent modes that are integral to each other and are thus dependent on each other. In a Deleuzian mode of thought, we would then suggest that listening, like creation itself, is a creative activity. But listening is also an activity in which, as musicians, we will sometimes engage in terms of its organisational principles. For Deleuze, the power of creation and the power of thought are immanent to life. To follow Carfoot, 'life is the creation of difference. In this sense, thought is not set over the world, as a representation of what exists; rather thought is part of life.'[31] As Colebrook puts it, 'to think is not to represent life but to transform and act upon life'.[32] Immanent listening, then, as the chapters in this part of the book attempt to show, is a continual openness to the not-yet-known. Immanent listening seeks to dissolve all boundaries, and the categorisations that divide the self from the other, and the self from sound object. On the immanent plane of listening, we are encouraged to think where thought has already started.

Deleuzian ontologies

Difference and differing motivate Deleuze's philosophical perspectives. As developed in *Difference and Repetition*, difference arises not as a relation between two existing things, each having a pre-existing identity. Rather, as Smith and Protevi observe, difference 'becomes a transcendental principle that constitutes the sufficient reason of empirical diversity'.[33] As such, the goal of philosophical thinking is, as Melissa McMahon writes, 'grasping things in their utter "thisness", in their empirical differing from other things'.[34] For Deleuze, difference is prior to identity and is the genetic principle for real experience.

As McMahon observes, concepts of identity function as a way to 'manage' differences: 'a concept subordinates differences by picking out qualities or things as "the same" or identical across (and despite) different cases'.[35] As ways of managing difference, concepts of identity provide habitual modes of engaging the world, but for Deleuze they do not constitute the essences or truths of existence. Rather, differential relations between things give rise to concepts of identity, such concepts serving to address specific problems. In addressing these concepts, thought turns away from questions of 'What?' and instead to 'Who?', 'How?', 'When?', and 'Where?'[36]

This ontology of difference runs throughout Deleuze's philosophical thought and generates a host of ways for thinking difference. As a genetic principle for real experience, ontological difference requires a turn toward immanence, toward the materialities of the world. In addressing the 'thisness' of things, it requires a non-representationalist thinking that turns away from a 'logic of *est* ("is")' and toward a 'conjunctive logic of *et* ("and")' — a dynamic logic of contingencies.[37] In turning toward the generative principles of differential relations in the material world, ontological difference requires an inquiry into how worldly things — human or non-human — affect one another, into how things affect and are affected. Such questions of affective powers entail a 'shift away from a *morality* to an *ethics*'.[38] And as a generative principle, ontological difference re-orients thinking to matters of temporality and becoming.

As a way of developing some aspects of the reorientations generated by ontological difference, we consider briefly the concepts of emergence and 'intra-activity' as they have been developed by recent authors who employ Deleuzian ontologies of difference: Manuel DeLanda and Karen Barad. DeLanda develops the idea of emergence focusing in particular on 'the creative powers of matter and energy'.[39] He approaches emergence through a consideration of non-linear systems in science studies, focusing on how the interactions of elements generate new, emergent properties of something that are irreducible to the properties of the interacting elements. DeLanda argues for a complex notion of causality, allowing for 'feedback loops in which one part that is affected by another may in turn react back and affect the first; other components may remain unaffected …'.[40] From Deleuze's ontology of difference, DeLanda develops an approach to emergence that acknowledges the dynamic and generative power of the material world.

Karen Barad, writing as well from a perspective of science studies and from feminist studies, advances a notion of 'agential realism' which takes account of 'matter's dynamism' and focuses on the 'intra-action' of agents that produce phenomena.[41] In Barad's theory, phenomena arise through the intra-actions of agents: '*phenomena are differential patterns of mattering* … produced through complex agential intra-actions of multiple material-discursive practices or apparatuses of bodily production'.[42] Denying on one hand, the pre-existence of objects and their properties and, on the other, the representationalist power of words to fix the object, Barad claims that 'it is through the specific agential intra-actions that the boundaries and properties of components of phenomena become determinate and that particular concepts … become meaningful'.[43] From Deleuze's ontology of difference, Barad develops a materialist approach in which matter is agential: 'neither fixed and given nor the result of different processes … [m]atter is produced and productive, generated and generative'.[44]

DeLanda's notion of emergence and Barad's notion of 'intra-action' themselves speak to the generative power of Deleuze's ontology of difference – an ontology that generates ontologies. These notions are used throughout the chapters of this collection, and indeed a philosophy of difference itself has a generative function, motivating new thought, new approaches, new forms of creativity. And as we mean to suggest with the title of this book, difference and differing direct thought toward the material and the new, toward immanence and the future.

The chapters

Each of the five parts of *Music's Immanent Future* includes a prefacing, 'folding' chapter and one or more chapters that intra-act around a particular theme. We provide a thumbnail sketch of those chapters to conclude the introduction.

Part I, 'The Academic Music Machine', includes three chapters that offer perspectives on music training in higher education. Two of the three chapters work with concepts that point to a Deleuzian way of thinking, and one engages with Deleuzian thought directly. In 'From the Universal and Timeless to the Here and Now: Rethinking Music Studies', McClary argues that the next generation of concert artists and orchestral players are trained almost exclusively on a diet of Western art music and that their training ignores music's socio-cultural context, treating it instead as timeless and universal. She invokes Small's concept of musicking to shift the focus from objects (that is, musical works) to the human activity of musicking. Shaw's chapter, 'Music and the Intertextualities of Listening, Performing and Teaching' asks why the academy persists in teaching music and musical works along canonical lines when postmodernist modes of thought have produced an array of different approaches to the study of music and other artefacts. She says that in the current time the autonomous musical work is a thing of the past, drawing on the concept of 'intertextuality' to open up a space for considering music as multi-faceted and multi-mediated. Williams examines three models of practice-led research in a critique that moves toward a Deleuzian articulation of theory and practice in the creative arts. Using Deleuze and Guattari's

12 *Sally Macarthur and Judy Lochhead*

concept of 'assemblage', he suggests that practitioner researchers mediate the flows of theory and practice into one another.

Part II, 'Deleuzian Encounters', includes three chapters that engage Deleuzian thought directly as a mode of encountering musical practices. In 'Chaotic Mappings: On the Ground with Music', Lochhead considers the music of Kaija Saariaho and Stacy Garrop, using a Deleuzian-inspired critical apparatus of chaotic mapping to produce knowledge about the specific works. Macarthur's chapter, 'Meeting the Composer Halfway: Which Anne Boyd?', addresses issues of identity for the woman composer, employing a Deleuzian-feminist approach to figure the multiplicity of identities and their political modalities. In 'Schaeffer's Sound Effects', Stevenson considers the thought and music of Pierre Schaeffer through the Deleuzian critique of identity, proposing a relational understanding of acousmatic sound.

Part III, 'Materialities of Sounding', comprises chapters by three composers residing in Australia, each addressing the sounding materiality of their compositional practice. In '*Living Colours*: An Asian-Pacific Conceptual Frame for Composition', Bruce Crossman addresses his music as a hybrid generated from the diverse aesthetic strands of Asian-Pacific and Western sound worlds. Paul Smith, in '*Kawaii* Aesthetics and the Exchange Between Anime and Music', uses Deleuzian thought to refigure the concept of compositional influence as a flow of affects between the Japanese *kawaii* aesthetic, Japanese anime, and his own musical creations. And in 'A Musical Portmanteau: Rock Viscerality, Juxtaposition and Modernist Textures in *Frumious*', Holly Harrison employs Lewis Carroll's concept of the portmanteau to approach the productive interactions of diverse musical aesthetics.

Part IV, 'Immanent Listening', includes two chapters that point to a Deleuzian re-imagining of listening. In 'Seeing the Sense: Imagining a New Approach to Acousmatic Music and Listening', Michelle Stead argues that the dominant ways of engaging music are through the sense of sight and that this has a negative impact on acousmatic music which is characterised by a lack of visual information. She offers some possibilities for rethinking the vision/audition opposition and for envisaging new ways of engaging with acousmatic music. Joseph Toltz's chapter, 'Listening to Ethnographic Holocaust Musical Testimony through the ears of Jean-Luc Nancy' engages an immanent listening approach to open up a very different kind of attentive space for thinking about Holocaust survivor testimonies. He draws on Nancy's philosophical meditation to ponder on the relationship of sound to the human body, arguing that sound produces powerful effects long after its sounding ends. Toltz shows that when Holocaust survivors recall in the present day the music they heard in the camps and ghettoes, it is as if they are hearing it for the first time. It thus resounds as a powerful memory in their lives in the present day.

Part V, 'Deleuzian Ontologies', includes Greg Hainge's 'Material Music: Speculations on Non-human Agency in Music'. In this chapter, Hainge thinks through a range of issues pertaining to music's ontology, proposing a relational ontology deriving from Deleuzian thought and resonant with recent philosophical work in speculative realism, object-oriented ontology, actor network theory and new materialism.

Notes

1 In addition to his several single-authored books, Gilles Deleuze co-authored several books with Félix Guattari. For the purposes of this collection, we will not always distinguish a Deleuzian philosophical perspective from a Deleuzian–Guattarian perspective. Sometimes we will simply refer to an idea as Deleuzian even if it has appeared in the shared work with Guattari.

2 Deleuzian philosophical perspectives have had far ranging implications for thought in other fields, including philosophy, mathematics, architecture, law, science, education, economics and the arts, prompting new heterogeneous visions of the world. The bibliography at the end of the volume gives an indication of the broad range of scholarship produced through Deleuzian perspectives.

3 For example, Susan McClary, recently quipped that: 'I think my body still has its organs, and I haven't yet reached the thousandth level of Angry Birds'. Susan McClary, email to Sally Macarthur, Monday 6 October 2014. Used with permission. The Deleuzian 'body without organs' is discussed later in this chapter.

4 See Gilles Deleuze, *Foucault*, trans. Sean Hand (Minneapolis: University of Minnesota Press, 1988); and Gilles Deleuze, *The Fold: Leibniz and the Baroque*, foreword and trans. Tom Conley (Minneapolis: University of Minnesota Press, 1993).

5 Claire Colebrook, *Understanding Deleuze* (Crows Nest, Australia: Allen & Unwin, 2002), 54.

6 Simon O'Sullivan, 'Fold', in *The Deleuze Dictionary*, ed. Adrian Parr (Edinburgh: Edinburgh University Press, 2005), 103.

7 On the eight postulates for the image of thought as a mode of representation see: Gilles Deleuze, *Difference and Repetition*, trans. Paul Patton (London: Athlone Press, 1994), 129–67; and for an overview of the image of thought see: Gregg Lambert, *The Non-Philosophy of Gilles Deleuze* (London: Continuum, 2002), 3–37.

8 Lesley Brown (ed.), *The New Shorter Oxford English Dictionary: Volume 1* (Oxford: Clarendon Press, 1993), 129.

9 Graham Livesey, 'Assemblage', in *The Deleuze Dictionary*, ed. Adrian Parr, 231.

10 It is important to note, however, that an assemblage is not necessarily restricted to a singular music institution. Camps that are constituted from the disciplinary expertise of their members, will often flow across a number of institutions simultaneously. The important point we are making is that the gravitation of like-minded bodies and their repetitive habits associated with the particular activity give rise to the assemblage.

11 Christopher Small, *Musicking: The Meanings of Performing and Listening* (Middletown, Connecticut: Wesleyan University Press, 1998).

12 James Williams, 'Identity', *The Deleuze Dictionary*, ed. Adrian Parr, 124.

13 Claire Colebrook, *Understanding Deleuze*, xx.

14 Anna Hickey-Moody and Peta Malins, eds., *Deleuzian Encounters: Studies in Contemporary Social Issues* (Houndmills, Basingstoke: Palgrave Macmillan, 2007), 5.

15 Williams, 'Identity', 125.

16 Bronwyn Davies, *Listening to Children: Being and Becoming* (London and New York: Routledge, 2014), 35.

17 Davies, *Listening to Children*, 35.

18 Davies, *Listening to Children*, 35.

19 Daniel W. Smith, *Essays on Deleuze* (Edinburgh: Edinburgh University Press, 2012), 55, 155.

20 Ronald Bogue, *Deleuze on Music, Painting, and the Arts* (New York and London: Routledge, 2003), 124.

21 The concept of 'body without organs' is typically abbreviated as 'BwO'. The term comes from Antonin Artaud's radio play *To Have Done with the Judgment of God* (1947).

22 Bogue, *Deleuze on Music, Painting, and the Arts*, 124–5.

23 Smith, *Essays on Deleuze*, 209.

24 Colebrook, *Understanding Deleuze*, xxiv.

25 James Williams, 'Immanence', in *The Deleuze Dictionary*, ed. Adrian Parr, 126.
26 Gilles Deleuze and Félix Guattari, *A Thousand Plateaus: Capitalism and Schizophrenia*, trans. Brian Massumi (Minneapolis and London: University of Minnesota Press, 1987), 265–6.
27 Deleuze and Guattari, *A Thousand Plateaus*, 266–7.
28 Gavin Carfoot, 'Deleuze and Music: A Creative Approach to the Study of Music' (Master of Music (Research) Thesis, University of Queensland, 2004), 14.
29 Carfoot, 'Deleuze and Music', 14.
30 Carfoot, 'Deleuze and Music', 14.
31 Carfoot, 'Deleuze and Music', 17.
32 Colebrook, *Understanding Deleuze*, xxiv.
33 Daniel W. Smith and John Protevi, 'Gilles Deleuze', *The Stanford Encyclopedia of Philosophy* (Spring 2013 ed.), ed. Edward N. Zalta, accessed 15 March 2015, http://plato.stanford.edu/archives/spr2013/entries/deleuze/.
34 Melissa McMahon, 'Difference, repetition', *Gilles Deleuze: Key Concepts*, ed. Charles J. Stivale, 2nd edition (Durham; Acumen, 2011), 44–5. In her article, McMahon uses the term 'thisness' as a translation of the Latin term 'haecceity' that Deleuze borrows from the Medieval philosopher–theologican John Duns Scotus.
35 McMahon, 'Difference, repetition', 45.
36 McMahon, 'Difference, repetition', 48. McMahon writes about how this series of questions functions in Deleuze's philosophy as a mode of 'dramatizing' thinking in her note 3 on p. 54.
37 Daniel W. Smith, 'Univocity', in *Essays on Deleuze*, 42.
38 Smith, 'Univocity', 41.
39 Manuel DeLanda, *Philosophy and Simulation: The Emergence of Synthetic Reason* (New York: Continuum, 2012), 6.
40 Manuel DeLanda, 'Emergence, Causality, and Realism', *The Speculative Turn: Continental Materialism and Realism*, ed. Levi Bryant, Nick Srnicek and Graham Harman (Melbourne: re.press, 2011), 385.
41 Karen Barad, *Meeting the Universe Halfway: Quantum Physics and the Entanglement of Matter and Meaning* (Durham: Duke University Press, 2007), 135 and 39.
42 Barad, *Meeting the Universe Halfway*, 140. Emphasis in the original.
43 Barad, *Meeting the Universe Halfway*, 139.
44 Barad, *Meeting the University Halfway*, 137.

Part I

The academic music machine

1 The academic music machine

Sally Macarthur

Is music academia a homogenising machine? Does it privilege particular kinds of music and exclude others? Does it treat music as a discrete category? Is music creation the same as researching music? These are just some of the questions addressed by the three authors in Part I of the book.

In the next chapter, McClary sketches the conditions of homogeneity in music academia, unfurling the territorialising processes of the machinic assemblage bound up with Austro-German music and its all-pervasive ideology. Although McClary does not explicitly engage Deleuzian concepts, in what I would argue is nonetheless a Deleuzian mode of thought, she maps a cartography of music academia and opens a space for the becoming of the music academy. In effect, McClary demonstrates the ways in which the conservatory model of training functions as a machinic assemblage. In Deleuze, and Deleuzian–Guattarian thought, the assemblage or the abstract machine is not concerned with what the thing is, or is like – in this case, the intrinsic properties or metaphors associated with institutions loosely labelled 'music academia' – but rather with what makes it function as a machine. McClary's cartography explores the political and social dimensions of the academic music machine. She demonstrates how these are driven by desire, exposing, in particular, their investment in and attachment to the Western art music canon. She shows how the conservatorium territorial assemblage[1] thrives on the power of negative difference: its territorialising mechanisms establish Austro-German music as supremely superior when compared with other kinds of music. But McClary also demonstrates that in each of these machinic operations there is always a deterritorialising impulse, a movement that seeks to undo and challenge the boundaries of the assemblage. She uses the deterritorialising term 'musicking' from Christopher Small to shift the emphasis from what music might mean to what it can do.[2]

McClary's chapter adds another important perspective to the burgeoning field of 'new musicology'.[3] Her work simultaneously shores up the new musicological assemblage while breaking apart the old assemblage. It does this through the operations of the collective assemblage of enunciation, which, for Deleuze and Guattari, are the 'acts and statements, of incorporeal transformations attributed to bodies'.[4] The collective assemblage of enunciation territorialises the machine by creating a set of signs that form the basis of an identity. Western art music

18   *Sally Macarthur*

history presents a set of markers that distinguish its music from other kinds of music. The standard history of Western art music, in a Deleuzian sense, is 'like a system of points and positions, which operates by cuts which are supposedly significant instead of proceeding by thrusts and crackings'.[5] Its linear narrative highlights innovative musical developments which give rise to new genres and styles. It expounds on these as significant but, in so doing, it potentially limits the possibilities for other machinic connections. McClary's chapter points to some of these other connections. She challenges the operations of canonical fetishism, critiquing the binary relationships that underpin the deeply ingrained positivist approaches to studying music and exposing how the apparatus of power for Western art music impacts negatively on all music. She then cracks the narrative open, modelling innovative ways in which to analyse music from different traditions and different time-periods side-by-side.

Small's concept of 'musicking' – in which music is conceived as an activity rather than an object – is proposed as a useful 'thinking' tool. As a verb, 'musicking' shares features with Deleuze's concepts, which are similarly active in conception. For Colebrook, Deleuzian 'concepts testify to the positive power of thinking as an event of life. We create concepts in order to transform life'.[6] Deleuzian concepts are not focused on what life means but rather on what it does. In McClary's hands, Small's concept of 'musicking' has the potential to activate a series of productive encounters with both canonical and non-canonical musics. In her teaching, she analyses Sardinian hymns and medieval organum together, juxtaposing sound clips (rather than scores) of Sardinians singing hymns in parallel triads with that of Notre Dame organum, and she shows that there are similar juxtapositions between Indonesian gamelan and Debussy. In so doing, she establishes a relationship between the sound of the music and the inaudible forces of the cosmos from which the music is actualised. Classical music begins to take on the character, to borrow from Hulse, of a 'pan-global environment … in which the connections and separations run along pathways too jumbled and multifarious to be understood in terms of structural positions or identities'.[7]

As with much of McClary's other work, she treats music as both a signifying system and a set of socio-political practices. McClary avoids the conception of music as a pre-determined, structural representation, taking into account the multiple ways in which it might be encountered by anyone in any given moment. This understanding of music as an activity or as an encounter lies at the heart of all her work. Beyond the pages of this book, her work has had far-reaching effects and, as I will elaborate below, it, too, functions like a machinic assemblage.

In a similar vein but with a slightly different orientation from McClary, Shaw addresses the issue of music as a discrete category, suggesting ways in which the divide between music and the other arts might be bridged. While Shaw, like McClary, does not directly engage with Deleuzian philosophy, her work holds out the prospect of escaping fixed positions, the already known and repetitive thinking. She canvases the work of recent post-structuralist theorists to address the focus on the great canonical works by most traditional music institutions and goes on

The academic music machine   19

to demonstrate how this focus might be disrupted by an awareness that music is always an encounter with multiple, multi-faceted, mediated and interpretative contexts.

Shaw takes up Kristeva's concept of 'intertextuality', which is tendered as 'an open discursive space', in order to resist the hierarchy of reading relationships within a given text. There has been a tendency in traditional accounts of music, such as opera, to privilege music over its lyrical content and other extra-musical parameters. Shaw posits the concept of the 'threshold' as a site of temporal connection, a spatial point of contact, and a site of social and political activity, suggesting that all the content – musical and extra-musical – is pertinent to the experience of the work.

In the third chapter in this part, Williams tackles the question of whether the practice of music can be regarded as a form of research. Creative artists often find it difficult to convince the more scientific-orientated disciplines that their research outputs generate new forms of knowledge. According to Smith and Dean, the relationship between creative practice and research is problematic because of the nature of the conventional definitions of research.[8] How do you measure the value and impact of so-called creative work? How do you answer social scientists who claim that their work is creative too? How do you answer the question that playing or composing music is not 'real' research? Williams puts forward the concept of the 'assemblage' from Deleuze as a model with a practical function, which, he argues, can be put to work by practitioner–researchers to connect their creative work to the problems they are attempting to solve and thus serve to validate their work.

As we read the three chapters in this part, it is possible to 'hear' Deleuze in the background, as in the work of McClary and Shaw, and to read his work foregrounded, as in Williams. In the remainder of this chapter, I want to think about how the three chapters bring together a collection of ideas and subject matter, coalescing around the music academy, that point to a series of becomings. What ties these chapters together are the workings of assemblages and the abstract machines that produce them. These chapters are not simply a series of reflections on themes relating to the curricula and research outputs of the music academy. As assemblages they themselves carve out territories while simultaneously engaging in deterritorialising processes. The Deleuzian concept of territory, as Message points out, is always a malleable site of passage. It is always in process, continually transforming itself.[9] The assemblage of the next three chapters, then, emerges through the processes of their connections and inter – (and 'intra'[10]) actions: with each other, and with the other assemblages into which they come into contact or are interlinked.

With this in mind, the present chapter performs the dual function of critique and multiplicity. It comments on some of the ideas of the three authors and introduces a plane of consistency conceptualised as the 'academic music machine'. In Deleuzian thought, the abstract machine is rhizomatic in conception. For Deleuze and Guattari, 'a rhizome ceaselessly establishes connections between semiotic chains, organizations of power, and circumstances relative to the arts, sciences,

20   *Sally Macarthur*

and social struggles'.[11] As a concrete example of this process, all of the chapters in this book can be understood as rhizomatic and machinic. To adapt an idea from Hickey-Moody and Malins, they are designed to function in practical, material ways, and to generate changes in the music academy.[12] Characterised as an assemblage, these chapters are at any point a rhizome connected with other assemblages, each characterised by diverse modes of coding (for example, political, musical, economic and social). There is a similarity between the assemblage in this part of the book and the book as generative object in the world. Deleuze and Guattari state that the book:

> necessarily acts on semiotic flows, material flows, and social flows simultaneously ... There is no longer a tripartite division between a field of reality (the world) and a field of representation (the book) and a field of subjectivity (the author) ... there is a collective assemblage of enunciation, a machinic assemblage of desire, one inside the other and both plugged into an immense outside that is a multiplicity, in any case.[13]

The assemblage of the book is produced by an elaborate machinery. According to Deleuze and Guattari, machines are everywhere, 'machines driving other machines, machines being driven by other machines, with all the necessary couplings and connections ... we are handymen: each with his little machines'.[11] This book, then, connects with those who read it and those who produce it, each with their different machinery to make it function as a book: the writing and editing machines, the marketing and publishing machines; the economic and political machines; and the reading machines, with their ever-changing, diverse perspectives, that couple with the book, producing it as a multiplicity.

The machinery of this book plugs into the McClary-machine, which is an apt concept that I have coined for considering how extensively her work has been taken up across the world.[15] In turn, the McClary-machine plugs into the assemblage of this book. As a dynamic instrument of possibility, the McClary-machine produces its own assemblage, emerging from the territorialising activities of the collective assemblage of enunciation. As an assemblage, the McClary-machine is simultaneously driving while being driven by the academic music machine. Her critique in this volume, deterritorialises the stable and seemingly unchanging large-scale assemblage of the conservatorium. It simultaneously shores up the sides of the new musicology assemblage, which sits inside the large-scale assemblage of the conservatorium. The conservatorium is viewed as a monolithic institution for which the wheels seem to turn very slowly. As Deleuze and Guattari point out, 'assemblages may group themselves into extremely vast constellations constituting "cultures" or even "ages"'.[16] One aspect of the conservatorium assemblage, then, as noted above, is that it makes the canon core to its educating role. However, focusing only on this facet of the assemblage means that we are likely to miss the larger connections and the criss-crossing between it and other assemblages. McClary draws attention to these other assemblages and the ways in which they point to becomings. For example, the audience for Austro-Germanic music is rapidly shrinking. Many orchestras and opera companies in North America are closing. The assemblages plugged into classical music are being deterritorialised by socio-economic forces. McClary's critique signals a deterritorialisation (and a becoming) of the conservatorium assemblage.

The McClary-machine also opens up a space for the work of the other two authors in this part. It propels their work into different relations within the new musicology assemblage and it tunes into the collective assemblage of enunciation. As an indirect, expressive discourse, as Deleuze and Guattari put it, the collective assemblage of enunciation 'explains all the voices present within a single voice'.[17] They insist that the work of a writer is already constituted as part of a collective assemblage of enunciation. The three writers in this part of the book, then, utter similar statements about the academic world of music. Shaw speaks with the collective in her suggestion that the model of the university as we know it today is changing. Her observation that the rise of online learning as one factor contributing to this change can be read as a deterritorialising impulse. Similarly, her 'intertextual' model of listening erodes the concept of the discrete discipline.

The concept of 'intertextuality' used by Shaw follows a line of movement, shifting from the conception of the musical work as static, autonomous, and fixed to considering it as a dynamic entity which interacts with bodies, convergent technologies, and a range of other artistic media. Shaw draws attention to the layers of strata involved in the intertextual experience. In her view, intertextuality is a set of processes involving reading and re-reading, and listening and re-listening to texts and their invariants. These ultimately produce an infinite intertextual space. As a multiplicity, the intertextual space thus becomes much more than a series of oppositions and differences. For Shaw, the intertextual space demands a different engagement from that of traditional analytical models that have been used to study the canonical musical works. In her view, the intertextual space prompts the discipline of music to become undisciplined. Shaw's work implies the production of a dynamic intertextual space that is unable to be rigidly contained by the category-producing analyses of structuralism. It suggests a deterritorialisation of music analysis.

Other voices from the collective assemblage of enunciation, present in the background of Shaw's chapter, tend to support the idea of an ongoing process of deterritorialisation for tertiary music institutions. Some of this work suggests that very few music graduates in Australia work exclusively in classical music.[18] As Bennett points out, employment opportunities increase if music graduates work in multiple genres.[19] The concept of the portfolio career is advanced as the most important change that has taken place in the music academy over the last decade. Following Deleuze, this would be understood as another deterritorialising impulse in the academic music machine.[20] According to research, however, the academic music machine continues to deliver a music curriculum that is: (a) based on a linear model of training in the belief that it leads to a life-long (mono) career; and (b) assumes that the appropriate repertoire for this training is the Western art music canon. As Letts, Schippers and Lancaster argue, the majority of undergraduate music courses – both in Australia and overseas – continue to prepare music students for nineteenth rather than twenty-first century careers and working environments.[21]

In different ways, McClary, Shaw and Williams have something important to say about musical training in the twenty-first century. Williams uses a Deleuzian framework whereas, as I have been suggesting, McClary and Shaw work with a Deleuzian mode of thought *sans* Deleuze. The collective assemblage of enunciation activates what Deleuze calls molar lines which, as Williams points out in his chapter, are the organising principles of the assemblage. Molar lines produce a relative stability within a territory or assemblage. The categories generated by the dominant structuralist approaches of music analysis can be understood as molar in conception. But the deterritorialising tendency is already underway, governed by what Deleuze calls molecular lines. Shaw's intertextual model, then, produces an organisation that is more flexible. Williams similarly enacts a deterritorialisation produced by molecular lines insofar as he challenges reflecivity as the dominant model for exegetical writing by creative practitioners. For Williams, drawing on Deleuze and Guattari, a territory is not a fixed space so much as it is a dynamic conversation between territorialising and deterritorialising forces. Furthermore, to draw on Davies, molar and molecular lines 'are not mutually exclusive lines of force and they simply cannot be mapped onto binaries such as good/bad, old/new. They continually affect each other and they depend on each other.'[22] Davies goes on to imply that molar lines 'may foreclose the emergence of new thought, but they may also create a coherent space in which the new can emerge'.[23] According to Williams, lines of flight have the capacity to break apart both molar and molecular lines in order to completely transform the assemblage from anything by which it might be recognised. Davies suggests that lines of flight are 'life-giving and powerful, but they are not always good and may sometimes be sad and even dangerous'.[24]

Considering the three chapters in this part as whole, there is the implication that danger is afoot in the music academy. Shaw says that to threaten the canon and canonical readings of texts is to threaten the music institution as we have come to know it. She adds that perhaps that is happening already through the government funding models for universities – in which less money is expected to go further – and through the emerging era of technological and operational convergence, and online learning. Perhaps, then, the transformation of the music institution will emerge as a line of flight, in which the bodies encountering other bodies, and ideas encountering other ideas, are carried away. And perhaps, as Deleuze and Guattari put it, the two relations will combine to form a more powerful whole, or one part might, instead, decompose the other, 'destroying the cohesion of its parts'.[25]

Williams goes on to argue for the important role of practice-led research. His cartography exposes some flaws in existing practice-led research models and suggests that there are emergent and self-generative qualities in creative work which, despite the scepticism in the collective assemblage of enunciation, suggest that artistic practice is capable of knowledge production. Williams shows how practice as knowledge production can be conceptualised as a becoming. He illustrates

The academic music machine   23

this idea with his own creative practice. As Massumi puts it, becoming 'always takes place in the world as we know it ... Bodies in flight do not leave the world behind ... they take the world with them – into the future.'[26]

I have illustrated the ways in which the traditional academic music machine, which is constituted from a number of territorial assemblages that are formed through the habitual activities of its members, moves across multiple and often overlapping spacio-temporal sites. According to Deleuze and Guattari, becoming implies 'two simultaneous movements, one by which a term (the subject) is withdrawn from the majority, and another by which a term (the agent) rises up from the minority'.[27] I have shown how each author has enacted a becoming by withdrawing from the majority and simultaneously rising up from the minority. As a musicologist in the 1990s, McClary withdrew from the majoritarian view, asking different kinds of questions that led to different kinds of solutions. These different questions gave different kinds of emphasis to music from those that had been given by the majority in her discipline. McClary was thus positioned as a minoritarian figure. From her minoritarian position, however, she brought about radical change in the traditional academic music machine through the creation of the McClary-machine. This single, minoritarian act interrupted the flow of the traditional academic music machine and set off multiple becomings. We see the fruits of some of these becomings in the work of Shaw and Williams (and numerous others) who stepped outside the traditional academic music machine by hooking up with the McClary-machine. I want to suggest that the folds in this chapter, then, will remain perpetually open, making way for multiple potential openings and becomings. The McClary-machine will forever go on being opened differently, producing an infinite array of other academic music machines that are yet to be imagined.

Notes

1   According to Macgregor Wise, the concept of assemblage in the work of Deleuze and Guattari refers to the 'play of contingency and structure, organization and change'. It is not a static concept. Rather, it is a *process* involving the 'arranging, organizing, fitting together' of that which is being assembled. See J. Macgregor Wise, 'Assemblage', in *Gilles Deleuze: Key Concepts*, ed. Charles J. Stivale (Chesham, UK: Acumen, 2005), 77.

2   See Christopher Small, *Musicking: The Meanings of Performing and Listening* (Middletown, Connecticut: Wesleyan University Press, 1998).

3   'Critical musicology' or 'cultural musicology' is the term used in the United Kingdom. In the United States it is known as the 'new musicology'.

4   Gilles Deleuze and Félix Guattari, *A Thousand Plateaus: Capitalism and Schizophrenia*, trans. Brian Massumi (Minneapolis and London: University of Minnesota Press, 1987), 88.

5   Gilles Deleuze and Claire Parnet, *Dialogues*, trans. Hugh Tomlinson and Barbara Habberjam (New York: Columbia University Press, 1987), 37.

6   Claire Colebrook, 'Key Terms', in *Understanding Deleuze* (Crows Nest, Sydney: Allen & Unwin, 2002), xxi.

7   Brian Hulse, 'Of Genre, System, and Process: Music Theory in a "Global Sonorous Space"', accessed 15 March 2015, https://www.yumpu.com/user/operascore.com.

8   Hazel Smith and Roger T. Dean, eds., *Practice-led Research, Research-led Practice in the Creative Arts* (Edinburgh: Edinburgh University Press, 2009), 3.

9 Kylie Message, 'Territory', in *The Deleuze Dictionary*, ed. Adrian Parr (Edinburgh: Edinburgh University Press, 2005), 275.

10 I am using the word 'intra-action' in the same sense as Karen Barad: intra-actions of material and non-material phenomena do not pre-exist each other but, in much the same way as a Deleuzian assemblage is constructed, they are mutually constituted in the moment of their connection. See Karen Barad, *Meeting the Universe Halfway: Quantum Physics and the Entanglement of Matter and Meaning* (Durham, NC and London: Duke University Press, 2007), 29–30.

11 Deleuze and Guattari, *A Thousand Plateaus*, 7.

12 Anna Hickey-Moody and Peta Malins, *Deleuzian Encounters: Studies in Contemporary Social Issues* (Houndmills, Basingstoke: Palgrave Macmillan, 2007), 18.

13 Deleuze and Guattari, *A Thousand Plateaus*, 23.

14 Deleuze and Guattari, *A Thousand Plateaus*, 1–2.

15 A recent review article focusing on McClary lends support to this idea of McClary's work, with its far-reaching political and social impacts, functioning like a machine. See Linda Kouvaras, '"Effing the Ineffable": The Work of Susan McClary and Richard Leppert and (Part of) their Legacy', *Musicology Australia* 36/1 (2014),: 106–20, accessed 14 February 2015, http://dx.doi.org/10.1080/08145857.2014.911059.

16 Deleuze and Guattari, *A Thousand Plateaus*, 406.

17 Deleuze and Guattari, *A Thousand Plateaus*, 80.

18 Dawn Bennett, 'What Do Musicians Do for a Living?', Music Council of Australia website, accessed 2 June 2014, http://www.musiccareer.com.au/index.php/What_do_Musicians_do_for_a_Living%3F.

19 Bennett, 'What Do Musicians Do for a Living?'.

20 Brydie-Leigh Bartleet et al., 'Preparing for portfolio careers in Australian music: Setting a research agenda', *Australian Journal of Music Education* 1 (2012), 35. For Bartleet et al., the portfolio career functions like a share portfolio in which musicians balance high- and low-risk ventures, and work in multiple employment activities concurrently. The skills needed for the portfolio music career are very different from those needed for the mono-employment model.

21 Richard Letts, Huib Schippers, and Helen Lancaster, *Submission to the Higher Education Base Funding Review* (Sydney: Music Council of Australia, 2011); and Huib Schippers, 'Blame it on the Germans! A cross-cultural invitation to revisit the foundation of training professional musicians', in *Preparing Musicians, Making New Sound Worlds*, ed. Orlando Musumeci (Barcelona: ISME/ESMUC, 2004), 199–208.

22 Bronwyn Davies, *Listening to Children: Being and Becoming* (London and New York: Routledge, 2014), 7–8.

23 Davies, *Listening to Children*, 8.

24 Davies, *Listening to Children*, 8.

25 Deleuze and Guattari, *A Thousand Plateaus*, 205.

26 Brian Massumi, *A User's Guide to Capitalism and Schizophrenia: Deviations from Deleuze and Guattari* (Cambridge, MA: MIT Press, 1992), 15.

27 Deleuze and Guattari, *A Thousand Plateaus*, 291.

2 From the universal and timeless to the here and now

Rethinking music studies

Susan McClary

Arnold Schoenberg once boasted that his invention of the twelve-tone system 'would ensure the supremacy of German music for the next hundred years'.[1] Of course, for all its influence within university composition departments, where it did indeed reign supreme in the middle decades of the twentieth century, Schoenberg's invention never truly made it into the hearts of listeners or standard concert programs. If the future supremacy of German music had depended on serialism, its legacy would have dried up long ago.

I want to draw your attention, however, to a detail in Schoenberg's statement: the word 'next'. If we might debate the second hundred years he anticipated, he was surely correct in classifying the previous hundred as one that saw German and Austrian music ascend to a position of unprecedented cultural authority worldwide. What he perhaps failed to see was that the canon he hoped to build upon had already closed, even for innovators such as himself.[2] And here we are, yet another hundred years along, still stuck in that same repertory and its pervasive – yet largely invisible – ideology.

I teach in a liberal arts university that provides the music history curriculum for a major conservatory, and a large part of my duty involves delivering the survey of Western art music to budding performers, some of them already accomplished concert artists and winners of international competitions. Unlike many musicologists, I actually love teaching the music history survey: tracing the ways European musicians developed the crafts of melodic invention, polyphony, dramatic representation, orchestration, techniques for simulating affect, and much more. I also examine with my students the reasons why certain changes in musical syntax, aesthetic priorities, and performance styles occurred. It's a great story, with great tunes all the way along. If I were put into a nursing home, I would immediately set about organizing music history courses for my fellow inmates.[3] In other words, I am not presenting my thoughts from a position of anarchy or boredom with my job. Rather I write as a music historian.

Recently in my class, we had occasion to discuss Felix Mendelssohn's 1829 revival of Bach's *Saint Matthew Passion* and the remarkable ramifications of that event: the concept of a core repertory, stretching from Bach through Brahms; the academic discipline of musicology; the theory and history curriculum that structures the lives of conservatory students. Next I moved from Mendelssohn to the

26 *Susan McClary*

canon building efforts of Robert and Clara Schumann and then to the vicious debate that broke out between defenders of 'absolute' music and advocates of the 'music of the future' — a debate that still determines what music is worthy of performing or analysing and what counts at best as guilty pleasure. My teaching assistants (professional musicologists in training) watched in horror as I deconstructed the ground under our collective feet. Is history survey — long the institutional *raison-d'être* for recruiting musicologists to the academy — really a product of nineteenth-century German ideology?[4]

Well, to certain extent: yes. For many of us, however, this is old news. The emergences of ethnomusicology, popular music studies and critical musicology have required that we lay bare the premises of the field as it had been constituted.[5] Why did professionals marginalize all non-European musics of the world, even that of Europeans other than Germans?[6] Why did they denigrate the soundtrack of people's everyday lives to the status of passing fads? Why do they protest so vehemently the notion of understanding the canonic masterpieces as expressions of particular places and moments?

Christopher Small did a great deal to reform music studies in his insistence that we shift our focus from objects (that is, works) to the indispensable human activity of musicking. A classically trained pianist who played Mozart sonatas when left to his own devices, Small argued that the contributions of African American musicians matter at least as much as this music — and perhaps more so, given our reluctance to engage with the standard repertory historically or culturally. And he contended that we should shift our attention away from the fetishising of composers to also pay heed to performers, listeners, and even ushers and agents in the ticket office, all of whom contribute to our ability to engage in the communal processes of music making. We usually notice the more lowly participants only when they go on strike and bring this sublime form of entertainment to a screeching halt.[7]

But for all the effort we have put into opening the discipline, the word has not trickled down to the conservatories in which we train our next generation of concert artists and orchestral players. Sound clips of Sardinians singing hymns in parallel triads in a session on Nôtre Dame organum or examples of Indonesian gamelan in a lecture on Debussy still provoke giggles; a 10-minute discussion of Clara Wieck Schumann and the cultural obstacles she faced as a woman daring to compose produces discomfort, even among the young women in the class.

For much like individuals consigned to monasteries before they have any idea of the stakes, our performance majors often need to believe that they have committed their lives and energies to the timeless and universal. Similarly, concert audiences resist spending their hard earned cash on anything that has not stood the test of time. In this chapter, I want to revisit the problems involved in dislodging 'classical' music's claim to a special status and to suggest ways in which we might move forward to a more inclusive study of music, one that acknowledges the urgency of concentrating on the here and now.

We have to start by recognizing how bizarre the conventions of the Classical music scene over the last hundred years clearly are. It happens that Bach — always the outlier in any historical narrative – knew a great deal of music written before his time, partly because he sang in choirs that drew on extensive library holdings and partly because he sought out as many sources for his musical inspiration as possible. But that means that although he may have studied Palestrina motets and Frescobaldi toccatas he also channelled the newest compositional devices as soon as they appeared: thus his thorough revision of all his formal processes when he first acquired a copy of Vivaldi's *Estro Armonico* or the ostentatious hand-crossing devices borrowed from Domenico Scarlatti that punctuate the *Goldberg Variations*. And for all the bad press he got from his critics who heard his work as too complex, he even penned some of the most exquisite of galant tunes.[8]

But, as I said, Bach was an outlier. Do not look for references of earlier styles in Handel or Haydn. A recent book by Christoph Wolff documents how Mozart first encountered Bach's music in Berlin when on tour a couple of years before his death.[9] The impact of that chance encounter on the younger composer's music is well known; less often realized is the extreme unlikelihood of such a bond forming between a celebrated cosmopolitan artist and a forgotten North-German provincial who had died nearly 40 years before.

We might want to sigh '… and the rest is history'. But not so fast! Even the music of Haydn and Mozart receded quickly into the unheard past. In the 1820s, Felix Mendelssohn not only resurrected the *Saint Matthew Passion*, but also staged several concerts of what he called 'ancient music' – by which he meant Bach and Handel, Haydn and Mozart, and even Schubert. It is no coincidence that Mendelssohn spearheaded this revival. The scion of the same socially prominent community of Jewish financiers responsible for first introducing Mozart to Bach's music, Mendelssohn devoted much of his energy to reconstructing *in sound* the monuments of German music history. As Applegate and Potter argue, 'Mendelssohn more consciously felt himself to be German than any composer of an earlier era and with more far-reaching consequences. … As an orchestral and festival director as well as founder of the Leipzig Conservatory, Mendelssohn went on to achieve a large measure of recognition for "our own" by placing the works of German composers in the center of the European concert repertory, where they have remained ever since.'[10] The great irony is that the man who singlehandedly launched the great German canon was himself erased from it by subsequent nationalists who saw him merely as a Jew.

Robert Schumann's incomparably influential journalism advised upwardly mobile audience members on what to listen to, and Clara Schumann's intellectually uncompromising piano recitals set the format for modern concert programming.[11] These efforts led to the rise of *Musikwissenschaft*, or music science: a new academic discipline that brought together the latest research techniques with an unapologetic focus on the music of German-speaking lands. Ever wonder why we have every jot of music ever written by Germans, in multiple scholarly editions, and no equivalent (until very recently) for the Italian, French or English? Or why the rigorous tools of Schenkerian analysis explicitly intend to offer scientific proof of German music's supremacy?[12]

Allow me to interject here that there is nothing unnatural about a cultural group assembling its own landmarks into a kind of historical narrative. We expect language programs to perpetuate such canons for each of the literatures involved. English departments typically begin with *Beowulf*, advance to Chaucer, then proceed through Shakespeare, Milton, Pope, Keats, and so forth; the same usually occurs in French, Spanish or Chinese. What does *not* happen is that they all divert to German literature around 1750. Yet this is precisely what we do in music studies.

A greater mystery involves why English-speaking cultures bought into this scenario in which German music held centre stage. The answer resides to some extent with suspicions harboured by the Puritans concerning the sensual arts, whether music or cooking. Musicologists Richard Leppert and Linda Austern have revealed deep-seated fears of music in England and its colonies — fears very often couched in profoundly homophobic language. In behaviour manuals dating back to the seventeenth century, English males were warned against serious involvement with music, which threatened their ability to propagate.[13] But if the English discouraged their own men from composing, they were all too happy to import music from the already-decadent continent. Handel, Haydn and (again) Mendelssohn helped forge an English predilection for the Teutonic repertories, and so it has remained.

The elevation of German music to transcendent status begins with Forkel's 1802 biography of Bach. Borrowing the term that literary historians had long applied to the works of Homer and Virgil, he declared that Bach was "'the first classic that ever was, or perhaps ever will be", and thus "an invaluable national patrimony, with which no other nation has anything to be compared"'.[14] A decade later, E.T.A. Hoffmann's notion of 'absolute music' gave rise to 'the gradual development of German music's reputation as superior precisely because of its universality and transcendence of national differences ...'.[15]

But perhaps most paralysing is the ideology articulated most forcefully by Eduard Hanslick, who postulated in 1854 that music could signify nothing other than music itself. In part a response to the collapse of liberalism following the failed revolution of 1848, *The Beautiful in Music* shifted the goal from the social activism characteristic of early Romantics to Art for Art's Sake.[16] After that moment, anything other than bare pitches, rhythms and abstract forms got relegated to the rubbish heap of the 'extramusical'. Used widely as a club with which to beat Liszt and others who advanced the cause of symphonic poems, this aesthetic position also made it impossible to take into account song lyrics, opera plots, or even the cultural web within any piece of music creates its meanings. Not coincidentally, the only music left standing that could be taken seriously was purely instrumental music, which attained its prestige precisely from its claim to have transcended its moment and place of origin — to have attained thereby the German Idealist dream of the timeless and universal. And we still bring this preposterous claim with us when we deal with any and all musics.

When I was in high school over 50 years ago, I was told that the popular music of my generation — Elvis, doo-wop, girl groups — was ephemeral, that we should

From the universal and timeless to the here and now   29

stick to music that had 'stood the test of time'. I think about that whenever I go to my neighbourhood grocery store, which features a steady stream of Elvis, doo-wop and girl groups, all of whom seem to have passed the test of time with flying colours.

Meanwhile, a recent piece in the *New York Times* reported that not even today's conservatory students have heard of Milton Babbitt, the bulwark of the North American postwar avant-garde who claimed to be saving music from oblivion.[17] In 2013 we saw many celebrations of the centenary of Stravinsky's *Rite of Spring*, and we felt smug in our ability to tolerate this clearly quite ancient music. What of anything more recent? How many conservatory students play anything composed within the last hundred years (except, perhaps, Rachmaninoff)?

We continually fall back on the tried and true – the repertories stockpiled from the nineteenth century. But it is no secret that symphony orchestras and opera companies across North America are failing. When I attend simulcasts from the Metropolitan Opera or concerts of the Cleveland Orchestra – long one of the great bands in the world – I find that I am among the very few members of the audience not using a walker. At age 68, I feel like a misplaced kid in those venues. Who, I wonder, will make up those audiences in 10 years, when even Mozart and Verdi have lost their ability to draw?

Thus far, our response to this obvious crisis is to shore up Classical music by continuing to preach its superiority and indispensability.[18] The old German discipline of musicology, ensconced in our music departments and conservatories, exists in order to perpetuate this canon and its values. And I'm afraid that much of my own teaching curriculum aids and abets this agenda.

So what can we do? Recognising the problem – how we got into this rather curious cultural situation – is but the first step, though an important one. No one would advocate just chucking that repertory; it is braided up with too many of our collective histories to make that possible or even desirable. Yet some change in orientation must take place or else music studies will go the same way as the aging audiences I just described.

Nineteenth-century German palaeographers had to scour countless archives and learn how to read long unintelligible notations in order to piece together the history of music narrative now seemingly set in stone.[19] No one at the time had heard the names Machaut or Josquin or Monteverdi. But with the proper incentive (nationalism, in their case), they set about recovering sources and drawing stylistic connections among them. The fact that we take the results for granted obscures how truly extraordinary that feat was, as is the cultural effort exerted to keep that canon in its supreme place.

If we really wanted to change the subject of music studies to the here and now, we would face a much easier task. A glance at YouTube attests to the exceedingly vibrant musical world we inhabit. Yes, thousands of performances of the Classics are posted there, but so is a flood of sonic expression from all over the world. I can count on finding the most obscure artists waiting there for me and for other listeners open to new experiences.

30   *Susan McClary*

We could do much worse than follow the model of Johannes de Grocheio. A pioneering sociologist, Grocheio decided around 1400 to write an inventory of the musics then circulating in Paris. After dismissing the metaphysical rubbish long parroted by theorists that prevented a clear view, he scrupulously listed all available genres, indicating for each the target audience. Thus elite intellectuals chose the complex motet, while young men leaned toward the athletic challenges of hocketing.[20] If we had had more Grocheios and fewer Hanslicks in our tradition, we might not be in our present circumstances.

A latter day Grocheio would pay attention to Lady Gaga as well as to Kaija Saariaho as prominent figures in our sonic world. She or he would also need to be place sensitive, assembling a picture of musical life specific to Cleveland, Sydney or Johannesburg. Some of those inventories would overlap, of course: we all still sponsor performances of Classical music. But imagine what our sense of possibility would be if those modes of expression typical of Australia or South Africa or Ohio became shared cultural property.

Occasionally something like this occurs. Recall how Paul Simon's *Graceland* made listeners all over the globe aware of South Africans 25 years ago. Although those sounds were initially filtered through Simon's hipster sensibility, many listeners turned quickly to buying recordings of undiluted Ladysmith Black Mambazo. For all *Graceland*'s many problems involving intellectual property and the breaking of boycotts, the music of South Africa suddenly not only emerged as an exciting cultural phenomenon but it also helped many to identify politically with the struggle against apartheid then in progress. It would be nice if we hadn't needed Paul Simon's intervention in order to have the music of Africa opened up to the wider world. But maybe we need more Paul Simons.[21]

In the 1980s MTV featured a number of artists such as Midnight Oil or Nick Cave that put Australia on the international cultural map. Sally Macarthur has sometimes risked disciplinary marginalization by writing on contemporary Australian female musicians   something many more of us ought to be doing.[22] For recall that not even those Universal and Timeless composers enshrined in the canon got to be there solely on their own merits; they required the concerted efforts of Mendelssohn, the Schumanns, and all the other writers, performers, and teachers who worked to make that music known and appreciated.

It is up to us, in other words, to change the subject. For every essay I write or course I teach concerning Classical music, I try to invent one that targets recent music, whether popular or concert oriented. That may seem strange, given that my principal research focuses on European musics of the sixteenth and seventeenth centuries. But, in fact, that background provided me with both the incentive and skills to interrogate later forms of expression, for both pre- and post-tonal   and even neo-tonal   repertories require questioning the monolith that is 'tonality'.[23] No less in my seminar on Renaissance madrigals than in one on Minimalism, I make the first order of business the rewiring of musicians who immediately seize onto tonal explanations for what 'works' and who tend to dismiss anything that doesn't fit into their pre-existing analytical categories. It turns out to be hard work disentangling the brain and the ear from habits instilled into them from childhood.

From the universal and timeless to the here and now 31

I doubt there has been any other time in cultural history in which professional artists have been so alienated – physically, mentally, experientially – from the musics of their own time.

It's an uphill struggle, however. My Bach seminar last year had an overflow enrolment of 40; the one on postmodernist operas (e.g., Glass, Adams, Saariaho, Adès) attracted five students. Compositions of the last 50 years still draw blanks among young professionals, whereas that early eighteenth-century repertory Mendelssohn rescued from the dustbin of history continues to hold pride of place. I suspect that Bach himself would advise students to take the other course. In any case, he himself would be eager to learn anything new and different, which accounts in large part for his extraordinary fertility. But then, I even have to battle students who resist understanding Bach as a creature of his own place and time. For all their devotion to music of past eras, few students know anything about the historical contexts within which their favourite composers worked.

What of cultural literacy? Don't we expect educated people (to say nothing of professional musicians) to know that core repertory? And isn't it the job of musicologists to ensure its perpetuation? Well, that was certainly the intention of the Schumanns. But several decades ago Virgil Thomson ridiculed what he called the Music Appreciation Racket, whereby upwardly mobile individuals were shamed into learning to identify the principal themes in Beethoven symphonies.[24] On the other end of the spectrum, Adorno derided the kinds of listeners who tune in only for the memorable melodies and then tune back out.[25] In *The Waves*, Virginia Woolf satirises the superficial concert audience of her day. Even the early Romantic Wackenroder sought to distance his own aesthetic hypersensitivity from the modes of consumption he witnessed at events.[26] For all the hue and cry about the demise of Classical music, it seems there has always been a sizable gap between the ideals of pure art and the conditions within which it circulates.

In any case, the Music Appreciation Racket largely collapsed in North America in the 1960s. Prior to that unruly moment, cultivated people accepted, however grudgingly, the claim that Classical music had greater ethical weight – or, as Roger Scruton never tires of arguing, that listening to it makes one feel noble.[27] But the moral outrages committed by the Germans during the Second World War put a dent in that line of persuasion, despite the concerted efforts of cultural pundits to deny any connection between context and 'the music itself'. And then came the responses to the Vietnam War: protest songs by Bob Dylan and other pop musicians on the one hand, and a tone deaf obtuseness in the continued assertions by the Appreciation Racketeers of Classical music's moral superiority. It just didn't hold water anymore.

Two generations later, today's cultural literacy should also include Louis Armstrong, Billie Holiday, George Gershwin, Miles Davis, Aretha Franklin, The Beatles, Led Zeppelin, Aerosmith, The Ramones, Prince, Metallica, Madonna, Public Enemy, Nicki Minaj, and so on. Contrary to what one might conclude reading the volumes devoted to twentieth-century music in Richard Taruskin's *Oxford History of Western Music*, the world of musicking has never been more exciting than today.[28] Recognising that, however, requires adjusting our sights.

For we cannot simply add these onto the tail end of what we present as the necessary backlog of music history — that backlog reconstructed so painstakingly since 1850. Rather, we have to review carefully what we want to emphasise in our training processes. English departments in North America have long since jettisoned the survey of English literature, leaving *Beowulf* for aspiring medievalists, and many foreign language programmes (for better or worse) now mostly offer courses in film. Only music departments insist on presenting that weird multi-language 'invented tradition' cobbled together from Latin responsories, Provençal troubadour songs, French chansons, Elizabethan anthems, Italian operas, German passions and Russian ballets.[29] And then the school year ends, perhaps with *Rite of Spring*, now over a hundred years old.

I still want to be able to introduce students to Josquin and Monteverdi, and their oeuvres should continue to belong to some part of the music curriculum. But as much as I love Josquin and Monteverdi, they cannot continue to take precedence over more recent playlists. We have bought the past at the expense of the present and future; we have achieved the internationalising of the German nineteenth-century symphony at the price of the rest of the planet's modes of cultural expression.

So let me return to Grocheio. A modern day Grocheio would certainly note that some segment of today's listeners and performers dedicate themselves to 'ancient music': that is (if we keep to Mendelssohn's timetable) music composed 40 or more years in the past. The Flemish music theorist Johannes Tinctoris, probably a student of Dufay, also set 40 years as his limit, when he said that nothing older than that had any value.[30] If we followed those models, we would relegate anything from before 1973 (including The Beatles) to history.

What if we left all that to the antiquarians — musicologists like me when I'm wearing my modal theory hat — and imagined a curriculum in which most courses would focus almost entirely on music of the late twentieth and twenty-first centuries? We would probably have to delete the courses in Renaissance counterpoint, Lutheran chorales and even orchestration. And what would we put in their place? Few of today's successful creative artists learn their craft in school. They're more likely to follow the model of garage bands: like minded musicians who get together to experiment and jam, first in private and then to a public, the feedback of which allows them to find what works and what doesn't. Robert Walser now has a programme in which students do this under his supervision, so as to earn them college credits and to give them the benefit of his own lifelong experience as a jazz and rock musician. Such pragmatic, hands-on training resembles the processes by which even the composers of the past acquired the skills necessary for their careers.

Given the extraordinary weight of the Classical tradition as it has developed and the profound inertia characteristic of academic curricula, we cannot hope to change the entire game plan by fiat. Perhaps, however, those of who care about these issues can push to have at least one course per programme dedicated to music of the last 40 years or so. Such a course would include in its historical account not only the minimalists and postmodernists of the concert stage but also punk, heavy metal, hip-hop, techno, music video, global pop, and YouTube. Its practical component would insist on improvisation and composition from all students. And it would necessarily engage with the explosion of new possibilities made available through digital technologies and the Internet.

But who will bell the cat? Who would teach such a course? The fear that we might have few volunteers speaks volumes to the long-term alienation of trained musicians from their own moment. Imagine asking Mozart or Brahms if they knew any experts on the musics of their particular times! The very idea is ridiculous; so why is it simply obvious in today's world?

I began this chapter by referring to Schoenberg's dream of a second hundred years of German hegemony. There was, of course, a second century of German dominated musicking – just not the kind Schoenberg had in mind. We're now a decade and a half into yet another such century, in which musicologists, theorists and major performing institutions continue to follow the script laid out by Mendelssohn and the Schumanns.

We need to develop new perspectives and turn our attention to today's creative artists, to the musicians who speak to our own times and locations. I dare say none of these composers will qualify as universal and timeless, in large part because such concepts themselves belong to nineteenth-century German Idealism. Far from timeless and universal, these criteria themselves bear the markings of a long outdated ideology, of a There and Then that somehow convinced the rest of the world of its transcendence. That ideology should now acquire the status of a blip on the screen and take its place in the ongoing narrative of cultural history. The subsequent chapters of that history are up to us.[31]

Notes

1   Schoenberg's student Josef Rufer reported that the composer told him this. As quoted in Hans Heinz Stuckenschmidt, *Schoenberg: His Life, World and Work*, trans. Humphrey Searle (New York: Schirmer, 1977), 277.

2   For more on the closing of the concert repertory, see particularly William Weber, *The Great Transformation of Musical Taste: Concert Programming from Haydn to Brahms* (Cambridge: Cambridge University Press, 2008), and 'Consequences of Canon: Institutionalization of Enmity between Contemporary and Classical Music, c. 1910', *Common Knowledge* 9 (2003): 78–99.

3   See my 'The Master Narrative and Me', introduction to *The Music History Classroom*, ed. Jim Davis (Farnham: Ashgate Publishing, 2012), 24–30.

4   For thorough and balanced discussion of this issue, see Celia Applegate and Pamela Potter, *Music and German National Identity* (Chicago: University of Chicago Press, 2002). See also Applegate, *Bach in Berlin: Nation and Culture in Mendelssohn's Revival of the St. Matthew Passion* (Ithaca, NY: Cornell University Press, 2005).

5   The Society for Ethnomusicology broke away from the American Musicological Society in 1953. Popular music studies began in disciplines outside musicology and began to be taken up in earnest in the 1990s, at the same time as critical musicology and the incorporation of concerns relating to race, gender and sexuality into serious research.

6   As Applegate and Potter put it: 'When musicologists place Finnish, Czech, Russian, or Spanish musical compositions under the heading of "musical nationalism", they implicitly compare them against a universally accepted German music and presume

34 *Susan McClary*

that other nations tried to distinguish themselves by deviating from the German standard.' *Music and German National Identity*, 1.

7   See particularly his *Musicking: The Meanings of Performing and Listening* (Middletown, CT: Wesleyan University Press, 1998), as well as his *Music, Society, Education* (Middletown, CT: Wesleyan University Press, 1997) and *Music of the Common Tongue: Survival and Celebration in African American Music* (Hanover, NH: Wesleyan University Press, 1987). The two latter books have been reissued along with *Musicking* by Wesleyan. See also Robert Walser, ed., *The Christopher Small Reader* (Middletown, CT: Wesleyan University Press, forthcoming).

8   Christoph Wolff has done a great deal to position Bach within his own cultural context. See his *Johann Sebastian Bach: The Learned Musician* (New York: W.W. Norton, 2001).

9   Christoph Wolff, *Mozart at the Gateway to His Fortune: Serving the Emperor, 1788–1791* (New York: W.W. Norton, 2012).

10 Applegate and Potter, *Music and German National Identity*, 9.

11 For more on Clara Schumann and her legacy, see Nancy B. Reich, *Clara Schumann: The Artist and the Woman* (Ithaca, NY: Cornell University Press, 2001).

12 See particularly the metaphysical rants excised from the translation of *Der freie Satz* but included in the back of the book. My favourite: 'Just as nature will always place elephants and crocodiles, for examples, where she can provide their life's necessities, so she will place a Beethoven – if indeed ever again – among the German People!' Heinrich Schenker, *Free Composition (Der freie Satz)*, trans. and ed., Ernst Oster (Vienna: Universal Edition, 1935; New York: Longman, 1979),160.

13 See Richard Leppert, *Music and Image: Domesticity, Ideology, and Socio-Cultural Formation in Eighteenth-Century England* (Cambridge: Cambridge University Press, 1989), and Linda Austern, "'Alluring the Auditorie to Effeminacie": Music and the Idea of the Feminine in Early Modern England", *Music and Letters* 74 (1993): 349–51.

14 Applegate and Potter, *Music and German National Identity*, 5.

15 Applegate and Potter, *Music and German National Identity*, 13.

16 Eduard Hanslick, *Von Musikalish-Schönen* (Leipzig: Rudolph Weigel, 1854).

17 Corey Kilgannon, 'A Composer's Best Friend', The *New York Times* 10 May 2013, accessed 15 December 2014, http://www.nytimes.com/2013/05/12/nyregion/lucy-mann-keeps-american-composers-spirits-alive.html.

18 Witness the endless procession of jeremiads lamenting the death of classical music, too well known and too numerous to list here.

19 For a critical account of the history of musicology, see Joseph Kerman, *Contemplating Music: Challenges to Musicology* (Cambridge MA: Harvard University Press, 1985).

20 Johannes de Grocheio, *De musica*, trans. Albert Seay (Colorado Springs, CO: The Colorado College Music Press, 1974). See the section excerpted in Piero Weiss and Richard Taruskin, *Music in the Western World* (New York: Schirmer, 1984), 63–7.

21 See particularly Louise Meintjes, 'Paul Simon's *Graceland*, South Africa, and the Mediation of Musical Meaning', *Ethnomusicology* 34 (1990): 37–73, and Charles Hamm, '*Graceland* Revisited', in his *Putting Popular Music in Its Place* (Cambridge: Cambridge University Press, 1995).

22 See Sally Macarthur, *Feminist Aesthetics in Music* (Westport, CT and London: Greenwood Press, 2001).

23 See my *Modal Subjectivities: Self-Fashioning in the Italian Madrigal* (Berkeley and Los Angeles: University of California Press, 2004) and *Desire and Pleasure in Seventeenth-Century Music* (Berkeley and Los Angeles: University of California Press, 2012). Thomas Christensen's new research on the nineteenth-century theorist François-Joseph Fétis demonstrates that the very concept of 'tonality' began as a way of documenting the superiority of Western classical music over the practices of Others. I wish to thank Professor Christensen for sharing some of this work with me.

24 See his 'Why Composer Write How', in *Virgil Thomson: A Reader*, ed. Richard Kostelanetz (Plume: 1984), 38–44.

25 See Theodor W. Adorno, 'Types of Musical Conduct', in his *Introduction to the Sociology of Music*, trans. E.G. Ashton (New York: Seabury Press, 1976), chapter 1.

26 Peter Franklin, *Reclaiming Late-Romantic Music: Singing Devils and Distant Sounds* (Berkeley and Los Angeles: 2014), chapter 1.

27 See Roger Scruton, *The Aesthetics of Music* (Oxford: Oxford University Press, 1999).

28 Richard Taruskin, *Oxford History of Western Music* (Oxford: Oxford University Press, 2005). See my review, 'The World According to Taruskin', in *Music and Letters*, 87 (2006): 408–15. A conference titled The End of Music History? was held in Taruskin's honor in Princeton in 2012.

29 See Robert Walser, 'Eruptions: Heavy Metal Appropriations of Classical Virtuosity', *Popular music*, 2 (1992): 265. Taruskin quotes Walser's claim disparagingly at the outset of the *Oxford History of Western Music* (vol. 1, xxii), but then proceeds to truck through precisely the hodgepodge Walser had critiqued.

30 Johannes Tinctoris, *Liber de arte contrapuncti* (1477), trans. Albert Seay (Rome: American Institute of Musicology, 1961), 14–15.

31 A version of this chapter was delivered at Western Sydney University and at the annual meeting of the South African Society for Research in Music in the summer of 2013.

3 Music and the intertextualities of listening, performing and teaching

Jennifer Shaw

Music often goes hand in hand with other artistic media: sung or spoken text; opera, film, music theatre and computer games are just a few examples. Those students who elect to study music at tertiary level are usually passionate about their musical activities. For those experiencing their first in-depth exposure to western art music and there are increasing numbers of such students in our undergraduate music courses it can be an overwhelming experience; occasionally transformative but often engulfing. In large part this is because the complex technical language of art music restricts its practitioners and audiences to those who possess that technical knowledge. So, in most undergraduate music programmes we struggle to find a common denominator in terms of the student knowledge base, and then the battle is on to fill them with enough content so they can graduate.

This context leads us to make choices about what is of shared importance and what can be omitted. It also has tended to mean that we have not had the resources to challenge nineteenth- and twentieth-century assumptions about content, pedagogy or theory. In terms of music analysis, for instance, as Jim Samson explained in an essay written late last century:

> Music analysis proceeds from a premise which underlies analytic aesthetics in general: namely, that objects of art share certain characteristics which define them as art and make them valuable to us, that they are determinate, and that they represent conceptual unities. In short, it is premissed as a closed, homogenous concept of the artwork. The most characteristic analytical mode is to equate concepts with objects, to allow fixed (or closed) representations of the object to stand for the object.[1]

Many undergraduate music programmes now take students not by individual audition or interview but via less conventional pathways for example, via audition by contemporary band recording or pathway from a music appreciation class. As this number increases, that divide between those who already possess specialist musical knowledge (and I will dub these the 'professionals') and those who do not (the 'generalists') is both critical and defining. The recent financial crisis faced by the School of Music at the Australian National University reinvigorated debate

Music and the intertextualities of listening, performing and teaching   37

about the merits of a professional tertiary music education over a generalist one; or what the university's Vice Chancellor, Professor Ian Young, dubbed in 2012 the 'conservatoire' versus 'university' model for music study.[2] Another way we might conceptualise this crisis is to ask whether, by turning out a select number of musicians who will gain long-term work as professional performers, composers and scholars, and a much larger body of generalist graduates who will go on to jobs and careers that have little to do with music, we are, in fact, failing our students.

My discussion in this chapter examines ways in which recent contributions to poststructural philosophy, and, in particular, to writings on and about intertextual practices, may help to bridge that divide in the way we share knowledge with our students and guide them in their listening to and performing of music. I argue that our understanding of intertextuality, with its roots in the writings of Julia Kristeva and through the intervention of literary and cultural scholars such as Jonathan Culler, John Fiske and Michael Riffaterre, has shifted. Moreover, while in the late 1960s and 1970s intertextuality was both a product of its time and ahead of its time, the aspects of it that have endured and developed over the last 50 years make it, in terms of music, a mode of listening that can be demonstrated to be 'in tune' with the way many students today encounter and approach music. In the second half of this chapter I explore how intertextual approaches to 'threshold' musical works, one by one of the 'great men' of Western art music and the other by an emerging female computer-game composer, can show us ways to bridge that gap.

The term 'intertextuality' was first coined by Bulgarian émigré-come-French national Kristeva in the late 1960s to refer to ways in which an author's text transforms elements of other texts. In her early formulations Kristeva, who, in her own words, arrived at her theories in attempting to read Mikhail Bakhtin and open up 'a new perspective beyond structuralism',[3] was not interested in source hunting and in fact suggested that intertextual readings operated in a vast, potentially infinite discursive space.[4] Her theories have been modified by many writers, including Barthes, Fiske and Riffaterre, most of whom have attempted to circumscribe that space or to impose a hierarchy of reading relationships within it.[5] As a result, although intertextuality is often grandly described as a theory of reading relationships between texts, many intertextual readings of both literary and musical texts focus, simply, on perceived instances of quotation. What I would like to suggest is that we go back to Kristeva's concept of an open discursive space and move away from more narrow readings.

I would also suggest that we contextualise intertextuality in its time and place: although intertextuality is often described as an intellectual product of the French formalists and poststructuralists, Paul De Man has pointed out that the focus on the reader and audience rather than on the work in Riffaterre's intertextual readings is particularly American;[6] and Riffaterre himself, while a French national, spent his entire academic life at Columbia University. Kristeva, in a 2002 essay, wrote expressly about this aspect of her relationship both with Riffaterre and with America, as she, too, although Paris-based, has been, since 1973, a frequent

38 Jennifer Shaw

visiting professor at Columbia and has been influenced both by Riffaterre himself and by the intellectual freedom that she experienced in the United States:

> Running away from communism to France, I did not encounter this [North American] hospitality over there, although France has given me my French nationality for which I will always be grateful. Paralyzed in its administrative and cultural tradition, and at the same time trying to free itself from this, my adoptive country promotes stunning innovations such as the artistic, philosophical and theoretical avant-gardes that have seduced me and have made its glory abroad. At the same time, it promotes a violent rejection, if not hatred toward these innovations. Contrastingly, America seems to me to be a territory that welcomes and even encourages grafts. This personal experience was the first kernel, the permanent basis for my interest in studying phenomena such as cultural and textual interaction, and above all intertextuality. This word is often taken as my creation and thus a term brevetted mostly by French literary theory. But at the same time I cannot but recognize how much this concept, especially when thinking of the works of Michael Riffaterre, is attuned to the American way of understanding literature by having a direct impact on the everyday reader in a given socio-political context.
>
> … For me, intertextuality is mostly a way of making *history* go down in us. We, two texts, two destinies, two psyches.[7]

As Jonathan Culler wrote in 1976, 'The notion of intertextuality emphasizes that to read is to place a work in a discursive space, relating it to other texts and to the codes of that space, and writing itself is a similar activity: a taking up of a position in a discursive space.'[8] I would add that this discursive space is not one populated by 'orphaned' texts as Kristeva has put it,[9] but it is a space defined by the socio-political and cultural contexts of its audiences.

Within this discursive space, intertextuality focuses on the reader's interpretation of a specific text within a network of other texts — a network created by the reader or listener: this, in turn, de-emphasises the literary or musical work as a completed, autonomous product of a particular author. In music studies the concept of intertextuality has been adopted in writings by a number of scholars, among them Christina Gier, Robert Hatten, Michael Klein, Kevin Korsyn, Lloyd Whitesell and Joseph Straus. Some (like Gier and Korsyn) have engaged with Kristeva's original concept.[10] Hatten, Klein, Straus and Whitesell have focused on later, modified versions of intertextuality as articulated, in particular, by Harold Bloom.[11] Many other music scholars, although using the term 'intertextuality' have not attempted to define its use in their work, and have tended to use it as a synonym either for 'extra-musical' or cross-referential sources. But what has been absent from all these discussions is a historicising and contextualising of the development of the concept of intertextuality, both in terms of its intellectual roots and its adaptation and transformation across non-literary media and genres.

Music and the intertextualities of listening, performing and teaching   39

Riffaterre's reformulation of Kristeva's theory – and one that in turn Kristeva has expressly acknowledged as an important dynamic in her own shifting understanding of intertextuality – is the one I find most useful. Riffaterre argues that intertextuality is a modality of perception. In other words, intertextuality should be practised as a way of reading literary texts or, as I have argued elsewhere, of hearing musical ones, through which readers/listeners open themselves to possible relationships between texts.[12] In this context, a musical 'text' can be read as a fixed object (e.g. a musical score) or experienced through time (e.g. through the act of listening to a recorded or live performance). Riffaterre's model, which he first developed through a series of writings in the late 1970s and early 1980s, focuses on two types of clues in the text: the first he classes as structural invariants, which may, for instance, be repeated motifs, characters, or themes; the second he terms 'ungrammaticalities', that is, moments that do not make sense within the framework of a given text.[13] For every ungrammaticality in a work Riffaterre claims that there is a grammaticality that lies elsewhere in a missing 'intertext' or 'ghost text'. It is important to stress that this is not source hunting for the elite audience (and Riffaterre makes this explicit in his writings). At times there will be a specific intertext capable of being identified; but often 'the ghost text may embody itself in potential but ready-made stereotypes within the range of any reader's linguistic competence'.[14]

In this model, reading or listening occurs in two stages: the first reading/ listening tends to be linear and representational, at the second stage, recognition of structural invariants and ungrammaticalities forces the reader to re-read, and the listener to re-listen, and, each, to employ their linguistic/musical competence in order to make sense of the significance of these moments.[15] This mode of reading/listening forces the hidden or 'ghost' intertext that is responsible for the structural invariants and ungrammaticalities to rise to the surface.[16] In the context of musical texts, the focus is on ways in which the composer transforms elements of other musical texts, whether known to the listener or not, and on the listener's interpretation of the text and competent reading of the text, along with its invariants and ungrammaticalities. So, while there is some circumscription of Kristeva's infinite intertextual space, in effect it is still wide open.

Looking back, in 2002, at her own development and wide-ranging intellectual interests and engagement, Kristeva identified one common point; that is, her search for the 'threshold' or in-between zone that 'is able to render not only a temporal connection or a spatial point of contact, but also a social melting pot, a political openness and most of all a mental plasticity'.[17] In that same essay she suggested that intertextuality should be 'conceived as a crossed threshold between languages and cultures'.[18] The focus of some of my recent work has also been on that concept of 'threshold' whether within a musical work (a concept I have borrowed from Julian Johnson) or, more aligned with Kristeva's conception, as applied to those musical works that don't fit neatly into our boxes of genre and style.[19]

My first example of a 'threshold' work is Austro-American composer Arnold Schoenberg's 1945 Prelude for the proposed *Genesis* Suite. In 1944 conductor and

40 *Jennifer Shaw*

composer Nat Shilkret, musical director at Metro-Goldwyn-Mayer movie studios, commissioned Schoenberg, Alexandre Tansman, Darius Milhaud, Mario Castelnuovo-Tesdesco, Ernst Toch and Igor Stravinsky — all émigré composers living in or close to Los Angeles at the time — to compose music for a proposed film setting of the Old Testament Book of Genesis. Each was tasked to write a piece for orchestra, with the Biblical texts to be sung/spoken by a male narrator and mixed-voice choir. Schoenberg agreed to write the Prelude to the *Genesis* movie: other movements completed included Shilkret's 'Creation' (setting verses from The Book of Genesis, chapters 1 and 2), Tansman's 'Adam and Eve' (chapters 2 and 3), Milhaud's 'Cain and Abel' (chapter 4), Castelnuovo-Tedesco's 'The Flood' ('Noah's Ark') (chapters 6, 7 and 8), Toch's 'The Covenant' ('The Rainbow') (chapter 9) and Stravinsky's 'Babel' (chapter 11). Other Los Angeles-based composers had agreed to write music for settings of later chapters in the Book of Genesis, but the *Genesis* movie itself was never made. Schoenberg completed his piece in September 1945, and in November 1945 the *Genesis* Suite, consisting of these seven completed works was premiered in Los Angeles at the Wilshire Ebell Theater by the Janssen Symphony Orchestra, conducted by Werner Janssen. In December 1945, the orchestral track, conducted by Janssen, and the choral track, conducted by Hugo Strelitzer, were recorded, with a narration track set down by actor Edward Arnold in 1946. Janssen and Shilkret pooled funds to self-publish.[20] After a couple of initial performances of the Suite in Salt Lake City and Portland and on radio, documented performances stopped. The full scores were rediscovered in the last decade of the twentieth century, and further commercial recordings have been released since then.[21]

The seven composers did not collaborate on the Suite nor did they alter their diverse musical languages, their styles or their signature textures. For example, in the final minutes of Schoenberg's *Genesis* Prelude, a vocalise chorus enters with a final statement of a fugue subject, with the twelve-tone row partitioned between the vocal and instrumental parts, before the Prelude ends on sustained C octaves that fade to a solo, sustained mezzo voice on C. In the Suite, this is followed immediately by Shilkret's 'Creation' setting, which, after shimmering tone-clusters, settles into predictable, C major film music with clichéd Hollywood voice-over.[22]

On the 1950/2001 recording, Schoenberg's *Genesis* Prelude bears the title 'The Earth was without form'; a reference to *Genesis* chapter 1, verse 2: 'And the earth was without form, and void; and darkness was upon the face of the deep.' But this is not a piece 'without form': nor does it depict a 'void'; its melodic and timbral content are intensely expressive; its 'space' filled with fugal imaginings. At the same time, the sub-title indicates the place of the Prelude in the Suite structure: that is, Schoenberg's music depicts a universal, creative state before a directed creative vision was realised.

But the 'C-ness' of his Prelude ending has continued to bother me. In the context of Schoenberg's aesthetic, this is an intertextual ungrammaticality: it bothered Shilkret, too, who moved it, in the initial recording, to the very end of the Suite and re-labelled it as a 'Postlude', even though at least one reviewer of that recording noted that 'Schoenberg composed his Prelude with the idea in mind

Music and the intertextualities of listening, performing and teaching   41

that it would lead to something else and wrote the end accordingly'.[23] Yet that 'something else' is also clearly not Shilkret's 'Creation'. So what is the missing intertext?

Some years ago, after hearing Schoenberg's Prelude for the first time, as an oboist I took part in a performance of Joseph Haydn's *Creation* oratorio and, for me, at least one of those intertexts became apparent. The famous 1798 oratorio depicts creation as described in three sources – the Book of Genesis, the Book of Psalms and John Milton's epic poem, *Paradise Lost* – and begins with a dramatic instrumental overture entitled 'The Representation of Chaos' ('Die Vorstellung des Chaos'), which precedes over 30 vocal movements. Both Schoenberg's Prelude and Haydn's overture last for just over 5 minutes; both use the winds, brass and percussion soloistically with an emphasis on dark tone colours. But what was most striking to me was again the 'C-ness'; those opening, uncontextualised C octaves in Haydn's *Creation*.[24] What Schoenberg gives us in his 1940s *Genesis* film piece is, I would suggest, a retrospective recontextualising of those C octaves in Haydn's *Creation* oratorio: before and after chaos there is and will be order: and Schoenberg's is a pre-chaos *chaosmos* exactly as Deleuze and Guattari conceived it, as a first level of 'absolute deterritorialisation'; infinite but not indeterminate; full of variety, variation and lines of flight.[25] We don't need to identify the Haydn intertext to make sense of Schoenberg's *Genesis* Prelude; nor do we need to be aware of Schoenberg's Prelude to appreciate Haydn's *Creation*, but recognition of this relationship adds another layer of richness to what is not 'mere' film music but a complex socio-political, end-of-war work and, in Deleuzian terms, one of many divergent responses to history that itself is a chaotic and active becoming.[26] This is not Schoenberg – or Haydn – attempting to experience, capture or express the beginnings of creation, but of them both attempting to conceptualise it; to *think* it.

My second example of a threshold work is the music written by young Japanese-American composer Laura Shigihara for *Plants vs. Zombies*, a computer game released in 2009.[27] If you have access to a 7–17 year old you'll know how popular and addictive this game is. In *Plants vs. Zombies* the gamers' aim is to cover their territory with plants to prevent the zombies entering their virtual house and eating their brains. The defined territory varies per level (in the 2009 version of the game, front and back yards and roof are used) as does the time of day or night and the plants, some of which are defensive and others that can be used more aggressively to destroy the zombie invaders. Aside from the never-seen 'you' inside (your) fortified Western-style slightly gothic suburban house there is one other live but insane human (Crazy Dave), waves of the undead that attack your house relentlessly (including your own zombie avatar) and the personified, solar-powered plants. Music features in the game itself as a subject: plants in a tranquil 'time out' Zen garden – the only place in which sustained major-key music is heard – request and thrive on music from an old phonograph; while, throughout the main game, Jack-in-the-Box Zombie plays an exploding wind-up jack-in-the-box and Disco Zombie and his all-male entourage disco relentlessly to your doorstep, if left unchecked.[28] And, of course, there are the obligatory musical clichés of the 'Hammer Horror' film genre if the zombies do make it into your house and eat

42   *Jennifer Shaw*

your brains. Shigihara herself makes a solo 'star' appearance as the singing sunflower in the extended music video at the game's end, which also features soloists and chorus from the singing undead.

What makes Shigihara's music stand out in comparison to most game musics is that it is quirky yet highly referential ('intertextual' in a loose sense) and, as it is on a loop in the game, listeners hear some pieces scores or even hundreds of times, so her music has to stand up to repetition.[29] In this era of technological convergence you can hear the music embedded in the game or download the 'authentic' digital version to your laptop or iPad as MP3 or ringtones; or listen to Shigihara's acoustic piano version (or covers by others) on YouTube, or watch the music video, or download the sheet music. 'Grasswalk', for instance, is a pastiche of cakewalk, tango, and funereal military march rhythms and melodies, replete (in the digital version) with snare drums, pizzicato high strings, and sinuous, lyrical lines for solo cello and oboe.[30] 'Choose your seeds' has elements of ragtime (reminiscent of William Bolcom's 1971 B♭ minor *Graceful Ghost Rag*) but it also layers references to classical pastoral and lament genres through instrumentation, chromatic harmony, minor tonality and elaborate 'baroque' ornamentation.[31] And while this piece might qualify as a 'motto' rather than a fully developed musical work, most of the other pieces on the digital recording are at least 4 5 minutes long and several are over 11 minutes, most with substantial melodic, harmonic, and textural variation and development. I don't think there is anything to be gained from identifying specific intertexts here, but the nostalgic reference to structural invariants from a common-practice vocabulary is clear, and the distinctive sharpened fourth degree (notated as B♭) and 'written out' ornaments in the melody of 'Choose your seeds', which I hear as ungrammaticalities, also have their common practice ghosts: among them, for example, the F♯ minor Adagio movement from Mozart's Piano Concerto No. 23 in A major K488. Again, in terms that both Deleuze and Kristeva would endorse, the importance is not the origins or representation of these intertexts, but on how they proliferate and are differentiated, and how we hear them as meaningful.

So, why not work backwards with both our 'generalist' and 'professional' music students from today's common practices to those less familiar intertexts? But where does this approach leave the nineteenth- and twentieth-century venerated concept of authorship? Is it still valid? While Shigihara, for instance, helpfully classifies her compositions with a range of online keywords classical, gothic, indie among them this is music that only makes sense in the context of the game or with knowledge of the game. It's also clear that gamers love the music: 7 year olds ('generalists' supreme!) don't need to identify the referential contexts outside the game to enjoy it. But it's also clear that while Shigihara is the composer, her role is one part of an elaborate collaboration and negotiation not just with the PopCap game designers and music arrangers but also with her online audiences. It is also clear that that is a dynamic relationship: in her chosen market she has opted to make herself accessible and responsive to her audiences through social media. She is very much 'the composer', but not the focus of interest for those who play the game and then buy the music.

Music and the intertextualities of listening, performing and teaching   43

Our students' focus, for the most part, in the music they listen to – whether art music or popular musics – has, through technological convergence and increased accessibility, shifted away from the composer alone to a range of performance and production options. Likewise, most students – generalists and professionals – will now search online for information about musical works and are used to following links, playing tracks and making the kinds of connections facilitated and encouraged by the web. This approach sits comfortably with presenting them with multifaceted, mediated interpretations of musical texts and their audiences. It also aligns with Deleuze's and Guattari's idea of perception as 'the interaction or connection of forces or codes'.[32] Yet, despite these dramatic shifts in the ways many of our students experience and comprehend music, the academy persists in teaching music and musical works along canonical lines.

In an article published in 1990 Riffaterre argued that, on the whole in the humanities, we are afraid to theorize about, and therefore risk challenging, our basic principles:

> [T]he role of the humanities is to preserve a tradition in order to better inform the present and to prepare the future. The liberal humanist teaches what is appropriately called a discipline attempting to maintain a culture and a social consensus or class consensus, by linking the concept of literacy to the concept of canon. It is only natural that the humanist should fear precisely that approach that questions the validity of a canon, or of oriented readings of that canon.[33]

Unfortunately this rings true. Universities in Australia oversee and support faculties and schools, in which sit disciplines or departments. Order is maintained in the disciplines/departments by discipline and department heads. Above the universities – the vast majority of which are publicly funded – the government requires all research and creative practice to be coded and ordered in established 'fields of research' or discipline areas: performing and creative arts, for instance, become coded as Field of Research (FoR) 1904 or placed under cultural studies FoR 2002; literary studies have their own recognized FoR 2005; and philosophy dominates FoR codes 2201–2203. To threaten the canon, and canonical readings of texts, is to threaten that established order.

But the established order is being transformed in any case – partly through government funding models for universities and a desire, on the part of government, to see universities increasingly source their funding from the private sector; partly through this emerging era of technological and operational convergence; and partly through new ways of learning: take, for instance, the rise of massive online open courses – anathema to the nineteenth- and twentieth-century concept of the music conservatorium. This is an era that is becoming undisciplined, but undisciplined does not mean unruly or directionless. Looking back on her own intellectual journey in 2002, Kristeva depicts her own constantly transformed understanding and application of intertextuality as a broad 'adventure'.[34] That adventure gives us the freedom to encourage students who choose to align

44 *Jennifer Shaw*

themselves with our disciplines to embrace that convergence and accessibility and, regardless of whether they take up professional music careers, to learn from and love the journey.

Notes

1 Jim Samson, 'Analysis in Context', in *Rethinking Music*, ed. Nicholas Cook and Mark Everist (Oxford and New York: Oxford University Press, 1999/2001), 43.
2 See David McLennan and Emma Macdonald, 'ANU reaffirms cuts to music', *Canberra Times* 16 June 2012, http://www.canberratimes.com.au/anu-reaffirms-cuts-to-music-20120615 20fuz.html and Peter J. Tregear, *Enlightenment or Entitlement? Rethinking Tertiary Music Education*. Platform Papers. Quarterly Essays on The Performing Arts 38 (Strawberry Fields, NSW: Currency Press, 2014).
3 Julia Kristeva, '"Nous Deux" or a (Hi)story of Intertextuality', *Romanic Review* 93/1–2 (2002): 8.
4 Kristeva, 'Problèmes de la structuration du texte', *Tel Quel: Théorie d'ensemble* (Paris: Éditions du Seuil, 1968), 298 317 and Kristeva, *La Revolution du langue poétique* (Paris: Éditions du Seuil, 1974); trans. Margaret Waller as *Revolution in Poetic Language*, with introduction by Leon S. Roudiez (New York: Columbia University Press, 1984).
5 See, for instance, Roland Barthes, *S/Z* (Paris: Éditions du Seuil, 1973); trans. Richard Miller (Oxford: Blackwell, 1990); John Fiske, *Television Culture* (London and New York: Routledge, 1987); and Michael Riffaterre, *Semiotics of Poetry* (Bloomington, Indiana: Indiana University Press, 1978/London: Methuen, 1980).
6 Paul De Man, 'Hypogram and Inscription: Michael Riffaterre's Poetics of Reading', *Diacritics* 11/4 (1981): 22.
7 Kristeva, '"Nous Deux" or a (Hi)story of Intertextuality', 7 8.
8 Jonathan Culler, 'Presupposition and Intertextuality', *Modern Language Notes* 91/6 (1976): 1382 3.
9 Kristeva, '"Nous Deux" or a (Hi)story of Intertextuality', 8.
10 Christina Bindslev Gier, 'Intertextuality in Music and Gender Ideology in Alban Berg's Modernist Aesthetics' (PhD thesis, Duke University, 2003); Kevin Korsyn, 'Beyond Privileged Contexts: Intertextuality, Influence, and Dialogue', in *Rethinking Music*, 55 72.
11 See, for instance, Robert S. Hatten, 'The Place of Intertextuality in Music Studies', *American Journal of Semiotics* 3/4 (1985), 69 82; Michael L. Klein, *Intertextuality in Western Art Music* (Bloomington, Indiana: Indiana University Press, 2005); Joseph N. Straus, 'The "Anxiety of Influence" in Twentieth-Century Music, *The Journal of Musicology* 9/4 (1991): 430 47; and Lloyd Whitesell, 'Men with a Past: Music and the "Anxiety of Influence"', *19th-Century Music* 18/2 (1994): 152 67.
12 Riffaterre, 'Syllepsis', *Critical Inquiry* 6/4 (1980): 625. The extension of Riffaterre's intertextual mode to musical texts is mine: See Jennifer Shaw, 'Arnold Schoenberg and the Intertextuality of Composing and Performing', *Context* 31 (2006): 110 12.
13 Riffaterre, 'Syllepsis', 625 6.
14 Riffaterre, *Semiotics of Poetry*, 91.
15 Riffaterre, 'Syllepsis', 626 7.
16 Riffaterre, *Fictional Truth* (Baltimore and London: Johns Hopkins University Press, 1996), 86.
17 Kristeva, '"Nous Deux" or a (Hi)story of Intertextuality', 9.
18 Kristeva, '"Nous Deux" or a (Hi)story of Intertextuality', 9.
19 Julian Johnson, *Webern and the Transformation of Nature* (Cambridge: Cambridge University Press, 1999).

Music and the intertextualities of listening, performing and teaching 45

20 In this recording, Schoenberg's Prelude was renamed 'Postlude' and moved to the last disc – this version has been re-released by the Pristine label in their *American 78rpm Rarities* Series (PASC306). Capitol Records reissued the Suite in 1950, with Schoenberg's Prelude name and position restored, and a new narration track featuring Pastor Ted Osborne.

21 EMI reissued the 1950 recording on CD in 2001. In 2005 Naxos released a new recording (Berlin Radio Symphony Orchestra and Ernst Senff Choir tracks recorded 2000; the narration track – with three male and two female narrators – was recorded in 2003).

22 The 1950/2001 recording can be accessed at https://play.spotify.com, https://www.youtube.com/watch?v=wyBtOstfcWo or http://www.simfy.de/artists/681153-Janssen-Symphony-Orchestra/albums/549323-The-Genesis-Suite-Nathaniel-Shilkret?locale=en (licence agreements permitting). Excerpts from the Naxos recording are also available on the Milken Archive and Naxos websites.

23 S.G.S., Review of Pristine Audio PASC 306, March 2012, accessed 3 March 2015, http://www.classicalcdreview.com/306.html.

24 There are numerous online excerpts of the opening of Haydn's *Creation*, and recordings of the entire oratorio, in the public domain.

25 See Gilles Deleuze and Félix Guattari, *A Thousand Plateaus: Capitalism and Schizophrenia*, trans. Brian Massumi (Minneapolis and London: University of Minnesota Press, 1987) and Claire Colebrook, *Gilles Deleuze* (London and New York: Routledge, 2002), 76–7.

26 Claire Colebrook, *Understanding Deleuze* (Crows Nest, Sydney: Allen & Unwin, 2002), xxxiv.

27 *Plants vs. Zombies*, developed by George Fan/PopCap Games, published by PopCap Games, 2009. *Plants vs. Zombies 2: It's About Time*, developed by PopCap Games, published by Electronic Arts, was released in 2013. Both games have won multiple industry awards.

28 The original Disco Zombie, who entered the lawn 'moonwalking', resembled Michael Jackson as Jackson appeared, as a zombie, in the 1983 MTV *Thriller* music video. After threatened legal action in 2010 by the estate of Michael Jackson, the character was changed to a generic 1970s disco dancer.

29 In *Plants vs. Zombies 2*, the music consists of remixes of tracks Shigihara composed for the 2009 game.

30 'Grasswalk' can be heard in many digital and traditional instrument versions online: http://laurashigihara.bandcamp.com/track/grasswalk (authorised digital excerpt); http://soundcloud.com/dren-mcdonald/plants-vs-zombies-from-the (string quartet arrangement, *The String Arcade*, 2014); https://www.youtube.com/watch?v=XSuv-dvqK9k (solo piano version performed by Shigihara); http://sebastianwolff.info/download/plants-vs-zombies/PvZ-Grasswalk.pdf (sheet music by Shigihara, arr. Sebastian Wolff).

31 'Chose your seeds' can be found at http://laurashigihara.bandcamp.com/track/choose-your-seeds-in-game (digital version); https://www.youtube.com/watch?v=c9yA_fqH9m0 (Shigihara, solo piano) and http://sebastianwolff.info/download/plants-vs-zombies/PvZ-Choose_Your_Seeds.pdf (piano/violin sheet music by Shigihara, arr. Wolff).

32 Deleuze and Guattari, *A Thousand Plateaus*, 147.

33 Michael Riffaterre, 'Fear of Theory', *New Literary History* 21/4 (1990): 921.

34 Kristeva, '"Nous Deux" or a (Hi)story of Intertextuality', 8.

4 An immanent approach to theory and practice in creative arts research

Joseph Williams

In the Australian higher education sector in recent years, considerable attention has centred on the relationship between traditional research outputs (books, book chapters, journal articles and conference publications) and non-traditional research outputs (including creative artistic works, performances, digital and other media art forms, and design). Both kinds of research generate measurable outcomes and these are evaluated through the Higher Education Research Data Collection (HERDC) system for traditional research and the Excellence in Research in Australia (ERA) initiative for non-traditional research. However, traditional research is recognised financially while non-traditional research is not. This matter has recently been made a point of focus in the newly established Australian Council of Deans and Directors of Creative Arts (DDCA)[1] and has generated much debate in the sector.[2] One of the contested issues is whether creative arts practice can be counted as research. Practitioner-researchers often face an uphill battle in having their work taken seriously alongside more traditional forms of qualitative, quantitative and conceptual research. Practice-led research outcomes within the creative arts are often difficult to express in qualitative or quantitative terms and, consequently, higher education administrators find the idea that art produces knowledge problematic.[3]

Obstacles to the acceptance of practice-led research in academia arise from the very characteristics that make it a valuable mode of knowledge production. As Barrett states:

> what may be argued to constitute the very strength of such research – its personally situated, interdisciplinary and diverse and emergent approaches – often contradict what is expected of research. This results in a continued devaluing of studio-based enquiry and research activities in relation to the more familiar methods of other disciplines.[4]

The need to demonstrate that artistic practice can be undertaken as a form of research has generated a conversation displaying extraordinary variation between authors regarding the objects, aims, methods and outcomes of creative-research projects. According to Biggs, however, the multiplicity of research methods and

An immanent approach to theory and practice in creative arts research   47

practices in the field should be regarded as an asset rather than a shortcoming.[5] In this chapter, I will focus on the ways in which practice-led research might be theorised without smothering the qualities that make it unique. I will critique three different models of practice-led research – Bolt's concept of 'handlability' borrowed from Heidegger,[6] Barrett's use of Foucault's 'author-function',[7] and Smith and Dean's model of the 'iterative cycle web'[8] – to demonstrate the distinctive ways in which these models enable knowledge-production through creative practice. Each model generates its own set of benefits while at the same time leaving space for new formulations of the relationship between theory and practice in creative work. Through a discussion of my own work, *Sillage* (2015), I will show how Deleuzian concepts can activate the idea of knowledge production as immanent in the creative process.[9] Throughout the chapter I will employ the Deleuzian–Guattarian concept of 'assemblage' to suggest that practice-led research projects can be understood as creative-theoretical assemblages.

Assemblage

According to Deleuze and Guattari, assemblages are formed through their complex relations and functions. They write that:

> On a first, horizontal, axis, an assemblage comprises two segments, one of content, the other of expression. On the one hand, it is a *machinic assemblage* … an intermingling of bodies reacting to one another; on the other hand it is a *collective assemblage of enunciation*, of acts and statements, of incorporeal transformations attributed to bodies. Then on a vertical axis, the assemblage has both *territorial sides*, or reterritorialised sides, which stabilise it, and *cutting edges of deterritorialisation* which carry it away.[10]

An assemblage is not merely a collection of parts, nor does it possess a stable identity of its own. As a machinic assemblage, it functions according to the connections it makes and any new connections will qualitatively alter the machine: quality and quantity are therefore not opposed in the assemblage but are ontologically entangled. Colebrook uses the example of the bicycle as a machine, with no fixed 'end' or intention, which becomes a vehicle only in connection with a human body, which itself becomes a cyclist.[11] A collective assemblage of enunciation territorialises the machine by attaching to it a regime of signs, so forming the basis of an identity, and potentially limiting the possibilities for connection on the machinic side. For example, if we think of bicycles primarily as vehicles, this image is a territorialisation produced performatively by a collective assemblage of enunciation. Territorialisations can be deterritorialised in various ways, such as through unusual connections that change the nature of the machine whereby 'the cycle becomes an art object when placed in a gallery'.[12] All of these functions – machinic assemblages, assemblages of

48 Joseph Williams

enunciation, and deterritorialisations — are part of the assemblage, including those that break it apart.

Deleuze and Guattari understand assemblages to be organised along lines that differ according to their function. Molar lines produce hierarchical relationships and rigid segments.[13] The molar is what is perceived and coded. It is the world of readily identifiable things. Molar lines work to produce relative stability within an assemblage. Molecular lines are associated with a relative deterritorialisation, organising in a more fluid and non-hierarchical way. The molecular both produces and escapes the molar. It is chaotic and imperceptible such that the molar is constituted in the organisation and extension of the molecular.[14] Lines of flight have the capacity to break apart both molar and molecular lines, drawing an assemblage away from known organisations. A line of flight is an absolute deterritorialisation, a pure and unpredictable movement of becoming. A territory, then, is not a fixed space so much as it is a process, a conversation between territorialising and deterritorialising forces that are subject to interruption by lines of flight.[15]

Practice-led research is just such a process, an assemblage with the capacity to produce territories, become deterritorialised and reterritorialised, and to crystallise in moments of relative stability, or to follow lines of flight in which they become radically other-than-themselves. Although practice-led research might already be considered a deterritorialisation of traditional research, my focus in this chapter is on the nature of practice-led research scholarship. I will aim to show that thinking in terms of assemblage — accounting for de/reterritorialisations, molar and molecular lines, lines of flight, machinic assemblages and assemblages of enunciation — is useful, not only for negotiating creative-research processes, but also for identifying broad contexts of significance in this scholarship.

Moving away from reflective practice

The dominant model of exegetical writing in practice-led research posits theory and practice in terms of an interactive relationship. This overlooks the productive forces that might emerge from a conception of theory and practice, to draw on Karen Barad, as 'intra-active', that is, as ontologically entangled in a reciprocally presupposing and mutually productive relationship. Barad writes that:

> The neologism 'intra-action' *signifies the mutual constitution of entangled agencies.* That is, in contrast to the usual 'interaction', which assumes that there are separate and individual agencies that precede their interaction, the notion of intra-action recognises that distinct agencies do not precede, but rather emerge through, their intra-action. It is important to note that 'distinct' agencies are only distinct in a relational, not an absolute, sense, that is, *agencies are only distinct in relation to their mutual entanglement; they don't exist as individual elements.*[16]

An immanent approach to theory and practice in creative arts research 49

The intra-action of theory and practice is immanent to creativity. The following examination of some existing models of practice-led research illustrates this principle in a movement away from reflective thinking.

Bolt draws on Heidegger's concept of 'handlability' to propose that we know the world theoretically only after we know it through handling it.[17] This implies a rethinking of human relations with technology and the world that moves away from mastery towards co-responsibility. She also questions the conventional model of 'cause and effect' by drawing on the ancient Greek concept of 'aition', meaning 'that to which something is indebted'.[18] Bolt builds on these notions of handling, co-responsibility, and indebtedness to re-situate the work of art as the particular form of understanding that the creative process enacts. Her model can be seen to share some qualities with the concept of 'assemblage'. First, it accounts for the influence of materials in collaboration with the artist (machinic assemblage). Second, it points to the artwork's indebtedness to the incorporeal, expressive aspects (collective assemblage of enunciation). However, while Bolt argues that knowledge flows from practice into theory, and not the other way around, she leaves the distinction between practical and theoretical processes in place. This distinction, as I will demonstrate, is dissolved when creative arts research is thought of as an assemblage. The intra-activity of theory and practice is necessary to the related movements of deterritorialisation and reterritorialisation. These movements continually carry the assemblage into the 'virtual' – the chaotic and unpredictable space which activates the potential for difference and becoming, where the assemblage is both no-longer-what-was and not-yet-what-will-be.

Barrett proposes a model for exegetical writing that draws on Foucault's notion of 'author function' and Haraway's 'situated knowledge'.[19] Foucault facilitates a conception of the author–work relationship that avoids situating the work as a discrete entity and the artist as 'unique creator'. Rather, the concept of 'author function' draws attention to the field of antecedent works and the discourse within which the artist and work function. Situated knowledge is suggested by Barrett as a complementary tool for re-inserting the self, providing a counterpoint to the critical distance of the Foucauldian approach. Situated knowledge is partial, locatable and critical, an antidote to reductionist and relativist approaches which endorse a 'gaze from nowhere claiming the power to see and not be seen'.[20] The primary distinction between Barrett's model and a creative-theoretical assemblage is that Barrett takes the creative process as given. Admittedly, her focus is on addressing the legitimate concern of auto-connoisseurship – the valorisation of artworks by their creators. However, the benefits of conceptualising arts research as a creative undertaking which is theorised retrospectively are limited. A model of assemblage requires a more holistic and integrated understanding of theory and practice.

Smith and Dean suggest an 'iterative, cyclic web' of practice-led research, into which the practitioner-researcher enters at any point and moves between interconnected phases of research, practice, and reflection (see Figure 4.1 for a visual representation).[21] The researcher navigates creative and theoretical processes either by following the cycle, traversing the web along connecting

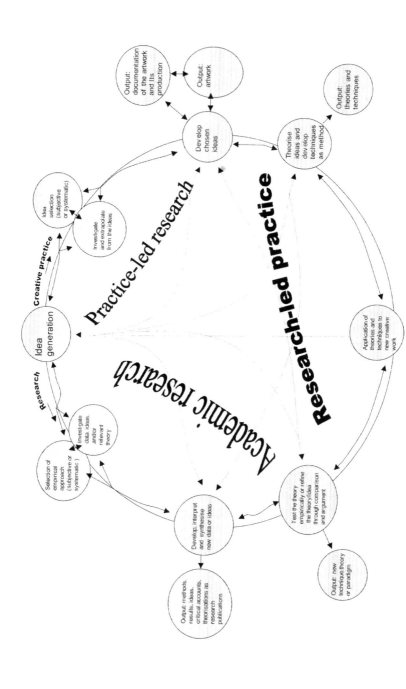

Figure 4.1 A model of creative arts and research processes: Smith and Dean's iterative cyclic web of practice-led research and research-led practice.[22]

An immanent approach to theory and practice in creative arts research 51

lines or repeating smaller cyclic arrangements of processes within the larger creative-research process.

Elements of Smith and Dean's iterative cyclic web hint at the concept of assemblage. They emphasise that 'although we might think of [artistically selective] choices as individually motivated, they are made in response to broader social and artistic forces'.[23] Arguments against the theorisation of creative practice, in their view, contribute to the mystification of the artist and perpetuate romantic ideals about the spontaneity of the creative process. They suggest a utility for their model in prompting researchers to experiment with different entry points into the iterative cyclic web. This latter point suggests the model's capacity to serve a deterritorialising function, destabilising habitual creative-research practices and opening new paths to creativity.

The key difference between a creative-theoretical assemblage and the models discussed above lies in the relationship between theory and practice. Theory and practice within the assemblage are intra-active. They are machinic assemblages in the sense that they consist in the formation of connections – antecedent works, materials and techniques, and influential theories – that determine the qualities of the assemblage. Creative-theoretical assemblages also need to be thought of dynamically. Theory sits on the virtual side of practice, continually undoing it, thereby opening the possibility of it becoming-other through reterritorialisations, or mutations of the assemblage. Simultaneously, the reverse process operates with practice occupying the virtual side of theory. Both researcher and assemblage, then, must always be creative-theoretical, as they only exist insofar as practice and theory become-one-another. The practitioner-researcher can here be distinguished from an author, since their role is not simply to produce and explain the work, but to mediate the flows of practice into theory, and vice versa.

Moving towards the immanence of theory and practice

The music for my album *Sillage*, for guitar, microphone and computer, draws influences from British and Irish folk music, soundscape music, and *music concrète*. The title is a French term for a wake, or trail, and is employed by perfumers to describe the extent to which a scent lingers in the air. The album's production might be thought of as a process of locating myself within a series of mediators. Of mediators, Deleuze writes:

> Whether they're real or imaginary, animate or inanimate, one must form one's mediators. It's a series: if you don't belong to a series, even a completely imaginary one, you're lost. I need my mediators to express myself, and they'd never express themselves without me: one is always working in a group, even when it doesn't appear to be the case.[24]

Forming a series of mediators as part of the assemblage involved the kinds of collaborative engagements with materials described by Bolt, as well as the connection to bodies of theory and knowledge, antecedent works and influences, and

52 *Joseph Williams*

the university environment as a place where people converge and influence one another. The series is theoretically infinite. It therefore becomes necessary for practitioner-researchers to identify those mediators that are best able to deterritorialise their habitual creative practices, as well as those that might extend the influence of their work as research into areas beyond the immediate context of the artwork's production.

One such mediator for the creation of *Sillage* was the guitar style known as 'folk-baroque'. This style briefly enjoyed popularity in the British folk revival of the 1950s and 1960s. The folk-baroque influence was significant in terms of its ethos. The collective assemblage of enunciation in the folk revival produced an association of folk music with an essential ethnic identity and an idealised pastness, engendering an overemphasis on the authenticity of its performance. As an exemplar of folk-baroque's revolutionary ethos within such a context, it is worth briefly mentioning Davy Graham's 1966 performance of 'She Moved through the Fair' at St Andrew's Folk Club.[25] In contrast to contemporary revivalist values of authenticity and transparency in the performance of traditional music, Graham's style is self-consciously hybrid. His opening remark, suggesting similarities between the modal qualities of the Irish air and some Indian music elicits laughter from the audience. Any attempt at authentic replication of either Irish traditional music or Indian music is obviously forsaken, and yet influences from the two styles sit alongside one another comfortably in Graham's blues-inflected fingerstyle. The modal tuning of the guitar — D A D G A D — was developed by Graham in order to accommodate a North African *oud* style of guitar playing, although its droning and suspended qualities are also apt for interpreting Irish traditional music. Graham's work thus seems to disrupt the traditional revivalist understandings of folk music that seeks to conceive of the music in terms of its fixed identity. Once the music's *raison d'être* as the representation of an ethnic essence is abandoned, its virtual power is unlocked, opening the way for new machinic connections. This virtual power of music to become-other, drawn from folk-baroque, informs the conceptual basis of *Sillage*. It is worth noting that, in identifying the influence of folk-baroque artists like Graham, however, I am placing myself in an *imaginary* series of mediators. It is imaginary in the sense that Graham's work informs my own through my particular interpretation of his work: that interpretation's tenability is less important than its productive power. This interpretation is itself contingent on the innumerable forces and connections that compose my creative-theoretical assemblage.

In tandem with the conceptual project of tapping the virtual force of folk-baroque, the creative processes of arranging, rehearsing, recording and editing *Sillage* are readily understandable in terms of a machinic assemblage. In recording and editing, the connection of acoustic guitar arrangements with found sound and soundscape elements necessarily mutated each tune-machine and the album-machine. However, the arranging and rehearsing processes brought about more volatile and unpredictable connections that warrant explication, especially, as I will now discuss, for my arrangement of two folk tunes, 'Londonderry Air' and 'Sakura', which were the starting points for two of *Sillage*'s tracks. The first, 'Londonderry Air', can be understood as enacting a becoming-other in which the processes of a

An immanent approach to theory and practice in creative arts research 53

relative deterritorialisation reorganised the tune-machine within its molar totality. The second, 'Sakura', is given licence to follow lines of flight, producing an absolute deterritorialisation that tapped into the virtual otherness of the tune-machine.[26]

'Londonderry Air' enacts the process of a relative deterritorialisation. The molar structure of the basic melody is given through its F Ionian modality and binary structure. The de/restructuring of the molecular elements – such as the harmony, texture, rhythm/meter, articulation, expression/dynamics, and duration – occurred in both the arranging process (in which a crude chance procedure was developed to build a harmonic scaffold), and the rehearsal process in which the arrangement was forced to bend to the practical concerns of its performability. My aesthetic choices accentuated the unforeseen outcomes of the chance harmony. Those aspects that pulled the tune into a new aesthetic space were intentionally foregrounded. Compared with the original tune, the arrangement recorded for *Sillage* displays a molar structure that is at once recognisable and other. The processes of molecularity forced the molar lines to bulge, contract and mutate, but without destroying them, allowing the tune-machine to become while maintaining the integrity of its borders.

The processes of arranging 'Sakura' opens up a different kind of becoming in which the virtual otherness of the tune was unfurled as a decomposition of itself. This was achieved by breaking apart the segments of the tune and varying them according to the principles of serial composition: inversion, retrograde, and transposition. The simple, modal quality of the original melody was crucial, imbuing the variations with a sense of continuity and preventing the line of flight from becoming a line of death. The latent virtuality of the original tune was used to stimulate a deterritorialisation of its own form, drawing the piece into a space between arrangement and composition.

The creative-theoretical assemblage can be understood as a becoming, driven by the machinic elements of theory and practice. In this view, *Sillage* is both an exercise of theory and practice: as theory, it interrogates the assumed correspondences between music and identity; and as practice it explores the possibilities of deterritorialisation as an approach to folk tune arrangement. Whereas existing models of practice-led research would understand theoretical knowledge as flowing from the practical work, or as vice versa, in this project, I am suggesting that the theory and practice reciprocally presuppose one another. *Sillage* is a machinic assemblage in which every part is necessarily mediated by every other part. Furthermore, as an assemblage it is meaningful only insofar as it forms connections with other assemblages. As an assemblage of enunciation it operates in a vast conversational realm in which the forms, expressions and functions of music are endlessly territorialised and de/reterritorialised, with future becomings at stake.

Conclusion

Thinking of practice-led research projects as assemblages entails a commitment to accounting for all the sides of the creative-theoretical assemblage. Such an approach produces a holistic view of theory and practice in which the

54 *Joseph Williams*

creative-research process is understood as immanent rather than consisting of distinct separations between the theoretical and practical elements of the work. Theory and practice are not separate, stable categories of knowledge. Rather, they are temporary crystallisations of active and ongoing processes, continually undoing and renewing one another. This intra-action in the theoretical-practical space animates the creative-theoretical assemblage and transforms it into a dynamic becoming, shifting it from the fixed object that is implied in reflective thinking. With his emphasis on difference and becoming, thus eschewing identity and being, Deleuze provides the conceptual tools that are apt for this challenging approach to creativity.

The case study of my album *Sillage* shows how the sides of the machinic assemblage and collective assemblage of enunciation might be understood, and provide creative fuel for a thinking about the dynamic aspects of the creative-theoretical assemblage. I have suggested that mediators are important, as is the need to locate the series into which a practice-led research project might fit. Mediators exist on many levels: as collaborators (human and non-human) within a machinic assemblage, as antecedent works, influential theories and as disciplines to which the research might be relevant. Locating mediators is a two-way process that both acknowledges the influence of areas beyond the immediate context in which artworks are produced and extends the significance of practice-led research into those areas. Finally, I have suggested that by forming connections within and outside their assemblages, practitioner-researchers have the potential to increase their productive power and creative potentials, and to participate in the ongoing processes of becoming-other-than-themselves.

Notes

1   See the Website of The Australian Council of Deans and Directors of Creative Arts, accessed 4 March 2015, http://ddca.edu.au/.
2   See, for example, the recent presentation canvassing some of the significant issues for practice-led research in Paul Gough, 'Research in the ERA Era', presented at the Deputy Deans of Creative Arts Inaugural Conference, The Victorian College of the Arts, University of Melbourne, 1 October 2014, accessed 4 March 2015. http://ddca.edu.au/wp-content/uploads/2014/10/Gough_DDCA-September-2014.pdf.
3   See Hazel Smith and Roger T. Dean (eds), *Practice-Led Research, Research-Led Practice in the Creative Arts* (Edinburgh: Edinburgh University Press, 2009), 3.
4   Estelle Barrett, 'Introduction', in *Practice as Research: Approaches to Creative Arts Enquiry*, ed. Estelle Barrett and Barbara Bolt (London: I.B. Tauris, 2007), 2.
5   Michael A. R. Biggs, 'Learning from Experience: Approaches to the Experiential Component of Practice-Led Research', in *Forskning, Reflektion, Utveckling*, ed. H. Karlsson (Stockholm, Sweden: Vetenskapsrådet, 2004), 9.
6   Barbara Bolt, 'Heidegger, Handlability, and Praxical Knowledge', presented at the Australian Council of University Art and Design Schools Conference, University of New South Wales, 25–27 September, 2013, accessed 22 October 2014, http://acuads.com.au/wp-content/uploads/2014/12/bolt.pdf.
7   Estelle Barrett, 'Foucault's "What is an Author": Towards a Critical Discourse of Practice as Research', in *Practice as Research*, 135–46.
8   Smith and Dean (eds), *Practice-Led Research*, 19–25.

An immanent approach to theory and practice in creative arts research   55

9   I will discuss my album *Sillage*, which blends folk-tune-based guitar solos with soundscape and *Musique Concrète* elements. I will show how this work arises from an immanent engagement of theory and practice.

10   Gilles Deleuze and Félix Guattari, *A Thousand Plateus: Capitalism and Schizophrenia*, trans. Brian Massumi (Minneapolis and London: University of Minnesota Press, 1987), 88. Emphasis in the original.

11   Claire Colebrook, *Gilles Deleuze* (London and New York: Routledge, 2002), 56.

12   Colebrook, *Gilles Deleuze*, 56.

13   Sally Macarthur, *Towards a Tweny-First-Century Feminist Politics of Music* (Farnham, UK and Burlington, VT: Ashgate, 2010), 7.

14   Colebrook, *Gilles Deleuze*, 82.

15   Brief introductions to these Deleuzian concepts and terminology can be found in Adrian Parr (ed.) *The Deleuze Dictionary*, 2nd ed. (Edinburgh: Edinburgh University Press, 2010).

16   Karen Barad, *Meeting the Universe Halfway: Quantum Physics and the Entanglement of Matter and Meaning* (Durham, NC and London: Duke University Press, 2007), 33. Emphasis in the original.

17   Bolt, 'Heidegger, Handlability, and Praxical Knowledge', 1.

18   Bolt, 'Heidegger, Handlability, and Praxical Knowledge', 5.

19   Barrett, 'Foucault's "What is an Author"', 135. See also Michel Foucault, 'What is an Author?', in *The Foucault Reader*, ed. Paul Rabinow (New York: Pantheon Books, 1984), 101–20; and Donna Haraway, 'Situated Knowledges: The Science Question in Feminism and the Privilege of Partial Perspective', *Feminist Studies* 14/3 (1988): 575–99.

20   Barrett, 'Foucault's "What is an Author"', 145.

21   Smith and Dean, *Practice-Led Research*, 20.

22   Reprinting, with kind permission of the Edinburgh University Press, of Figure 1.1 from 'A model of creative arts and research processes', p. 20 in Hazel Smith and Roger T. Dean (eds) *Practice-Led Research, Research-Led Practice in the Creative Arts* (Edinburgh: Edinburgh University Press, 2009).

23   Smith and Dean, *Practice-Led Research*, 22.

24   Gilles Deleuze, 'Mediators', in *Zone 6: Incorporations* ed. Jonathan Crary and Sanford Kwinter (New York: Urzone, 1992), 285.

25   An influential figure in the mid-twentieth-century British folk revival, Graham is credited with popularising the DADGAD tuning. Although he never achieved widespread popularity outside of musicians' circles, his influence can be detected in the music of Pentangle, Fairport Convention, John Martyn, Martin Carthy and Jimmy Page (Led Zeppelin). See Jon Pareles, 'Davy Graham, 68, Widely Influential British Guitarist: [Obituary (Obit)]', *New York Times*, 21 December 2008. The recording can be accessed online at http://www.youtube.com/watch?v=U0h-XICWlSA.

26   For a recording of these tracks see: Joseph Williams, arrangement of 'Londonderry Air', https://www.youtube.com/watch?v=fznYNygYAIk; and Joseph Williams, arrangement of 'Sakura', https://www.youtube.com/watch?v=5bs3pvkEb7Q&feature=youtu.be.

Part II
Deleuzian encounters

5 Intra-active soundings

Becoming-woman, becoming-minor

Sally Macarthur and Judy Lochhead

The three chapters in Part II encounter Deleuzian thought in three distinct ways. Lochhead directs Deleuze's philosophical thought about Francis Bacon toward a critical approach to music, focusing on music's sounding as the production of sensation. Macarthur addresses issues of a feminist approach to compositional identity from the Deleuzian perspectives of becoming and becoming-woman. Much as Deleuze re-read earlier philosophers, Stevenson rereads the writings of a mid-twentieth-century composer's thinking about music, mining them for their Deleuzian implications. All three chapters address the music of composers who assume a minoritarian position in the larger field of twentieth- and twenty-first-century Western classical music: Lochhead and Macarthur address the music of living women; and Stevenson addresses the musical thinking of a man positioned as a technician. This confluence of Deleuzian thought in the context of minoritarian music, thought and creators raises questions about the ethical implications and potentials not only of Deleuze's philosophy but also of the new thought it has produced.

This chapter engages the idea of becoming-woman as a central – and sometimes problematic – concept of Deleuzian thought while also addressing the becomings of women – the composers and the two authors. It also extends these observations to the concept of becoming-minoritarian in light of an ethics of thinking about music. In order to address these various matters, we have staged this chapter in terms of our personal scholarly narratives. Each of us recounts our paths to writing about composers who are women and about our Deleuzean encounters. Through these two narratives we hope to demonstrate how Deleuzian philosophy itself produces diverse modes of thought which through their intra-actions proliferate into new thought. First, Macarthur relates her path toward the chapter, 'Meeting the Composer Halfway: Which Anne Boyd?'. Lochhead then relates hers toward the chapter 'Chaotic Mappings: On the Ground With Music', and finally we consider the minoritarian implications of Stevenson's 'Schaeffer's Sound Effects'.

Politics as the orientation of a 'Dividual' assemblage[1]

Sally Macarthur

In 'Meeting the Composer Halfway', I demonstrate the difficulty of working with Deleuze when identity issues take centre stage. In the dominant account of identity in Western art music, the composer-being is pivotal but, as I argue, its construction as a masculine identity works to exclude women composers. I explore the possibility of an entangled intra-action[2] between the two seemingly contradictory tendencies of 'being' and 'becoming'. On the one hand, the composer has a recognisable identity, and on the other hand, the composer-figure is not so much a fixed identity as it is a process. In the spirit of Braidotti, I view the woman composer as a 'becoming other-than-itself, suspended between the no longer and the not yet'.[3] I approach Boyd, then, with questions of a diffractive subjectivity and the becomings of the composer-identity.[4]

In this present chapter, I want to think further about identity given that, for the best part of my career, I have been effectively writing about identity politics. In view of Deleuze's rejection of human beings as pre-established, autonomous individuals, however, my encounter with women's music and feminism is necessarily complicated. The political nature of my work means that it holds itself between two possibilities: actualising solutions to the problems encountered; and imagining the potentialities of problems on the plane of the virtual. In this account of my own story, apart from this introduction, I will avoid using the first person pronoun, 'I'.[5] This is partly because the social formations of the music world have produced a particular kind of political subject in what I currently regard as the divided person of myself. To follow Roffe, as a 'dividual' (as distinct from 'individual'), my being is necessarily 'divided rather than fundamentally unified'[6] and, following Deleuze and Guattari, like all beings, I regard myself as a multiplicity. Paying attention to Davies, however, I note that multiplicities are not 'discrete entities existing side-by-side or even bouncing off each other'.[7] For Deleuze, beings 'continually transform themselves into each other ... so that becoming and multiplicity are the same thing'.[8] In bringing about new ways of thinking about the individual, it is important to consider how it is bound to particular conceptions of identity, self and agency. I will invoke the concept of 'dividuality' in the manner of Roffe to disrupt the discourses and practices of identity which sustain the individual.[9]

The story given here is also necessarily selective, not least because it is only a recollection. But this personal story is further complicated by the fact that, on the one hand, as a musician, I am compelled to negotiate the pre-existing world of music with its institutionalised striations and collective assemblage of enunciation while, on the other hand, through the processes of connection, I am subjected to the lines of force that escape these striations, deterritorialising the assemblages through which my personal assemblage is constituted. I have chosen to work with the concept of 'assemblage' to mobilise my personal account. As Colebrook says, 'a human body is an assemblage of genetic material, ideas, powers of acting and a relation to other bodies ... the assemblage is created from its connections'.[10] The work in which I have been engaged over several decades,

Intra-active soundings 61

has had both political and ethical implications but, as Davies writes, politics and ethics are not independent of each other. They are coproduced through emergent and multiple encounters.[11] In the spirit of Davies, I see my work as 'questioning what is being made to matter and how that mattering affects what it is possible to do and think'.[12] I will discuss my encounter with feminist theory and women's music in terms of a cartography of assemblages. Following Bergen, I will argue that feminist politics in music is grasped by understanding how the assemblage of the dividual operates according to the typology of lines: molar, molecular, and lines of flight.[13]

My commitment as a dividual subject to women's music and feminist theory stems back to the 1970s and, in some ways, the narration of the dividual's story parallels that of the feminist trajectory as outlined by Colebrook.[14] The dividual assemblage (which I view as a body in a 'condition of permanent dynamism'[15]) begins as a simple political adherence to liberal emancipation. In those early days, the feminist territorial assemblage focused on equality in the belief that it would liberate women. When feminism was protesting on the streets against women's oppression, demanding equal social, legal and political rights, the dividual, dynamic assemblage was in Adelaide connecting with the higher education assemblage where it was completing an undergraduate music degree, majoring in musicology. At this time, women composers were completely absent from the curriculum. The dividual assemblage, then hooking up with the feminist assemblage, enquired as to their whereabouts. The institutional assemblage, disconnected from gender issues, dismissed the question. At that time in Australia, as far as it was known, there were only two such identities who were emerging: Anne Boyd, then poised on the edge of her career; and New Zealander Gillian Whitehead (who was to later work at the Sydney Conservatorium for many years), who had been a recent guest at the University of Adelaide.

In 1976, the dividual, dynamic, emergent assemblage began to loosen, stepping out of its classical music comfort zone into a more formal engagement with feminism. As an amateur drummer, it plugged into a set of rehearsals for a feminist cabaret show, *The Carolina Chisel Show*, which was being produced to mark International Women's Year in Adelaide (1977).[16] This was a collaborative work about women's struggles and, for the most part, drew on the popular music of the day. The dividual assemblage, then preoccupied with the molar identities of women, however, was limited by what it could do at that time. It understood that a 'real' instrument was the piano (on which the personal assemblage had been trained), 'real' composers were men, and popular music did not count as ('good') music. These ideas of the institutional assemblage, intersecting with the dividual assemblage, were accentuated by the musicological focus of the dividual to medieval music and the serial compositions of Webern.

As a consequence, the dynamic, dividual assemblage was dominated by what Bergen, following Deleuze, calls 'break lines' (or molar lines), 'leading to hard segmentation, implicated in binary divisions … actualised at the level of history'.[17] The lines in the dividual assemblage were being pulled between two opposing forces: that of a supposedly political feminism versus a seemingly apolitical music.

As a revolutionary movement, feminism, as expressed in the production of *The Carolina Chisel Show*, mobilised identity politics for the purposes of raising awareness about the very personal nature of the political. In contrast, the University of Adelaide music department, presenting (Western art) music in terms of a rational, neutral (or apolitical) system, detached itself from anything remotely personal.

In the 1980s, the 'dividual' musicking assemblage continued to be connected with the assemblages of higher education, hooking up with them as a sessional lecturer in two of its institutions, the Sydney Conservatorium of Music and the University of Sydney. During this period, the 'dividual's' machinic assemblage began to change the nature of the musicological assemblage, also plugged into the assemblages of the conservatorium and the university. Ideas drifting around these assemblages claimed that the absence of women composers from musicological curricula was more a matter of individual women choosing not to be composers than it was a matter of their discrimination. The dividual assemblage persisted with the equality argument, not yet being familiar with the feminist counterargument as outlined by Colebrook much later. As Colebrook writes, the problem with the liberal ideal of equality is that it renders women equal to (or the same) as men.[18] In this view, being equal amounts to being majoritarian or masculinised or normalised. Back in the 1970s, the molar line prevailed in the liberal dividual assemblage and, with the crack line (or line of flight) nowhere yet in sight, it embraced the binary emancipation politics of the day, keen to see more women represented in music. At this same time, the dividual assemblage was also challenged to 'prove' that women's music was original and innovative. On this latter point, colleagues in the musicological, compositional and music performance assemblages subscribed to the view that women composers were not very good at creating structure for their music. Clara Schumann's piano concerto was often cited as an example: its lopsided structure was deemed to be not very good.

In the 1990s, the dividual assemblage attended the first ever music and gender conference at Kings College, University of London, and became involved as an artistic adviser and organiser of the four women's music festivals and conferences held in Australia. During the same decade, it enrolled in a PhD (University of Sydney). Addressing the challenges mentioned above, the dividual subject that was bigger than the dividual's own self (but nonetheless channelled through the self), embraced the molar identity politics of the collective assemblage of enunciation and wrote a thesis, demonstrating that women composers were disadvantaged and that their music was not inferior to but simply different from their male counterparts.[19] At this time, to follow Colebrook's sketch of feminism, the collective assemblage of enunciation had also moved on to radical or difference feminism, which highlighted women's specific identities.[20] In the difference argument in the dividual's thesis, the assemblages of the French feminists, particularised to the figures of Irigaray and Cixous, were engaged and the concept of *l'écriture féminine* (which loosely translates to mean 'writing from the feminine body') was applied to music. As Colebrook points out, however, the problem with radical or difference feminism is its assumption that women's identity exists and is knowable.[21] Furthermore, difference feminism ends up being essentialist. As Hickey-Moody and Malins comment, much later, identity categories are too restrictive for making sense of the idea that bodies exist in a state of continuous change. According to these authors, bodies become stratified 'when they are arranged into grid-like categories, such as sex, gender, colour, ethnicity, religion, sexuality, age and ability'. As they continue:

> Such categories can be extremely useful, for they create a stable sense of 'self', and enable the production of the thinking, speaking, political subject. Yet they are limiting, for they reduce the body to particular modes of being and interacting.[22]

And as they also observe, bodies will often traverse multiple categories at once.[23] The dividual's thesis, later published as a book,[24] straddled the two kinds of feminism on offer in music in the 1990s: egalitarian feminism and difference feminism. The equality issues were captured in an extensive quantitative survey that it conducted, showing that women's music was, indeed, absent from concert programmes. The difference issues were dealt with through the analyses of selected women composers' music in which the dividual subject, bigger than that of the dividual (but nonetheless channelled through the dividual-self) argued that women's music was different from men's but not less worthy in the aesthetic stakes. The problem with all of this work, as the dividual makes the point in its chapter in this part of the book, is that it relies on negative difference. The dominant account of identity, which is dependent on the molar line, polarises woman against man. It is discursively situated on a representational matrix organised within oppositional categories and yields to the law of normativity in which difference from the male norm is understood as negative.

According to Colebrook, even although feminism has attempted to create its own genealogy, its theoretical heritage does not really yield to the principles of the progress narrative that underpins the philosophical tradition. She makes the point that feminist 'questions have always been voiced in terms of what thought might become (rather than the correctness of this or that model)'[25] and she goes on to say that 'feminist questions have more often been directed to interventions, encounters, formations of identity and productive becomings'.[26] She suggests that feminist work, like Deleuzian work, is about 'the creation of new terrains, different lines of thought and extraneous wanderings that are not at home in the philosophical terrain'.[27]

In 2008, one of the dividual's graduate students completed a PhD thesis which drew on Deleuze for the analysis of Australian women's music theatre and radiophonic work. During the student's candidature, the dividual began to read Deleuze and realised the enormous potential of this work for feminist musicology. This led to the publication in 2010 of a second monograph, *Towards a Twenty-First-Century Feminist Politics of Music*.[28] It is at this point, in the dividual's account, that the state of things are reconfigured. While the book plugs into the collective assemblage of enunciation caught up with Deleuzian thought, it abandons some, but not all, of the work that had preceded it, experimenting with potentialities and possibilities

64   *Sally Macarthur and Judy Lochhead*

on the plane of the virtual. It enters the haze of the imaginary sphere. The dividual, political assemblage dissipates the subject. It maps a cartography of becoming: the fixed identity undergoes a brutal transformation. The line of flight radically composes new thought for the identity of the woman composer. This new conception of the woman composer finds its way into this personal account in which the dividual maps a cartography of assemblages, including the feminist and musicological assemblages. In Deleuzeian Guatarian style, the account does not concern itself with questions of interpretation but, instead, following Bergen, investigates 'the singular operation of assemblages'.[29] The book from 2010 stages a line of rupture in the manner described by Bergen: it is as if 'nothing has happened, but everything has changed'.[30] Likewise, in this present chapter, 'a becoming-minor, a becoming-imperceptible' dissipates the subject.[31] The dividual has moved on.

'The Flap of a Butterfly's Wings': Producing knowledge/affecting change

Judy Lochhead

In 1963 Edmund Lorenz published his now famous paper 'Deterministic Nonperiodic Flow' theorising the sensitive dependence on initial conditions in non-linear systems, a theory that developed from his work in meteorology. About a decade later, another paper, 'Predictability: Does the Flap of a Butterfly's Wings in Brazil set off a Tornado in Texas?', gave poetic force to this theory.[32] As is well-documented this research contributed to non-linear dynamical systems theory and to what is now called chaos theory.[33] Also well documented are the interactions between Deleuze's philosophical thought on difference and becoming and these developments in mathematics and science.[34] In both the scientific and philosophical domains of thought, there is a focus on how parts of a system 'interfere, or cooperate, or compete' with one another such that their interactions produce something new.[35] DeLanda, in particular, has focused on how emergence within such non-linear dynamic systems has been central to science as well as Deleuzian philosophy.[36] From the seemingly innocuous flapping of the butterfly's wings in Brazil, then, a tornado emerges in Texas: small events can produce new emergent effects over time.

Here I focus on how the intra-actions of diverse events, circumstances and dispositions in my life have, at least partially, affected my chapter for this part of the book that is, how the intra-actions of initial and changing circumstances produce new knowledge. I map out the intra-acting events, circumstances and dispositions from which my chapter emerged not to demonstrate a progress from cause and effect. Rather, this mapping suggests that for the three chapters in Part II, the differing approaches to minoritarian musical practices emerge from the differing situations of their authors and that the differences between them exemplify the multiplicity of ways that a problem may be addressed and confronted by means of Deleuzian concepts. Further, the intra-actions of these chapters themselves have the potential to produce new becomings: to produce knowledge and affect change.

'Chaotic Mappings' models an approach to music-thinking, targeting the 'logic of sensations' in the context of sonic experience. Deleuze's writing on Francis Bacon, with its emphasis on the material aspects of art-thinking, inspired my approach – his writing also infused with concepts of difference and becoming. My chapter addresses the music of two women who are active creators in the twenty-first century. As women working (1) in a field that is and has been dominated by men (2) in the tradition of classical music often described as being on its deathbed, and (3) in the style of contemporary classical music, these two composers occupy creative places that, in at least three ways, are on the fringe. My goals in addressing the music of Saariaho and Garrop are locally modest but globally ambitious. Locally, I hope to open a public discourse on the music of these composers in terms that focus on their creations as music-thinking. Globally, I hope to contribute to ongoing processes of deterritorialisation by producing knowledge about the music of those whose creative work is marginalised by the historical, social and cultural forces that afford preferences according to gender, race, sexuality and ethnicity. In other words, my global ambitions are to affect change by producing knowledge.[37] My decision to employ this strategy of using the local to effect global change – a strategy akin to the 'flap of a butterfly's wing' effecting a tornado – is fraught with challenges, a topic I will return to at the end of my contribution.

The events, circumstances and dispositions affecting my local and global aspirations for 'Chaotic Mappings' entail several intra-acting strands: music with an emphasis on contemporary classical music, philosophy with a particular interest in feminist theory, and critical study of music from both historical and music theoretical/analytical perspectives. Both the music and philosophy/feminist theory strands invited me into their spheres, almost as if I had no choice. Music's invitation was intense and I gladly accepted, taking up performance as my mode of participation. While I remember no conscious decision to accept the invitation of music, I now know matters of class, race and gender most certainly helped to create the opening for my acceptance. The affective force of music was not to be denied and there was no one in my life deflecting that force. When serious music study began in college at UCLA I felt the force of other invitations. From the privileged place of college, the buffet of diverse domains of knowledge was enticing to me and the summons of philosophy was particularly strong, launching me into its conceptual modes of thought. As I gained more experience and knowledge, my occupations with music and philosophy became more focused. My musical activities were targeted on performances of contemporary music, which offered a particular reward because of my interactions with composers. My philosophical interests turned toward the then burgeoning field of feminist studies, an interest kindled by the protest activities both on campus and in greater Los Angeles. At the time, these protests focused on the human rights of African-Americans, women and gays, and the protests were themselves fuelled by theories that legitimised the protests and that extended their reach into other domains of activity – such as music scholarship. Toward the end of my undergraduate music studies, I had two professors who explicitly encouraged my music analytical and theoretical work, suggesting I combine my interests in contemporary music with music theoretical work in graduate school. Their encouragement toward music theory resonated with my own interests in philosophical concepts and a growing sense of the need for extending feminist thought into thought about music. And so, I set off with these goals in mind.

Once in graduate school the trajectories of my musical activities became more intentional. Music and philosophy had invited me into their thinking through sensations and concepts, and these two modes of thought intra-acted through my scholarly work. Combining these two strands of music and philosophical scholarship, my work targeted contemporary music. In particular I focused on the mismatch between, on one hand, existing analytical concepts and the types of music structures they addressed with, on the other, the aesthetic goals and sounding designs of much contemporary music, especially that which I played. In philosophy, I turned to phenomenological thought, especially the work of Merleau-Ponty with its emphasis on embodied knowing, as a basis for developing new music analytical tools. An additional focus on feminist theory directed my work toward critiques of existing scholarship on Berg's *Lulu* and to practices within the still male dominated field of music theory in the United States.[38] In the early years of the new millennium, the philosophy of Deleuze, and Deleuze and Guattari, offered another invitation into a new philosophical world of strange terms and challenging concepts. And it became quickly clear, that these terms and concepts provided effective tools for addressing a range of issues that had been confronting me over many years, including: art is a form of thought through sensations; territorialisation/deterritorialisation as a way of addressing the mismatch between contemporary music and analytical concepts; minoritarian musical practices and the roles of thought in destabilising majoritarian perspectives; the becoming of musical works as an ongoing temporal process; the intra-actions of listeners, performers, creators, material aspects of sound in the production of music; the production of knowledge as a means of affecting change. Deleuzian concepts have and continue to be productive for developing new thought about music.

The intra-actions of these life events, circumstances, and dispositions flow through my chapter for this part of the book. I employ the philosophical thought of Deleuze as a tool for addressing the music-thinking of particular works, attending to the sonic materiality of each work's 'logic of sensation'. My focus on music created by women engages the goals of feminist political action by producing knowledge about their music-thinking. My local goal is to produce knowledge about works of music that occupy the fringe places of contemporary classical music by women. By producing knowledge, I hope to open a discourse about the music of these women, and also about contemporary classical music. The production of knowledge and the ensuing discourse about it will, hopefully, have a broader affect. In global and long-range terms, the production of knowledge about the music of women will contribute to processes of deterritorialisation that fosters new music-thinking and new knowledge. My global aspirations are to encourage creative activities by those who occupy minoritarian places according to their gender, race, ethnicity, sexuality or economic circumstances and to encourage the production of new thought about recent creative practices by attending to the material details of music-thinking – to the sensations of musical sounds. These local and global goals may seem 'Polyanna-ish' and a form of unrealistic wishful thinking not sufficiently involved in the messy and sometimes nasty details of everyday life – a reaction I have shared in the past and even do now. But then there is the flap of the butterfly's wing ...

Earlier, I referred to the challenges of the strategy I have chosen in my chapter of employing the local to effect global change. This strategy does not address the problems confronted by those marginalised by matters of gender, race, ethnicity, sexuality, and economic circumstances in the professional world of music, nor does it directly theorise the problems. Further, if using the local to affect the global fails at the local level to, in my case, get readers and hence open up a discourse, then the strategy will fail. These are real problems and challenges. Another strategy is to address a problem directly, naming it and theorising it: this is Macarthur's strategy in her 'Meeting the Composer Halfway' chapter. Our two strategies are not, however, at odds with one another. We both conduct scholarship focused on the situation of composers who are women as a way to address their minoritarian places in contemporary music practices. There are multiple strategies that can be employed to address the problems confronting the creative practices of women. Following the Deleuzian emphasis on becoming and the production of new forms of thought, the chapters in Part II together may be understood to intra-act and to – hopefully – generate new strategies and ways to address problems of gender, race, ethnicity, sexuality and economic disadvantages. The flapping of many butterfly wings may produce real change.

'Chaotic Mappings' addresses musical works by Saariaho and Garrop in terms of the materiality of their sounding affects, that is, how the works achieve their music-thinking. In such an address, I focus on how musical sounds function as sounding sensations. This kind of address positions the chapter within the traditions of music theory and analysis, but at the same time, my chapter offers new ways to use terms and concepts in the effort of producing new knowledge. These non-canonical uses of existing approaches, terms, and concepts align the chapter with the Deleuzian concept of the 'minor'. In their book on Kafka, Deleuze and Guattari define a 'minor literature' in terms of how its 'language is affected with a high coefficient of deterritorialization' and how it is 'political'.[39] In general terms, the Deleuzian concept of the minor is associated not with the numerical differences between identity groups but rather with the activities of those operating within the power relations of a dominant constellation of perspectives and institutions. Specific activities – such as writing, composing – create a minority 'on lines of flight, which are also its ways of advancing and attacking'.[40] Becoming-minor then is a deterritorialising activity of existing modes of thinking, acting, and its associated power relations by, as Bogue observes, 'inducing processes of becoming-other, by undermining stable power relations and thereby activating lines of continuous variation in ways that have previously been restricted and blocked'.[41]

Becoming-minor: Political/ethical

Sally Macarthur and Judy Lochhead

Stevenson's chapter in this part demonstrates the Deleuzian implications of Pierre Schaeffer's concept of the 'sound object', framing it as a way of understanding the 'unbound potentiality of musical sound'.[42] In focusing on how Schaeffer uses his experiences in the electronic music studio to approach timbre in positive terms, unlike his contemporaries, Stevenson characterises Schaeffer's concept of the sound object in minoritarian terms.

As a white man working in France within the traditions of Western classical music during the middle years of the twentieth century, Schaeffer does not fit into a numerical minority. But, nonetheless, he is even today framed as an outsider. The *Grove Music Online* entry by Francis Dhomont makes this clear: 'A man who had studied science at the Polytechnique and who looked askance at established ideas, a philosopher of art and science, a controversial anti-authoritarian, ever active, quick to question routine practices, Schaeffer was always a disturbing figure.'[43] This 'disturbing' presence derives from both Schaeffer's interdisciplinary training and his challenges to established, majoritarian practices. Compare this to Bogue's summary of how Deleuze and Guattari characterise Kafka's creation of a minor literature: it 'experiments with language, ignores canonical models, fosters collective action and treats the personal as something immediately social and political'.[44] Schaeffer's activities of musical creation, conception and listening disturbed existing practices, and in their affects, these activities enacted a becoming-minor. The recent scholarly interest in Schaeffer's concepts at the turn of the millennium makes manifest the deterritorialising affects of this 'disturbing' figure.[45]

As a deterritorialising activity within the context of the existing power relations, becoming-minor has both political and ethical ramifications. It produces actions and practices that are blocked by a dominant, majoritarian perspective. The processes of becoming-minor, as Smith observes, are 'an act of resistance whose political impact is immediate and inescapable, and that creates a line of flight on which a minority discourse … can be constituted'.[46] The three chapters in Part II encounter Deleuzian thought in differing ways and each addresses the becoming-minor of musical creation and thought. In doing so, the three chapters have political ramifications in both their topics and the lines of flight they propose. In drawing attention to the minoritarian activities of composers, the chapters also pose ethical questions about the choices scholars of music make and how these choices recognise and react to multiplicity and difference. Along with Erinn Cunniff Gilson, we affirm that 'the question of how to live ethically is fundamentally a political question'.[47]

Notes

1   This subtitle has been adapted from Bergen. See Véronique Bergen, 'Politics as the Orientation of Every Assemblage', trans. Jeremy Gilbert, *New Formations* 68/2 (2009), 34–41. The concept of 'dividual' is borrowed from Roffe who, as I explain in this chapter, uses 'dividual' to indicate a divided rather than unified subject. See Jonathan Roffe, 'The Revolutionary Dividual' in *Deleuzian Encounters: Studies in Contemporary Social*

Issues, ed. Anna Hickey-Moody and Peta Malins (Houndmills, Basingstoke: Palgrave Macmillan, 2007), 40–49.

2   'Intra-action' is a key element in Barad's methodological toolkit and, as indicated in several places in the present book, it works in well with Deleuze's philosophy of immanence. As Barad points out, 'the notion of intra-action constitutes a radical reworking of the traditional notion of causality' (33). It recognises that distinct agencies, which 'are distinct only in a relational, not absolute, sense' emerge through their mutual entanglement. See Karen Barad, *Meeting the Universe Halfway: Quantum Physics and the Entanglement of Matter and Meaning* (Durham, NC and London: Duke University Press, 2007), 33.

3   Rosi Braidotti, *Transpositions: On Nomadic Ethics* (Cambridge, UK and Malden, MA: Polity, 2006), 156.

4   I use the concept of a diffractive subjectivity in the manner proposed by Barad. She argues for a diffractive versus reflexive methodology. The reflexive researcher seeks to represent the subject as if it is independent of the researcher's gaze. Diffractive researchers are not interested in *representing* the subject but understand that they are implicated in its ongoing production. For Barad, a diffractive approach does not 'map where differences appear, but rather maps where the *effects* of differences appear' (72). It is thus focused on the processes that give rise to the subject's emergence. See Barad, *Meeting the Universe Halfway*, 71–94.

5   I will adopt the strategy of employing the concept of the 'dividual', as well as that of 'assemblage' (as I discuss below), in place of the first person 'I'. This is a political move. There was a time when first person pronouns were discouraged in academic writing. At later time, they were encouraged, especially for work that addressed feminist concerns given feminism's mantra of the 'personal is political'. What this personal pronoun approach seemed to accomplish, however, was the creation of a minor discourse. Feminist work in music was viewed as being less important than work – for example, music theory – that used the distancing devices of a third person mode of address. In this chapter, then, I problematize the notion of the first person narrative by referring to myself as a 'dividual' subject or an 'assemblage'.

6   Roffe, 'The Revolutionary Dividual', 41.

7   Bronwyn Davies, *Listening to Children: Being and Becoming* (London and New York: Routledge, 2014), 9.

8   Gilles Deleuze and Félix Guattari, *A Thousand Plateaus: Capitalism and Schizophrenia*, trans. Brian Massumi (Minneapolis and London: University of Minnesota Press, 1987), 249.

9   Roffe, 'The Revolutionary Dividual', 40–49.

10 Claire Colebrook, *Understanding Deleuze* (Crows Nest, Sydney: Allen & Unwin, 2002), xx.

11 Davies, *Listening to Children*, 10.

12 Davies, *Listening to Children*, 10–11.

13 Véronique Bergen, 'Politics as the Orientation of Every Assemblage', 34–41.

14 Claire Colebrook, 'Introduction' in *Deleuze and Feminist Theory*, ed. Ian Buchanan and Claire Colebrook (Edinburgh: Edinburgh University Press, 2000), 1–17.

15 Bergen, 'Politics as the Orientation of Every Assemblage', 35.

16 In late 1975, Australian actor Jude Kuring received an International Women's Year grant for a cabaret performance. As Moss writes, *The Carolina Chisel Show* was 'a series of songs, from rock to musical comedy, strung together on a story line about three sisters – all called Grace, who inherited the possibility of putting on a show' (143). It had a plot that allowed for anything. Actors and singers could bring along something they knew well – like 'Bobby's Girl' – and it was slotted into the performance/story. This show, and others like it, were a vehicle for the expression of feminist politics. See Merrilee Moss, 'Puppets to Playwrights: Girls on Stage', in *Australia for Women: Travel and Culture*, ed. Susan Hawthorne and Renate Klein (Melbourne: Spinifex Press, 1994), 142–8.

70 *Sally Macarthur and Judy Lochhead*

17 Bergen, 'Politics as the Orientation of Every Assemblage', 36.
18 Colebrook, 'Introduction', 10.
19 The dividual's thesis was completed in 1997. See Sally Macarthur, 'Feminist Aesthetics in Music: Politics and Practices in Australia', PhD Thesis, University of Sydney, 1997.
20 Colebrook, 'Introduction', 10.
21 Colebrook, 'Introduction', 10.
22 Anna Hickey-Moody and Peta Malins, *Deleuzian Encounters: Studies in Contemporary Social Issues* (Houndsmills, Basingstoke: Palgrave Macmillan, 2007), 5.
23 Hickey-Moody and Malins, *Deleuzian Encounters*, 5.
24 Sally Macarthur, *Feminist Aesthetics in Music* (Westport, CT and London: Greenwood Press, 2001).
25 Colebrook, 'Introduction', 10.
26 Colebrook, 'Introduction', 10.
27 Colebrook, 'Introduction', 10.
28 Sally Macarthur, *Towards a Twenty-First Century Feminist Politics of Music* (Farnham, UK and Burlington, VT: Ashgate, 2010).
29 Bergen, 'Politics as the Orientation of Every Assemblage', 38.
30 Bergen, 'Politics as the Orientation of Every Assemblage', 36.
31 Bergen, 'Politics as the Orientation of Every Assemblage', 36.
32 Edward Norton Lorenz, 'Deterministic Nonperiodic Flow', *Journal of Atmospheric Science* 20 (1963): 130–41; Lorenz, 'Predictability: Does the Flap of a Butterfly's Wings in Brazil Set Off a Tornado in Texas?' Paper for the American Association for the Advancement of Science, December 1972. This latter paper is reportedly the source of the popularity of the term 'butterfly effect'.
33 James Glieck's *Chaos Theory: Making a New Science* (New York: Viking, 1988[1987]) has become the classic work on the history and impact of chaos theory for general audiences.
34 Manuel DeLanda, along with others, has developed the interactions between philosophical and scientific thought on dynamical systems. See in particular: DeLanda, *Intensive Science and Virtual Philosophy* (London: Continuum, 2009[2002]).
35 Steven H. Strogatz, *Nonlinear Dynamics and Chaos: With Applications to Physics, Biology, Chemistry, and Engineering* (Boulder, CO: Westview Press, 2001), 9.
36 DeLanda's definition of emergence is: 'a property of a whole is said to be emergent if it is produced by causal interactions among its component parts. Those interactions, in which the parts exercise their capacities to affect and be affected, constitute the mechanism of emergence behind the properties of the whole.' 'Emergence, Causality and Realism', in *The Speculative Turn: Continental Materialism and Realism*, ed. Levi Bryant, Nick Srnicek and Graham Harman (Melbourne: re.press, 2011), 385.
37 This is also a goal of my book, *Reconceiving Structure in Contemporary Music: New Tools in Music Theory and Analysis* (New York: Routledge, 2015). There I address music by Sofia Gubaidulina and Anna Clyne as well as different works by Kaija Saariaho and Stacy Garrop.
38 See Lochhead, 'Lulu's Feminine Performance', in *Cambridge Companion to Berg*, ed. Anthony Pople (Cambridge: Cambridge University Press, 1997), 227–46; and 'Hearing *Lulu*', in *Audible Traces*, ed. Elaine Barkin and Lydia Hamessley (Zurich: Carciofoli Verlagshaus, 1999), 231–56. A group of young music theorists in the mid 1980s actively promoted discussions about feminist music theory and about scholarly biases within music theory. This work eventually led to the establishment of the Committee on the Status of Women in the Society for Music Theory in 1986.
39 Deleuze and Guattari, *Kafka: Toward a Minor Literature*, trans. Dana Polan (Minneapolis: University of Minnesota Press, 2003[1986, French 1975]), 16–17.
40 Gilles Deleuze and Claire Parnet, *Dialogues*, trans. Hugh Tomlinson and Barbara Habberjam (New York: Columbia University Press, 1987), 43.

41 Ronald Bogue, 'The Minor', in *Gilles Deleuze: Key Concepts*, ed. Charles J. Stivale, 2nd ed. (Durham, England: Acumen, 2011), 135.

42 Stevenson, this volume, pp. 102–15.

43 Francis Dhomont, 'Schaeffer, Pierre', *Grove Music Online. Oxford Music Online* (Oxford: Oxford University Press), accessed 31 January 2015, http://www.oxfordmusiconline.com/subscriber/article/grove/music/24734.

44 Ronald Bogue, 'The Minor', 131.

45 For a recent scholarly study demonstrating the later affects of Schaeffer's work, see: Brian Kane, *Sound Unseen* (New York: Oxford University Press, 2014).

46 Daniel W. Smith, 'Life', in *Essays on Deleuze* (Edinburgh: Edinburgh University Press, 2012), 215.

47 Erinn Cunniff Gilson, 'Responsive Becoming: Ethics between Deleuze and Feminism', in *Deleuze and Ethics*, ed. Nathan Jun and Daniel W. Smith (Edinburgh: Edinburgh University Press, 2011), 66.

6 Chaotic mappings
On the ground with music

Judy Lochhead

In *What is Philosophy?* Deleuze and Guattari maintain that there are three fully equal yet distinct modes of thinking the world: philosophy, science and art.[1] Philosophy is the production of concepts, science the production of functions or propositions and art the production of sensations. Some ten years prior in his book on the painter Francis Bacon, Deleuze presents the theme of art as a mode of thinking the world and in particular seeks to establish a 'logic of sensation' as it arises in the colours, textures and gestures of Bacon's paintings.[2] About his writings on art, Deleuze claims, however, that they are philosophy — and only philosophy — in as much as he produces concepts about art and develops a philosophy of art. In the introduction to his translation of the book on Bacon, Daniel Smith warns readers that this is not a work of 'art criticism' since 'there is little discussion of the socio-cultural milieu in which Bacon lived and worked; nor of his artistic influences or contemporaries, nor of his personal life …'.[3] Yet, when Deleuze was asked if one of the 'goals of his book is to make readers see better', he agreed that it would have that 'effect if it succeeded'. But he also claimed that it has a 'higher aspiration', which is to 'approach something that would be the common ground of words, lines, colours, and even sounds'.[4]

From these statements by Deleuze and Smith we know the following: Deleuze's writing on Bacon's paintings is philosophy and not art criticism, and the goals of such writings include making an improved or better apprehension of art and getting at the 'common ground' of thinking the world. Here I use these observations as a springboard for exploring the prospects of writing about music and for proposing a particular sort of music criticism, what I call chaotic mappings.

While Smith understands art criticism as necessarily addressing the biography, influences and cultural context of the artist, the term 'criticism' has a broader reference and often entails writing or work whose goal is to enhance or sharpen apprehension. The term also sometimes refers to evaluative writing, which may focus on the effectiveness of the work or performance. And while it is typical in music studies to distinguish between writings that are historical, theoretical or analytical, journalistic, or critical, sometimes all of these are lumped together under the broader category of 'criticism'. The point here is not to define what criticism is or isn't, but rather to demonstrate that a possible goal of critical writing about music is to affect musical experience — recalling Deleuze's statement that his writing on Bacon's art would make 'readers see better' if it were successful. Criticism then may have a productive goal.

As a genre, however, critical writing about music sits uncomfortably within the three ways of thinking the world that Deleuze and Guattari propose. On one hand, a thinker whose mode of formulation is linguistic might create concepts about music, those concepts operating in the domain of philosophy. (This is apparently what Deleuze means to assert about his writings on Bacon's art.[5]) On the other hand, a thinker, whose primary mode of formulation is quantitative, might create functions that operate for a specific musical work or a proposition about a system of musical organisation. Those functions or propositions would be understood to operate in the domain of science. But in the last instance, a thinker whose mode of formulation is sensations would need to create sensations about sensations. While not impossible, such thinking *about music with music* highlights an expectation about music critical thought: that it reflects upon musical experience and musical works in non-musical modes.[6]

Music critical writing typically operates as either a form of philosophical or scientific thinking, but its topic is the thinking of sensation – of affects and percepts. This address of music from the perspective of a non-musical mode of thinking raises a number of questions and it generates scepticism from many. Such scepticism (and often hostility) seems to be generated by the assumption that philosophical and scientific thinking about music offer to explain it, to provide a better mode of understanding. And from that assumption, the scepticism carries some weight. But if music criticism serves the goal of affecting musical experience, of shaping or even enhancing it, then its function is to produce more experiential engagements with music.

However, if we are to follow Deleuze and Guattari on the distinctions between the three ways of thinking the world, we must also be mindful of the gaps between them and thus of how these distinct modes might be put into a productive relation with one another. A music criticism that is multi-faceted, approaching its topic from multiple perspectives, might well then be a creative one in which we can 'approach … the common ground of words, lines, colours, and even sounds' in Deleuze's terms.

The productive music criticism I sketch here will – if it succeeds – shape musical experiences, no matter whether these are the experiences of listening, performing or creating. This potential for a productive music criticism is irrespective of the writer's intention and, of course, dependent on receptive readers/listeners. And as a generative project, such music criticism does not set itself against any other existing approaches but rather focuses its means and goals on the production of new musical experiences.

A productive music criticism takes as one of its central premises the Deleuzian-Guattarian idea of chaos – that 'common ground' that is the material of art, philosophy, and science. In her excellent book on art and Deleuzian philosophy, Elizabeth Grosz writes that 'chaos may be understood not as absolute disorder but rather as a plethora of orders, forms, wills … it is the condition both for any model or activity and for the undoing and transformation of such

74   *Judy Lochhead*

models or activities'.[7] The philosopher, the scientist and the artist all 'struggle against chaos' but in differing ways. In the face of the encounter with chaos, the philosopher produces variations manifest in concepts and the scientist produces variables in the form of functions: that is, the philosopher and the scientist think through the plethora of orders, producing conceptual variations and proliferating functions. The artist, on the other hand, produces varieties that 'illuminate [chaos] for an instant, [in] a Sensation'.[8] In these distinct forms of thinking the world, the artist, philosopher and scientist struggle with chaos by way of a creative encounter.

A productive music criticism approaches music as such an 'illumination' of chaos via 'sensation', and takes the musical sounds of a particular work not as a fixed bundle of properties but rather as a web of emergent structurings of sound. So not only does the artist struggle against chaos but also those who engage musical works as sensations similarly struggle with sounds as emergent structurings of the plethora of orderings. Productive musical criticism addresses itself to the musical work as a web of emergent structurings and considers the creative roles of all who struggle against chaotic sensations of musical soundings.

The productive potentials of art-critical writing were recognised by Deleuze, as evidenced in his wish to affect a viewer's seeing of Bacon's art. But at the same time his claim that his own writing on Bacon is philosophy – only philosophy – reflects a discomfort with the idea of art criticism, a discomfort that is certainly not unique to Deleuze. The general ambivalence about art criticism arises in part from the sense that such writings, using modes of philosophical or scientific discourse, are an attempt to explain art from the outside – from perspectives alien to the practice and apprehension of art as sensation. As an incursion from the outside, art-critical writing is sometimes understood to tell us something that we don't or can't know in artistic experience directly – suggesting the inadequacy of art to generate its own comprehension. The kind of productive criticism I propose aims not at explanation but rather at possibilities.

Rather than an explanatory incursion, art criticism may better be understood in terms of its production of new possibilities for seeing or hearing, as was Deleuze's wish for his writings on Bacon. But since art criticism uses concepts and functions from the domains of philosophy and science, questions arise about the relations between art, philosophy and science as ways of thinking the world – questions about both the gaps between them and the productive outcomes their encounters may generate. A full accounting of these questions is well beyond my task here, but of particular significance for my project here is how to engage the 'languages' of philosophy or science in ways that affirm the nature of artistic thinking – that is, in ways that take account of the 'language' of sensation. In *What is Philosophy?* Deleuze and Guattari assert the differences between the three forms of thought but also assert the possibility of a reflexive relation between them.[9] Deleuze's claim that his writings on Bacon are 'philosophy, nothing but philosophy' and that they have the potential to make viewers 'see the paintings better' is already a recognition of this reflexivity. In other words, concepts can play a generative role in inducing new sensations.

Nonetheless, the challenge for the arts and music in particular – a challenge that is echoed in typical complaints about the relation of critical thought to musical apprehension – takes on three forms.[10] One is how to address the 'language' of sensation through the 'languages' of philosophy or science in ways that affirm the nature of artistic thinking. The second is for critical writing to support the nature of art works as themselves continuously productive of new sensations. And the third is the question of how to approach (to use Deleuze's term) the sensations of art in modes of presentation that are themselves productive. Let me briefly consider each of these challenges.

First, the languages of philosophy or science may be utilised in relation to art, not to capture its essence or meaning, but rather as a spur to new engagements and hence sensations. And it is perhaps in just those modal differences between philosophy, science and art that something new can be produced in artistic thinking – be it the creation or apprehension of art works. Problems may arise if art is understood to operate as philosophy or as science since at that point it ceases to function as art. The trick is to use philosophical concepts or scientific formulas to approach the particular ways that art generates and thinks through sensation. The second challenge involves the issue of how an art work functions in general and what might be accomplished in any writing about it. Following Deleuze and Guattari, I understand the art work as both the product of artistic thinking by its creator and as a multiplicity whose functioning entails the production of sensations. And as such a multiplicity, experiential encounters with an art work engage viewers/listeners in creative involvements which are themselves a mode of artistic thinking. The trick is to affirm this continuously productive mode of engagement by means of a critical address that itself refreshes the work's multiplicity. The third challenge of art criticism entails the problems of how to approach the art work as an ongoing production of sensation, problems that vary depending on the artistic media. For music, the temporal transiency of its sounding as well as matters of performance pose particular challenges of reference – which sound, when and in what performance?

While significant, these three challenges are not insurmountable but do require a mode of critical address that is mindful of them. In what follows, I exemplify a critical address that I conceive as chaotic mapping.

Chaotic mappings

For present purposes chaotic mappings are a descriptive mode of address of a musical work whose primary aim is not judgment but rather an account of music as sensation. The descriptive mode I develop here maps out the chaotic potential of a musical work, exploring and discovering aspects of the work's 'logic of sensation'. I do not claim a fixed structure for a work but rather show the work's musical terrain with a descriptive mapping.[11] The music critical task is to explore the many – but certainly not all – of the multiple pathways of

76   *Judy Lochhead*

musical sounding that constitute a work. And such descriptive mapping tends to music as sounding through the various dimensions of its sounding presence, that is through its tones, rhythms, dynamics, textures, timbres, gestures, forming, affects, and so on.

The mappings themselves take a graphic form that combines symbols, colours, shapes, words and various other means in order to evoke the sensations of musical sounding. The mappings do not 'represent' the work as such but rather evoke its sounding potential in an effort to generate new sonorous engagements with a work and to approach, in Deleuze's terms, 'the common ground' of musical sensation — or in other words to approach the work as a mode of 'thinking the world'.

I demonstrate two different approaches to chaotic mapping by considering parts of two works: *Prés* for cello and electronics by Kaija Saariaho and String Quartet no. 3, 'Gaia' by Stacy Garrop. These mappings exemplify the possibilities for chaotic mapping and are not meant to address each work in a comprehensive way.

Kaija Saariaho: **Prés (1992); movement 1, for cello and electronics**

Saariaho's *Prés* is a work combining the sounds of a live cello with electronically generated sounds projected through speakers. The electronic sounds include computer-generated sounds, sampled sounds and real-time processing of the live cello. I consider here only the first of this three movement work.

About *Prés* Saariaho writes that it relates to the 'experience of the sea itself and waves, their different rhythms and sounds, stormy weather and calms. In other words: material, wave shapes, rhythmic figures, timbres.'[12] This evocative description provides a fruitful pathway into the movement. My mapping of the music depicts its simultaneous musical currents that surge and crest in formal cross-rhythms, creating a complex musical surface which can be suggested by an analogy with the breaking of waves along a rocky and broken sea shore. Like the multiple sea currents that create the wave-surges that consistently break along the shore but whose frequency and intensity are muted and increased according to the action of the multiple underlying currents, the music of Saariaho's *Prés* has musical cross-currents that result in a formal rhythm of surges of intensity and calmness.

Figure 6.1 depicts the movement according to several simultaneous strands of musical events. The top two rows show bar numbers and a timeline based on a performance by Anssi Karttunen.[13] The bar numbers and vertical stiches of the timeline mark the beginning of events within the six simultaneous strands shown horizontally on the map of Figure 6.1.

Figure 6.2 provides more detail on the six strands, indicates the types of events occurring within each, and shows the symbols used in Figure 6.1 to denote the type. The Electronics strand comprises electronic sounds of four types: electronically generated (or synthesised) sounds; sampled and transformed cello sounds;

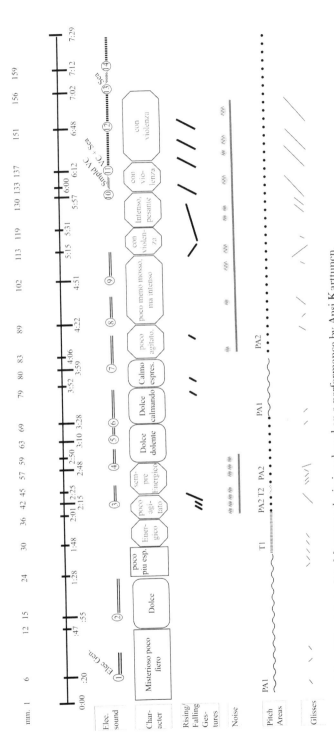

Figure 6.1 Map of Saariaho's *Près*, Movement 1, timings based on a performance by Anssi Karttunen.

Strands	Types			
Electronic Sounds Symbol	Electronically Generated sounds ═══	Sampled and Transformed Cello sounds /////////	Sampled and Transformed Cello plus Sampled Sea sounds ▮▮▮▮▮▮▮	Sampled Sea sounds ～～～～
Character Symbol	Mysterioso/Espressivo Type: *Mysterioso poco fiero; Poco più espressivo* □	Dolce Type: *Dolce; Dolce dolente; dolce calmando; Calmo espressivo* ○	Energico Type: *Energico; poco agitato; poco meno mosso, ma intenso; con violenza; intenso pesante* ⬡	
Gestures Symbol	Rising /		Falling \	
Noise Symbol	~~~~~~~~~~~~~			
Pitch Areas Symbol	PA 1 ～～～ F-D-A-B♭-F♯-A	T1 G-F♯-G-A-B♭	PA 2 • • • • • • • • C-C♯-D-A-E-F♯-G♯-C♯	T2 E-F-F♯-A-A♯-C♯
Glisses Symbol	Upward Gliss		Downward Gliss	

Figure 6.2 Prés. Movement 1, six simultaneous strands and types within each strand.

sampled and transformed cello sounds combined with sampled sea sounds; and sampled sea sounds. The circled numbers in this strand refers to the sound files that are activated by either the performer or sound engineer.[14] The Character strand refers to expressive musical types which are indicated in the score as directions to the performer. There are three Character types, each of which includes several related expressive directions as listed on Figure 6.2: *Mysterioso/Espressivo* type; *Dolce* type; and *Energico* type. The Gestures strand comprises prominent rising or falling movements that span more than an octave and involve three or more discrete events. Example 6.1 cites bars 33–46 and shows three instances of Rising Gestures at bars 37, 39 and 42.

The Noise strand comprises noisy timbral events created by bow pressure and placement of the bow on the bridge (*sul ponticello* – S.P). Example 6.1 shows five instances of Noise events starting at bar 36. The Pitch Area strand indicates that there are two primary pitch areas (PA 1 and 2) and two transitional areas (T1 and 2). Example 6.2 shows that the Pitch Areas consist of registrally fixed collections of 5 and 7 pitches. The Transition collections serve a kind of 'filling in' function, consisting of mostly semi-tones and tones, and they serve to transition from one pitch area to the next. Finally, the Gliss strand comprises continuous rising and falling pitch movement. Example 6.1 shows one instance of a Gliss at bar 43.

These simultaneous strands form musical cross-currents whose interactions generate surging and ebbing formal flows. The formal rhythms of such surging and ebbing have the expressive force of intensity and calmness. The next section of my mapping of this movement of *Prés* takes account of the sounding potentials of this surging and ebbing.

Figure 6.1 surveys the details of sounding events, and Figure 6.3 provides a critical account of potential phase grouping within each strand and of how these

Chaotic mappings 79

Example 6.1 Prés, Movement 1, instances of Noise events, Rising Gestures and Glisses, bars 33–46.

groupings create the surging and ebbing of the musical flows of *Prés*. The phase groupings indicate a clustering of events that have some similarities, and the surging and ebbing refers to how the phases of each strand interact.

The Electronic strand consists of two phases, indicated by grouping circles. An extended opening phase (20–5:15) uses electronically generated sounds, and a concluding phase (5:57–7:29) uses sampled and transformed cello and sea sounds, these two used either singly or in combination. Groupings of the Character strand are shown at the top of Figure 6.3 as Character Phases. The movement begins with the *Misterioso/Espressivo* type followed by an alternation of *Dolce* and *Agitato* types. The duration of these four phases are relatively similar at 47, 61, 60, and 67 seconds, creating a regular success of changes. A long *Agitato* phase follows, lasting nearly 3 minutes, and is followed by a short *Dolce* phase of 27 seconds.

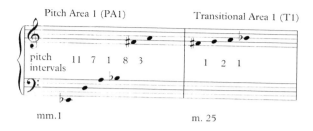

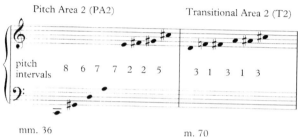

Example 6.2 Prés, Pitch Areas 1 and 2 and Transitions 1 and 2.

The Gestures strand comprises three phases, the first two consisting of only Rising Gestures, and the third a mix of Rising and Falling Gestures. The first and third phases (starting at approximately 2:15 and 5:15) coordinate with the *Agitato* Character type, and the second (starting at approximately 3:45) moves across the change from the *Dolce* and *Agitato* Character type at 4:06. As Figure 6.3 shows, two Noise phases shape this strand, and both are coordinated with the *Agitato* Character phases. The initial Noise phase starts about halfway through the first *Agitato* phase, and the second Noise phase begins and ends with the long *Agitato* phase.

The Pitch and Transition Areas are indicated in Figure 6.3 by arcs. As the map of Figure 6.3 suggests, PA1 and T1 occur successively, followed by the alternation of PA2 T2 PA2 and a reoccurrence of PA1. Starting at 3:59 PA2 reoccurs and remains through the movement's ending, creating a sense of pitch stasis over its last 3 minutes and 30 seconds. Finally, the bottom row of Figure 6.3 shows the frequent occurrences of Glisses and their phase groupings. The arrow at the bottom also points to the increasing frequency and increasingly wider pitch span of the Glisses over the duration of the movement.

As Figure 6.3 shows, the phase groupings of each strand are unique, creating several simultaneous rhythmic flows. There are three moments in the movement, however, when there is a convergence of either the beginning or ending of phases within each strand. These convergences create wave-like rhythmic surges, and Figure 6.3 depicts these convergences by vertical or horizontal barbell lines. Surge 1, indicated by a vertical line, occurs around 2:00, with

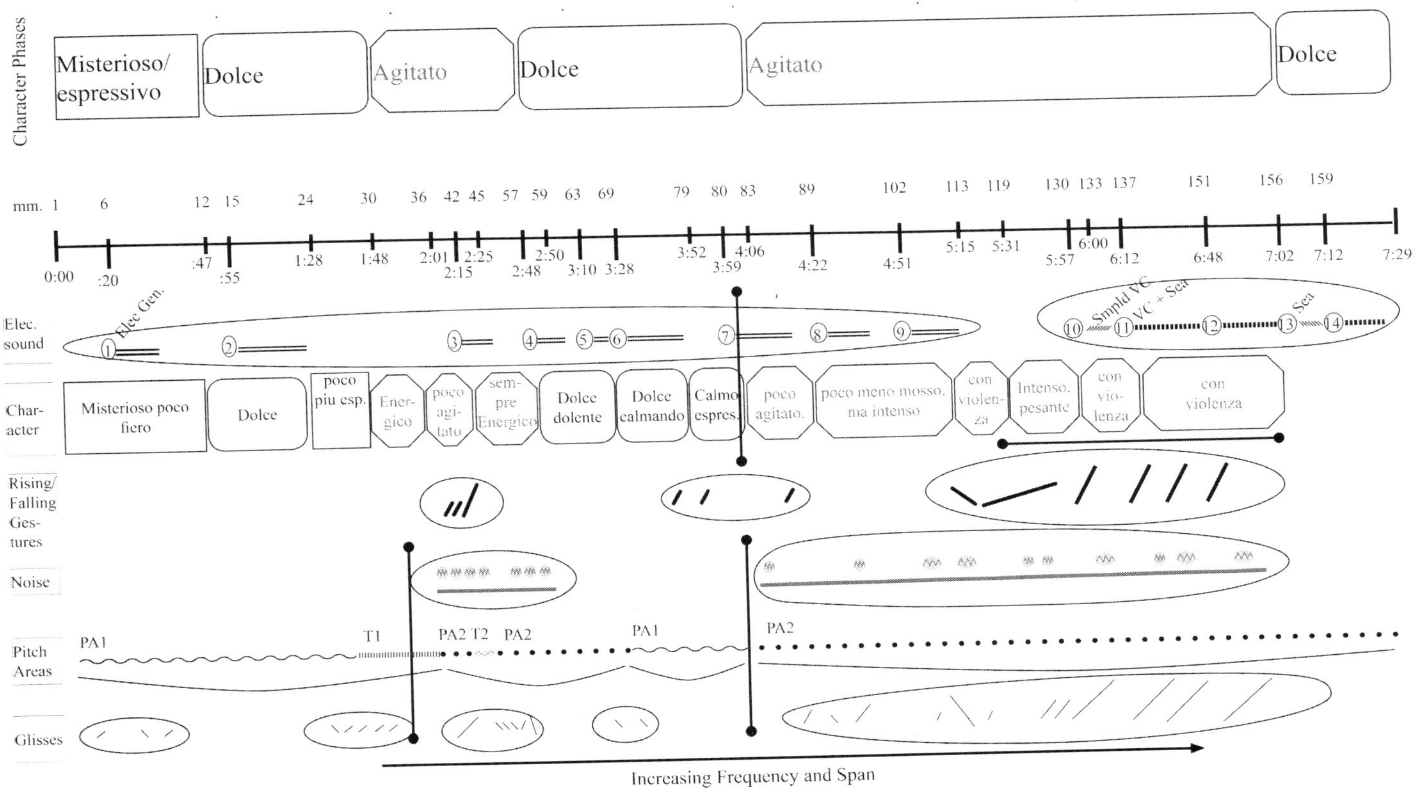

Figure 6.3 Map of converging processes and surges, *Prés*, Movement 1.

convergences between four strands: Gestures, Noise, Pitch Area and Glisses. Surge 2, also a vertical line, occurs around 4:00 with convergences between: Electronics, Noise, Pitch Area and Glisses. Surge 3 is depicted with a horizontal line spanning about 5:30–7:00, with convergences between Electronics, Gestures, Noise, Glisses.

Surges, intensity, calm. While these three surges arise from the convergence of simultaneous phases between strands, the phase groupings within each strand also generate less intense surges which contribute to the ongoing sense of the movement's flow.

Stacy Garrop, third string quartet, 'Gaia' (2008), fifth movement

Garrop's third string quartet is subtitled 'Gaia' after the mythical Greek goddess of the Earth, and my mapping focuses on the fifth and final movement titled '… et in terra pax'. About the movement, Garrop writes: it 'represents what so many of us hope and want both in the world, as well as for the planet itself'. While the work as a whole traces all the dimensions of the goddess Gaia, 'her creativ[ity] and kindness as well as her anger and vengeance', the last movement is wary yet hopeful about the fate of the Earth.[15]

Garrop identifies a generative motive for the work, what she calls the 'Gaia' motive, which consists of a rising tetrachord: A B C D. My mapping of the fifth movement focuses on the becoming of this motive and how it embodies Gaia's wary hopefulness. I trace the motive through three moments in the final movement, which are shown in Figure 6.4 along the character associated with each moment: Stasis and Equilibrium, Direction and Movement, and Ekstasis.[16]

The generative power of the Gaia motive resides partially in its intervallic arrangements and the sensations they produce. My mapping of the motive traces movements from intervallic symmetry in the moment of Stasis/Equilibrium, to asymmetry in Direction/Elation, and finally to a transcendence of this opposition in Ekstasis. Intervallic symmetry is associated with 'limited transposition' arrangements, asymmetry with diatonic arrangements and transcendence in an arrangement of harmonic openness. In other words, the musical sensations generated by the symmetries of limited transposition arrangements are opposed to asymmetries of the diatonic arrangements, and this opposition is transformed into a sensation of sonorous openness in Ekstasis.

Figure 6.4 Map of Garrop, Third String Quartet, three moments of the Gaia motive's becoming.

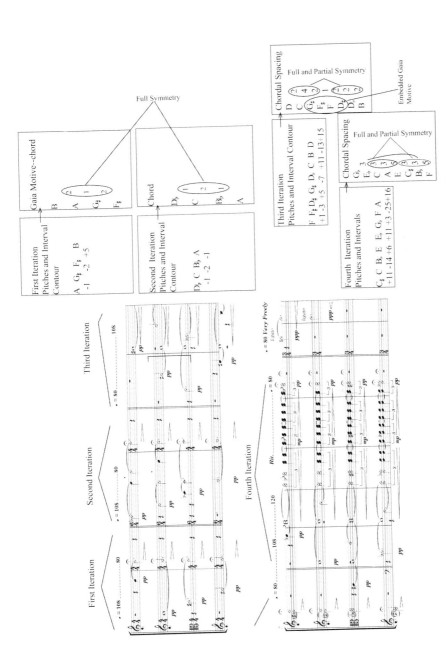

Example 6.3 Third String Quartet, four iterations of the Gaia motive: Intervallic arrangements, bars 1–12.

84   *Judy Lochhead*

Example 6.3 shows the moment of Stasis/Equilibrium and labels four iterations of the Gaia motive. The boxes on the right excerpt pitches as letter names, and for each iteration one box shows the sequence of pitches and its interval contour and the second box shows the pitches and intervals of the *fermata* chords. Iteration 1 is a straightforward presentation of the motive and the second, third and fourth iterations form a chain of transformations that preserves the sensation of symmetry while refreshing its details. Figure 6.5 provides the details of this chain: brackets show the intervallic symmetries and the annotations under each iteration summarise the transformations. Iteration 2 is an interval exchange (1 becomes 2 and 2 becomes 1); Iteration 3 embeds the Gaia motive and extends the intervallic symmetry both above and below it; and Iteration 4 amplifies the intervallic symmetry of Iteration 3 by expanding the intervals (2 becomes 3 and 4 becomes 5). These intervallic symmetries generate the sensations of stasis and equilibrium during the opening of the movement.[17]

Example 6.4 cites and annotates bars 197–211, the moment of Direction/Elation. As the map of Example 6.4 indicates, the music presents a succession of parallel major triads, moving stepwise through the Gaia motive: F♯ G♯ A B. The succession of chords continues to a C♯ root, but the triad is rendered initially as a minor chord which transforms to major in bar 205, the minor/major sequence repeating in bars 208–209. By overshooting the Gaia motive to a triad on C♯, the passage articulates an F♯ minor diatonic sequence, an asymmetrical sequence of pitches matched by the implied asymmetry of the major triads.

Intervallic arrangements of symmetry and asymmetry characterise these first two moments of the becoming of the Gaia motive. Figure 6.6 provides critical interpretation of how the symmetries of the Stasis/Equilibrium moment become the asymmetries of the Direction/Elation moment. The figure traces the intervallic symmetries of Iterations 1 and 2 of the Gaia motive to the intervallic symmetries of the octatonic collection, and the specific pitch formations of these iterations to octatonic collections I and II.[18] The figure also shows the asymmetrical diatonic sequences of F♯ major and minor during the Direction/Elation moment, indicating how the diatonic minor embeds the Gaia motive.[19] During this transformation from Stasis/Equilibrium to Direction/Elation, the Gaia motive serves as the generative thread between these oppositional arrangements. By means of these interactions and transformations, the Gaia motive generates the sensations of Direction/Elation, or in other words, the symmetries of the opening moment become the asymmetries of second moment.

Example 6.5 cites and annotates the Ekstasis passage, bars 267–282, that ends the movement and work. The passage continues the process of the Gaia's motive's becoming in a moment that transcends the symmetrical/asymmetrical opposition of the previous moments. The whole passage is played with the high

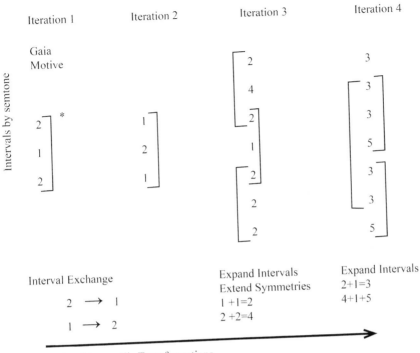

Figure 6.5 Third String Quartet, iterations of the gaia motive and chain of intervallic transformation, bars 1–12.

and soft ethereal sounds of string harmonics. This timbral and registral quality along with the details of the passage's intervallic arrangements generate a sensation of Ekstasis – a standing apart that emerges from but does not replicate the oppositions of the preceding two moments. The Gaia motive occurs during bars 267–268 in an intervallic and rhythmic configuration replicating the movement's beginning but in a timbral and registral transformation. Bars 269–277 present a sequence of seven distinct contour transformations of the Gaia motive, as indicated by the contour annotations on Example 6.5. The Violin I part leads this sequence with a slowly rising line that articulates an F♯ natural minor diatonic collection. The map of Example 6.5 shows and annotates this collection, showing how it embeds two versions of the Gaia motive and both major and minor pentachords. These differing implications of Violin I's melodic sequence are each activated by the sequence of differing Gaia motives, and by activating these differing features from the Stasis/Equilibrium and Direction/Elation moments, the music of this passage dissolves their oppositions. The concluding sonority of the movement emerges from this slow activation of intervallic implications

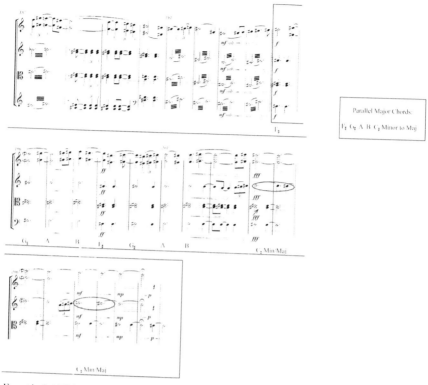

Example 6.4 Third String Quartet, bars 187–212: Parallel major chords, bars 197–211.

and concurrent transformations of the Gaia motive, and the final iteration of the Gaia motive in bar 277 is sustained in the closing passage. As Example 6.5 shows this final sonority, what I refer to as the Ekstasis chord, has an intervallic spacing of 2, 5 and 7 semitones. This open sonority has implications of both symmetrical and asymmetrical intervallic arrangements: it draws on the pitches of an F♯ minor diatonic sequence yet suggests symmetry with the inversionally related intervals of 5 and 7.

The sensation of 'standing apart' of this moment of Ekstasis emerges from several factors: the nearly equal rhythmic articulation of events, the ethereal timbre and dynamics, the succession of Gaia transformations that proliferate diverse intervallic arrangements, the slow upward movement of Violin I through an F♯ minor line, and the reiterations of the concluding open chord from bars 278–281. Overall, these sensations of Ekstasis materialise from the oppositions of the Stasis/Equilibrium with the Direction/Elation moments but not as a function of resolution. Rather, the moment of Ekstasis emerges from the oppositional details as something new, as a standing apart.

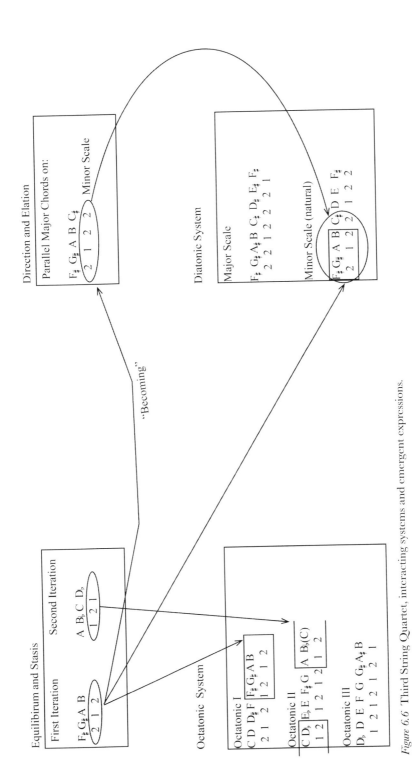

Figure 6.6 Third String Quartet, interacting systems and emergent expressions.

88 *Judy Lochhead*

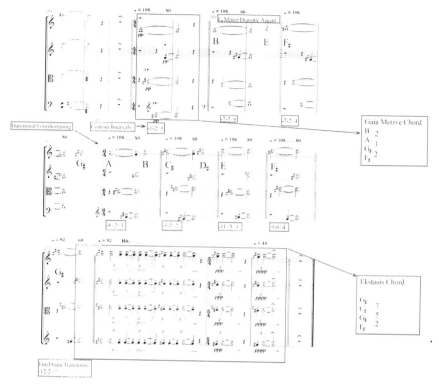

Example 6.5 Third String Quartet, bars 264–283, Ekstasis and the Transcendence of Opposition during bars 266–282.

Conclusion

If art is a form of thought, as Deleuze and Guattari maintain, then the question of whether it is possible to amplify artistic thought through philosophy or science is vital. On one hand, as a form of thought our experiential engagements with art should be sufficient; but on the other hand, there has always been art-critical engagements with art using the tools of philosophy and science. The forms of thought that characterise art, philosophy and science are not exclusive and can have a generative force on each other. So, art criticism may be understood not as an explanation of art practice but rather as means of intensifying and generating new experiences of art. The question of how art-critical work goes about this is crucial. And one of my goals here is to exemplify a process of chaotic mapping for music that will – if it is successful – encourage and intensify the experiences of specific musical works. What I propose is a kind of productive criticism that begins with the sensations of music's sounding and has the goal of generating new experiential sensations.

Notes

1. Gilles Deleuze and Félix Guattari, *What is Philosophy?*, trans. Hugh Tomlinson and Graham Burchell (New York: Columbia University Press, 1994[1991]).
2. Gilles Deleuze, *Francis Bacon: The Logic of Sensation*, trans. Daniel Smith. (New York: Continuum, 2003[1981]).
3. Daniel W. Smith, 'Translator's Introduction. Deleuze on Bacon: Three Conceptual Trajectories in *The Logic of Sensation*', in Deleuze, *Francis Bacon: The Logic of Sensation*, ix.
4. Smith, "Translator's Introduction", xx.
5. In another article, Smith and Protevi sustain the interpretation of Deleuze's writings on the arts (his Bacon book as well as several on film) as philosophical thought in aesthetics. Daniel W. Smith and John Protevi, 'Gilles Deleuze', *The Stanford Encyclopedia of Philosophy*, ed. Edward N. Zalta, accessed 15 March 2015, http://plato.stanford.edu/archives/spr2013/entries/deleuze/.
6. There are some notable exceptions: Hans Keller created analyses of pieces by composing a score that was to be performed. See: Hans Keller, *Functional Analysis: The Unity of Contrasting Themes: Complete Edition of the Analytical Scores*, ed. Gerald W. Gruber. (Frankfurt am Main: P. Lang, 2001). And some assert that all art is itself a form of critical reaction to previous works of art, the most notorious formulation of which is Bloom's 'anxiety of influence'. See: Harold Bloom, *The Anxiety of Influence: A Theory of Poetry* (New York: Oxford, 1979).
7. Elizabeth Grosz, *Chaos, Territory, Art: Deleuze and the Framing of Earth* (New York: Columbia University Press, 2008), 26–7.
8. Deleuze and Guattari, *What is Philosophy?*, 202–6.
9. Deleuze and Guattari, *What is Philosophy?*, 202–3.
10. I am thinking here about complaints that may be expressed in such statements as: 'But can you hear it?' or 'Words cannot capture musical signification'.
11. Such a descriptive mapping is not the same as the notation of the work since that notation is prescriptive for the performer. Chaotic mappings are descriptive of a work's potential soundings.
12. Kaija Saariaho. "Program Notes", *Prés* for cello and electronics (London: Chester Music, 2004[1992]).
13. The timings utilised in the maps are from the recorded performance by Anssi Karttunen: Kaija Saariaho, *Prés*, on *Private Gardens* (Helsinki: Ondine, 1997). While there will be some temporal variation between performances because of the way the sound files are triggered, the durations of those sound files limit the amount of variation.
14. These sound files are indicated with numbers in the score, and Saariaho provides a general descriptive account of the music in the file as a cue for the performer.
15. Stacy Garrop, 'Program Notes', String Quartet no. 3, 'Gaia'. (King of Prussia: Theodore Presser, 2010[2008]).
16. The timings in Map 6.3 are taken from the recording by the Biava Quartet: Stacy Garrop, String Quartet no. 3, on *In Eleanor's Words* (Chicago: Cedille, 2011).
17. Other factors, such as dynamics, rhythm, duration, and the registral disposition of pitches, play a role in this sensation, but for present purposes, I focus on intervallic arrangements only.
18. For present purposes I have chosen to focus only on Iterations 1 and 2 of the Gaia motive, primarily because Iterations 3 and 4 are transformational extensions.
19. A full critical account would also comment on the moment when a major chord is replaced by a minor/major sequence – a moment corresponding to an overstepping of the Gaia motive into the F♯ minor pentachord.

7 Meeting the composer halfway
Which Anne Boyd?

Sally Macarthur

There is an image of the Australian composer Anne Boyd (b. 1946) that is at once stable and predictable, and pointing to the unceasing movement of difference in which there is no stable centre. The flux of movement in the identity of Boyd, to draw the words from Deleuze, 'implies a plurality of perspectives, a tangle of points of view, a co-existence of moments which essentially distort representation ... forcing us to create movement'.[1] At the same time, there is a tendency in the collective assemblage of enunciation[2] to stabilise and fix the image of Boyd and, in so doing, to reinforce her negative opposition to the male composer and thus her inferior membership of the category 'composer'. In this way, her identity works against Deleuze's philosophy of difference, in which difference is always dynamic, and in which 'difference is shown differing'.[3] Representational images of Boyd fail 'to capture the affirmed world of difference',[4] for representational logic mediates and treats identity as static and stable, and 'moves nothing'.[5] The concept of identity has always been fundamental to musical composition, forming the trope of the heroic master composer. As I will argue in this chapter, the ideology of the heroic composer inhibits the productive functioning of the woman composer.

I will explore the processes that give form to the identity of the woman composer, focusing on Boyd. A perennial problem for feminist theory has been how to break with the binary system of thought which conceives of man as the 'universal ground of reason and good thinking'[6] and woman as the Other. The challenge, then, is how to engage Deleuze's concept of 'becoming-woman' to counteract the implied negativity of 'being-woman'. The point of departure for much feminist work is that women's subjugation is taken as a given. The Deleuzian-feminist perspective, however, shifts from this negative idea, suggesting that feminists have always looked for solutions outside the standard modes of philosophical questioning. As Colebrook argues, feminism has been more interested in 'what a philosophy might do, how it might activate life and thought, and how certain problems create (rather than describe) effects'.[7] When feminists have been confronted with theories of the body, they have tended to ask 'an intensely active question, not "What does it mean?", but "How does it work?"'[8] This leads Colebrook to argue that 'any movement of utopianism or any politics of the future is ... best thought of through a Deleuzian notion of becoming'.[9] For Colebrook,

Deleuze encourages different kinds of questions: 'questions beyond determinations of identity, essentialism, emancipation and representation'.[10] In particular, Deleuzian philosophy 'provides a way of understanding the peculiar modality of feminist questions and the active nature of feminist struggle'.[11] In the philosophy of Deleuze and Guattari, 'all becomings begin with and pass through becoming-woman. It is the key to all other becomings'.[12] Grosz stresses, however, that 'becoming-woman' is not based on the recognition of woman as a molar identity, that is, on her definition as a fixed, physical, female form. According to Grosz, 'for women, as much as for men, the process of becoming-woman is the destabilisation of molar (feminine) identity'.[13] Becomings can never be determined in advance and nor can we necessarily know what a becoming might be moving towards. Becomings are always double: they have the potential both to affirm change and to engender further becomings elsewhere.

Representation and identity

The concept of identity is central to how we think and write about music. It functions as a boundary marker, distinguishing one kind of music from another, one genre or style from another, and one composer or performer from another. In the system of binary logic, musical genres and composer-identities yield to the law of normativity. Composers are recognised over time because they become associated with a set of identity markers in the category of composer. Similarly, musical genres emerge through a set of characteristics that are repeated over a period of time. The woman composer is also recognised when she adopts the qualities associated with the composer identity. According to Colebrook, the law of normativity 'maintains the necessary and essential tension between subjection (to the norm) and activation'.[14] The norm comes into existence through various repetitive performances but, as Colebrook also makes the point, such repetitions will 'introduce differences and instabilities'.[15] Despite this, representational models of authorship define identity in narrow terms, constructing the composer from a pre-existing form in which it is also determined. Through the act of composing, a personal territory is established which is defined by the composer's 'unique' voice. The act of territorialising is grounded in habit: the composer's subjectivity is formed through the repetition of action and thought.[16] Music begins to be composed of what Deleuze refers to as molar lines in which it is reduced to hierarchical relationships and divided into rigid, over-coded segments.[17] These lines territorialise music, regulating the way we think about it.

The image in circulation of Anne Boyd as a solitary figure has territorialised and regulated the way we think about the composer. The narrative of Boyd's life associates her work with the Australian landscape.[18] It implies a causal link between her early childhood life, which is depicted as solitary and sad, and her adult composing life. It explains that shortly after Boyd's birth, her father died prematurely, leaving her mother in difficult financial circumstances. At the age of four, Boyd was sent to live with relatives on a remote sheep station not far from Longreach in central, outback Queensland. Most of her childhood was

92   *Sally Macarthur*

spent separated from her mother and siblings. When eventually Boyd returned to Sydney to live with her mother, her mother committed suicide and, aged 12, she was an orphan. This story of Boyd's childhood, now familiar in Australian music circles, is often proffered as the reason for her 'truly original voice in Australia'.[19] It suggests that the desolate child finds solace in music and in the Australian landscape where she looks for comfort. In the composer's own account, the landscape gives form and purpose to her life: it is bound up with her identity; it becomes a substitute for her mother; and it gives her a sense of belonging.[20] Boyd writes that 'the landscape of my early childhood ... became etched with a kind of sorrow, but also great beauty'.[21]

The unfolding story of Boyd draws a link between her childhood and adult life. It suggests that as a student of Peter Sculthorpe (1929–14) at the University of Sydney in the early-to-mid-1960s, she was introduced to the music of Southern and South East Asia. The encounter with this music re-enlivened the memories of her childhood experiences of the flat, Australian landscape and soon she began to craft music that broke new ground in its 'sounding of Australian landscape' through its embrace of 'ancient Japanese traditional music'.[22] While studying for her doctorate at the University of York, it notes that Boyd had an epiphany: the score of a 'hit tune' of the Japanese court repertory, *Etenraku*, which was hanging on the wall of her study-bedroom, was transformed magically (with Boyd in a self-induced hallucinatory state having unknowingly consumed cookies laced with marijuana) into images of 'country' that she recognised immediately from her days as a small, lonely child in remote, rural Australia.[23] She says that: 'Suddenly the connection between the "sacred" other of Japanese ritual music and these vast, flat and often forbidding spaces that had provided the backdrop for my childish imagination, was clear.'[24]

The image of Boyd as a solitary figure connected with the Australian landscape and Japanese ritual music has, over the years, become repetitive, gathering momentum and acquiring significance.[25] Boyd writes that her 'personal interest in Oriental philosophies and leanings towards mysticism separate her work from the compositions of her Australian contemporaries'.[26] The various writings on Boyd heighten her recognition as an individual who stands apart[27] and normalises her identity, overriding other ways to think about the composer. The familiar description of Boyd as a solitary figure is based on a model of identity that is grounded in representational thought which imagines that the world lends itself to being re-presented. In this view, the landscape also lends itself to being represented by Boyd's music.

In the classificatory system of representational thought, identities are hierarchically ranked. One composer is better than another. A younger Boyd aspires to be like her teacher, Peter Sculthorpe, whom she holds in high esteem.[28] Yet, Boyd also searches for her unique identity, the thing that distinguishes her from Sculthorpe.[29] She explores what it means to be Australian and turns to the music of South East Asia. In 1994, she writes that: 'Western harmonic concepts were always foreign to me.'[30] She explains that: 'tonality is replaced by modality. In organising pitch I have chosen modes, often oriental modes such as are common in the cultures of Japan, Korea, China, Bali and Java.'[31] Like Sculthorpe, she believes she is intensely Australian[32] and writes that: 'I have always considered the landscape of central Queensland an extremely important formative influence upon my personal, imaginative and compositional development'.[33] She discusses her musical aesthetic in terms of its distinctiveness, and that of other composers with whom she is aligned.[34] Her writings circulate in the public domain and begin to regulate the way we experience and make sense of her music and that of the other composers about whom she writes. And yet, in a Deleuzian sense, the ideas in Boyd's writings are always already constituted in the public domain. Deleuze and Guattari write that: 'There is no individual enunciation. There is not even a subject of enunciation.'[35] For Deleuze and Guattari, writings that appear under the name of an individual are already part of the 'collective assemblage of enunciation'.[36] Boyd's individuated writings give the appearance of contributing to our recognition of her and the composers about whom she writes as unique individuals but they are simply an effect of the collective assemblage of enunciation.

The classificatory system that organises identity into a hierarchical structure differentiates Anne Boyd according to her gender. According to Deleuze, she is the minority in a category in which the majority are male. As a member of the category 'woman composer', Boyd's music is assessed according to its resemblance: to that of other female composers; and to that of the supreme (male) standard. As Massumi puts it: 'The modus operandi is negation: x = x = not y (I = I = not you).'[37] In this formulation, Anne Boyd is 'not Sculthorpe' and her music is 'not (men's) music'. For Deleuze, the concept of identity invokes the most general principle of representation: the Cogito ('I think') – 'I conceive, I judge, I imagine, I remember and I perceive' – 'form quadripartite fetters under which only that which is identical, similar, analogous or opposed can be considered different'.[38] The representations of Boyd compare her with other composers. As a composer who works with the aesthetic materials of South East Asia, she is judged as similar to Sculthorpe. As a woman composer she is regarded as different from Sculthorpe.

In Deleuzian thought, the plane of representation is a restricted form of thinking and acting: it relies on a world that consists of the known and of fixed norms, including static conceptions of identity that are unable to acknowledge the idea of pure difference or difference-in-itself. Difference-in-itself is opened up by the plane of immanence. According to Stagoll, Deleuze's concept of difference-in-itself is not grounded in anything else.[39] The reiterative images of Boyd repress difference-in-itself, yet it is no easy task to reconstruct Boyd's identity in terms of its specificity and particularity while, at the same time, conceiving of it as a dynamic movement, or as a becoming. In representational thought, the individual identity of Boyd is judged as the same or equivalent to other women composers and, by inference, different from men composers. The act of identifying the composer involves the act of classifying: Boyd is classified as a *woman* composer. As Colebrook argues, 'the condition of being a self – that one remain the same through time – requires a certain iterability: what one is must be repeated or maintained'.[40] Against this idea, she says that 'Deleuze does not allow a system or form of differentiation to exhaust the real or potentiality of being'.[41] Deleuze wishes to

94 *Sally Macarthur*

give primacy not to categories but to movement and differenciation (continuous difference), to becoming different rather than being categorised as different.

What happens to our capacity to perceive difference-in-itself when we engage in representations as inevitably we must? How do we avoid pressing the composer towards the norm, even while she is recognised in her specificity and difference? Deleuze offers a radical reframing of the question of difference, focusing on 'how things become different, how they evolve and continue to evolve beyond the boundaries of the sets into which they have been distributed'.[42] For Deleuze and Guattari, the body is a dynamic movement and a flow of affective capacities. They write that: 'We know nothing about a body until we know what it can do.'[43] In the next section I will shift from the epistemology of representation to the plane of immanence, performing a series of experimental encounters involving Boyd and her music. My aim is to break open the territorial composer-assemblage, and to conceive of it as movement in which it is continuously subjected to the processes of differentiation.

The plane of immanence and Anne Boyd

The proposition that life is immanent, resembling nothing outside itself, is captured by Deleuze and Guattari as follows:

> The plane of immanence is not a concept that is or can be thought but rather the image of thought, the image of thought gives itself of what it means to think, to make use of thought, to find one's bearings in thought … Thought demands 'only' movement that can be carried to infinity.[44]

The plane of immanence is conceptualised by Deleuze and Guattari in two ways: as a hidden principle 'which makes visible what is seen and audible what is heard';[45] and as deeply rooted in Nature, where, as they state:

> There are no longer any forms or development of forms; nor are there subjects or the formation of subjects. There is no structure, any more than there is genesis. There are only relations of movements and rest, speed and slowness, between unformed elements.[46]

On the plane of immanence, Deleuze conceives of music as a 'haecceity' which, in Hainge's words, 'is a becoming, a certain kind of affect at varying degrees of intensity … a this-ness'.[47] Deleuze and Guattari suggest that the visible and invisible dimensions of the plane of immanence continually pass 'from one to another, by unnoticeable degrees and without being aware of it, or one becomes aware of it only afterward. Because one continually reconstitutes one plane atop another, or extricates one from another',[48] Deleuze's work is a radical intervention into thought in that it understands life itself to be a process of creative power.

In representational thought, an event is often understood as a bounded entity within a determinate structure. In relation to a composer, an event might be marked by her/his birth and death, or it might be understood as a narrative structure in which the unfolding life of the composer contributes to its overall plot which, in turn, is determined by the events along the way. In contrast, Deleuze's treatment of the concept 'event', which follows the work of the Stoics,[49] makes a distinction, as Patton says, 'between a material or physical realm of bodies and states of affairs and non-physical realm of incorporeal entities'.[50] The incorporeal realm is unseeable and unknowable, and yet, in Deleuzian thought, everything we know and experience in the world moves around this realm. When something shifts in the moving around, we glimpse or grasp what is otherwise hidden. It is also important to note that the incorporeal realm is not conceived as a binary, dividing the unseeable and the unknowable from the physical reality of the world. What is represented in the actual world is dependent upon the unseen forces of the immaterial, incorporeal realm: both realms influence each other and are dependent upon each other.

Given this, it becomes possible to argue that the whole of Boyd's oeuvre straddles two readings of time as they relate to the event: *Chronos* time and *Aeon* time. *Chronos* is concerned with the material or physical realm, and *Aeon* with the non-physical realm of incorporeal entities. Whatever happens always occurs within this double dimension. In Deleuzian thought, *Chronos* time passes into the present. It is the time in which an event unfolds, including the idea of a past and future relative to it. And yet, to draw this idea into Boyd's oeuvre, each musical work passes into the present, but the present is never actually present. In Bidima's view, the event is never the present. It is always eternally that which has happened and which will happen in the future. It is never that which is happening.[51] As Zepke puts it:

> On the one hand, the event is actualised within a state of affairs, within a present whose duration includes a past and future relative to it, while on the other it remains a purely virtual and incorporeal 'idea' expressed in an infinitive verb (e.g. 'to cut'), which is either already over or still to come in relation to embodiment.[52]

Deleuze and Guattari suggest that *Aeon* is 'the indefinite time of the event, the floating line that knows only speeds and continually divides that which transpires into an already there that is at the same time not-yet-here, a simultaneous too-late and too-early, a something that is both going to happen and has just happened'.[53] The event, according to Bidima, is also a call from the future. It directs itself forward.[54] It is never backward-looking or nostalgic for things of the past.

Deleuze illustrates how both these readings of time are mutually implicated in his discussion of 'Alice's Adventures in Wonderland' and 'Through the Looking-Glass'.[55] The example of Alice, paradoxically, is that she is 'becoming smaller with respect to the bigger Alice who is growing away from her; but she is becoming bigger with respect to the Alice she is growing away from'.[56] Deleuze's argument is that Alice is never 'at a point, an instant, called the "present" Alice'.[57] And, furthermore, 'even in the present she is a stretch forward and back in time, becoming bigger and smaller and many other things'.[58] When emotions are added to the mix of this two-directional concept of time, they betray the many dimensions of becoming. There is 'never a single direction in time, or a single movement, or one alteration, but all of them at different degrees of intensity, selected and expressed by our emotions and the ways we replay complex events'.[59]

Since the mid-1990s, Boyd's musical aesthetic seems to have shifted. It is no longer, as it once was, predominantly based on a South East Asian aesthetic. Instead, it has begun to take up a post-minimalist aesthetic based in Western tonality. Despite this shift in the music's actual aesthetic, so forceful is the collective assemblage of enunciation in associating Boyd's music with the earlier aesthetic that it assumes dominance. Yet, it is possible to reconceive Boyd's music along the lines of Deleuze's Alice as both simultaneously: the older music tied up with South East Asia is receding with respect to the post-minimalist, tonal music which is growing away from it; and the post-minimalist, tonal aesthetic is becoming more prominent with respect to the South East Asian music it is growing away from. As in the analogy of Alice, the newer music is never in the present but a stretch forward and back in time simultaneously, becoming more prominent and receding, and many other things.

Furthermore, in a Deleuzian sense, the musical works in Boyd's oeuvre are not inert and passive with the capacity to only come to life through the actions of the composer. The works themselves are capable of acting on the world with transformative effects. Boyd's music is in a process of continuous transformation in every dynamic encounter: when it alters course and meets up with minimalism and Western tonality, it potentially encounters a different version of landscape from the version it takes up in the earlier music. It is possible to affect a transformation when the music alters a chord to include a major third in which previously her music had avoided such an encounter. To illustrate this point, I will now discuss the chronologically earlier, modally conceived *Meditations on a Chinese Character* (1996) and the later tonally-conceived *Serafin Canticles* (2008). These two works open up notions of the landscape, transforming the visual dimension of landscape into sonic material through their liberal use of drones and pedal points punctuated by silence. But the earlier work assiduously seems to avoid diatonic harmony. In contrast, the later work captures the landscape as a rising A major chord. Both works use silence and pedal points but in the actualisation of these works, the A major chord of the later work can be understood as a becoming-A major chord of the earlier work. The visual landscape understood as a sonic metaphor in both works might also be understood as a becoming-landscape for both works.

Boyd's music will potentially alter direction again when it encounters the future, which is, as yet, unknown. Through each encounter the music changes its properties. Through each encounter, those who listen to the music change their properties. The multiplicity opened up by the music, including its encounters with the composer, the listener, the landscape, South East Asia, modality, tonality and minimalism, are in a perpetual state of change and transformation.

I will now argue that, from the moment of the connection of her music with the Australian landscape, an infinite variation is opened up. The music composes changes to the landscape, and the landscape composes changes to the music.

In other words, the pre-established practices involving South East Asian music introduce change into Boyd's music through the landscape, and her music introduces change into the pre-established idea of landscape remembered from her childhood, and into the musical palette that responds to landscape. The event of music and landscape, colliding as a confluence of forces, involve a shift that gives rise to a becoming-landscape-becoming-music.

Each new work composed by Boyd, as I am suggesting, is never a completely new beginning and nor is it a brand new invention. Yet, referring to an early work, *As it Leaves the Bell* for percussion and harp (1973), Boyd believes that she is 'inventing music again, from scratch, from essence'.[60] She suggests that her music captures 'feelings of loneliness and sadness connected to landscape'.[61] The gong, in particular, is imagined to conjure these feelings as well as to depict the landscape. As Boyd writes, 'a whole series of vibrations seemed to come out of the gong sound onto paper'.[62] She says that 'it came out as a graphic score, mostly blank paper. It was not really a chord but a resonance and I approached it and retreated from it using different sonorities from the instruments available'.[63] She attempts to express the inexpressible. And yet, it is in the inexpressible – in the gap that has no words – that the multiplicity is opened up for this music.

The individuated statements, or what Deleuze refers to as the assemblage of enunciation, focus on Boyd's music as a programmatic representation of the landscape. The assemblage of enunciation focuses on a romanticised idea of landscape: a flat, arid landscape occupying a vast space. The assemblage of enunciation equates the romanticised landscape with Boyd's music: the slow-moving, static chunks of sound are understood to represent the landscape. More than three decades after its composition, Boyd reflects on *As I Crossed a Bridge of Dreams* for 12 unaccompanied voices (1975), in a similar manner, suggesting that the work is a synthesis of Japanese music and landscape, and 'an authentic expression of Australian cultural identity'.[64]

Shifting from these representational images, however, it becomes possible to conceive of a dynamic movement in *As I Crossed a Bridge of Dreams*: its difference in terms of itself might be understood as less about the expression of a prior or grounding substance and more about the capacity of the music and listener and composer to respond to multiple feelings and connections, some of which have nothing to do with the landscape. And yet, we might also argue that it is possible to conceive of the becoming-landscape in this work as altering what happens to the music: elements of the music are changed to accommodate different conceptions of landscape which, in turn, accommodate different conceptions of music. The multiplicity opened up by the concept of becoming-landscape-becoming-music as a set of multiple interactions pass through the bodies engaged with the music, and through actual and virtual (unknown) structures. According to Williams, these virtual structures can be understood as 'relations of emotional investment considered in abstraction from the bodies that carry them'.[65] As virtual structures, they are ongoing and unpredictable.

Boyd's individuated statements about her music and musical processes are deeply integrated in the collective assemblage of enunciation. According to

Deleuze and Guattari, however, as an indirect discourse, the collective assemblage of enunciation 'explains all the voices present within a single voice'.[66] As they put it, 'the notion of collective assemblage of enunciation takes on primary importance since it is what must account for the social character'.[67] The verbal accounts of the music opened up by the collective assemblage of enunciation, however, is insufficient and unable to account for the ways in which Boyd's music potentially transforms the bodies that listen to it. It cannot account for those aspects of the music that escape articulation, such as the completely unexpected 'shivers down the spine' or 'being moved to tears'. There are no words to describe unpredictable experiences like these. Yet, it is possible to observe palpable transformations that are opened up by the music in the non-physical realm. The incorporeal realm brings about observable changes through the expressive dimension of the music; the virtual realm of becoming and the actual realm of embodied events that emerge from listening to Boyd's music are intimately enmeshed through their connections.

Which Anne Boyd?

In this chapter, I have worked with the doubleness of identity. On the one hand, identity is reiterative, recognisable, stable and coherent. On the other hand, it is imagined as a dynamic movement, and immanent. The represented, unique identity of the composer is captured through repetitive, habituated acts that surface in collective assemblage of enunciation. On the plane of representation, Boyd's subjectivity is formed through territorialising acts. These territorial acts enclose her music in molar lines and reduce it to hierarchical relationships. The habitual acts that territorialise music regulate the way we think about it. I have suggested that the assemblage of collective enunciation spins on the plane of representation. In this mode of thought, we conceive of Boyd's music as representing a pre-existing, static landscape. The landscape is drawn into the present through the composer's memory: she nostalgically reflects on her childhood experience of landscape and represents her particular vision of the landscape in her subsequent music. The representational world is actualised as music. The representational world relies on fixed norms, including static conceptions of identity that stifle the idea of difference-in-itself.

Shifting from a representational mode of thought, I have drawn on the concept of evental time, which conceives of time as simultaneously occupying the space between the material or physical realm of bodies and states of affairs, and the non-physical realm of incorporeal entities. Thinking about Boyd's music through the concept of the 'event' dislodges it from the reiterative thought patterns that circulate through the collective assemblage of enunciation. The event is not what evidently occurs. Boyd's music can be understood as an event when each new work effects a transformation through the potential immanent within the momentary gathering together of unseen forces. I have argued, to draw on Stagoll, that the event 'is not a disruption of some continuous state, but rather the state is constituted by events "underlying" it that, when actualised, mark every moment of the state of transformation'.[68] For Deleuze, an event is neither a beginning nor an end point, but rather always in the middle, an ongoing process that is related to the idea of dynamic change or 'becoming'. Boyd's music is thus never in the present, occupying a static position on a chronological timeline, but constantly moving forwards and backwards in time.

Finally, I have posited Boyd as a composer whose life unfolds as infinite variations of movement. I have suggested that the multiple variations of Boyd are opened onto the plane of immanence. I invoked the concept of becoming to disrupt the binary system on which negative difference (and woman's subjugation) is founded. The power of Boyd's music lies in its production of the multiplicity of relations in a multiplicity of time zones. The becomings opened up by Boyd's music potentially affirm change while engendering further becomings elsewhere. In the final analysis, Boyd's music opens a window onto the infinite as pure sensation.

Notes

1 Gilles Deleuze, *Difference and Repetition*, trans. Paul Patton (New York: Columbia University Press, 1994), 56.
2 According to Deleuze and Guattari, a collective assemblage of enunciation is always already constituted as a set of acts and statements that circulate in the public domain. What a given individual says is already part of the collective unconscious. These pre-existing set of actions and statements infiltrate the languages and statements of the individual. See Gilles Deleuze and Félix Guattari, *A Thousand Plateaus: Capitalism and Schizophrenia*, trans. Brian Massumi (Minneapolis and London: University of Minnesota Press, 1987), 80, 85, 88.
3 Deleuze, *Difference and Repetition*, 56.
4 Deleuze, *Difference and Repetition*, 55.
5 Deleuze, *Difference and Repetition*, 55–6.
6 Claire Colebrook, 'Introduction', in *Deleuze and Feminist Theory*, ed. Ian Buchanan and Claire Colebrook (Edinburgh: Edinburgh University Press, 2000), 2.
7 Colebrook, 'Introduction', 7.
8 Colebrook, 'Introduction', 8.
9 Colebrook, 'Introduction', 17.
10 Colebrook, 'Introduction', 15.
11 Colebrook, 'Introduction', 7–8.
12 Deleuze and Guattari, *A Thousand Plateaus*, 277.
13 Elizabeth Grosz, 'A Thousand Tiny Sexes: Feminism and Rhizomatics', *Topoi*, 12 (1993), 177, accessed 5 May 2014, http://link.springer.com/article/10.1007%2FBF00821854#page-1.
14 Claire Colebrook, 'On the Very Possibility of Queer Theory', in *Deleuze and Queer Theory*, ed. Chrysanthi Nigianni and Merl Storr (Edinburgh: Edinburgh University Press, 2009), 14.
15 Colebrook, 'On the Very Possibility of Queer Theory', 14.
16 For Deleuze, a territorialisation of a space is created when people relate to it in habitual ways. The space associated with composing is not in itself a territory but the activity is, such as composers who compose music in particular kinds of ways. Deleuze and Guattari provide a detailed account of the concepts of territorialisation and deterritorialisation. See Deleuze and Guattari, *A Thousand Plateaus*, 311–50.
17 According to Woodward, Deleuze and Guattari conceptualise three lines of force, molar lines, molecular lines and lines of flight: 'Molar lines organize by drawing strict boundaries, creating binary oppositions and dividing space into rigid segments with

a hierarchical structure. Molecular lines organize in a more supple way, interlacing segments in a non-hierarchical fashion. The line of flight is ... the line of change and metamorphosis.' See Ashley Woodward, 'Deleuze and Suicide', in *Deleuzian Encounters: Studies in Contemporary Social Issues*, ed. Anna Hickey-Moody and Peta Malins (Houndmills, Basingstoke: Palgrave Macmillan, 2007), 69–70.

18 See, for example, Rosalind Appleby, 'Anne Boyd', in *Women of Note: The Rise of Australian Women Composers* (Fremantle: Fremantle Press, 2012), 89.

19 Appleby, 'Anne Boyd', 78.

20 Anne Boyd, 'Dreaming Voices: Australia and Japan', in *Intercultural Music: Creation and Interpretation*, ed. Sally Macarthur, Bruce Crossman and Ronaldo Morelos (Sydney: Australian Music Centre, 2006), 10.

21 Boyd, 'Dreaming Voices', 10.

22 Appleby, 'Anne Boyd', 80–81.

23 Boyd, 'Dreaming Voices', 10. Also, see Appleby, 'Anne Boyd', 80.

24 Boyd, 'Dreaming Voices', 10.

25 Among the research that discusses Boyd in these terms are: Deborah Crisp, 'Elements of *Gagaku* in the Music of Anne Boyd' (Honours Thesis, University of Sydney, 1978); Kathryn Tibbs, 'East and West in the Music of Anne Boyd' (Honours Thesis, University of Sydney, 1989); Joy Sotheran, 'Concepts as Organising Elements in Selected Works of Anne Boyd' (Master of Music Thesis, University of New South Wales, 1992); and Rita Williams, 'Asian Influences are Integral to the Music of Anne Boyd' (Honours Thesis, University of Sydney, 1996). See also Sally Macarthur, 'Women, Spirituality, Landscape: The Music of Anne Boyd, Sarah Hopkins and Moya Henderson', in *The Soundscapes of Australia: Music, Place and Spirituality*, ed. Fiona Richards (Aldershot: Ashgate, 2007), 51–74.

26 Anne Boyd, 'Draft Biography', unpublished, 1983, 2. Anne Boyd file, Australian Music Centre.

27 See, for example: Crisp, 'Elements of *Gagaku*'; Tibbs, 'East and West'; Sotheran, 'Concepts as Organising Elements'; Williams, 'Asian Influences'; and Macarthur, 'Women, Spirituality, Landscape'.

28 The esteem Boyd had for Sculthorpe as a student is demonstrated through her analytical writings on his music. See Anne Boyd, 'Peter Sculthorpe's *Sun Music 1*: An Analysis', *Miscellanea Musicologica: Adelaide Studies in Musicology* 3 (1968): 3–20.

29 Some years later, Boyd discusses her work in terms of its uniqueness. See, for example, Boyd, 'Dreaming Voices'.

30 Anne Boyd, 'A Solitary Female Phoenix Reflects on Women in Music', *Contemporary Music Review* 11 (1994): 41.

31 Boyd, 'A Solitary Female Phoenix'.

32 See Peter Sculthorpe, *Advertiser* (9 June 1967), cited in Graeme Skinner, *Peter Sculthorpe: The Making of an Australian Composer* (Sydney: University of New South Wales Press, 2007), 482.

33 Anne Boyd, 'Listening to the Landscape', Interview with Geoff Watt, *POL* (1977): 89.

34 See, Anne Boyd, 'Writing the Wrongs? A Composer Reflects', *Sounds Australian: Igniting the Flame—Documentation & Discourse* 67 (2006): 18–23; and Anne Boyd, 'To *didj* or not to *didj*: Indigenous representation in Margaret Sutherland's *The Young Kabbarli* and Andrew Schultz's *Journey to Horseshoe Bend*', in *Opera Indigene: Re/presenting First Nations and Indigenous Cultures*, ed. P. Karantonis and D. Robinson (Farnham, UK and Burlington, VT: Ashgate, 2011).

35 Deleuze and Guattari, *A Thousand Plateaus*, 79.

36 Deleuze and Guattari, *A Thousand Plateaus*, 79.

37 Brian Massumi, 'Translator's Foreword' to *A Thousand Plateaus*, by Deleuze and Guattari, xiii.

38 Deleuze, *Difference and Repetition*, 138.

39 Cliff Stagoll, 'Difference', in *The Deleuze Dictionary*, ed. Adrian Parr (Edinburgh: Edinburgh University Press, 2005), 72–3.

40 Colebrook, 'On the Very Possibility of Queer Theory', 14.

41 Colebrook, 'On the Very Possibility of Queer Theory', 16.

42 James Williams, *Gilles Deleuze's 'Difference and Repetition': A Critical Introduction and Guide* (Edinburgh: Edinburgh University Press, 2003), 60.

43 Deleuze and Guattari, *A Thousand Plateaus*, 257.

44 Gilles Deleuze and Félix Guattari, *What is Philosophy?*, trans. Hugh Tomlinson and Graham Burchell (New York: Columbia University Press, 1994[1991]), 37.

45 Deleuze and Guattari, *A Thousand Plateaus*, 265.

46 Deleuze and Guattari, *A Thousand Plateaus*, 266.

47 Greg Hainge, 'Is Pop Music?', in *Deleuze and Music*, ed. Ian Buchanan and Marcel Swiboda (Edinburgh: Edinburgh University Press, 2004), 36.

48 Deleuze and Guattari, *A Thousand Plateaus*, 269.

49 See Gilles Deleuze, *The Logic of Sense*, trans. Mark Lester with Charles J. Stivale and ed. Constintin V. Boundas (London: Continuum, 2004[1969]).

50 Paul Patton, *Deleuzian Concepts: Philosophy, Colonisation, Politics* (Stanford: Stanford University Press, 2010), 12.

51 Jean-Godefroy Bidima, 'Intensity, Music and Heterogenesis in Deleuze', trans. Michael Wiedorn, in *Sounding the Virtual: Gilles Deleuze and the Theory and Philosophy of Music*, ed. Brian Hulse and Nick Nesbitt (Farnham, UK and Burlington, VT: Ashgate, 2010), 152.

52 Stephen Zepke, 'Becoming a Citizen of the World: Deleuze Between Allan Kaprow and Adrian Piper', in *Deleuze and Performance*, ed. Laura Cull (Edinburgh: Edinburgh University Press, 2009), 110.

53 Deleuze and Guattari, *A Thousand Plateaus*, 262.

54 Bidima, 'Intensity, Music and Heterogenesis in Deleuze', 152.

55 Deleuze, *The Logic of Sense*, 3–5; and James Williams, *Gilles Deleuze's Logic of Sense: A Critical Introduction and Guide* (Edinburgh: Edinburgh University Press, 2008), 28–9.

56 Williams, *Gilles Deleuze's Logic of Sense*, 28.

57 Williams, *Gilles Deleuze's Logic of Sense*, 28.

58 Williams, *Gilles Deleuze's Logic of Sense*, 29.

59 Williams, *Gilles Deleuze's Logic of Sense*, 29.

60 Appleby, *Women of Note*, 82.

61 Appleby, *Women of Note*, 82. Boyd is referring to being sent to live with her relatives in Queensland as a very young child following the death of her father.

62 Appleby, *Women of Note*, 82.

63 Boyd, 'Dreaming Voices', 12.

64 Boyd, 'Dreaming Voices', 9.

65 Williams, *Deleuze's Logic of Sense*, 1.

66 Deleuze and Guattari, *A Thousand Plateaus*, 80.

67 Deleuze and Guattari, *A Thousand Plateaus*, 80.

68 Stagoll, 'Event', in *The Deleuze Dictionary*, ed. Adrian Parr (Edinburgh: Edinburgh University Press, 2005), 87.

8   Schaeffer's sound effects

Ian Stevenson

In this chapter, revisiting the innovative approach to musical research undertaken by the French pioneer of *musique concrète*, Pierre Schaeffer (1910 95), I show how Schaeffer's humanistic modernism can be understood in the light of the post-structural critique offered in the works by Deleuze[1] that were published in the years following Schaeffer's *magnum opus*, the *Traité des objets musicaux* (*Treatise on Musical Objects*, hereafter *Treatise*).[2] With the first English translations of Schaeffer's works only now becoming available,[3] we have an opportunity to reassess his contribution.

There are many similarities between the approaches taken by Schaeffer and Deleuze. While their subject matter and methods could not be more different, there are many features of their thought that resonate. As Deleuze suggests in *Difference and Repetition* the subjects he deals with were, at the time, 'manifestly in the air'.[4] What makes Deleuze's approach useful for my engagement with Schaeffer is his method of productive reading or conceptual appropriation. This approach allows me to interrogate Schaeffer's conceptual apparatus and suggest new perspectives on the problems with which he was dealing. This reveals Schaeffer as a much more open thinker than he is generally portrayed in the literature, and shows the lasting value of his thinking on the problems of musical sound and listening.

One of the innovations in Deleuze's early original philosophy is the description of the objects of knowledge and experience as sets of relations. In his critique of Aristotelian logic he shows that these relations obtain not between entities of fixed identity but between entities that are themselves sets of relations. This form of thought challenges the very notion of relation that we usually take to exist between 'things'. Deleuze suggests that relationship or the state of being in relation is at the very core of the things we encounter. In common usage, a relation is 'the way in which two or more people or things are connected, [or] a thing's effect on or relevance to another'.[5] Putting these concepts together we find that things 'are' ways of being connected, effects or relevance to other things. This implies that when we look closely we find that things are different from how they first appear: they are different from themselves because wherever we look we find that we are observing connections to the influences or effects of other things.

Two particular forms of relation are subject to the most intense critique by Deleuze. The relation of identity or the identical, and the relation of opposition, on which Aristotelian logic are based are shown to be effects in themselves.[6] Deleuze indicates that, for Aristotle, the specific form of difference – which is logical opposition – becomes an absolute ground to which all forms or degrees of difference must be referred. However, the principle of non-contradiction, which states that a proposition cannot be both true and not true, or a thing cannot be both itself and its opposite, only operates at the abstract level of formal logic. At the level of the general, identity and opposition are abstractions from the reality of the particular in which there is no absolute opposition, only degrees of difference. However, the apparent logical truth of the principles of identity and non-contradiction become the basis of common sense through which we make claims about the world of particular entities. For Deleuze this sleight of hand,[7] which, crudely speaking, amounts to superimposing the abstract conditions of the domain of formal logic on the concrete world of particulars, is a form of sense-effect; a way in which we discover sense in the world or the world makes sense. Thus, in Deleuzian philosophy, sense is prior to truth.

At the level of particulars, Deleuze's approach mirrors Aristotle's in that the essence of the real is made up of two complementary dimensions: the actual and the virtual.[8] The virtual refers to all the sets of relations between and within an actualised entity, other actual entities, and the realms of the abstract and ideal, which produce or motivate the actualisation of particulars. The virtual is always present in the real actualised individual entity as it undergoes change and as it stands in relation to others of its kind.

Relations, then, which lie at the heart of real phenomena, are connections, relevancies or effects. For Deleuze, the effect is a relation of special importance. While his analysis of material cause and effect is not directly relevant to this discussion, it is his use of the effect as it is related to special effects, optical effects and, importantly, sound effects that is most instructive. Deleuze highlights the rise of the effect as a category of description and explanation in the material sciences of the nineteenth century. He cites the Kelvin and Seebeck effects, describing phenomena associated with relations between materials:[9] rather than being effects in the abstract which arise subsequent or consequent to a cause, these named effects – like musical effects – name the conditions that arise when a set of relations are brought bear. Deleuze invokes the image of a surface-effect that enfolds a set of relations that we can name and that makes sense of a state of affairs.[10]

How, then, is this rather arcane critique of reality related to the work of Schaeffer? First, this relational world-view was very much 'in the air' in the French intellectual *milieu* of the late 1960s and can be identified in the series of descriptive and explanatory terms in Schaffer's musical research. Second, the Deleuzian concept of the effect has been taken up in the field of sound research by French philosopher, urbanist and musicologist Jean-François Augoyard to bridge the gap between the specific sonic context of experimental music in which Schaeffer's theories of sound and listening develop, and the more general context of sounds in the environment and the everyday.[11] It is these two key ideas – a reappraisal of Schaeffer's theories of musical sound and listening, and the concept of the sonic effect – that are the main focus of this chapter.

104   *Ian Stevenson*

Schaeffer's interdisciplinary method

During the mid-twentieth century, Schaeffer worked as an innovative technocrat and administrator at France's national broadcaster. There, Schaeffer's engagement with recording technologies led him in 1948 to develop the avant-garde style known as *musique concrète*. While his contribution to the fields of electronic and experimental music has been widely publicised, his pioneering, innovative work in musical research is less well-understood in the Anglophone world.

Schaeffer's principal writing on music spans the period 1948 to 1966 and reveals the philosophical influences of phenomenology and structuralism. Schaeffer claimed to be developing a musical *interdiscipline* between the boundaries of composition, instrument building, musicology, physics, psychology, phenomenology and linguistics;[12] an endeavour prefiguring interdisciplinary research in urban ambiences and sonic effects led by Augoyard.[13]

With the pitched tone as its archetype, Schaeffer speculated on a basic unit of musical organisation that he called the musical object. A musical object is the correlate of an appropriately musical listening and a suitable acoustic action. Schaeffer argued that musical objects could include and extend beyond the domain of the pitched sound that underpins conventional musical practices. He was wary of producing a set of fixed theoretical structures that would too pre-emptively constrain any potential musical practice that might arise from his intervention. While his writings are saturated with structural devices for the description and clarification of these ideas, he appears to have viewed these structures as methods of articulation for the concepts he was developing. I use the term 'articulation' in two senses. First, articulation is 'the action of putting into words an idea'; and, second, it is 'the state of being joined'.[14] In the first sense, the structures of Schaeffer's thought that arose from his practical experiences in the studio brought about new contrasts and associations. They produced new ways of conceiving musical sound that he expressed in his writing. In the second sense, Schaffer joins together various ideas to produce series of inter-related concepts. These ideas arising from various disciplinary domains produce new concepts through their connections or intersections between successive pairs or series of conceptual entities. This method of serial thought is examined in Deleuze's *The Logic of Sense*.[15]

In amplifying these aspects of Schaeffer's research I have chosen to engage in a Deleuzian re-reading of Schaeffer's writing.[16] Deleuzian reading, as a form of portraiture, understands the concepts developed by any writer as already multiple and capable of producing new perspectives on a subject. This productive mode of reading is demonstrated in Deleuze's early writings on historical philosophers and his approach to structuralist thought as outlined in the essay: 'How Do We Recognize Structuralism?'[17] This productive spirit also characterises Schaeffer's project; a project that encompasses new forms of music and sound production, new modes of listening and, importantly, an influential body of writing. Often regarded as a polemic against the excessive abstraction of European modernism, a close reading of Schaeffer's output reveals a non-prescriptive reappraisal of the musical or *musicianly*[18] as a system of differential relations with no pre-determined end-point.

Part of Schaeffer's project was to re-engage with phenomenology. His *Treatise* represents the culmination of 20 years of empirical, experimental, creative and theoretical work that attempted to suspend both common sense and scientific assumptions about the materials he was exploring. His theories are often charged as exhibiting essentialism,[19] but there is very limited evidence for this assertion; rather, his work demonstrates a thorough-going pluralism. This view is supported not only by a careful analysis of the symbolic relations within his apparently structuralist system, but also by numerous comments by Schaeffer that showed he was attuned to the unbound potentiality of musical sound.[20]

Schaeffer's musical object is an eminently flexible entity that will be shaped by, or will shape, whatever set of specialist listening practices are applied to it. The underlying sound object and its correlated sounding and listening are, appropriately for sonic phenomena, an event or an effect of musical sound, or more simply a sound effect. Deleuze introduces the concept of the effect as he develops a theory of the production and circulation of sense. Deleuze's event-effect is 'co-present to, and coextensive with its own cause'.[21] In Schaeffer there is a parallel working out of the production of musical sense in the emergence of the musical object as the proper object of musical audition. The musical object makes musical sense within in its musical context.

As an example of how Schaeffer's interdisciplinary approach uncovers a range of sonic effects it is instructive to consider his phenomenological exploration of how the concept of *timbre* stands for our tendency to think-perceive identity. In its everyday usage, timbre is a form of auditory cognition at work, conforming to the conventional 'image of thought' that Deleuze attacks in *Difference and Repetition*.[22] Timbre is a tautological concept, a phantom that vanishes when pursued through the systematic musical experiments conducted by Schaeffer. Few theorists at the time recognised this.[23] Most employed a negative definition of timbre, characterising it as the perceivable differences in musical sounds when pitch and loudness are kept constant. And many theorists persisted with Helmoltz's spectral definition that formed the basis of then contemporary musical acoustics.[24]

The understanding of the complex multi-dimensional nature of timbre emerged slowly,[25] and a more nuanced and critical view only became mainstream in psychoacoustics in the last decade of the twentieth century.[26] In Schaeffer's system, because timbre is not susceptible to use as a differential function or unitary perceptual dimension, it is replaced by the more subtle concepts of 'genre' or 'criterion'.[27] In developing his unique terminology for the characterisation of sounds, Schaeffer recognised the concept of 'timbre' as shorthand for what Merleau-Ponty described as consciousness of 'what things mean'.[28] In this view, perception is bound up with the 'world-as-meaning' that becomes apparent through the process of phenomenological reduction. This world of sonic meanings is evident in Schaeffer's identification of such musical typological criteria as *facture*,[29] which is both a quality of perceived variations in the sustained portion of a sound and a clue as to the material and energetic aspects of sound production. The French word *facture* shares a common root with the English word manufacture.[30] The sonic sense bundled within the effect of facture is as relevant to the apprehension of a passage played on a violin as it is to the manipulated sound of a ball rolling in a bowl.[31]

The acousmatic

A key moment in Schaeffer's exposition is the discovery of so-called 'reduced listening'. This revelation came about as a result of experiments with radio production equipment available in 1948, particularly the lacquer disc recorder. When the groove in the disc is accidentally closed by scratching the disc's surface, a repeating sound fragment is produced. After a short period, the sound appears to lose its inherent connection to its material acoustic source and becomes an independent sound phenomenon or pure acousmatic event. This revelation highlights the differences in the objects of perception of the various senses and our naive assumptions about the nature of those objects. Whereas the unities of vision and touch seduce us into assuming the objects of perception are physical objects (despite the everyday presence of such phenomena as sky and rainbows), reduced listening reveals the object of audition as an entirely different type of entity that Schaeffer terms the 'sound object' that is the correlate of acousmatic listening.

Schaeffer explains that the term acousmatic is borrowed from the Pythagorean cult in which the master is hidden behind a sheet to allow the disciples to focus on the aural transmission of the teaching rather than the master's presence.[32] In the electroacoustic sound studio, recording media and the loudspeaker provide the necessary isolation from the physical source of a sound, which encourages us to focus on its form and matter. As Schaeffer claims, however, it is the repetition of the sound that allows us to lose our normal conditioned interest in the source and become fully aware of the sound object itself and the details of its audible features.

Schaeffer's sound effects

The term 'sound effect' has several uses in Schaeffer's lexicon that all link to the idea of an effect as a relationship that forms a type of listener or listening and a certain listening context. Schaeffer's first engagement with sound effects was with a collection of sound-making devices used to illustrate the scenes of radio drama production with which he hoped to develop his first concrete musical compositions. These included 'clappers, coconut shells, bicycle horns, … door bells, alarm clocks, rattles, [and] whirlygigs'.[33] Schaeffer retains the pejorative use of the term 'mere sound effects' but also indicates that such sounds can move 'from being an effect to being a means of discovery'.[34] In defining the sound object, Schaeffer elaborates on the longstanding distinction between sound and noise. This distinction commonly differentiates the organised sounds of musical instruments, characterised by identifiable pitches and timbres of variable duration, from all other environmental noises.[35] Schaeffer suggests that in concert music, audio or audio-visual media, an ordinary listener will listen for a musical or a dramatic context in which to situate each type respectively. In this way the sound effect has a dramatic or dramaturgical function. Its effect is to orient the listener towards a particular form of sonic discourse or structure of audible sense, either musical or dramatic.

In his earliest experimental concrete studies, such as the seminal *Étude Aux Chemins De Fer* (1948),[36] Schaeffer notes that his use of the sounds of the railway station produce a 'monstrous result' juxtaposing 'dramatic sequences' with other more musically successful sequences.[37] The dramatic sequences in which 'we witness events, departures, stops', and so on, achieve 'popular appeal' but 'constrain the imagination',[38] He notes that the possibly more musically successful sequences occur 'where the train must be forgotten and only sequences of sound colour, changes of time and the secret life of percussion instruments are heard'.[39] For Schaeffer, the techniques of isolation and repetition have the potential to transform the anecdotal into the musical, resulting in a new principle of sound organisation. The sound object, isolated from its function in a conventionally dramatic context, invites attention to its intrinsic sonic properties alone, producing an entirely new musical effect. This effect arises as the relationship between a particular form of listening and a sonic context. Unlike a cause and effect relationship, this musical effect produces both the context and the listening, as musical.

A further use of the term 'sound effect' is revealed in Schaeffer's description of the compositional process of the later concrete studies. One of the principles of Schaeffer's compositional approach was the discovery of sound characteristics that retained perceptual permanence but that could be subject to variation such that sequences or passages of musical values could be produced, resulting in abstract structures of musical meaning.[40] The model or archetype of this principle is the relationship between timbre and pitch. In conventional music, variations in pitch that make up a melody are made salient when produced by a single instrumental timbre. In this case, the identity of the instrument timbre remains permanent while the pitch is varied. This permanence of the characteristic instrument timbre is the *effect* of, or is produced by, variations in pitch and, conversely, the relative values of successive pitches are produced through the apparent permanence of the timbre.[41] This structural relation of permanence–variation is essential to the definition of instrument, musical object and to the concrete music that Schaeffer was attempting to develop. Once again we see the reversible nature of Deleuzian effect at work, in which the musical note, the melody and the instrument are both cause and effect of their musical sense. In Deleuzian terms the identity or permanence of timbre is brought about by the repetition of differences in pitch, showing the central role of difference or relation in the determination a phenomenon.

Schaeffer is explicit in his development of this aspect of sonic effect. By uncovering the acousmatic sound object as the primary object of audition he brings attention to our typical everyday manner of ascribing a physical cause (e.g. knocking) as the name of a sound. If the sound is the effect we perceive, 'it is through [this] effect ... that we can go back to' the cause. These causes are 'dominated by structures which, before being linguistic or acoustic, dramatic or prosaic, detective or medical, or, finally, musical properly speaking, are the structures of sonority'.[42] While the causes in all their structural complexity are the sense that is produced through the sonic event-effect, it is the structures of sonority and listening that Schaeffer endeavours to explicate.

Ordinary and specialist listening

The significance of Schaeffer's acousmatic revelation was to hear, clearly, everyday listening in all its naivety, multi-modal and differential complexity.[43] For Schaeffer, ordinary listening is a dynamic process that is energised by a 'two-fold tension' between, on the one hand, the objective and the subjective dimensions, and, on the other, the abstract and concrete dimensions. This pair of dualities resolves into the four series or modes that comprise the quadrants of Schaeffer's model of ordinary listening. Schaeffer's ordinary and specialist listening modes comprise a potentially open-ended series of effects through which a listener is formed. For Schaeffer, the ordinary and the specialist are not poles in opposition but are co-constitutive. Ordinary listening is not a unitary universal phenomenon; rather, it is unique in each case determined by the particular specialisms or intentions that characterise or form each listener and each listening.

Reduced listening is only one form of specialised listening. Other forms of disciplinary expertise produce the specialised listening of the ornithologist, musician, poet or technician. Paraphrasing Schaeffer, Chion offers the following explanation:

> Specialist listening concentrates on a particular manner of listening. For example, the sound of galloping: ordinary listening hears it as the galloping of horses, but different specialised listenings hear it differently; the acoustician seeks to determine the nature of the physical signal, the Native American Indian hears 'the possible danger of an approaching enemy', and the musician hears rhythmic groupings.[44]

Chion makes the point that it is not so much the expertise of the listener which allows them to recognise or identify a certain sound or sound value; instead, it is the sound object that invokes that expertise or listening intention of which it is the correlate.[45] The process of recognition and identification run both ways as both the potential of the sound and the listener is actualised in a certain direction. The sound becomes fixed under a certain aspect, as does the listener as a specialist in their field. In the galloping example, the disciplinary knowledge of the musician identifies rhythms as objects of auditory knowledge that may be transcribed with more or less precision. The existence of rhythmic groupings within this discipline allows the musician to take their place within the realm of musical listening.

Many subsequent researchers have proposed models of listening to environmental sounds. Gaver, for example, considered listening to sounds in the environment, suggesting two modes of listening: everyday listening, which identifies sound sources as objects or events; and musical listening, which focuses on the intrinsic properties or features of sounds.[46] Schaeffer provides a more detailed and flexible model of everyday listening which attempts to capture more of the complexity and dynamism of listening experiences without tying them to fixed identities. Table 8.1, adapted from Chion's *Guide to Sound Objects*, presents the four modes or quadrants of Schaeffer's listening model including summary details taken from the book that Schaeffer devotes to the topic.[47]

Schaeffer's sound effects 109

Table 8.1 Four quadrants of Schaeffer's listening model

Quadrant 4. COMPREHENDING [COMPRENDRE] for me: signs before me: values (meaning-language)	Quadrant 1. LISTENING [ÉCOUTER] for me: indexes before me: external events (agent-instrument) *Emission* of the sound	(1) & (4) OBJECTIVE because we turn towards the object of perception.
Emergence of a sound continuum and *reference to, confrontation with* extra-sonorous notions. Comprehending means grasping a meaning, values, by treating the sound as a sign, referring to this meaning through a language, a code.	Listening means listening to someone, to something; and through the intermediary of sound as an index, aiming to identify the source, the event, the cause, it means treating the sound as a sign of this source, this event.	
Quadrant 3. HEARING [ENTENDRE] for me: qualified perceptions before me: qualified sound object *Selection* of certain particular aspects of the sound	Quadrant 2. PERCEIVING [OUÏR] for me: crude perceptions, rough outlines of the object. before me: crude sound object *Reception* of the sound	(2) & (3) SUBJECTIVE because we turn towards the activity of the perceiving subject.
Hearing, here, according to its etymology, means showing an intention to listen, choosing from what we perceive what particularly interests us, using selective perception in order to make a "description" of it.	Perceiving means perceiving by ear, being struck by sounds, the crudest, most elementary level of perception; so we "hear", passively, lots of things which we are not trying to listen to or understand.	
(3) & (4) ABSTRACT because the object is stripped down to qualities which describe perception (3) or constitute a language, express a meaning (4).	(1) & (2) CONCRETE because the causal references (1) and the raw sound data (2) are an inexhaustible concrete given.	

Instead of being a process that is carried out by the listener, Schaeffer's model suggests the way in which listening is something that happens to or through the listener. This is not to assert that we could not direct our listening attention in certain ways by exercising expertise or habits of listening of one sort or another, but rather, when we do so, we are inserting ourselves into these processes without fully being in control of them: we take our place within something called listening.[48] While Schaeffer's description of everyday listening remains anchored in the Husserlian language of subjects and objects,[49] it is clear from what I have already indicated that the subjective is partly determined by objective disciplinary practices, and what shows up as the objects of audition are conditioned by listening subjectivities.

Similarly, Schaffer's concrete refers to entities actualised as events or causes or as perceptive capacities, each of which is conditioned by the abstract or virtual dimension of listening practices. On the other hand, the abstract nature of technical hearing intentions and the comprehension of language can only be realised within actual concrete instances of sound. The parallels with the Deleuzian analysis of the real comprising virtual and actual dimensions is apparent and, like Deleuze, Schaeffer escapes the representational logic of identities and oppositions that might otherwise limit his system of thought.[50]

Table 8.1, quadrant 1 describes the most apparent mode of listening to the objective and concrete sources or causes, a mode captured by the idea of *hearing the door slam*. In this mode, the intentionality of my listening is directed towards external objects. In this case, sound is an index not only to the external events indicated by Schaeffer but also to a 'larval' subjectivity.[51] This listening subject is passively synthesised but has the potential of morphing into a fully formed Cartesian or Husserlian subject as the effect of being oriented towards the recognised objects whose representations apparently occupy or form consciousness.[52]

In the second quadrant perceiving is represented as a subjective and concrete experience of sound in everyday listening. In this mode, sound is actualised not as some abstracted form but related to its reception as a raw and crude outline of the object. We could think of this as the Heideggerian moment of the every-day in which being and listening are united. As Heidegger suggests 'this potentiality for hearing … is existentially primary',[53] and in our everyday being 'the swirl of sensation'[51] is not necessarily consciously organised to give shape to what is understood.

The third quadrant is the first moment of abstraction in which subjective, descriptive categories are invoked, leading to a dynamic focus on the object structure relation within which any sound is actualised.[55] In this mode, new values or descriptive categories of sound emerge through the opening of audition to the productive force of difference in relation to the repetition of previously acquired subjective or inter-subjective values.

Finally, the fourth quadrant is the fully abstract and semiotic mode of comprehending sound in which pre-existing objective values offer reference to and confrontation with the extra-sonorous. In this mode, the virtual takes hold of listening. As Nancy points out, the two poles of 'sense (that one listens to) and a truth (that one comprehends)'[56] are inseparable and when mapped onto Schaeffer's modes we see that moving around the circuit from 1 to 4 we arrive where we left off. The truth of a verbal assertion is not so very different from the truth of a correctly identified sound source. This truth or the sense that is made by the apprehension of the sounding life-world establishes it as a material fact.[57] There is a germ of Husserl's definition of the task of transcendental philosophy, as pursued by Kant, in this observation, which 'undertakes to understand the existing world as a structure of sense and validity'.[58] The structure of this life-world (its ontic meaning) as a set of validities is brought into relief in the apprehension or intrusion of illusion, ambiguity and confusion, or in the form of the acousmatic revelation.

Schaeffer's model of everyday listening contains the representational elements through which the listening subject can be assembled at the subjective terminus of sonic experience with the sound object or event as its objective correlate.[59] In introducing the idea of a listening assemblage I am borrowing from Deleuze's notion of the assemblage as an articulation of various heterogeneous series including the 'human, the social, technical machines',[60] and organised *abstract machines* such as professional disciplines or other forms of organisation and regulation. Schaeffer shows how this differential system produces types or domains of listening expertise located at any of the four poles of, or indeed, actualised at any point along the series of listening modes. He maintains that the specialist listener is produced only in differential relation to the other three poles, since the listener is unable to escape 'going around the four quadrants' in any listening process.[61]

Understanding Schaefferian structuralism

Like Deleuze, Schaeffer was concerned with relations rather than fixed identities or oppositions. The terms in Schaeffer's apparently structuralist system and the models or structures themselves are a form of infra-structure not actual in themselves, but only in the listening intentions, sounds and musics that they produce and that make them apparent. Borrowing Proust's phrase, originally used to describe the revelatory experience of a particular sound, these structures are 'real without being actual, ideal without being abstract'.[62] As Schaeffer asserts, if listening is a creative act then it will only ever be partially susceptible to scientific investigation, and only partially susceptible to the methods of hermeneutics, and an analysis of a musical composition may well be seen as an analysis or interpretation of a listening strategy.[63] Thus musical composition is strategic listening or an embodiment of a listening theory.

The Schaefferian lexicon is one of terms in differential relations. These are not grounded in opposition or identity but are often complementary or coextensive terms, and in Schaeffer's *Treatise* the terms are assembled in series that compose its inter-related episodes. Each episode is concerned with the development of a new aspect or sound effect from which a new musical discourse may be constructed. Examples of key concept pairs highlight the extent of Schaeffer's lexicon (see Table 8.2).

Following Deleuze I note that 'the fact that the two [terms in a] series cannot exist without each other indicates not only that they are complementary, but that by virtue of their dissimilarity and their difference in kind they borrow from and feed into one another'.[64] Each of these series narrates an aspect under which the sonic domain may be mapped. The intersection of any two or more series suggests a novel perspective from which sonic experience may be viewed. For example, the trajectory from the musical to the musicianly traverses the conventions of musical culture at one extreme to the perceptive attitudes or awareness which discovers

112 Ian Stevenson

Table 8.2 Key concept pairs in Schaeffer's lexicon

Accident	Incident
Analysis	Synthesis
Balance	Originality
Composed	Composite
Context	Contexture
Continuous	Discontinuous
Criterion	Dimension
Density	Volume
Description	Identification
Duration	Variation
Making	Hearing
Mass	Facture
Meaning	Event
Meaning	Index
Musical	Musicianly
Musicality	Sonority
Natural	Cultural
Object	Structure
Ordinary	Specialist
Permanence	Variation
Polyphony	Polymorphy
Prose Composition	Translation
Site	Calibre
Value	Characteristic

or produces the musical detail in both conventional and in unexpected sources. Schaeffer provides these structures to help us listen with fresh ears; effectively, to postpone the premature operation of the imagination filling our ears with what it expects or with the disappointment or lack of what our expectation demands. In practice, this involves listening to what is present or actualised in a composition, performance, environment or sound, rather than critically hearing what is not present. This suggests that there is an infinite scope for learning new parameters of listening. There is also endless potential both as listeners and as music makers for the production of new sonic effects. Like Deleuze, Schaeffer invites us to imagine or even practise an immanent listening that frees us from transcendent categories or moderates the tendencies, habits and constraints of expertise or the everyday. Rather than prescribing an ideal music of the future, Schaeffer's didacticism requires us to submit to a process in which sound is re-imagined or experienced anew, and new effects of listening are discovered and learned.

Notes

1 The two key texts are Gilles Deleuze, *Difference and Repetition*, trans. Paul Patton (London: Athlone Press, 1994), and Deleuze, *The Logic of Sense*, trans. Mark Lester with Charles J. Stivale, ed. Constantin V. Boundas (London: Continuum, 2004[1969]).

2 Pierre Schaeffer, *Traité des objets musicaux: Essai interdisciplines*, 2nd ed. (Paris: Editions du Seuil, 1966).

3 Schaeffer, *In Search of a Concrete Music*, trans. Christine North and John Dack. California Studies in 20th-Century Music. (Berkeley CA: University of California Press, 2012[1952]).

4 In particular he refers to trends then current in phenomenology, structuralism, and modernism in the arts: Deleuze, *Difference and Repetition*, xviii.

5 'relation, n'., *Oxford English Dictionary Online* (Oxford: Oxford University Press, 2011), accessed 5 March 2014, http://www.oed.com.

6 Deleuze, *Difference and Repetition*, 117, 145.

7 Deleuze, *Difference and Repetition*, 32.

8 Aristotle uses the term 'potential' alongside actual to refer to a thing's dynamic potential to affect or be affected. See S. Marc Cohen 'Aristotle's Metaphysics', *The Stanford Encyclopedia of Philosophy* (Summer 2014 ed.), accessed 5 March 5 2014, http://plato.stanford.edu/archives/sum2014/entries/aristotle-metaphysics/.

9 Deleuze, *Difference and Repetition*, 228.

10 Deleuze, *Difference and Repetition*, 117.

11 Jean- François Augoyard and Henry Torgue, *Sonic Experience: A Guide to Everyday Sounds*, trans. Andra McCartney and David Paquette (Montreal: McGill-Queen's University Press, 2005).

12 Michel Chion, *Guide to Sound Objects. Pierre Schaeffer and Musical Research* (Leicester: EARS De Montfort University, 2009[1983]), accessed 8 October 2015, http://ears.pierrecouprie.fr/IMG/pdf/Chion-guide/GuidePreface.pdf, 96.

13 Augoyard and Torgue, *Sonic Experience*.

14 'articulation, n'., *Oxford English Dictionary Online* (Oxford: Oxford University Press, 2011), accessed 5 March 2014, http://www.oed.com.

15 Deleuze, *The Logic of Sense*, 29–34.

16 Gilles Deleuze and Félix Guattari, *What Is Philosophy*, trans. Hugh Tomlinson and Graham Burchell (New York: Columbia University Press, 1994[1991]), 54.

17 Deleuze, 'How Do We Recognize Structuralism?', trans. Michael Taormina, in *Desert Islands and Other Texts, 1953–1974*, ed. David Lapoujade, *Semiotext(E) Foreign Agents Series* (Cambridge, MA: Semiotext(e), 2004[1972]).

18 Chion, *Guide to Sound Objects*, 85.

19 Seth Kim-Cohen, *In the Blink of an Ear: Towards a Non-Cochlear Sonic Art* (New York: Continuum, 2009), 94.

20 For examples, see Chion, *Guide to Sound Objects*, 188.

21 Deleuze, *The Logic of Sense*, 70.

22 Deleuze, *Difference and Repetition*, 129.

23 John David Puterbaugh, 'Between Location and Place: A View of Timbre through Auditory Models and Sonopoietic Space' (PhD dissertation, Princeton University, 1999), 63.

24 Hermann von Helmholtz, *On the Sensations of Tone as a Physiological Basis for the Theory of Music*, trans. Alexander John Ellis, 2nd English ed. (New York: Dover Publications, 1954).

25 D. Wessel, 'Timbre Space as a Musical Control Structure', *Computer Music Journal* 3/2 (1979), 45–52.

26 Albert S. Bregman, *Auditory Scene Analysis: The Perceptual Organization of Sound*. 2nd MIT Press paperback ed. (Cambridge, MA: MIT Press, 1999), 92.

27 Chion, *Guide to Sound Objects*, 114.

28 Maurice Merleau-Ponty, *Phenomenology of Perception*. Routledge Classics (London: Routledge, 2002[1945]), xv.

114 *Ian Stevenson*

29 Chion, *Guide to Sound Objects*, 129.
30 John Dack and Christine North, 'Translating Pierre Schaeffer: Symbolism, Literature and Music', in *Conference of the Electroacoustic Music Studies Network*, Beijing, 2006, accessed 8 October 2015, http://www.ems-network.org/IMG/EMS06-JDack.pdf.
31 This was a key musical element in Schaeffer's 1958 work *Étude Aux Sons Animés* in Schaeffer and Pierre Henry, *L'œuvre Musicale* (Paris: INA-GRM 6027/6029, 1998), CD sound recording, (disc 3, track 2).
32 Schaeffer, *Traité Des Objets Musicaux*, 92.
33 Schaeffer, *In Search of a Concrete Music*, 4.
34 Schaeffer, *In Search of a Concrete Music*, 31.
35 Schaeffer, *In Search of a Concrete Music*, 134.
36 Schaeffer and Henry, *L'œuvre Musicale*, (disc 1, track 1).
37 Schaeffer, *In Search of a Concrete Music*, 12.
38 Schaeffer, *In Search of a Concrete Music*, 14.
39 Schaeffer, *In Search of a Concrete Music*, 14.
40 Chion, *Guide to Sound Objects*, 70.
41 Chion, *Guide to Sound Objects*, 48.
42 Schaeffer, *Traité des objets musicaux*, 337.
43 Chion, *Guide to Sound Objects*, 11.
44 Chion, *Guide to Sound Objects*, 25.
45 Schaeffer, *Traité des objets musicaux*, 123.
46 William W. Gaver, 'How Do We Hear in the World? Explorations in Ecological Acoustics', *Ecological Psychology*, 5/4 (1993): 285–313. See also Eric J. Clarke, *Ways of Listening: An Ecological Approach to the Perception of Musical Meaning* (New York: Oxford University Press, 2005).
47 Chion, *Guide to Sound Objects*, 21.
48 This paraphrases Williams's description of Deleuze's conception of thinking: 'The Thinker Deposed' in Williams, *Gilles Deleuze's 'Logic of Sense': A Critical Introduction and Guide* (Edinburgh: Edinburgh University Press, 2008), 175.
49 Schaeffer refers to philosopher Husserl's *Cartesian Meditations* as the text by which he came to understand his enterprise to be essentially phenomenological: Chion, *Guide to Sonic Objects*, 29.
50 Deleuze, *Difference and Repetition*, 208.
51 Deleuze, *Difference and Repetition*, 78.
52 Deleuze, *Difference and Repetition*, 133.
53 Martin Heidegger, *Being and Time*, trans. John Macquarrie and Edward Robinson (Oxford: Blackwell, 2005), 207.
54 Heidegger, *Being and Time*, 207.
55 Chion, *Guide to Sound Objects*, 58.
56 Jean-Luc Nancy, *Listening*, trans. Charlotte Mandell (New York: Fordham University Press, 2007), 2.
57 Edmond. Husserl, *Crisis of European Sciences and Transcendental Phenomenology*, trans. D. Carr (Evanston: Northwestern University Press, 1970), 104.
58 Husserl, *Crisis of European Sciences*, 99.
59 Deleuze and Guattari, *A Thousand Plateaus: Capitalism and Schizophrenia*, trans. Brian Massumi (Minneapolis and London: University of Minnesota Press, 1987), 71.
60 Deleuze and Guattari, *A Thousand Plateaus*, 40–41.
61 Schaeffer, *Traité des objets musicaux*, 120.
62 Deleuze, 'How Do We Recognize Structuralism?' 179; Deleuze, *Difference and Repetition*, 208.
63 This point is taken up by Peter Szendy in *Listen: A History of Our Ears* (New York: Fordham University Press, 2008), 35.
64 Deleuze, *Difference and Repetition*, 100.

Part III
Materialities of sounding

9 Applied aesthetics

Judy Lochhead

In Part III, three composers focus their creative energies toward a conceptual articulation of the materialities of their sounding creations. On one hand, these authors might be understood to reorient their activities from the imaginative realm of aural sensation to the conceptual realm of thought with the goal of offering insight into the creative process. Or, on another hand, they might be understood to offer an authorial template for how to listen to and understand their music, as did many composers in the middle years of the twentieth century. In this chapter on applied aesthetics, I pose an alternate way to understand these sound-conceptual chapters using perspectives from a Deleuzian and Deleuzian–Guattarian philosophy of becoming and relating the applied aesthetics of Crossman, Smith and Harrison to the allied movements of practice-led research and new materialism in the arts.

The term 'applied aesthetics' itself suggests this alternate approach. Within the philosophical domain, aesthetics is focused on a philosophy of art and on the nature of beauty and taste. Since it implies a retrospective vantage, it is not typically understood as something that can be applied. Similarly, we sometimes think of artists as creating 'an aesthetic', referring to the style of existing works from a retrospective vantage. The aesthetic in both of these instances tends toward a retrospective perspective, aiming to *reflect* something already created as a static entity. Rather than mirroring existing things or practices, applied aesthetics implies an *intra-active* relation between creation and thought, between sensation and concept.[1] The term captures the dynamic relation between doing and knowing as an embodied and productive mode of thinking the world. It dissolves distinctions of theory and practice, form and content, mind and body, and other such oppositional formations.

I return to a fuller discussion of applied aesthetics toward the end of this chapter after some preparatory discussions. These preparatory sections focus, first, on Deleuze's logic of sensation with respect to art and, second, on the materialities of sounding in general and specifically with respect to the music of Crossman, Smith and Harrison.

Art and the logic of sensation

As Deleuze and Guattari maintain, thinking the world assumes three distinct modes, as philosophy, science and art.[2] All three modes of thinking struggle with chaos but in differing ways: philosophy produces concepts, science produces function and art produces sensations. In their struggles with chaos, the philosophers, the scientists and the artists produce ways of encountering or grappling with it. Such productive encounters with chaos as a thinking of the world are ongoing, they are in a constant process of becoming. In this formulation, art-thinking is a 'sibling' of philosophy- and science-thinking, as Elizabeth Grosz points out.[3] These three modes of thinking operate on the same plane of creative engagement with the chaos of the world but they accomplish their thinking in different ways.

In his book on Francis Bacon, Deleuze addresses the painter's art-thinking, demonstrating how the materials of painting together with the embodied actions of the artist accomplish a logic of sensation.[4] While specific to the materials of painting, Deleuze's account of Bacon's art-thinking provides a rich context for approaching the materialities of music. Of particular significance here is Deleuze's attention to the link between the materials and actions of painting and the sensations they may produce, and to the nature of these sensations and how they enact a logic, an affective logic. Attending to the specifics of how the artist works, Deleuze focuses on how Bacon uses paint, canvas, brush, and cloth and how his hand, arm, and body interact with these materials to enact art-thinking. Through these materials Bacon creates the painting and its sensations of figure, line, shape; of colour, light and darkness; of depth and relief; of movement. Together these sensations enact a logic, what Deleuze refers to as the 'Rhythm ... that runs through a painting just as it runs through a piece of music.'[5] Or, in other words, this logic of sensations is enacted temporally through the dynamic relations of affects. For painting, Deleuze notes the particular relation of 'eye and hand' and remarks on how the pictorial image produces 'a third eye, a haptic eye, a haptic vision of the eye'. Through such a haptic vision the painter 'makes visible a kind of original unity of the senses' of the body.[6] The logic of sensation then operates through the intensities of bodily affects as a totality. An address of this logic   this art-thinking   strives not only to intensify sensation but also to elucidate the rhythms of art-thinking, rhythms that themselves 'illuminate ... [chaos] for an instant'.[7]

Deleuze's writings on Bacon and his elucidation of art-thinking in the context of painting are suggestive for an address of music-thinking. This is not to imply that discussion of music and sound are missing in the writings of Deleuze, Deleuze and Guattari, and many others embracing a Deleuzian philosophical perspective.[8] My own address of music-thinking here is generated from this existing work, and in particular by Deleuze's attention to the materiality of artistic creation. The translation to music-thinking is, however, not straightforward. While music's sounds produce the sensations of line and shape; of colour, light and darkness; of surface and depth; of movement as does painting, their occurrences as events heard over time pose a special problem for the address of music's sound-thinking. These problems notwithstanding, the possibility of developing a concept of a 'third ear' or a 'haptic hearing' for music seems within reach. The vibrations of musical sound have a palpable affect on the bodies of creators, performers, and listeners and by attending to the logic of these sounding sensations, we may aspire to elucidate a music-thinking of the world.

In order to address music-thinking it is necessary not only to begin with the 'materials' of sound as Deleuze began with Bacon's paint, canvas, brush, cloth and hand but also 'to listen closely to what painters [or composers] have to say'.[9] In the next section, I consider in general terms the materials of music-thinking and then turn to a consideration of how Crossman, Smith and Harrison address the materials of their music.

Materialities of sounding

Composers work with sounds that have timbre, pitch, duration, dynamics and articulation, these parameters of sound constituting the materials of musical crea-tion.[10] While it is possible to distinguish these parameters of sound, any particular sound has sonic presence as a totality – the parameters are facets of sounding sensation. Not simply through the sense of hearing, these sounding sensations are felt throughout the body. As Deleuze observes about painting, in a sounding sensation there is 'an existential communication … of color, taste, touch, smell, noise, a weight'.[11] Even further, sound sensations engage the body not only in sensory domain but also in domains of memory, culture, history, and so forth – all inhabiting the felt reality of sensation. These sound materials are the stuff used by creators to enact the sensations of music-thinking.

The sensations of music have some affinities with the sensations of painting as Deleuze articulated them and the terms employed to evoke these sensations are familiar, playing a role in our everyday address of musical experience. These include: sound colour, including features of brightness and darkness; rhythm and velocity of movement; spatial placements with respect to the body, such as high and low sounds, and sounds that pierce or envelope; degrees of dynamics, includ-ing the absence of sound as silence; degrees of warmth and cold; characters of sharpness and softness; fullness or sparseness of texture; depth and surface; shapes, such as contour, lines, blocks; memories of places or events; historical evocations; and so on. Such sounding sensations are sometimes dismissed as merely meta-phorical, as operating in the subjective domain of experience and hence not real. Others give more credence to such accounts of musical experience, either under-standing metaphors as intersensory forms of cognition or as a result of embodied cognition.[12] From a Deleuzian perspective, such terms address the sensations that sounds produce, and their reality is manifest in the vibratory affects on bodies, animate or inanimate.

I turn now to the composers, paying attention to what they say about their music and what their 'saying' illuminates about their music-thinking from a Deleuzian perspective. Eventually this discussion will take me back to applied aesthetics and

120 *Judy Lochhead*

an alternate way to understand their sound-conceptual chapters. All three of these composers, Crossman, Smith and Harrison, reside and compose in Australia.

Writing about three works composed in the first two decades of the twenty-first century, Bruce Crossman conceptualises a motivating force for his aesthetic as *living colours*. Two events impacted his music-thinking about this aesthetic. One was the event of hearing Cantonese opera and the other an event of seeing the calligraphic gestures of the hand on the page. Together these events generated an awareness of an underlying and vital force. As Deleuze puts it 'music ... render[s] nonsonorous forces sonorous, and painting ... render[s] invisible forces visible' and it is these forces that animate the aesthetic of *living colours*.[13] Crossman's attention to silence as a force — a force he senses in the Japanese concept of *Ma* or as residing in the Chinese concept of *Qi* or in the Judeo-Christian idea of the spirit. Musical silence then operates within a broad sense of geopolitical awareness. And in his mingling of tuning systems from the Filipino, Chinese and Western practices, Crossman's music generates a tonal colouring that vibrates with places. Crossman's aesthetic of *living colours* makes palpable this multi-placial, geopolitical situation of the twenty-first century. Music-thinking becomes hybrid, multiple, and situational.

Paul Smith addresses a single piano work from 2010, composed during a period of time in which his working in musical sound focused on issues of childhood. Turning to his own experiences as young person, he wrought his music-thinking through the *kawaii* aesthetic of Japanese practices of anime. Smith worked with the ideas that inhabit this aesthetic of cuteness and the visual narratives of animation, giving them sonorous form in his musical thinking. He refers to his musical materials and their sensations as simple harmonies and bright sonorities, rendering sonorous the visual aesthetic of cuteness and anime. Smith himself links the interactions of the visual and the sonic through the concept of exchange — a differential interaction that produces something new.

In her 2012 orchestra work, Holly Harrison thinks musically through the opposing forces of interacting rhythmic streams, of Lewis Carroll's word constructs and of music stylistic juxtapositions. Carroll's notion of the portmanteau provides the conceptual hook for what she thinks of as the 'combative' interactions of these forces. Harrison constructs chords by stacking together power chords from rock styles with chromatic configurations, embedding the tonal within the atonal. Musical textures entail juxtapositions of differing 'sound slabs', creating sharp disjunctions during the musical flow, which give way to sound 'scatters'. The work's rhythmic energy emerges from the opposition of a 'vernacular groove' with constantly changing meters of contemporary classical music. In her musical thinking, Harrison deploys sonorous disjunction and opposition as a means of producing the new while retaining the sense of originals as does a portmanteau word.

In writing about their music, the three composers address their music through ideas, concepts and prior experience using language that speaks to the materials of creation but more significantly to the sensations of their music-thinking. The references to sensations of energy, brightness, sound slabs, *living colours* — to name just

Applied aesthetics 121

a few – provide a glimmer of the various ways that the music of these composers accomplishes its sound-thinking. In the next section on applied aesthetics, I argue that the writings of these composers need not be read as an instruction on how to listen to their music or as a reflectively conceptual account of the creative process. Rather, they can be read as an account of applied aesthetics.

Applied aesthetics

Deleuze's philosophy of becoming focuses on temporal relations between diverse things and from these differential relations the new emerges. This philosophical perspective directs attention to questions of how from questions of what, to the event rather than to essence. This emphasis on what something does through differential relations draws attention to the materials of relational difference and of the emergent new. The term applied aesthetics signals a philosophy of art-becoming. With this term, I mean to draw attention to how the practices of art creation – here specifically music creation – are a becoming; that is, musical works arise from the differential relations between materials, concepts, sensations, memories, bodily memories, and so forth. 'Applying the aesthetic' is to create the things that produce sensations through a process of differential becoming from which the art work emerges. The writings of artists then are an address of this process of becoming. Such writings need not be read as a philosophy of the particular art work (or works) but rather as a mode of addressing the becoming of art, a process that with each writing about art proliferates into newly emergent forms of aesthetic creation or conceptual thought.

The focus on the materials of becoming in Deleuzian perspective recognises, according to Coole and Frost, that matter has 'an excess, force, vitality, relationality, or difference that renders [it] active, self-creative, productive, unpredictable'.[14] While not aligned explicitly with work in what is called the 'new materialisms', the chapters by Crossman, Smith and Harrison reveal another dimension to this turn in recent scholarship – in particular the dimension of sound materials. This turn toward 'material thinking' acknowledges that things themselves have forces, what Jane Bennett refers to as 'thing-power', that affect human behaviours; or in other words, the new materialist scholarship moves away from a subject–centred philosophy and toward an intra-actional philosophy of becoming.[15] Such a new materialist turn has resonance in thinking about art. As Barrett and Bolt observe: 'Methodologies of artistic research [creations] have the capacity to produce new knowledge and to shift understandings of the way in which knowledge emerges and functions.'[16] In Deleuzian terms, the materials of artist practice are the means for art-thinking through the production of sensations.

The recognition of art as a form of thinking the world and as a mode of knowledge production has ramifications for how the arts are regarded in broader cultural issues of education and scholarship. For instance, in the United States the models for training musicians are undergoing transformation, the conservatory model of shaping 'musical technicians' is no longer viable even in conservatories.

122 *Judy Lochhead*

And in Europe and Australia a whole new research area on practice-led research in the arts has emerged, partly in response to changes in government educational policies and partly as a result of changes toward 'reflection and research' in art practices themselves as Henk Borgdorff has observed.[17] If art creation and apprehension is construed as a form of knowing the world then its particular forms of engaging the world through sensation have broad effects not only on humans but all beings — animate or inanimate — in the world. For instance, to name just one instance of such effects, recent neuroscience research on memory has demonstrated that early training in music affects neural plasticity and improves memory in later life.[18] The findings of such neuroscientific research approach the topic of memory in the mode of science, and they confirm that art-thinking — thinking with sound, with paint — is indeed a productive way of engaging the world with far-reaching implications

Conclusion

Writing about music and about art of any kind tends to get a bad rap. As I pointed out in my chapter for this collection, Daniel Smith disavowed Deleuze's book on the paintings of Francis Bacon as any form of art criticism. There seems to be a fundamental discomfort about using words as a means of engaging art. Despite this discomfort, we still write about art, we discuss it, we debate it. Imagine a situation in which after a performance of Caroline Shaw's *Partita* all members of the audience said nothing, not in a moment of awe before applause begins but said nothing ever.[19] No comments were offered on whether this person liked it, or that person didn't, or this person complained about the poor acoustics in the building – and does applause count as a kind of speaking?

Deleuze's philosophy of becoming provides some illumination of these issues. If art is a mode of thinking the world through its materials — of sound, of colour, of line, and so on — then those who experience it think along and generate their own forms of thinking the world, through art, concepts, formulas, or perhaps all together. The chapters of this part on the materialities of sounding operate within this mode of becoming as each of the composers addresses those sounds, concepts, experiences, feelings, memories, and so forth that play and continue to play in their creative process of sound-thinking.

Notes

1 As already discussed in the introduction to this collection, the term 'intra-active' was coined by Karen Barad in reference to relations through which things emerge as things, such relations working through complex feedback loops. Some authors use the term 'reflexive' in characterising similar relationships that are dynamic and generative. The term reflective, on the other hand, refers to a mirroring relation, what Deleuze and Guattari refer to as tracing, and is distinct from the productive relation between things and events suggested by the terms reflexive or intra-active.
2 Gilles Deleuze and Félix Guattari. *What is Philosophy?*, trans. Hugh Tomlinson and Graham Burchell (New York: Columbia University Press, 1994[1991]). In my earlier

Applied aesthetics   123

chapter for this collection, I take up this issue with respect to the idea of music criticism. Here I turn the matter toward the creative process.

3   Elizabeth Grosz, *Chaos, Territory, Art: Deleuze and the Framing of the Earth* (New York: Columbia University Press, 2008), 2.

4   Gilles Deleuze, *Francis Bacon: The Logic of Sensation*, trans. Daniel Smith (New York: Continuum, 2003[1981]).

5   Deleuze, *Francis Bacon*, 37.

6   Deleuze, *Francis Bacon*, 129 and 37.

7   Deleuze and Guattari, *What is Philosophy?*, 204.

8   Some of the works addressing music from a Deleuzian perspective are: Brian Hulse and Nick Nesbitt, eds, *Sounding the Virtual: Gilles Deleuze and the Theory and Philosophy of Music* (Farnham, UK and Burlington, VT: Ashgate, 2010); Edward Campbell, *Music After Deleuze* (London: Bloomsbury, 2013); Ronald Bogue, *Deleuze on Music, Painting and the Arts* (New York and London: Routledge, 2001); Ian Buchanan and Marcel Swiboda, eds, *Deleuze and Music* (Edinburgh: Edinburgh University Press, 2004). In 2008, *Perspectives of New Music* published a collection of essays around the topic 'A Thousand Plateaus': see 46/2 (Summer).

9   Daniel Smith, 'Translator's Preface', *Francis Bacon*, xi. Smith is paraphrasing an interview Deleuze gave about painting: 'La Peinture enflame l'écriture', interview with Gilles Deleuze by Hervé Guibert, *Le Mode*, 3 December 1981, 51.

10   For the present context, I consider music creators defining themselves as composers. This should not be taken as an exclusionary move. Music creators of any sort are engaged in activities similar to composers.

11   Deleuze, *Francis Bacon*, 37.

12   Authors such as Lawrence Zbibkowski and Janna Saslaw are notable for their work in conceptual metaphor in relation to music. For instance, see: Lawrence Zbikowski, *Conceptualizing Music. Cognitive Structure, Theory, and Analysis* (New York: Oxford University Press, 2002) and Janna K. Saslaw, 'Forces, Containers, and Paths: The Role of Body-derived Image Schemas in the Conceptualization of Music', *Journal of Music Theory* 40/2 (1996): 217–43. Arnie Cox and Thomas Clifton are notable for their work in embodied cognition (for Clifton in its early phenomenological guise). For instance, see: Arnie Cox, 'Hearing, Feeling, Grasping Gestures', in *Music and Gesture*, ed. Anthony Gritten and Elaine King (Aldershot: Ashgate, 2006), 45–60, and Thomas Clifton, *Music as Heard: A Study in Applied Phenomenology* (New Haven: Yale University Press, 1983).

13   Deleuze, *Francis Bacon*, 48.

14   Diana Coole and Samantha Frost, 'Introducing the New Materialisms', in *New Materialism: Ontology, Agency, and Politics*, ed. Diana Coole and Samantha Frost (Durham, NC: Duke University Press, 2010), 9.

15   Jane Bennett, *Vibrant Matter: A Political Ecology of Things* (Durham, NC: Duke University Press, 2010), chapter 1 passim. Since research in the 'New Materialism' is a large and fast–growing field, I list two references here: Bill Brown, *A Sense of Things: The Object Matter of American Literature* (Chicago: University of Chicago Press, 2003), and Rick Dolphijn and Iris van der Tuin, *New Materialism: Interviews & Cartographies* (Ann Arbor: Open Humanities Press, 2012).

16   Estelle Barrett and Barbara Bolt, 'Introduction', in *Material Inventions: Applying Research in the Creative Arts*, ed. Barrett and Bolt (London: I.B. Tauris, 2014), 1. Interested readers should also see: Estelle Barrett and Barbara Bolt, eds., *Carnal Knowledge: Towards a 'New Materialism' Through the Arts* (London: I.B. Taurus, 2013).

17   Henk Borgdorff, 'The Debate on Research in the Arts', *Dutch Journal of Music Theory* 12/1 (2007). 1–2. See also *Studies in Material Thinking*, a journal that began in 2007: accessed 13 October 2015, https://www.materialthinking.org.

18   See in particular, Christopher J. Steele et al., 'Early Musical Training and White-Matter Plasticity in the Corpus Callosum: Evidence for a Sensitive Period', *Journal of*

124 *Judy Lochhead*

Neuroscience 33/3 (2013): 1282–90 (doi:10.1523/JNEUROSCI.3578–12.2013); and Travis White-Schwoch et al., 'Older Adults Benefit from Music Training Early in Life: Biological Evidence for Long-Term Training-Driven Plasticity', *Journal of Neuroscience* 33/45 (2013): 17667–74 (doi:10.1523/JNEUROSCI.2560–13).

19 Caroline Shaw, *Partita for 8 Voices* (2009–11). The score of the *Partita* is not yet published, but the work has been recorded: *Roomful of Teeth* (Brooklyn, NY: New Amsterdam Records, 2012). Information about the *Partita* can be accessed at: accessed 16 March 2015, http://carolineshaw.com/hear/partita-for-8-voices/.

10 *Living colours*

An Asian-Pacific conceptual frame for composition

Bruce Crossman

Mind and spirit

The raucous barrage of metal sounds of *The Drunken Emperor Orders to Have His Brother Executed* as performed by the Paichangxi Repertoires of Cantonese Opera jolted me alive. Hearing this riotous interpretation in Hong Kong's Ko Shan Theatre resonated with an earlier experience of Japanese calligraphy I had witnessed some years earlier in Tokyo that struck me as similarly spirited.[1] Miyata Ryohei's vigorous calligraphical strokes demonstrated how character is embodied in the creative actions of calligraphy. These two aesthetic experiences made palpable for me a duality that resides in all creative actions and their resulting artefacts. This duality may be suggested by the concepts of the unspoken mind of the artist and of the moving spirit. On one hand, the unspoken mind has historical bases in the Greek idea of the 'unspoken word'[2] or the Chinese idea of the 'mind of the artist'.[3] And on the other hand, the moving spirit has bases in the Judeo-Christian idea of the 'living word' (or spirit)[4] or in Chinese thought the *dao* 'which moves amongst things'.[5] This creative duality is refracted through and resident in the artist and gives rise to both 'irreducible individuality'[6] of the creative work and its embodiment of the cultural identities of the artist. Not a simple fixed binary, this duality generates works of a complex hybridity involving both the 'spirit-led' and the identity formations of the artist.[7]

As a composer based in Australia, I consider my own compositional voice as shaped by the complex hybridity that characterises Australia as a place of Asian-Pacific cultures. As I conceive it, the hybridity of my compositional practice is formed from several features of the Asian-Pacific. These include: the Japanese concept of *ma*, the blending of nature and art in Chinese thought, sonorities of East and Southeast Asian music, and Chinese musical aesthetic of a multi-art form.[8] I conceive this musical hybridity with the metaphor of *living colours*, and in my music I engage with *ma* and its exploratory space, with the colours of eastern Australia's bush; the instrumental materials of traditional Chinese move about as a metaphor and embodiment of *spirit* and specifically engage with: *ma*'s exploratory space and shifting colour; the colours of east coast Australian bush; the musical modes and instrumental resources (especially gongs) of traditional Chinese, Korean, Filipino and Japanese music, and the gestural aesthetic of Chinese opera traditions that is both visual and sonic. The hybridity of my compositional language is also shaped by recent Western practices of composition, including their notational conventions, instrumental resources, and harmonic rhythmic features.

In this chapter I consider three recent compositions, tracing the hybrid aesthetic each embodies. The works are: *In Gentleness and Suddenness* (2003), *Not Broken Bruised Reed* (2009) and *Gentleness Suddenness* (2012). In particular, I trace how my aesthetic of *living colours* emerged from my experiences of Cantonese opera and Japanese calligraphy, and how it reflects an attitude of openness or friendship, an attitude requiring 'lateral thinking'.[9] In another context, Steven Nuss has referred to such an aesthetic hybridity as 'cross-cultural action and interaction', drawing attention to the resonant cultural flux of such creative actions.[10] For me, the cultural interactions of the Asian-Pacific are a confluence of place and individual creative actions that resonate in contemporary compositional practice as *living colours* of musical sound.

Asian-Pacific context, connections and concepts

Within the Australian context and its region of the Asian-Pacific rim, a new vision of connection between geopolitical entities has emerged recently. The Australian Government's 2012 White Paper re-envisages Australia as an integral part of Asia, calling for greater connectedness within the region and a consequent diminishing of connections with Europe.[11] My musical aesthetic of *living colours* echoes this geopolitical awareness in the cultural plane. *Living colours* draws both on the early twentieth century emphasis amongst some French composers on a sensuous colouring of the sound palette and on Asian-Pacific sonic references. Unlike the French composers of the last century, however, my music does not build from music of an exoticised Other but rather is generated from the sonic place of Australia within the broader Asian-Pacific context or as Said suggested, *living colours* is generated from a 'geopolitical awareness into [the] aesthetic'.[12]

The *living colours* aesthetic has links with more recent musical practices that emphasise sonic colouring. For instance, in the latter half of the twentieth century composers of the Spectral School, notably Tristan Murail and Gérard Grisey, approach sound colour through the analysis of the spectral structure of specific sounds.[13] My own approach to sonic colour is more intuitive drawing generally from the Asian-Pacific sound world. In the Australian context, Peter Sculthorpe and Percy Grainger both engaged with this sound world, and my approach to *living colours* extends this engagement but within a specific Confucian philosophical context. Overall, the aesthetic of *living colours* draws on sonorities of the instrumental and harmonic resources of the Asian-Pacific and on the function of silence as a manifestation of Japanese *ma*. For me, as an Australian composer, *living colours* embraces multiple regional strands of thought, including: Judaic-Christian thought from Australia's British colonial roots; Confucian philosophy of ancient China; and Zen Buddhism of Japan. I conceive my approach not as one of cultural domination or absorption of the Other but rather as one of a fluid crossing between cultural borders and prominent beliefs within the Asian-Pacific – a crossing that manifests as *living colour*.

Lateral thinking, mind of the artist, and spirit

My compositional activity is grounded in a philosophical position that embraces both Chinese and Judeo-Christian thought. I derive three tenets from this thought, which have been briefly introduced earlier. These are: lateral thinking, mind of the artist, and spirit. In the following, I consider each tenet in more detail.

Lateral thinking

In his discussion of cross-cultural interactions, Steven Nuss builds upon ideas of Michel Foucault and introduces the possibility of 'thinking Chinese', a possibility that arises from the refusal to think through a politics of cultural boundaries.[14] Foucault questions the assumption that we cannot think as the Other. In *The Order of Things* he writes: 'But what is it impossible to think, and what type of impossibility are we faced with here?' In this he suggests that these impossibilities, these boundaries are porous and can be broken down to allow a flow between self and Other.[15] Nuss employs this idea of thinking as the Other in his approach to hearing Japan in the music of Takemitsu and he generalises it as a model of cross-cultural hybridity.[16] Through the lateral thinking of these border crossings new possibilities of thinking emerge.

My aesthetic of *living colours* resonates with the lateral thinking of such mid-twentieth century, French philosophical thought, even though it did not originate from it. This thought has some useful parallels to the Daoist and Judeo-Christian threads of my aesthetic. In particular, I draw attention to my engagements with the knowing calligraphical actions of Miyata Ryohei and the riotous sounds of Cantonese opera – both mentioned earlier. These lateral engagements have been reinforced by other artistic encounters I have had in the past: the fusion of modernist and traditional painting in the work of Wu Guanzhong and Lui Shou-Kwan,[17] and the abstract brush-stroke paintings of my father, the New Zealand artist Wallace Crossman.[18] Edmund Capon makes explicit the link between such lateral engagements and the thought of Confucius through the idea of the horizontal:

> The great thing about Confucius is that he was a generalist – he practiced horizontal thought, and I've always had it firmly fixed in my mind that great ideas are horizontal in form, not vertical.[19]

The significance of such a lateral approach to creativity in Chinese thought is developed further by Edward Ho. He observes that the ancient Chinese literati were expected to master the 'four activities of calligraphy, painting, *qin* playing and chess playing'.[20] The venerable Chinese-American scholar and composer

128 *Bruce Crossman*

Chou Wen-Chung also observed that the practices of poetry, painting and music in the Tang Dynasty employed the same aesthetics across the art-forms, and he used this as a model for his own calligraphical-inspired music.[21] And in a recent article on practice-led research, Hazel Smith and Roger Dean observe that knowledge is something 'generalisable ... and transferable ...' between domains of research, for instance between science and art, or calligraphy and music.[22] Such lateral thinking is an integral component of creative activity that gives rise to an aesthetic of *living colours*.

Mind of the artist

The second tenet of my creative process, mind of the artist, builds upon the activities of lateral thinking and focuses them specifically on the unspoken mind of the artist expressed musically. This unspoken mind is something that I sense, which I touched on earlier, as the Greek 'unspoken word'[23] and discuss later as Chinese *deyi*,[24] which is expressed in sonorous musical gestures. For me this is a process grounded in the sonic places of the Asian-Pacific with its rich confluences and juxtapositions. My experiences of the music-sonorous places of the Asia-Pacific include Taiwan, Hong Kong, Japan, Korea, the Philippines and Australia. Nuss nicely observes that cross-cultural border crossings move toward a new hybrid space that does not entail negation of the self but rather the building of a new self from the confluence of our own 'personal baggage' and the new encounters.[25] In my own music, a unique hybridity arises from the trace elements of Chinese and Filipino modes in harmonic colour constructions, the melodic lines and noise of Chinese opera, especially that of *Kunqu* and Cantonese practices, the metal sonorities (especially the undampened vibration characteristic) emanating from Southeast Asian musical practices, and the musical gestures that embody Asian-Pacific calligraphic movements.[26]

This hybrid sonic palette arises from unspoken thought, from the creative actions of me as the artist. Such unspoken but creative thought has a parallel in the Chinese literati painter — both contemporary and ancient. Capon observes that with the ancient literati painter 'the landscape was but a metaphor — no artist sought to record what the eye saw; it was all about how the mind and the heart responded'.[27] And in a more recent context, the new ink painter Lui Shou-Kwan emphasises this tradition's 'painting from the heart'.[28] Curator Tang Hoichiu reformulates the idea that art is generated from the heart as: the freedom 'to use different techniques and expressive devices to convey [one's] own personality and that of nature'.[29] Changing the perspective from creator to participant, art historian Yang Xin focuses attention on the 'mind of the artist': '*Deyi*, "getting the idea" of the image in the artist's mind, becomes the chief point to grasp when looking at a painting. The viewer has to go beyond the image to the implied meaning'.[30] In my own creative practice and aesthetic, I strive to have in mind a sonic thought — a sonic essence — that embodies the complex cultural hybridity of the Asian-Pacific and that arises from my own unspoken thought within this context.

Spirit

The third and most important tenet of *living colours*, spirit, extends the issues of the cultural hybridity residing and expressed through the mind of the artist into the domain of the creative artefact. In short, sounding music emerges as a moving labyrinth of colours, both timbres and interval-colours, embodied by a heart-felt impulse acting as spirit. This sense of the moving spirit resonates with the Judeo-Christian idea of 'hovering over the waters' and the Jewish association of the word with 'God' as spirit.[31] This notion of spirit also finds expression in Chinese thought, as Chou Wen-Chung observes, in the idea of *dao*. According to philosopher Zhuang Zi *dao* is that which 'moves amongst things'.[32] Further, Chou understands creative activity as 'achieving the ultimate truth or the supreme understanding' – as achieving *dao*.[33] In both Judeo-Christian and Chinese thought, creativity is related to the movement of the spirit toward an ultimate being or enlightenment. In musical terms this movement generates specific musical gestures, for instance gestures which may be described on one hand in my own words as 'sudden sensuousness amid silence' or on the other as a paraphrase of Chinese scholar Edward Ho's ideas of 'forceful energy with residual resonance'.[34] These differing energy levels play a generative role in Chinese thought. Ho clarifies with reference to the concept of *qi*:

> *Qi* is air in motion or energy with the power to transmit force, to sustain a motion and to communicate between realms; it is vitality; it essentially involves breathing … *Qi* is the creative force that begins, sustains and completes a work of art, without which there is no life.[35]

In summary, my creative process is itself a hybrid within the place of the Asian-Pacific, moving laterally across boundaries, resonating with the unspoken mind of the artist, and guided by the spirit. Reframing Nuss's idea of 'thinking Chinese', I strive to be a 'participating Asian-Pacific' though an intercultural journey of friendship.[36]

My music

In the following discussion, I consider specific instances in my music that point to the aesthetic of *living colours*. The discussion is organised around three themes deriving from the Asian-Pacific context: *ma*, sounding materialities, and colour confluences.

Ma: Musical structure

Writing about the Japanese *shakuhachi honkyoku* tradition, Jim Franklin provides an elegant entry into the concept of *ma* in a musical context:

> The word *ma* means 'interval' in many contexts, one of them being an interval of time. This interval is not simply of physical duration, but is also a gateway through which a possibly undefinable 'something' may present itself.[37]

My creative awakening to 'hearing Japanese', following Nuss, was through friendship with two distinguished *shakuhachi* performers: Jim Franklin is from Australia and Kawamuru Taizan is from Japan. From 2002 to 2003, Franklin, a *shihan* (or master) *shakuhachi* player, had an office adjacent to me at Western Sydney University. Our friendship involved the sharing of ideas and sound, and I was particularly interested in how Franklin articulated the Zen Buddhist idea of exploring 'inside-the-note'. In my music, I approached this exploration of sound through the single musical moment as a form of *ma*. A musical interval of time then serves as a 'gateway' through which subtle timbre changes take performers and listeners 'inside-the-note' in Franklin's sense. As a gift to Franklin, I composed a solo *shakuhachi* work, *In Gentleness and Suddenness* (2003). Example 10.1 cites the opening 12 bars of the piece, exemplifying the various timbral features that allow the *shakuhachi* player to explore inside-the-note. The music combines this momentary focus on sound with a large-scale structuring, a compositional trace of my prior training in recent Western compositional practices.[38]

A couple of years later, I had the opportunity to meet and work with Kawamuru Taizan at the 2010 Asian Music Festival in Tokyo. In preparation for a performance of *In Gentleness and Suddenness* (*shakuhachi*), I met with Taizan and the festival director and composer Matsushita Isao who acted as translator. After moments of friendship over green tea, we collaborated on the interpretation and sense of the music. Taizan gave an impassioned and spacious performance that intensely projected the *living colour* aesthetic, and in particular I was impressed by how he created a noise component of high upper partials which sounded like a pure whistling.[39] My score calls for the use of noise within

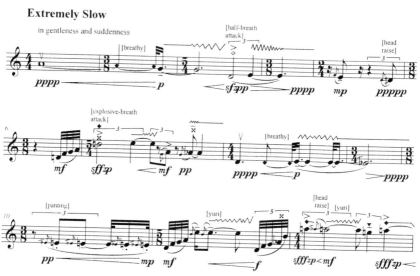

Example 10.1 Crossman, *In Gentleness and Suddenness* (*shakuhachi*), inside-the-note, bars 1–12.

the notes, but I was particularly delighted by how Taizan explored inside-the-note with this whistling upper partial. My musical exchanges with Taizan affected me profoundly and influenced a later work *Gentleness–Suddenness*, which I discuss shortly.

Sounding materialities: The Asian-Pacific

The materiality of music is an important indicator of place as a geographical and cultural site. In my own music my situation as a resident of the Asian-Pacific resonates in what I earlier referred to as the unspoken mind of the artist. The musical materials of the Asian-Pacific are such things as the ancient Filipino *kulintang* gong-chimes and the small Japanese Temple Bowl, both imbued with placial associations retained in a hybrid context.[40] The placial materiality of sounds is also traceable to the modal structures of Southeast and East Asian music; structures that are inscribed in instrumental design and that generate identifiable sonorities. My use of these materialities allows me to enter into a mode of 'participating "Japanese"' (following Nuss).[41] These modes of participation extend even further into to the rhythmic fluctuations of *ma*, the wriggling gestures of Japanese calligraphy and silences of Chinese landscape painting.

Such materialities of sound may be traced in my work *Not Broken Bruised Reed* (violin, piano, percussion) (2009) through the particular concept of resonance.[42] At the centre of this piece is an exploration of resonance – either through the brutal excitation of dampened strings or the gentle vibrations of a Southeast and East Asian gong.

The harmony of *Not Broken Bruised Reed* is characterised by two principles of resonance: interval-colour and altered timbres. Interval-colours are generated by mixing the Filipino *kulintang* gong-chime mode, the pentatonic Chinese *Shang-tiao* mode, and Western chromatic sonorities.[43] I use the tuning of the Atherton *kulintang*[44] and one additional gong-chime from Western Sydney University set as part of the basis for my harmonic language. I drew from these pentatonic and whole-tone sounds. These *kulintang* materials are juxtaposed against chromatic sonorities using overtone structures, in a French spectral-like approach, as an approximate guide to the spacing of the pitches. The interval-colours (m3, M2) recur across both sonority types to unify the overall resonance (see Examples 10.2 and 10.3).

Example 10.2 Philippine *Kulintang* (Atherton and Western Sydney University gong-sets) – pentatonic and whole-tone materials.

Example 10.3 Crossman, *Not Broken Bruised Reed*, resonance reduction diagram, bars 95–100.

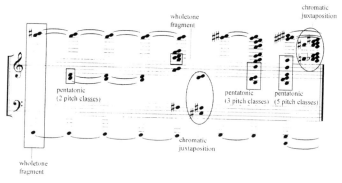

Example 10.4 Crossman, *Not Broken Bruised Reed*, altered resonances, bars 1–6.

The second principle of resonance involves altered timbres to intensify the effect of *living colours* in *Not Broken Bruised Reed*. In order to alter the timbres of the piano, a sound also inspired by Asian gongs, the pianist stops a string inside the piano while simultaneously striking the corresponding key and holding the sustain pedal down. I conceive of this as a 'bruised sound' since harmonics are added to the natural resonance of the piano sounds. Example 10.4 cites the opening six bars of the piece, showing the performance details of this technique. The effect of *living colour* is enhanced by changes in where the piano string is stopped inside the piano, eliciting changes in the upper partials, and the string is brutally excited by a *sforzando* attack which generates a sustained resonance. The brutal attack and its subsequent lingering resonant tension draw on two Asian-Pacific concepts in particular, Japanese *ma* and Korean after-tone.[45] In *Not Broken Bruised Reed*, the resonant principle of altered sounds finds inspiration in the Japanese concept of *ma* in *Noh* theatre when after the actor's gesture '[a] feeling of concentrated intensity in the depths of the actor's heart is sensed by the audience, and thus the silent pauses are made interesting'.[46]

Colour confluences

Gentleness–Suddenness, a work for mezzo-soprano, violin, percussion and piano, my aesthetic of *living colours* develops from the vibrancy of cross-art practices in an East Asian context.[47] The second movement, entitled 'Spirit', is particularly noteworthy since it was composed after my experiences with Cantonese opera, Japanese calligraphy and a Japanese *shakuhachi* master discussed above. The music is characterised by raucous juxtapositions and wriggling lines and there is a strong timbral presence of metal gongs – all sounds reflective of my recent experience. And at around the same time, I also became interested in nature and abstract painting as sources for musical creativity.

Overall, *Gentleness–Suddenness* is a meditation on the nature of love and creativity. The text for the work brings together passages from the classic *Kunqu* opera *The Peony Pavilion: Mudan ting* by Tang Xianzu,[48] and from *Genesis, Song of Songs, Psalms* and *Revelation* of the Judeo-Christian Bible.[49] The work focuses on a specific part of the *Peony Pavilion*'s story of love between two young people and links this story to the Judeo-Christian idea of spiritual life in the Biblical passages.[50] The text of the *Peony Pavilion* story is both sensual and spiritual in nature, and echoes closely the Judeo-Christian idea of spiritual life. These characteristics are present in the short passage cited here from the English translation by Lindy Li Mark:

> This brief moment is made in heaven,
> Pillowed on grass, bedded among flowers.
> Red petals dot billowing hair,
> Jade hairpin loose to one side.
> Holding you tight, ever so tenderly;
> Flesh to flesh …
> Such sun rouged blush, damp with rain.[51]

One short passage from the second movement, 'Spirit', of *Gentleness–Suddenness* demonstrates the confluence of ideas. Example 10.5 cites bars 127–131, which juxtapose the text 'Zhe yi sha tian' (This brief moment) with 'The angel showed me the river' from the *Peony Pavilion* and *Bible* respectively.[52] These texts of sensuous spirituality create cross-cultural confluences that are echoed sonically by my own personal interval-colour sonorities, *Kunqu* inspired-melodic fragments, metal timbres from the Japanese Temple Bowl, the soft *kulintang* gong-chimes, and the wriggling Chinese opera-influenced vocal lines.

Example 10.5 Crossman, *Gentleness Suddenness*, 'Spirit', intense confluence, bars 127–131.

This confluence of multiple Asian-Pacific features in *Gentleness Suddenness* echoes the *qiyun* philosophy of the Chinese literati: the vigorous energy of *qi* in the metal timbres and the figures of Chinese opera is juxtaposed with the *yun* in the resonant sounds of the *kulintang* gongs and mezzo-soprano line.

This brief moment of Asian-Pacific confluence of sounds and words also draws inspiration from nature and abstract art. In the realm of abstract art, I found creative energy from the pastel *Shanghai Marks II* by Wallace Crossman.[53] The painting has several upward spurting gestures of reds, pinks and blues that I rendered musically in the juxtapositions of several wriggling instrumental and vocal lines. And in *Gentleness Suddenness* the juxtapositions of colour confluences amidst moments of pregnant silence echoes the juxtapositions I experience in nature. For instance, in the Mulgoa Nature Reserve the early flowering of vibrant pink flowers singing amidst green foliage stands in stark contrast to the muted colours of the bush.[54]

Concluding remarks

My compositional practice over the last decade grows from a broad philosophical, material, and placial context of the Asian-Pacific. The multiplicity of changes within and across the sounds of the music seem to me as if they brood, as if they respond to the spiritual hovering described in *Genesis* or the movement of *dao*. My musical creations arise from an intuitive approach — an 'unspoken' and 'living' word — which situates itself as Judeo-Christian knowing or as a Zen Buddhist '*isness*'.[55] This latter concept is further developed by Suzuki in reference discussing Zen artistic practices:

> The artist's world is one of free creation, and this can only come from intuitions directly and immediately rising from the isness of things, unhampered by senses and intellect.[56]

My music embodies not only Suzuki's sense of the creative freedom of intuition but also Nuss's sense of the freedom from cultural silos and freedom toward cross-cultural interactions of 'constant flux'.[57] Such a freedom of constant flux takes shape in a personal hybridity arising from the Asian-Pacific context. I conceive my music as free-spirited yet anchored in the living colours of the Asian-Pacific and its philosophical, material and placial confluences. It is from these confluences that my aesthetic of *living colours* thrives.

Notes

1 *The Drunken Emperor Orders His Brother's Execution*, Paichangxi Repertoires of Cantonese Opera, Ko Shan Theatre, Kowloon, Hong Kong, 13–14 October 2010.
2 Kenneth Barker, ed., *The NIV Study Bible: The New International Version* (Michigan: Zondervan, 1985), 1593.
3 Yang Xin, 'Approaches to Chinese Painting: Part 1', in *Three Thousand Years of Chinese Painting*, ed. Richard Barnhart et al. (New Haven: Yale University Press, 2002), 2.
4 Barker, *Study Bible*, 1593, 1600.
5 Chou Wen-Chung, '*Wenren* and Culture', in *Locating East Asia in Western Art Music*, ed. Yayoi Uno Everett and Frederick Lau (Middletown, Connecticut: Wesleyan University Press, 2004), 213.
6 Frederick Lau, 'Context, Agency and Chineseness: The Music of Law Wing Fai', *Contemporary Music Review* 26/5 (2007), 588.
7 Steven Nuss articulates a similar idea using somewhat different terminology in his: 'Hearing "Japanese", Hearing Takemitsu', *Contemporary Music Review* 21/4 (2002), 44.
8 For more on the concept of *ma* see: Shimosako Mari, 'Japan: Philosophy and Aesthetics', in *The Garland Encyclopedia of World Music: East Asia: China, Japan, and Korea*, ed. Robert Provine et al. 7 (New York: Routledge, 2001), 553. For more on the Chinese blending of nature and art see: Chou Wen-Chung, 'The Aesthetic Principles of Chinese Music: A Personal Quest', *Canzona* 7/4 (1986), 76–8 and Tang Hoichiu 'The Way of Ink Painting: The Origin and in Search of Zen' in *Lui Shou–kwan: New Ink Painting*, ed. Tang Hoichiu (Hong Kong: Leisure and Cultural Services Department, 2003), 13, 15; For more on sonority see: Lau, 'Context, Agency and Chineseness', 600. For more on the multi-art aesthetic see: Edward Ho, 'Aesthetic Considerations in Understanding Chinese Literati Musical Behavior', *British Journal of Ethnomusicology* 6 (1997), 36 and Chou, 'Aesthetic Principles', 74.
9 Edmund Capon, *I Blame Duchamp: My Life's Adventures in Art* (Victoria, Australia: Lantern, 2009), 16.
10 Nuss, 'Hearing "Japanese"', 64.
11 In 2012, the Australian government commissioned a white paper subsequently published as 'Australia in the Asian Century', accessed 1 December 2014, http://asialink.unimelb. edu.au/media/media_releases/media_releases/Australia_in_the_Asian_century. Prior to its publication, one of the authors, Ken Henry, delivered a speech about the commission titled 'Australia in the Asian Century: Reflections on the Australian

136 *Bruce Crossman*

Government White Paper' at the *Knowing Asia: Asian Studies in an Asian Century, 19th Biennial Conference of the Asian Studies Association*, Parramatta Campus, Western Sydney University, 12–13 July 2012. For the entire speech, see, accessed 1 December 2014, http://www.uws.edu.au/ics/events/past_events/asaa_conference/asaa_video_15.

12 Edward Said, *Orientalism* (London: Penguin, 2003), 12.

13 The interested may read more about Murail's reflections on his compositional aesthetic in Ronald Bruce Smith and Tristan Murail, 'An Interview with Tristan Murail', *Computer Music Journal* 24/1 (2000), 11.

14 Nuss, 'Hearing "Japanese"', 38, 40, 43–4.

15 Michel Foucault, *The Order of Things: An Archaeology of the Human Sciences* (New York: Vintage, 1973), xv.

16 Nuss, 'Hearing "Japanese"', 44.

17 Lui Shou-Kwan (b. 1919, Guangzhou, Guangdong Province, China; d. 1975, Hong Kong) was an innovative Chinese painter who combined techniques from traditional Chinese ink painting with abstract art; his spirit and gestural approach were closely allied to Zen Buddhism. For more on his style and biography, see: Tang Hoichiu, ed., *Lui Shou-kwan: New Ink Painting*.

18 In October 2010 I served as a composer participant at the Asian Music Festival in Tokyo and as a Scholar-in-Residence at the David C. Lam Institute for East–West Studies, Hong Kong Baptist University. While in Hong Kong I attended a showing of art by Wu Guanzhong: *Lofty Integrity: Wu Guanzhong*, 26 March–4 July and October 2010, Hong Kong Museum of Art. Some instances of the paintings influential for *Gentleness Suddenness* by Wallace Crossman are posted on my website: http://brucecrossman.com/.

19 Capon, *I Blame Duchamp*, 16.

20 Ho, 'Aesthetic Considerations', 36.

21 Chou, 'Aesthetic Principles', 74. And for the calligraphical nature of Chou's music see: Yayoi Uno Everett, 'Calligraphy and musical gestures in the late works of Chou Wen-Chung', *Contemporary Music Review* 26/5 (2007), 570.

22 Hazel Smith and Roger Dean, *Practice-led Research, Research-led Practice in the Creative Arts* (Edinburgh: Edinburgh University Press, 2009), 3. In their introduction, Smith and Dean quote the ideas of Sharon Bell who, in her chapter of their book, 'The Academic Mode of Production', refers to the proliferation of lateral thinking as 'generically disrespectful and promiscuous', 258–9, 261.

23 Barker, *Study Bible*, 1593.

24 Yang, 'Approaches to Chinese Painting', 2.

25 Nuss, 'Hearing "Japanese"', 44.

26 José Maceda, 'A Concept of Time in a Music of Southeast Asia (A Preliminary Account)', *Ethnomusicology*, 30/1 (1986), 11–53. Ethnomusicologist Maceda understands metal sonorities 'allowed to vibrate freely with one stroke' (12) as characteristic of Southeast Asia music. For additional discussion of these matters, see: Bruce Crossman, 'Spiritual Essences: Sounds of an Asian-Pacific Place, Personality and Spirit in *Double Resonances*', in *Music of the Spirit: Asian-Pacific Musical Identity*, ed. Michael Atherton and Bruce Crossman (Sydney: Australian Music Centre, 2008), 21.

27 Capon, *I Blame Duchamp*, 221.

28 Tang, 'The Way of Ink Painting', 12.

29 Tang, 'The Way of Ink Painting', 13.

30 Yang, 'Approaches to Chinese Painting', 2.

31 Barker, *Study Bible*, 6, 1593, and 1600.

32 Zhuang Zi quoted in Chou, 'Wenren and Culture', 213. Also see Chou in notes and glossary of terms in *Locating East Asia in Western Art Music*, ed. Yayoi Uno Everett and Frederick Lau, 261, 289. Zhuang Zi's philosophical thought is contained within the book *Zhuangzi* [also known as Chuang tzu], which is the second key text of Daoism.

In his commentary and translation of the Daoist classic by Chuang Tzu, David Hinton clarifies the Tao as a spiritual concept, which is a type of process or way that moves through things. See Hinton's The *Four Chinese Classics: Tao Te Ching, Analects, Chuang Tzu, Mencius* (Berkeley: Counterpoint, 2013), 133 and 138. In his essay 'A Little Talk About Evening Things Out', Chuang Tzu describes the 'Way' (Tao) as a state where 'all things move freely as one and the same', in Hinton, *The Four Chinese Classics*, 152.

33 Chou, '*Wenren* and Culture', 213.
34 Ho uses these phrases in his 'Aesthetic Considerations', 37–8.
35 Ho, 'Aesthetic Considerations', 37–8.
36 Nuss, 'Hearing "Japanese"', 44.
37 Jim Franklin, 'Japanese Shakuhachi Honkyoku Tradition and its Reinterpretation into a Contemporary Composition Practice', in *Music of the Spirit*, 96.
38 *In Gentleness and Suddenness* was premiered by Franklin in 2006 at the Brunei Gallery Theatre at the University of London. For a performance, see, accessed 11 December 2014, http://brucecrossman.com/media/. Excerpts from *In Gentleness and Suddenness* and *Not Broken Bruised-Reed* are used with kind permission of Wirripang Pty Ltd.
39 This whistling reminds me of *Kokû-Reibo*, a work from the *honkyoku* repertoire which employs high bell-like overtones. A recorded performance of *Kokû-Reibo* by Judo Nôtomi may be heard on: *Shakuhachi: Japan* (CD), Victor HMV.
40 Lau makes this point in: 'Context, Agency and Chineseness', 598, 600.
41 Nuss, 'Hearing "Japanese"'.
42 This concept of resonance was picked up by Stephen Adams, the new music curator of an ABC Classic FM radio program. He described the piece as having 'Asian-inspired sudden brutal gestures and gentle, exposed resonances of [a] Pacific composer'. See Adams, 'The 2010 World New Music Days: Hear the World's Best New Music Festival on Your Radio', in *Limelight: Music Arts, Culture*, ed. Diane Parks and Marija Beram, Australian Broadcasting Corporation, May 2010, 94.
43 I accessed this Chinese Shang-tiao mode through Korean scholar Lee Kang Sook's discussion of Korean modes in 'An essay on Korean modes', *Asian Music* 9/2 (1978), 42–3. Lee Kang Sook relates Korean modality to five Chinese modes, drawing on the work of Lee Hye-Ku.
44 The Atherton *Kulintang* is an ancient gong-set procured by Australian ethnomusicologist Michael Atherton in his travels through the Philippines. I used six of these gongs (C, C♯, F, G, A♭, A). For further discussion of this gong-set, see: Michael Atherton, 'At the Edge of What Comes Next: "Comprovised" Meaningfulness in Jiriyai, a New Work for Percussionist and Dancer', in *Intercultural Music: Creation and Interpretation*, ed. Sally Macarthur, Bruce Crossman and Ronald Morelos (Sydney: Australian Music Centre, 2007), 84. The UWS *Kulintang* is a modern gong-set at Western Sydney University that was procured in San Francisco, USA. I used one gong (D) from this set.
45 For more on Korean aesthetics see: Byung-ki Hwang, 'Philosophy and Aesthetics in Korea', *The Garland Encyclopedia of World Music: East Asia: China, Japan, and Korea*, 813.
46 Shimosako, 'Japan: Philosophy and Aesthetics', 553. This sense of an 'interesting silence' was present in the 2010 performance of the piece by Anna mcmichael, violin, Claire Edwardes, percussion, and Zubin Kanga, piano, as part of the ISCM World New Music Days. The performance took place at Verbrugghen Hall, Sydney Conservatorium of Music and was broadcast by ABC Classic FM Radio. A For a portion of the performance see, accessed 10 December 2014, http://www.abc.net.au/classic/iscm2010/.
47 *Gentleness–Suddenness* was performed by Lotte Latukefu, mezzo-soprano, James Cuddeford, violin, Claire Edwardes, percussion, and Michael Kieran Harvey, piano at Campbelltown Arts Centre, Sydney, New Music Series, 29 June 2013 and recorded live by ABC Classic FM radio, with producer Stephen Adams and Filigree Films, with director Iqbal Barkat. See Bruce Crossman, *Gentleness–Suddeness* (Sydney: Filigree

Films, 2014). For a first draft of the video, see, accessed 11 December 2014, http://www.filigreefilms.com/corporate/gentleness suddeness/.

48 For the entire text see: Tang Xianzu, *The Peony Pavilion: Mudan ting*, trans. Cyril Birch, 2nd ed. (Bloomington: Indiana University Press, 2002).

49 My source for the Biblical texts was Barker, *Study Bible*.

50 I was assisted in preparation of the Chinese text by two people. I relied on Lindy Li Mark's translation: *Peony Pavilion: Young Lovers' Edition: A life-affirming legend of love and resurrection*, UCLA International Institute, Asia Institute, accessed 31 May 2011, http://www.international.ucla.edu/china/mudanting/. And Hong Kong linguist Cheung Man Shan assisted with pronunciation and romanisation of the Chinese text.

51 Lindy Li Mark, 'The Opera: Book 1 Script: Part 1', *Peony Pavilion*, 16. This passage is used in my musical score *Gentleness Suddenness* (2012) utilising both Lindy Li Mark's translation and Milky Shan Man Cheung's romanisation of the Chinese script, preface, 3.

52 The excerpt from *Gentleness Suddenness* is used with the kind permission of the Australian Music Centre.

53 The pastel can be viewed at, accessed 11 December 2014, http://brucecrossman.com/2011/10/22/gentleness-suddenness/.

54 For a picture of the scene I have in mind, see, accessed 11 December 2014, http://brucecrossman.com/2011/10/22/gentleness-suddenness/.

55 Barker, *Study Bible*, 833.

56 Daisetz Taitaro Suzuki, *Zen and Japanese Culture* (Princeton: Princeton University Press, 2010), 17.

57 Nuss, 'Hearing "Japanese"', 64.

11 *Kawaii* aesthetics and the exchange between anime and music

Paul Smith

While many composers find inspiration in the musical works of others, a recent period of my compositional work has been interested not in the musical but in rendering the visual as musical. Going against the dominant musical pedagogy of studying composers and musical techniques, I have looked to Japanese anime, animated cartoons, as my source of artistic influence and found in the shapes, colours, tones and contours of animation everything I need to compose music. An added benefit of this is that it forces a correlation and consideration between the boundaries of artistic languages and sensory media. For a period in 2010 I was specifically interested in the way anime portrayed the Japanese aesthetic known as *kawaii*, which translates approximately as cuteness or cute. Writing for the Italian pianist Antonietta Lofreddo at this time, I was interested in composing music that explored childhood. As my own childhood was populated with cute anime characters, I took this as my creative impetus. The result was a four movement suite for piano I named the *Kawaii Suite*. The artistic act of writing four pieces of music drawing on *kawaii* aesthetics has forced me as a composer to consider the dynamic relationship between music and source material, particularly as the source material in this case is two-fold involving both the *kawaii* aesthetic more generally and the specific anime characters. To destabilise any formal qualities of authorship that may be used to view my process, I prefer to consider my music from this period as similar to a work of translation, which Zeller defines as 'a work of art emanating from another author's context'.[1]

I qualify my act as 'artistic' to distinguish it from creative acts that exist outside art, and to affirm that a theoretical relationship between material and act was not at the front of my mind while composing. During the artistic act I was composing and being inspired by the visuals; now I consider my process from a critical perspective. In some ways, then, I explore my music as an outsider who objectively assesses the music and its relationship with anime and the *kawaii* aesthetic, but I am also privy to the specific compositional choices that occurred – choices that are central to this discussion.

Rather than writing music that drew on the *kawaii* aesthetic broadly, I chose specific iterations of the *kawaii* aesthetic and used these as the impetus for my music. This has had surprising effects on how my music relates to and communicates with both the *kawaii* aesthetic and the original Japanese anime characters. Rather than a direct flow of influence, *kawaii*-ness to anime to music, I suggest that a more dynamic and communicative dialogue exists between the three.

140   *Paul Smith*

This act of remediating a work of art by another work of art has an established discourse around the concept of ekphrasis. Much of the writing on ekphrasis, which originates as a literary device, is centred on inter-medial representation and re-presentation. Given the charged debate surrounding music and representation, musical ekphrasis challenges 'those who persist in treating music as standing apart from the other arts'.[2] A major proponent of musical ekphrasis, Siglind Bruhn, states that composers 'may transpose aspects of both structure and content; they may supplement, interpret, respond with associations, problematise, or play with some of the suggestive elements of the original image'.[3] For this chapter, I have chosen another way to approach the exchange between art forms. I adopt the Deleuzian concepts of exchange and the fold to further challenge the perceived hierarchy of meaning, authorship and form that still strongly dominates the musical arts. Exchange and the fold allow the three parties in play – *kawaii* aesthetics, anime and my music – to be viewed equally or even inverted so that backwards ascriptions of meaning can be traced from my music to anime and even further to the *kawaii* aesthetic. There is interplay here between the actors of musical meaning and artistic language.

Moving between visual and aural is a political process. Under the scrutiny of representation a majoritarian/minoritarian dichotomy is created that positions the assertive and focused visual as majoritarian and sound as minoritarian. Al-Nakib outlines Deleuze and Guattari's premise on the political nature of language, which I feel extends to artistic languages.

> It is political because it draws attention to the conditions that make one language or form of expression majoritarian and others not. It is collective because it expresses shared resistance, which inevitably occurs in response to domination, linguistic or otherwise, and because it embodies an emergent sensibility while pointing to the possibility of a community to come.[4]

My compositional process is then a deterritorialising of that which is visual. There is a strong argument to be made positioning the aural as minoritarian to the visual.[5] This assessment under an immanent politics of music does not negate potential meanings or dialogues but rather 'asks how [these] systems can be other than they are'.[6] My goal in this chapter is to show how visualist and aural systems dialogue. I approach this dialogue of the visual and aural by considering three strands: *kawaii* aesthetics, their use in anime, and how anime and the *kawaii* aesthetic have informed my music in the *Kawaii Suite*, focusing in particular on the opening movement, 'Mokona'. I then discuss how Deleuzian concepts can recalibrate consideration of the three strands.

Kawaii aesthetics and anime

The breadth and character of the *kawaii* aesthetic is much debated within the academic sphere and challenges theorists for whom 'cute' does not properly convey its conceptual Japanese understanding. In general terms, *kawaii* culture, which denotes the practice and presence of *kawaii* in Japan and other countries, 'celebrates the material as opposed to the abstract side of existence insofar as cute images explicitly eschew metaphysical aspirations'.[7] Characteristically, *kawaii* is associated with youthfulness, vulnerability, innocence, gentleness and immaturity. The way these combine 'encompasses a multiplicity of meaning'.[8] Despite its contemporaneity, artist Takashi Murakami links *kawaii* with the historical term *yurui* (lethargy). Papp explains Murakami's theory and claims that 'the contemporary transition to *kawaii* from *yurui* indicates a sense of sexual incapacity and impotence'.[9] Since the end of the Second World War and the symbolic naming of the atomic bomb dropped on Hiroshima in 1945 as 'little boy', Japan has undergone an infantilisation. The metaphor of 'little boy' aptly characterises a significant turning point in twentieth-century Japan and it also addresses another complexity associated with the notion of *kawaii*. The juxtaposition of an infantile name for such a catastrophic instrument of power highlights the contradictions that characterise *kawaii*. Osama Tezuka's iconic *manga* (and then anime) character, Astro Boy (1952–68), epitomises this contradiction through the slight and juvenile figure that wields considerable power.

Anime are not only produced as children's entertainment in Japan: they often depict complex adult themes for a mature audience. Napier argues that '[anime's] complex story lines challenge the viewer used to the predictability of Disney while its often dark tone and content may surprise audiences'.[10] The anime boom of the 1990s in Australia and the United States located this practice as a unique artistic articulation of the world different from other forms of Western animation; this difference arose not simply from the cultural allusions to bento-boxes and the depiction of cherry blossom leaves cascading to the ground but rather from anime's unique mode for figuring bodies and things. According to Hu, anime may be characterised by the term 'medium-genre'.[11] The term acknowledges anime's distinctive visual aesthetic but also that it can be adopted to convey specific messages or articulate a variety of visual gestures. It is a platform for expression where animators, authors, writers, composers and actors come together to create visual narratives. Since different groups of people use it in quite disparate ways, anime can be productively viewed as a platform for expressive articulation of concepts and objects.

The corporeal modes of expression that anime employs both require and create a discourse of their own. Brophy argues that in anime 'the dynamic interaction between gesture, event, sound and image reaches its apogee'.[12] Such dynamic interactions generate new observations and perspectives on such concepts as technology, nature, gender and identity. Brophy maintains that anime's use of mannequin-like forms re-envisions the human figure and that the body underneath the animated kimono or warlord's armour is not a body as it might 'appear' in our world.[13] In fact it does not appear at all, the drawn part of the anime, the kimono or the armour only suggest that a body is underneath and we infer that there is a human figure behind what has been animated since it is never really drawn. This inferred space behind the animated mannequin-like figure is in many ways a potential space – a virtual space. It is for this reason that characters' identities in anime are rarely territorialised. The human figure in anime is extended and altered; characters can change size, hair colour, gender or even become animals, and they often do. An extension could be made to the Deleuzian notions of the 'actual' and the 'virtual' where the actual denotes what is drawn and appears within the anime, and the virtual describes the potential space behind what is animated. Bost and Greene assert that 'from an immanent standpoint, the virtual and the actual affect and are affected by the assembly of a body'.[11] Their observation applies well to anime: the literal re-drawing/re-creation of the human body; the hair is hair but not an anthropological hair; tears are tears but not as humans would normally cry. In this way the source material that I draw from underscores my research as a deterritorialising of the sensorial boundaries of art.

Anime, as Brophy suggests, forces the 're-imagining, re-inventing and reconfiguring of all we assume humanity and humanism are',[15] and through these interactions, anime generates a new species — the anime species, which plays an important role in my compositional process. The insertion of anime into my working process as a mediated form of *kawaii* creates layers of form around the piece of music. It is possible for me to draw directly from *kawaii* discourse and take definitions such as gentle, cute, naive or others and use this as the impetus for my compositions but I was more interested in how different anime directors have used the *kawaii* aesthetic in their works and how I could then respond to this musically.

Kawaii **and power**

Scholars who analyse *kawaii* in the context of anime deal with two things in a complex relation. When employed within anime *kawaii* becomes the visual veneer of a character. What is presented as cute, naive and vulnerable may in fact be malicious, mature, powerful or dangerous. The *kawaii* aesthetic does not always match the internal personality. Barber, Bryce and Davis describe this relation as 'a resounding visual and psychological clash'.[16] These instances are not rare, and in one particular instance of this complexity, Brophy points out that 'this is the deeper meaning of *kawaii* culture ... nothing is singularly gendered; everything is multi-sexed'.[17] The power contained within a cute design can be unexpectedly disproportionate.

My piano music responds to this 'visual and psychological clash' within the *kawaii* aesthetic in anime by avoiding a character that could be heard as simply cute. Rather than trying to write cute music, I explored the specific ways that cuteness might be used within anime. Throughout the suite moments of clear harmonic movement, phrases with only one clear melodic line, thinly textured sections and the use of the piano's upper and brighter register are juxtaposed with other moments of dissonance, aggression, unclear voice leading and unexpected harmonic progressions. The juxtapositions of these sound characters express the *kawaii* aesthetic in anime.

Next I turn to a more detailed analysis of how *kawaii* is employed and circumvented by the specific anime character I drew on when composing 'Mokona', the opening movement of my *Kawaii Suite*.[18] The movement is based on the character Mokona from the anime series *Tsubasa Chronicle* (2007–08), which in turn is based on the *manga* created by the all-female manga group CLAMP. The story follows a group of travellers searching for the memories of one of their friends who cannot remember her past. Mokona's purpose in the show is to take the travellers from one world to the next, to move them to new environments and new challenges while also acting as the comic foil and *kawaii* mascot of the series.

I structured the piece of music around the three events that take place when Mokona and the travellers are moving to a new world. First, Mokona grabs the travellers' attention by yelling the word 'me-kyo' repeatedly in a high-pitched voice. Second, Mokona summons a portal through which the travellers are chaotically transported from the world they inhabit. And third, the characters arrive in a new and unfamiliar world. This progression inspired me to compose three sections, which respond to these events in the anime. Of these three sections it is the first and second, titled 'the herald' and 'the portal', which most closely articulate the contrasting nature of Mokona's *kawaii* characteristics.

The 'Mokona' movement opens with heralding, repetitive semiquavers, a fanfare influenced by Mokona's relentless use of word 'mek-yo'. The semiquavers move over different chords and time signatures suggesting different inflections and intentions. During the anime, the portals Mokona conjures are a vortex of swirling masses of brightly coloured patterns that appear dangerous and moderately aggressive in how they transport the travellers between worlds. There is a level of uncertainty and danger in this process since the travellers are unsure of where they are being taken. The 'portal' section of the movement uses a repeated note pattern in the bass over which a number of chords and scale passages from different key areas are played depicting the variety of visual patterns and textures used when animating the vortex. Example 11.1 cites bars 38–41 showing how the bass pattern is disrupted sporadically by a number of syncopated bars. These syncopations become more frequent, building to a low resounding chord cluster, which signifies that the travellers have arrived at their new destination. In this new environment they are left to discover the intricacies of a new reality.

Mokona's cute and entertaining nature is what inspired the melody-dominated homophony between bars 16 and 34. Example 11.2 cites bars 18–21, showing the bright melody played in octaves and accompanied by arpeggiated D major triads. I purposefully composed little harmonic complexity in this section since Mokona can appear quite vague and often verbalises the most mundane observations. This rollicking homophony is slowly broken down during the second section with bars of rhythmic syncopation and additive rhythms, which give way to harsh gestures played against a bass ostinato. This music captures the unlikely powerful ability that comes from the somewhat dim-witted Mokona. The character of the music is not violent or aggressive but rather tumultuous and unpredictable; and I meant to draw out musically the subtle forms of power that the *kawaii* aesthetic can project.

Example 11.1 Smith, *Kawaii Suite*, 'Mokona', bars 38–41.

Example 11.2 Smith, *Kawaii Suite*, 'Mokona', bars 18–21.

Exchange and the fold

As outlined above it is the insertion of an existing art medium between inspiration and music that results in a multi-layered, potentially hierarchical, order of actors in my musical process. It is not uncommon for composers, particularly those working within the Western musical canon, to draw inspiration from some non-musical source. Typically, composers abstract ideas from the source material. For example, Vivaldi used the idea of the seasons, Holst the idea of the planets, and Sibelius and Wagner used ideas about mythological figures; and in each of these instances the compositions make musically concrete the abstracted ideas. In the examples discussed in this chapter, my music is a second iteration of artistic form. There exists a *kawaii* aesthetic outside anime, and it is employed and mediated by anime. In my music, I draw on a hybrid of this abstract aesthetic and its manifestation in anime during my compositional process. As mentioned earlier, the concept and practices of ekphrasis as articulated in post-structuralist thought have played a central role in my musical thinking for all the movements of the *Kawaii Suite*. While it is accepted that literary ekphrasis is a common tool, the avenues for musical ekphrasis are narrower and more arguable. The difficulties associated with musical ekphrasis suggest questions regarding the flow of abstract idea and material between the three parties, especially as it invites the problematic aspects of representation. The imposed hierarchy of the three parties means that the one directional nature, or flow, of representation will result in the problematic search for comparative articulations between modes of expression. This flow is not to be ignored, as Doel suggests that representation is second nature, it is part of everything we do, and everything we are subject to. He observes that 'there is an original and a copy, and the relationship between the one and the other lends itself to an evaluation in terms of the degree of similarity'.[19] When analysing two art works that are of the same medium it is arguably easier to find the similarities than when looking at art works that are of different media. As such, despite the argument that representation underscores any and all evaluations, two art works that are related but are of different media (especially different sensory media) will require non-representational considerations. I argue that my music adds to and informs the original anime as much as the original anime has informed my music. There are two Deleuzian concepts I employ to assert this and to move away from the problem of representation.

In an attempt to address the hierarchical implications of ekphrasis Al-Nakib uses the notion of exchange to move away from a direct one-to-one correlation of parts, exchange involving an interaction between separate and unrelated things. Al-Nakib states that 'what can occur in an exchange is not simply a quantitative trade of elements reduced to a single unit of measure but, rather, a qualitative transformation or deterritorialisation that affects both sides and creates something altogether different in the process'.[20] Depending on the different ways this process occurs, the exchange is altered producing different effects on both sides and expanding different aspects of the source material. Rather than understanding a work of art as limited by its sensory borders, a deterritorialising exchange highlights the work's mutability. The visual can be unvisual and the musical can be unmusical. In the instance of two interacting art works in differing media, exchange does not subtract from the work created first; rather, the exchange invites a proliferation of media, expression and meaning. The assertion that music can deterritorialise the visual suggests that 'the world no longer appears fixed or ordered in quite the way we had imagined',[21] and in this disorder there is potential. It is then not only appropriate to explore what visuals are rendered musical – such as which chord or melody corresponds to which image – but also the reverse: what in the images is

146 *Paul Smith*

revealed by the music. The nature of *kawaii* aesthetics and the anime characters in their visual milieu are musically understood as a harsh juxtaposition of gestures. The simple major melody gives way to the chord cluster just as the playful anime figure gives way to the massive swirling portal. The actual — the anime characters as they appear — and the virtual — the anime characters as they *are* — are both made musically real.

In addition to such a consideration of the one-to-one relation between events of the anime and the music, it is worth considering how the *kawaii* aesthetic more broadly operates within the exchange. 'Any truly effective deterritorialisation remains doubly entangled, in part to the territory it happens to escape or detach from and, in addition, to the new territory it happens to become or assemble with'.[22] The nature of *kawaii* then functions, in Deleuzian terms, as a 'double-capture' or 'double-theft' where the connection between the two art mediations inform each other as they contribute to the overall meanings of *kawaii*. Mediation could be considered a form of representation. Such a consideration, however, prohibits the potential for unique dialogical structures, especially when music is used to mediate an abstract idea and would benefit from non-comparative scrutiny. It is important to note that the rhetorical is not only linguistic — it exists across media, and because of this it is necessary to abandon the 'tendency to register rhetorical effects on the plane of representation and signification'.[23] Doel warns of the problem of representation because it 'is bound to a specific form of repetition ... the problematic is constrained to keep these repetitions in order to ensure that they do nothing more than return originals, identities and givens'.[24] The exchange enacted between the diverse parts of my compositional process is not to a return to originals: my music does not return to identities but adds layers of potential meaning.

In addition to exchange, I draw on the fold as a figure through which we can assess the relationship between *kawaii*, anime and my music. As Kaufman has noted, the concept of exchange lends itself to a Saussurean structuralist opposition between the signifier and the signified — or in this instance the original and a copy. Drawing on Deleuze, Kaufman notes that the signifier and signified persist 'even if these roles are interchanged as we change points of view'.[25] The concept of the fold provides a productive way to comprehend the integration of *kawaii* aesthetics, anime and the *Kawaii Suite*. Rajan describes the figure of the fold as 'a form of involution and complication, turning and returning, the fold gathers differences into an enigmatic continuum'.[26] The ever-changing nature and organisation of the fold allows the inside to become the outside at any moment. When applied to the music of the *Suite*, the *kawaii* aesthetic and anime, the decentring processes of enfolding allows for a malleable conception of the musical work and its core. The *kawaii* aesthetic does not stand as the core from which new iterations are generated. Neither is it that a single work of music or anime may be understood as the departure point from which we could compare or contrast ascriptions of meaning. The fold changes and evolves with each addition of information or of unique approaches by performer, composer, animator or audience member. That is, the fold reorganises and redistributes, blurring the boundaries of signifier and signified.

The application of these post-structural notions to my creative processes occurs within a context of differing approaches. My traversing of the planes of virtuality and actuality within the realms of both anime and music invite responses from positions of music compositional habit. Deleuzian territories are contested fields between the 'double entanglement of potentiality with the often overpowering pressure of habit'.[27] My compositional practice, however, leads me to potentiality. Within a musical pedagogy that promotes the idea of an absolute music, I draw instead on and follow ekphrastic works of art that challenge the autonomy of musical form. Further, I have chosen as my inspiration a medium that challenges normative conceptions of biological sex. In the multi-sexed, visually clashing, re-figured reality of anime I find what Lewis Carroll called the 'unanswerable cryptic cipher whose conditions of openness are also the conditions of its infinite enfolding'.[28] Form and expression are not bound in anime but diverse and changing, the visual can logically be musical.

Notes

1 Beatriz Zeller, 'On Translation and Authorship', *Meta: Journal des Traducteurs* 45 (2000), 139 (doi:10.7202/004640ar).

2 Lydia Goehr, 'How to Do More with Words. Two Views of (Musical) Ekphrasis', *The British Journal of Aesthetics* 50 (2010), 389 (doi:10.1093/aesthj/ayq036).

3 Siglind Bruhn, 'A Concert of Paintings: "Musical Ekphrasis" in the Twentieth Century', *Poetics Today* 22 (2001), 551.

4 Mai Al-Nakib, 'Assia Djebar's Musical Ekphrasis', *Comparative Literature Studies* 42 (2005), 257.

5 See Stead, pp. 179–187. And Jonathan Crary, *Suspensions of Perception: Attention, Spectacle and Modern Culture*, An October Book (Cambridge, MA and London: The MIT Press, 2001), 2–3.

6 Matthew Bost and Ronald Walter Greene, 'Affirming Rhetorical Materialism: Enfolding the Virtual and the Actual', *Western Journal of Communication* 75 (2011): 443 (doi:10.1080/10570314.2011.588902).

7 Dani Cavallaro, *Art in Anime: The Creative Quest as Theme and Metaphor* (Jefferson, NC: McFarland & Co., 2012), 24.

8 Christie Barber, Mio Bryce and Jason Davis, 'The Making of Killer Cuties', in *Anime and Philosophy*, ed. Joseph Steiff and Tristan. D. Tamplin, (Chicago, IL: Open Court, 2010), 23.

9 Zilia Papp, *Anime and its Roots in Early Japanese Monster Art*, (Folkestone: Global Oriental, 2010), 6.

10 Susan Napier, *Anime from Akira to Princess Mononoke: Experiencing Contemporary Japanese Animation* (New York: Palgrave Macmillan, 2001), 9.

11 Tze–yue G. Hu, *Frames of Anime: Culture and Image-Building* (Hong Kong: Hong Kong University Press, 2010), 2.

12 Phillip Brophy, *100 anime: BFI Screen Guides* (London: BFI Publishing, 2005), 6.

13 Brophy, *100 Anime*, 6.

14 Bost and Greene, 'Enfolding', 443.

15 Brophy, *100 Anime*, 8.

16 Barber et al., 'Killer Cuties', 23.

17 Brophy, *100 Anime*, 118.

148 *Paul Smith*

18 *Kawaii Suite*, in *Childhood in Music*, piano Antonietta Loffredo (Wollongong, NSW: Wirripang, 2011), CD.

19 Marcus A. Doel, 'Representation and Difference', in *Taking-place: Non-Representational Theories and Geography*, ed. Ben Anderson and Paul Harrison (Farnham, England and Burlington, Vermont: Ashgate, 2010), 119.

20 Al-Nakib, 'Musical Ekphrasis', 259.

21 Al-Nakib, 'Musical Ekphrasis', 258.

22 Al-Nakib, 'Musical Ekphrasis', 258.

23 Bost and and Greene, 'Enfolding', 443.

24 Doel, 'Representation', 117.

25 Eleanor Kaufman, 'Levi-Strauss, Deleuze and the Joy of Abstraction', *Criticism* 49 (2007): 453 (doi:10.1353/crt.0.0045).

26 Tillotama Rajan, 'The Phenomenological Allegory: From Death and the Labyrinth to The Order of Things', *Poetics Today* 19 (1998), 440.

27 Al-Nakib, 'Musical Ekphrasis', 258.

28 Alan Lopez, 'Deleuze With Carroll', *Angelaki: Journal of Theoretical Humanities* 9 (2010): 118 (doi:10.1080/09697250420003076664).

12 A musical portmanteau

Rock viscerality, juxtaposition and modernist textures in *Frumious*

Holly Harrison

Inspired by the nonsense literature of Lewis Carroll, my orchestral work *Frumious* (2012) reimagines the portmanteau word as a musical portmanteau, a concept referring to the coexistence of musical oppositions through the reorganisation of structure.[1] A portmanteau word is a fusion of two distinct words, where two meanings are *packed up* as one; it maintains the original meanings, whilst creating a new meaning. Musically, my aesthetic is energised by the stylistic collisions occurring in the music of John Zorn, Michael Torke, Charles Ives, Igor Stravinsky and Louis Andriessen. Each of these composers challenges the dichotomous dynamic between art and popular worlds, producing music that I consider to be musical equivalents of Carroll's portmanteaus. Like nonsense, my aesthetic aims to flatten, invert and manipulate stylistic hierarchies via juxtapositional sound-blocks to question the idea of hierarchy itself. Embracing the portmanteau as a metaphor for the convergence of musical oppositions, my music reorganises hierarchies through nonsense juxtapositions to form a new kind of 'sense': the logic of nonsense. By doing so, my compositional voice works towards a combative, energised sound-world with an architectural design of rhythmic vitality and visceral sonorities.

Frumious positions oppositional ideas against each other as stylistic juxtapositions, borrowing structural techniques from *musique concrète*, Ives and Zorn, to experiment with a mosaic, non-linear design. These juxtapositions collide horizontally and vertically, appearing as either successive or superimposed sound-blocks, organised as portmanteaus. Within these blocks, *Frumious* is driven by a series of dichotomies involving rhythm and sonority, the dichotomies generating different types of musical motion. The piece also blends the rhythmic viscerality and vernacular language of rock and post-minimalism (Andriessen/Torke) with the architectural design of late Modernism (Stravinsky) and early American Experimentalism (Ives), each of these strands invigorating the other. *Frumious* juxtaposes sonorities by pitting the functional chords and triads from rock against the atonal, chromaticism of contemporary art music. As an extension of sonority, textural density gives way to visceral sound-slabs, which are contrasted with an almost pointillistic, scattering effect.

Portmanteau and musical rebellion

Susan Stewart, a scholar of nonsense, maintains that one of its main features is the intersection of disparate domains. Humour is generated when differences are found in domains thought to be compatible, and similarity found in domains thought to be incompatible.[2] Carroll's use of portmanteau words demonstrates this idea by joining two existing words together to create a new word that evokes multiple meaning. The most famous examples of portmanteaus come from Carroll's poem *Jabberwocky* (1871); for instance, 'frumious', 'galumphing', 'slithy', 'chortle', and 'mimsy'.[3] At first the words appear to make little sense, to be gibberish, but this is part of the concealed sense that nonsense enjoys. What is most striking about portmanteau words is how easily they demonstrate the joining together of two ideas, whether perceived as compatible or incompatible, to express a new meaning that preserves the essence of each of the original parts. 'Slithy' is a combination of lithe and slimy; 'mimsy', miserable and flimsy; 'galumph', gallop and triumph, and 'frumious', a blending of the words 'furious' and 'fuming'. In this way, nonsense is also polyphonic, making use of a plethora of materials that borrows from different worlds to flatten hierarchies. As Lecercle observes: 'nonsense as a genre is the weaving together into a tradition of two different, even opposed threads, one literary, the other folkloric, one poetic, the other childish, one "high", the other "low"'.[4]

Traversing art and popular worlds, the music of Zorn, Ives and Andriessen epitomises the idea of the musical portmanteau by rebelling against the perceived hierarchy between art and vernacular worlds and harnessing the polyphony of nonsense. Zorn's rapid genre shifts are split into sound-blocks, which suggest a successive channel-surfing effect akin to *musique concrète*. Despite their chaotic exterior, Zorn's works are meticulously structured and toggle between fierce oppositions of 'the improvisational and the imitative, the creative and the derivative, the chaotic and the parodic' as McNeilly points out.[5] By comparison, Ives's works are more concerned with superimposed juxtapositions, where several stylistic streams occur simultaneously to create a portmanteau effect. Peter Burkholder discusses how within single works Ives embraces multiple styles, where 'modernistic passages can give way without warning to traditional-sounding music, or vice-versa, or that strikingly different styles can even occur simultaneously'.[6] Andriessen's aesthetic is anti-orchestral and Marxist; he challenges the orchestral model via rock-inspired elements, where unusual ensemble combinations, amplified instrumentation, repetitive, ruthless rhythms and dense unison textures define his post-minimalist language. Andriessen talks openly about the loudness and use of amplification for balance in *De Staat* (1976) as stemming from rock'n'roll, and how American orchestras were unable to play *De Snelheid* (*The Velocity*, 1984) without the use of earplugs.[7] Each of these composers harnesses a designed double energy where, by flattening and reorganising stylistic hierarchies, they create engaging combative sound-worlds, parallel to Carroll's nonsense.

Musical portmanteaus

Rhythm

I see the combative nature of *Frumious* as being intrinsically linked with rhythmic energy, where stylistic juxtapositions are driven and defined by a series of rhythmic dichotomies that contribute to the portmanteau effect. These dichotomies are listed in Table 12.1. The juxtaposition of rhythmic dichotomies generates a dual-energy and friction, which propels the blocks forward; it is both relentless and interruptive, creating a combative motion, which pulls in opposing directions. *Frumious* uses visceral rock gestures and drum kit techniques of hockets and paradiddle rudiments, inspired by my own experience as a rock drummer and structured via an architectural design. Since my goal here is not to discuss rhythm exhaustively, I have chosen to focus on rapidly changing time signatures, syncopation and groove.

Shifting time signatures play an essential role in dislocating rhythmic energy throughout and creating a non-linear sense of time throughout *Frumious*; repeated patterns and vernacular grooves are continually disturbed by changing tempo, metre, accents and pulse. Example 12.1 shows a short excerpt from the end of the piece, which comprises three main sound-blocks. I use the term sound-block to refer to sections of distinct stylistic character, which appear and sometimes recur, as either variations or verbatim, throughout the piece. Each block has its own rhythmic character, defined by metre and tempo changes. Example 12.1 cites bars 174–184, showing three blocks: The first begins at bar 174, the second at 178 (Rehearsal T), and the third at 180 (Rehearsal U). Throughout *Frumious*, the $\frac{5}{8}$ sections are frenetic and restless, with a stop–start energy and unison texture (see bars 180–181), while the $\frac{4}{4}$ sections are fluid and funky (bars 178–179), with independent lines. Earlier in the piece during the $\frac{4}{4}$ block of bars 124–29 stabbing chords and splattering sounds interrupt continuous lines, blending both fluid and frenetic energies.

The passage shown in Example 12.1 also demonstrates the rapid alternations between odd and even time signatures and the various combinations of syncopated and 'straight' rhythms, as the downbeat is continually displaced. The effect

Table 12.1 Dichotomies as an oppositional music aesthetic

Rhythmic oppositions
Pulsed
vs.
Pulse-less
Manic bursts
vs.
Stillness
Wild syncopations
vs.
Rigid rhythms
Continual motion
vs.
Rhythmic hiccups
Rapid-fire
vs.
Extreme slowness

152   *Holly Harrison*

is of jolting, spiky rhythms contrasted with smooth and fluid rhythms. The alternation of music having odd time signatures ($\frac{7}{8}$, $\frac{5}{8}$) in bars 174–177 and 180–183 with music having an even time signature ($\frac{4}{4}$) in bars 178–79 suggests a hiccupping effect. The music of the even bars seems either truncated or extended. Odd metered bars play this shortening game too; for instance, in bars 175 and

Example 12.1

(Continued)

A musical portmanteau   153

Example 12.1 *Frumious*, changing time signatures, bars 174–184.

182, the $\frac{7}{8}$ rhythm is suddenly truncated to $\frac{3}{4}$ and the $\frac{5}{8}$ rhythm to $\frac{2}{4}$, disrupting the phrase. Just as a pattern is established from bars 174–177, the block suddenly gives way to a heavier duple feel in the $\frac{4}{4}$ metre at Rehearsal T. The previous block's syncopation is replaced by straight, rigid march-like rhythms, a change amplified by a dramatic drop in tempo. At Rehearsal U the music snaps back into the initial $\frac{5}{8}$ meter of the piece at the original tempo of q = 115 and the

154　*Holly Harrison*

semiquaver bursts here conjure up a stop start frenetic energy. Again, just as a pattern is established, the energy is interrupted by a pause at bar 183 and a brief clarinet solo. The final bar recalls the 5/8 block, now extended to 4/4, and is followed by a silent pause and a cheeky pizzicato chord. The handful of pauses that appear in the piece serve as another way to disturb the energy of the music. The recurrence of distinct sound-blocks throughout *Frumious*, with opposing metres and tempos, such as those found in Example 12.1, set up different types of grooves that explore the relationship between syncopated and straight rhythms another portmanteau. This characteristic of frequent metre changes occurs throughout *Frumious*, and Table 12.2 shows these changes from bars 22 117.

The phenomenon of groove is an implicit part of all music and yet difficult to define. It plays an important role in *Frumious*, arising from the repeated use of syncopated rhythms. Musicologist Richard Middleton discusses how groove is produced by rhythmic patterns that shape the rhythmic character of the piece: 'different configurations of note placing, articulation and accent from the various components of the percussion kit, at specific tempi, play a large part in defining styles'.[8] He examines how groove is created according to how rhythmic gestures respond to and behave with other gestures, resulting in movement from the listener which is either real or imagined. In thinking about how groove is created by the interlocking of different but related rhythmic layers, I have looked to Michael Torke's *Adjustable Wrench* (1987), an amalgam of chamber, pop and jazz styles; it was first performed by the British ensemble Lontano led by Odaline de la Martinez. The piece is driven by a repeated syncopated vamp, which is continually displaced and transformed throughout. As John Roeder has noted, there are frequent shifts and reversals in syncopation where accents that once sounded strong or 'on' the beat suddenly sound 'off-beat'; and during the first 24 bars the lack of regular accents only imply rather than fix a metre, despite its notation in ¦.[9] Example 12.2 cites Roeder's analysis of the *Adjustable Wrench*'s opening 24 bars.[10] It demonstrates how, as the four syncopated layers are added sequentially, they lock in together at various points and phase in and out on odd and even stresses to create a groove. The absence of bar lines in the example allows for multiple metric interpretations.

The first four bars show the opening vamp, which is then joined by a second layer in the bass clef from bars 5 8. The annotation above the staff highlights the new layer's shared accents with the first, and how the accent points of the new layer fall mostly on the odd quaver beats. Bars 9 16 introduce the third layer, the melody above, and the annotation highlights how the end of each the three melodic phrases lock in with the previous layers on the odd stresses. Bars 17 24 show the fourth layer, which interjects on (mostly) even quaver beats, supporting alternative accent points of the melody from bars 9 16. Here, the introduction of a second set of accents reverses the previous syncopation, so that the long notes of the melody now sound 'on' the beat, as reflected by Roeder's choice of beaming. This reversal in syncopation allows the stresses of the melody to be heard in two distinct ways, generating a shifting groove that moves in and out of phase, as hinted at by the title of the piece: 'adjustable wrench'.

Table 12.2 Changing metres of *Frumious*, bars 22–117

Bars and rehearsal	A 22–23	24–27	28–29	30	31	32–33	34	B 35–36	C 37–38	39	40	41	42	43–44
Metre	5/8	4/4	5/8	3/8	5/8	4/4	3/4	4/4	5/8	2/4	4/4	5/8	2/4	4/4
Tempo	♩= 115							♩= 105	♩= 115					

Bars and rehearsal	45	46–47	48	E 49–71	G 72	73	74–75	76	77–78	79–80	H 81	82	83–84	85–88	89
Metre	5/4	5/8	3/4	4/4	5/8	3/4	4/4	5/8	3/4	7/16	3/4	7/8	3/4	7/8	3/4
Tempo			Rit.	♩= 88–115 –110	♩= 115		Poco rall.	♩= 115							

Bars and rehearsal	90–91	92–93	94	95	96	97	98	I 99	100	101–105	106	107–108	109	J 110–116	K 117 (18")
Metre	7/8	7/16	5/8	4/4	2/4	5/8	4/4	3/4	7/8	4/4	5/4	4/4	2/4	4/4	N/A
Tempo								Molto rall.						♩= 90 Molto rall.	Free–time

Example 12.2 Michael Torke, *Adjustable Wrench* layers, John Roeder analysis, bars 1–24.

What I refer to as the 'Funky' blocks of *Frumious* (at rehearsals D, F, I, second part of L, and M) generate groove in a similar way to Torke's *Adjustable Wrench*. Example 12.3 is a rhythmic reduction of bars 124–129 of *Frumious*, using Roeder's model, which demonstrates how repeated syncopated patterns lock together within the same pulse division. In opposition to the rapid time signature changes of other blocks, the coordinated rhythmic simplicity amplifies the groove, harnessing the continual motion, clearly defined pulse, and cyclic repetition of pop music.

As Example 12.3 shows, there are three syncopated layers, each with a distinct rhythmic and timbral character; these three layers are: the insistent bass line, the melodic pattern with wide leaps, and the *sforzando* events – what I'll refer to as splatters – played by the ensemble. These latter events create the effect of a 'splatter' because of the fleeting dissonance of their accents, variegated timbres and irregular timings. Each of the three layers lock together at various points on shared accents and stresses, toggling between emphasis on the strong beats of 1 and 3, and weak beats of 2 and 4. The insistent bass line alternates between quaver and crotchet values to create a syncopated effect; and though its two-bar unit gives the impression of repeating, it is never the same. The quaver register leaps of the vibraphone and trumpet melody create two distinct rhythms. One by the leap from high to low, and the other from low to high, such that the high and low notes alternate between being on and off the beat.

In Example 12.3, the rectangular boxes show the number of quaver rests between each woodwind, brass and string splatter accent. Each group plays a ratio

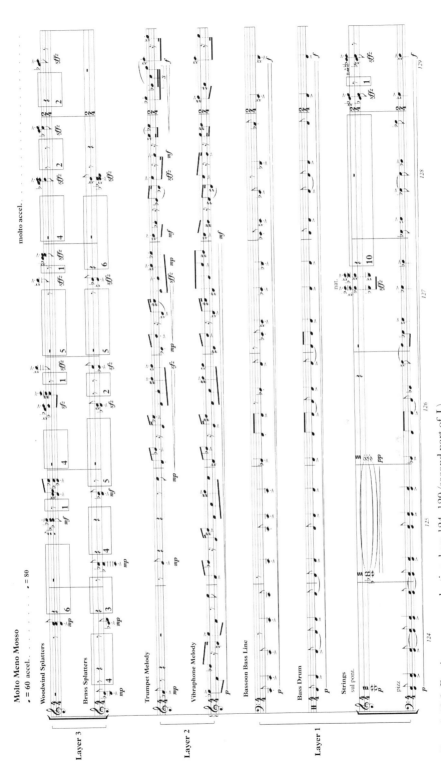

Example 12.3 *Frumious*, groove reduction, bars 124–129 (second part of L).

158   *Holly Harrison*

game, as each accent occurs irregularly, toggling back and forth between expanding and truncating ratios of odd and even length. No two ratios are repeated in a row, except at the end of the section with the woodwinds in bars 128–129, but even here the last accent of bar 128 is off the beat, and the first of bar 129 is on the beat. This ratio game propels the section forward, in tandem with the accelerating tempo, whilst simultaneously thwarting it as ratios are suddenly elongated.

The changes in colour of the *sforzando* splatters also intensify the syncopated interjectory effect, where in bars 124–129 different instrument groupings interlock and alternate timbrally as well as rhythmically. There is another ratio game at play here, too, where, when all instruments are grouped together, the number of quaver rests before each accent is also irregular, as shown in Table 12.3. The vibraphone is the only instrument heard on each of these splatter accents, and the bass drum, which is present on all but six of these 14 accents, produces a constant drone-like effect. Pitch also plays an important role in accentuating syncopation; the most dissonant splatters occur on off-beats, giving additional weight to the accent with minor second clashes. The interplay between, on one hand, the seemingly regular and irregular syncopated figures, with variegated timbres, dissonant accents and a clearly defined pulse, and, on the other, a sense of 'back-beat' generates a pointillistic type of groove.

Sonority juxtapositions: Pitch and rock-inspired textures

In terms of sonority, *Frumious* blends the atonal sound-world of contemporary art music with the tonal world of rock to create a harmonic portmanteau, juxtaposing playful and dark moods, dissonance and consonance. My tonal harmonic language often eschews traditional chord hierarchies in favour of a vertical stacking technique. From the very first chord, there is a vertical emphasis on major and minor seconds. Throughout the piece, seconds are repeatedly stacked and reorganised into different octaves creating a kind of layered cluster effect. These cluster chords give way to visceral sound-slabs, capturing the timbral rebellion of rock. The clusters quite literally act as chordal portmanteaus, fusing multiple chords or triads together to create a new chord. As Example 12.4a shows, the first chord of the piece uses tones from the whole-tone series stacked from E through to C (E, F♯, G♯, A♯, C), with additional tones of F and B creating semi-tone clashes. The chord plays with space by assigning each of these notes into different octaves and alternating instrumental colours. Yet, within some stacked chords, there is also a 'hidden' functional chord and triadic element at work. Embedded seconds and sevenths 'disguise' and colour thirds, fourths and fifths. Example 12.4b, from rehearsal A, shows a series of chords, which also use this atonal stacking technique. Within these interval stacks are 'hidden' chords that are defined by their spacing within the sonority, but the fast pace of these sound-slabs makes it difficult to distinguish these chords unless they are played in isolation. As Example 12.4c shows, the first chord is a B♭ major chord and a C power-chord, the second a 'disguised' C dominant seventh chord, coloured by stacked seconds, while the third and fourth are atonal stacks, comprising of whole-tone series and semi-tone clashes. In the first two chords, open notes show functional chords and closed

A musical portmanteau   159

Table 12.3 Frumious – Groove variegated timbre accents

Bar	Beat	Instrument groupings	Number of quarter rests before next accent
124	1	Trumpets, trombone, bassoon, bass drum, and double bass	4
124	3.5	Oboe, clarinets, horns, bassoon, bass drum and double bass	3
125	1.5	Horns, trumpets, trombone, bassoon, bass drum and double bass	2
125	3	Oboe, clarinets, bassoon, bass drum and double bass	1
125	4	Oboe, clarinets, horns, bassoon, bass drum and double bass	0
125	4.5	Oboe, clarinets, and trumpet	4
126	3	Oboe, clarinets, horn and trumpet	0
126	3.5	Oboe, clarinets, trumpet, bassoon, bass drum and double bass	1
126	4.5	Piccolo, trumpets, trombone, bassoon, bass drum and double bass	4
127	3	Strings	0
127	3.5	Piccolo, trumpets, trombone and strings	1
127	4.5	Oboe, clarinets and trumpet	4
128	3	Piccolo, oboe, clarinets, horns, trumpets, and trombone	2
128	4.5	Oboe, clarinets, trumpet, bassoon, bass drum and double bass	0
129	1	Trumpet, strings, bassoon, bass drum and double bass	1
129	2	Oboe, clarinet, trumpet, strings, bassoon, bass drum and double bass	

notes show additional stacked intervals, while in the third and fourth chords, open notes show whole-tone series and closed notes, clashes.

Throughout *Frumious* I use fifths and octaves in the French horns, low brass and low strings to reimagine the ubiquitous rock power-chord by colouring it with atonal stackings. The preponderance of augmented fourths throughout the piece further enhances the sense of an ambiguous sonority, allowing a quick alternation between dark and playful moods. In opposition to the atonal chords, some sound-blocks have tonal centres, or implied tonal centres, and make use of (almost) functional chord progressions at Rehearsals B, E, F, J, M, and T. While being inspired by rock sonorities, my vertical stacking and hidden chord techniques also resonate with Igor Stravinsky's harmonic concepts. The well-known opening passage of

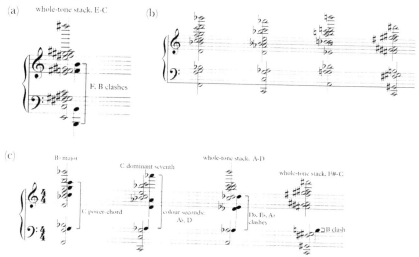

Example 12.4a–c *Frumious*, interval stacking: Atonal stacks and 'hidden chords'.
(a) Chord reduction, bar 1; (b) Atonal stacks, bars 22–23;
(c) 'Hidden chords', bars 22–23.

'Augurs of Spring: Dances of the Young Girls', from *The Rite of Spring* (1913), stacks an E♭7 chord in the violins and violas over an F♭ major chord in the lower strings to create a menacing dissonance.[11] In Stravinsky's orchestration, the French horn stabs highlight the displaced accents in the percussive string line, also voicing the two distinct chords. In *Frumious*, I use Stravinsky's stacking technique to create new sonorities and combine that with the power-chord stacks from rock music to create a harmonic portmanteau.

Frumious also employs various timbral and articulatory techniques to create a rock-influenced 'dirty' sound, including flutter-tonguing, glissandi, trills, slides, lip bends, Harmon mute wah wahs and trills. As Example 12.5 shows, the repeated rhythmic figure in the unison strings at bar 145 resonates with the 'breakdown' section synonymous with progressive rock and metal styles. Here the staccato strings imitate the palm-muted accents of guitar and double-kick bass drum and the double bass plays the main accents of the phrase with a percussive slap pizzicato articulation. The tonal centre hovers around D, which pays homage to the de-tuned guitars of progressive rock and heavy metal. The percussion also emulate timbral rock techniques and conventions with the frequent use of cymbal chokes, rimshots and clicks, flams, hi-hat doubling sticking, and clamorous half-opened hi-hats, along with rhythmic techniques of repeated figures and use of a backbeat. *Frumious* becomes a timbral portmanteau, as rock-inspired timbres and techniques are performed by orchestral instruments in a concert setting.

Musical design

The rhythmic and sonority juxtapositions of *Frumious* are regulated by a series of carefully designed structural juxtapositions. At first, the rapid shifts from sound-block to sound-block appear disorienting and make little sense, but as the piece

Example 12.5 Frumious, rhythmic textures and slap pizzicato, bars 145–150.

continues, the recurrence and manipulation of each of these opposing blocks constructs a new type of sense via reorganisation to create a musical portmanteau. Figure 12.1 schematises the global design of *Frumious*'s juxtapositions. As the figure suggests, each block has its own rhythmic character and, like the polyphony of nonsense, follows a different 'thread' of the patchwork structure. Throughout *Frumious*, the sense of opposing blocks lurks under the surface or it is overtly present as conflict, and in all instances, the blocks maintain their original meanings as do the meanings in Carroll's portmanteau words. During *Frumious*'s rapidly changing textures dense timbral slabs are pitted against small group interjections, frequently toggling between colour combinations in an almost pointillistic way. This call and response behaviour generates a textural portmanteau, where different textural characters collide vertically and horizontally; relentless density coexists with nervy note splatters, and sustained lines are superimposed with vertical stabs. Instrument groups and sound-blocks cut in and out of the texture as material is tossed about the orchestra in a combative call and response way creating a spattering of different timbral layerings. Example 12.6, citing bars 134–144, exemplifies this textural portmanteau. The excerpt is built from two wedge-like shapes positioned either side of a two bar sound-slab (bars 137–138). The first block quickly accumulates in density, reaches its peak texture, and then dissipates as a scattering of colour group fragments. *Frumious*'s visceral energy, captured by dense unison rhythms and atonal stacks, draws influence from rock band textures and is set against interruptive and fragmented textures which resonate with Zorn and Ives.

Block organisation of time

Rapidly changing time signatures, frequent tempo fluctuations, pauses, rallentandos and accelerandos contribute to a playful rhythmic elasticity, which teases the listener. These changes act as tools to both connect and disrupt sound-blocks, working to intensify or disperse energy. Some of these changes are gradual but for the most part they are sudden, harnessing the abrupt juxtapositional channel-surfing techniques of Zorn. As Table 12.4 shows, *Frumious* continually changes tempo throughout, alternating blocks of speed with funky and dreamy blocks,

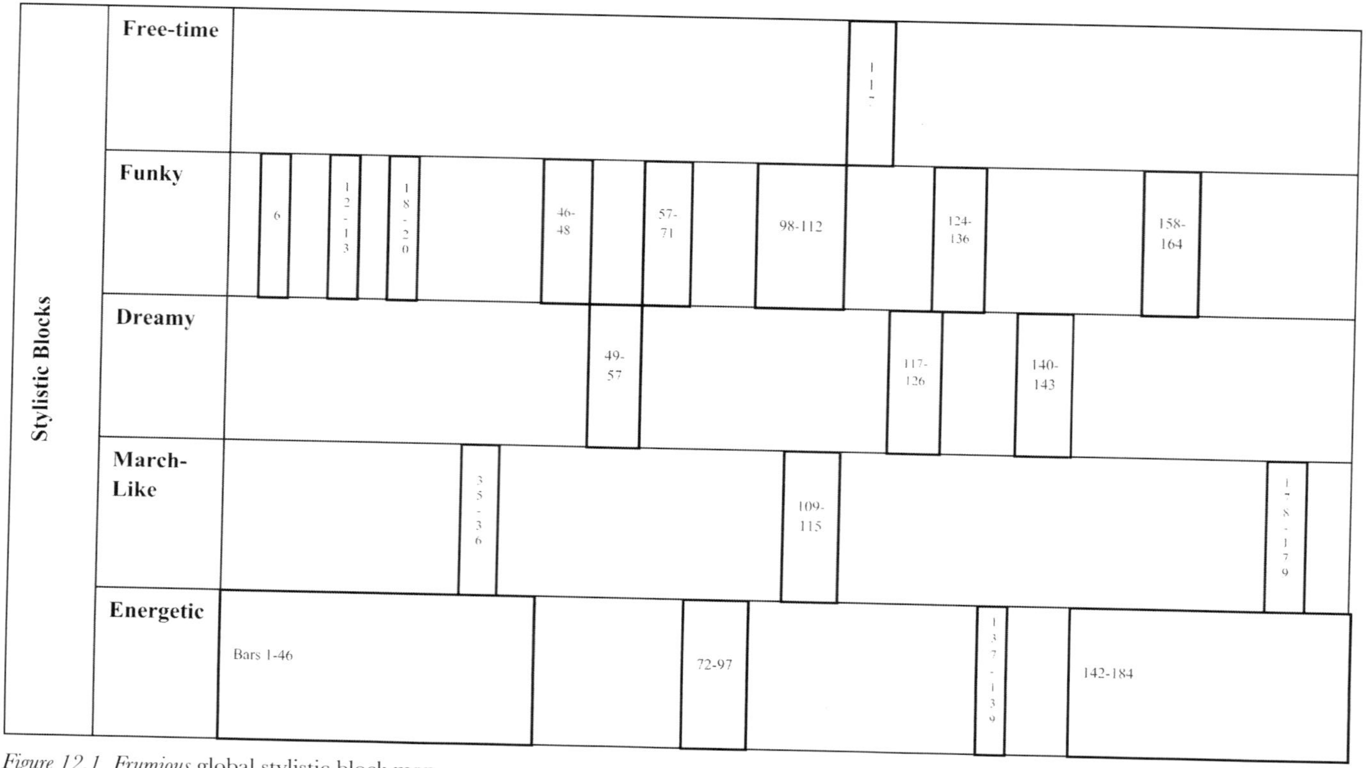

Figure 12.1 Frumious global stylistic block map.

Table 12.4 *Frumious* tempo map

Bar	1	21	22	35	37	46	49	58 60	61	64	72	75	76	97	99
Tempo	♩ = 110	G.P	♩ = 115	♩ = 105	♩ = 115	Rit.	♩ = 88	Accel.	♩ = 115	♩ = 110	♩ = 115	Poco rall.	♩ = 115	Molto rall.	q = 115
Mood Indication	Energetic		Energetic	Suddenly Slower	Energetic	Funky	Dreamy			Funky	Energetic		A Tempo		Funky

110	113 116	117 (18")	118	119 123	124	125	126 133	137	139	140	145	174	178	180	Fine.
♩ = 90	Molto rall.	Free-time	♩ = 80	rall.	♩ = 60	♩ = 80	Molto Accel.	♩ = 115	Molto rall.	♩ = 80	♩ = 115	♩ = 110	♩ = 75	♩ = 115	
Meno Mosso Subito		Solo Piccolo	Dreamy		Molto Meno Mosso			Energetic			Driving	Slightly Slower	Heavy and Suddenly Slower	Energetic	

164 *Holly Harrison*

from the fastest tempo of q = 115 to the slowest of q = 60, to the free-time piccolo solo of Rehearsal K. In contrast to hard-edge juxtapositions, accelerandos and rallentandos occur over a series of bars helping to connect disparate sound-blocks by providing a common denominator of pulse that prepares the listener for change.

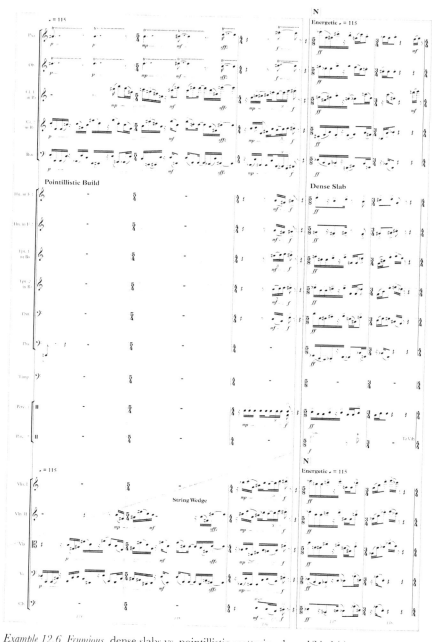

Example 12.6 *Frumious*, dense slabs vs. pointillistic scattering, bars 134–144.

A musical portmanteau 165

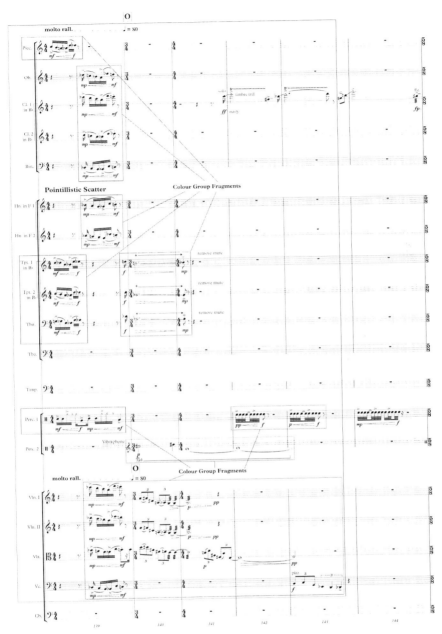

Example 12.6 *Frumious*, dense slabs vs. pointillistic scattering, bars 134–144.

Conclusion

By pitting musical oppositions against each other to form musical portmanteaus, *Frumious* flattens the hierarchy between popular and art musics to question the idea of hierarchy itself. The sound-blocks' antagonistic interactions aspire to challenge the perceived incompatibility of conflicting ideas, whilst also demonstrating their compatibility. As Susan Stewart discusses, nonsense emerges from the real and imagined friction between the collision of similar and dissimilar worlds. Born from a series of dual processes and inspired by the intersection of disparate sound-worlds, my aesthetic embraces a designed double energy of rhythmic vitality and visceral sonority. This duality extends to the interaction between music and literature, where Carroll's portmanteau words have provided an imaginative springboard for seemingly incompatible worlds and the convergence of musical oppositions. The intersection of rock and art music domains, via drum kit and hocket techniques, grooves and disruptions, rapid tempo and time signatures changes, textural density and call and response, and interval stacking and posttonal densities, are continually rearranged by a carefully designed juxtapositional architecture. My aesthetic further extends the metaphor of Carroll's portmanteau words by reimagining them in a three-dimensional setting, where musical portmanteaus function horizontally and vertically, with differing densities, as successive and superimposed blocks. The friction created by musical portmanteaus enriches my emerging aesthetic; it posits nonsense as the disorganisation and reorganisation of sense and brings together polyphonic threads to produce a designed double energy.

Notes

1 Holly Harrison, *Frumious* (Sydney, unpublished, 2012). An excerpt of *Frumious* may be heard at SoundCloud, accessed 5 March 2014, https://soundcloud.com/hollyharrisoncomposer/frumious-excerpt.

2 Susan Stewart, *Nonsense: Aspects of Intertextuality in Folklore and Literature* (Baltimore: Johns Hopkins University Press, 1989), 35.

3 Lewis Carroll, *Alice's Adventures in Wonderland* and *Through The Looking-Glass And What Alice Found There* (London: Vintage Books, 2007 [first published in 1865 and 1871]), 180-82.

4 Jean-Jacques Lecercle, *Philosophy of Nonsense: The Intuitions of Victorian Nonsense Literature* (London and New York: Routledge, 1994), 179.

5 Kevin McNeilly, 'Ugly Beauty: John Zorn and the Politics of Postmodern Music', *Postmodern Culture* 5/2 (1995): para.8 (doi:10.1353/pmc.1995.0005).

6 J. Peter Burkholder, *Charles Ives: The Ideas Behind the Music* (New Haven: Yale University Press, 1985), 3.

7 Louis Andriessen, *The Art of Stealing Time*, ed. Mirjam Zegers (Todmorden, UK: Arc Music, 2002), 148, 178.

8 Richard Middleton, 'Popular Music Analysis and Musicology: Bridging the Gap', *Popular Music* 12/2 (1993), 180-81. Ethnomusicologists Steven Feld and Charles Keil have also written extensively about groove. Feld writes that groove is an 'intuitive sense of style as process, a perception of a cycle in motion'. See Feld, 'Aesthetics as Iconicity of Style, or "Lift-up-over Sounding": Getting into the Kaluli Groove', *Yearbook for Traditional Music* 20 (1988), 74. And for Keil a concept of 'participatory discrepancies'

documents how being somewhat 'out of time' and 'out of tune', especially in jazz and folk music, generates its own kind of groove. See Keil, 'Participatory Discrepancies and the Power of Music', *Cultural Anthropology* 2/3 (1987), 275–83.

9   John Roeder, 'The Craft of Hybrid Composition: Meter, Tonality, and Grouping in Michael Torke's "Adjustable Wrench"', *Perspectives of New Music* 41/22 (2003), 135 and 127. Reproduced with kind permission.

10 Roeder, 'The Craft', 127.

11 The bitonality of the opening of 'Augurs of Spring' had a precedent in Stravinsky's earlier ballet *Petrouchka*, which juxtaposes triads on C and F♯.

Part IV
Immanent listening

13 Immanent listening

Sally Macarthur

Listening is vital to music but to pin it down to a definition has proven difficult because what is 'heard' by any one person is unverifiable and has no specifiable correlation with the acoustical properties of sound. Listening, along with hearing and the 'ear', turn out to be metaphors for a complex constellation of physical, psychological, historical and cultural factors. Listening assumes a range of engagements, encompassing varying degrees of attention across a variety of sounding phenomena and raises a number of questions. Does sound exist independently of anyone who listens? Where does the ear begin and sound end, and vice versa? To complicate matters even more, are our engagements with sound solely a matter for the sense of hearing? What role do our other senses, such as touch and sight, play in listening?[1] Is listening a passive or active engagement with sound? Might we imagine that sound attends to us? How might listening play a role in subject formation? How might listening be caught up with an ideological agenda, or are sounding phenomena necessarily non-ideological as physical entities in the world? These are just some of the contested issues in the research about listening, which have produced a diversity of opinion and some of this opinion is captured in the next two chapters in Part IV of this collection.

Despite this diversity of thinking in the field of listening, much of the research tends to view it as a more or less stable activity and to think of sounding phenomena as fitting neatly into ready-made categories. These categories – such as music, noise, natural and synthetic sounds, and spoken, sung and vocalised language – are then taken as givens. When sound is treated as an object, it is defined, standardised, measured and manipulated. In Deleuzian thought, this produces the figure of the Same. Sound becomes homogenised and our ways of engaging with it set in train endlessly recurring patterns of listening, diminishing the possibilities for difference. Such approaches to sound fail to acknowledge the heterogeneity of sound, and the fact that it will continuously spill out of its categories and/or overlap with other categories.[2] Deleuze's philosophical framework provides a productive alternative approach to such representational modes of listening. In representational modes, the listener is trained to reproduce an existing model of 'what sound is' – thus *re*presenting that which is prescribed by, for instance, musical notation or theoretical systems of musical organisation. But what happens to listening if these requirements to 'hear correctly' are lifted? What happens when the trained ear and sounds disengage from one another, becoming discrete entities, bouncing off each other and 'continually transform[ing] themselves into each other, cross[ing] over into each other'?[3] Such a question highlights

172 *Sally Macarthur*

the complexity of listening and the difference between listening as a mode of representation and immanent listening. In this chapter, I will map some of the research on listening, interspersing it with a Deleuzian critique.

In a mode of immanence, listening makes perceptible what is as yet imperceptible. From a Deleuzian perspective, such listening oscillates between the real and the possible, and the actual and the virtual. These ontological couplings capture the complexity of listening. Listening may entail the possible when sound is comprehended as familiar or as a resemblance to other sounds that pre-exist it. For example, the sound of white noise imitating the wind, to draw on O'Sullivan, is 'a kind of representation of the real [wind] that appears to pre-exist it'.[4] It is not the wind itself but rather an 'isotope of the real inasmuch as it only lacks reality'.[5] It thus 'doubles like with like'.[6] The virtual, in comparison, excludes the notion of the identical as a prior condition and, as O'Sullivan, drawing on Deleuze, explains, it 'names a real place but one which has yet to be actualised'.[7] Actualisation of the virtual is thus a creative act, which opens up difference and, as Deleuze puts it, produces 'a pure multiplicity'.[8] The actualisation of the virtual as the sound of white noise, then, will produce limitless, dynamic engagements and responses 'which correspond to without resembling a virtual multiplicity'.[9]

Listening moves between representation and immanence. When listening encounters the sonic object as immanence, as Deleuze writes of the encounter with any object, 'it forces us to think. This something is an object not of recognition but of a fundamental encounter … its primary characteristic is that it can only be sensed.'[10] When listening treats sound as an object of recognition, to draw on O'Sullivan, it 'is a *re*presentation of something always already in place'.[11] Listening, in this sense, remains anchored to the plane of representation. The primary characteristic of the object of recognition is that we are already familiar with it. Our listening will therefore affirm and reinforce our habitual ways of listening. In a music aural skills class the typical mode of listening is recognition. For example, trained listeners will listen for the familiar in order to reproduce the training. In the second movement of Webern's Variations for Piano, op. 27, they will notate the first eight bars of the inverted row and its movement canonically against the retrograde inversion. However, in the process of executing this intricate task, the listener may not register having heard other aspects of the music (or that the music is itself hearing itself). In the academic setting, such listening would not necessarily be encouraged. The novice listener outside the context of the aural skills class, who is unfamiliar with Webern's musical style and lacking the skills to notate the music, might be able to represent the music using descriptive language, suggesting that it sounds like 'mosquitos darting chaotically about the room'. But like the expert listener, the novice will not necessarily notice that had heard other aspects. In both examples, the listener attempts to reflect the music, illuminating it with notated or verbal representation. But neither the expert's nor the novice's account is complete or correct.

From these examples, it becomes clear that listening establishes a relationship between the listener and the sounding phenomenon, shaping the listener as much as the listener shapes the sound. But much of the research on listening has been invested in maintaining a clear ontological separation between sound and listener. The image of thought that produces this separation is concerned with identity: it gives rise to an assumed human listener who is privileged over a non-human sound object. In this portrayal, the listener identifies the music; the listener identifies *with* the music; and the music identifies itself to the listener. And yet, in all these encounters, as implied by the title of an essay by Murphy, as a virtual phenomenon, music 'is thinking too'.[12] The notion of listening as an experimental mode opens up the plane of immanence. As immanence, listening resembles nothing outside itself. From a Deleuzian perspective, immanent listening (as with thought) 'demands "only" movement that can be carried to infinity'.[13]

Listening as an infinite multiplicity in the Deleuzian framework contrasts the avalanche of research in empirical studies that defines listening as a rigidly differentiated field.[14] One of the common assumptions is that, unlike seeing, in which 'the gaze' is understood as a central trope, there is no central auditory trope that is equivalent to 'the listen'. In its place, Sterne argues, 'there are dozens of figures and figurations of audition'.[15] Some of these are that listening is immersive, attentive, semantic, causal, deep, reduced, heightened, active, passive, virtuosic and ubiquitous. The attempts to organise listening into these types of identity categories, however, conceal as much as they reveal about listening. Furthermore, individuals engaged in particular types of listening will inevitably exceed the categories that seek to contain them. Chion, for example, characterises listening in terms of three modes: causal, semantic and reduced listening.[16] Causal listening involves associating sounds with their cause. Semantic listening assumes that we listen for the meaning of the sound or that we listen to gain an understanding of what is being transmitted. But, as Chion also points out, semantic and causal listening will often overlap when they are employed simultaneously. Reduced listening, which is a concept attributed to Pierre Schaeffer, focuses on the traits of the sound object itself 'independent of its cause and of its meaning'.[17] According to Schaeffer, reduced listening is a 'listening attitude which consists in listening to the sound for its own sake'.[18] This idea, discussed earlier in this volume by Stevenson, proposes that the concrete qualities of sound can be isolated from their meanings and that the listener would be unable to identify the basis or origin of the sound. And yet, for Schaeffer, listening and the sound object are correlates of each other, defining 'each other mutually and respectively as perceptual activity and the object of perception'.[19] Given that the listener and the sound object are co-implicated in this way, as Voeglin points out, reduced listening is not actually 'reducing but freeing [the sonic] and opening it up to a multitude of possibilities'.[20] Voeglin, then, alludes to the immanent listening that I have been discussing above.

According to Deleuze, every object is defined by the qualities it possesses and the extension that it occupies. Hughes suggests that in Deleuze's philosophy these two characteristics – quality and extensity – are 'the basic elements of representation'.[21] As representations, then, Schaeffer's sonic object and the listener's perceptual activity are categorised, each with well-defined borders. The sonic object functions as individuated matter in that it occupies an actual temporal space and is defined by a particular set of qualities such as timbre, pitch and

174 *Sally Macarthur*

duration. However, the undifferentiated state of sonic matter is simultaneously present, characterised by a permanent becoming which draws its power from the virtual. In the process of actualisation, to follow Hughes, the sonic object is shaped into extensive parts from which its qualities are determined.[22]

This understanding of Schaeffer's sound object and perceptual activity has implications for other distinctions such as those drawn between hearing and listening, and hearing and vision. A widely held view is that it is possible to hear something without listening to it, and that hearing is active and listening is passive. These terms of hearing and listening toggle back and forth between active and passive. Jean-Luc Nancy, for example, argues that there is a difference between listening and hearing, and that the habituated practices in philosophy privilege hearing. Typically, philosophy hears in order to make meaning of what is being said and, in this sense, hearing is active. Nancy goes on to explore whether it is possible to listen (in philosophy) while simultaneously addressing hearing and understanding, or whether listening can simply resound and not direct itself to meaning. This question is considered by Toltz who, in this part of the book, revisits some earlier research he conducted with Jewish Holocaust survivors. He explains that he asked his participants about the role of music in their lives during their time of incarceration. It becomes apparent in Toltz's chapter that there is 'listening and listening'. As Davies puts it elsewhere, we either listen 'to fit what we hear into what we already know' or we listen as an activity involving a continual openness to the not-yet-known.[23] Listening as a continual openness to the not-yet-known is what Davies describes as 'emergent listening'. It is the kind of listening that is about being 'open to being affected' and 'about being open to difference and, in particular, to difference in all its multiplicity as it emerges in each moment in between oneself and another'.[24] Indirectly, Toltz's work embraces this idea of emergent listening while also engaging Nancy to consider how the Holocaust survivor testimonies in his own study might be understood as powerful memories resounding in the present day. As he makes the point, these are not merely memories, for in the accounts of the survivors, music is recalled as it was imagined to have been heard in the past and, at the same time, as if it is being heard again in the present day for the first time. This kind of immanent listening, as taken up by Toltz from Nancy, produces an active, resonant space.[25]

The active/passive distinction between hearing and listening in Nancy's meditation also finds resonance in Sterne's differential between vision and hearing. For Sterne, 'hearing is primarily a temporal sense, vision is primarily a spatial sense; hearing is a sense that immerses us in the world, while vision removes us from it'.[26] Sterne's model of listening treats the sonic object, like that of Schaeffer above, as a separate and differentiated entity, which is distinct from other entities. In so doing, it produces an act of thinking that reflects sameness. Music studies are abundant with examples of reflective (sameness) thinking. The score is typically treated as a mirror image of the music's sound, and the use of visual and spatial metaphors, such as high and low for pitch qualities, collapses the sense of sight into that of hearing. For Stead in this part, the dominance of reflective listening in music scholarship has negative ramifications for acousmatic music.[27] Such listening perpetuates the ideology of the autonomous work, treating it as a reified, visual object. In Stead's analysis, music is seen rather than heard. Unlike Western art music with its visual documents (scores), bodies (performers) and objects (instruments), as she makes the point, acousmatic music includes very little – if any – visual information.

It is clear that this visual rendition of music produces a comparison between sound and sight. In a Deleuzian sense, such a comparison is based on an external, negative notion of difference: vision as positive versus audition as negative. These identity categories of difference rely on their ontological separateness. In this style of thinking, difference is always constructed as negative. It suggests a difference in a system that is reliant on separation and division. Contrary to this, positive difference opens it up as an effect of connections and relations within and between sound and bodies such that each is affected and goes on continuously being affected by each other. Positive difference, in Deleuze's relational ontology, is like life itself: a continuum and a multiplicity in a constant state of becoming or differentiation in relation to each singular body, as it affects other bodies and is itself affected.[28]

Stead asks whether Deleuze and Guattari's concept of the desiring-machine would offer a more productive theoretical model for listening practices in the academy. While Stead is not arguing to replace or overthrow the dominant visual model, she is suggesting that institutions need to address this issue. It would seem that Stead has an ally in Kassabian who asserts that our listening practices in institutions and music scholarship need to acknowledge the '*range of engagements* between and across human bodies and music technologies, whether those technologies be voices, instruments, sound systems, or iPods and other listening devices'.[29] In Kassabian's view, tertiary music institutions continue to train musicians to listen to music as if none of these technologies had been invented. Like Stead, Kassabian argues that theories of narrative are the culprit, which she says is the dominant listening paradigm favoured in the modern music institution.[30] The narrative paradigm, which undergirds Adorno's typology of listeners, privileging the expert listener above all others, imagines that this individual is 'fully conscious, fully attentive, and able to hear longitudinal, structural relationships in large-scale musical works … [such a listener] hears the sequence, hears the past, present and future moments together so that they crystallize into a meaningful context'.[31] For Kassabian, this approach to listening is problematic because it does not encompass the range of music in the present day and the ways in which listeners engage with this music. Given that musicology has shown how particular practices of listening produce the canon, predisposing listeners to the very musics of their training – which is a point made by McClary earlier in this volume – then it follows that other modes of listening would produce and reproduce other repertoires.[32]

Kassabian insists that 'all listening is physiological and that many kinds of listening take place over a wide range of degrees or kinds of consciousness and attention'.[33] She challenges the routine uses of listening in music and sound studies scholarship. Because our sonic environments have radically changed it follows that our listening habits have also changed.[34] While attentive listening is

176 *Sally Macarthur*

appropriate for some music it is not appropriate for all music. Different kinds of listening encounters are entailed in music for film and television, iPods and smart phones, and video games and audio books. Such listening has barely made an entrance into the curricula of tertiary music institutions. Institutions still seem to be focused on the acoustic properties or aesthetic values or being able to reproduce the music in notated form, thus representing the music.[35]

In this short chapter, I have critiqued some of the listening models that are widely used in music institutions. In effect, I have shown that these are bound up with politics. In Deleuzian thought politics is not a separate field. As Bergen writes, politics is 'an orientation operating at the heart of every assemblage; its lines meeting everywhere where an assemblage individual or collective, of thought or of desire operates'.[36] The assemblage constituted as listening, then, can be understood as continually arranging and rearranging itself in terms of this political cartography. The movement between the actual and the virtual are entangled in 'intra-active' flows, to borrow the term from Barad.[37] These are opened up by encounters in which listeners and listening objects construct diagrams as they are affecting and being affected by one another. This gives rise to a double process that avoids fixing listeners and sound objects in a duality because the pole that draws hard boundaries around the sonic object and the pole that seeks to break free of these borders 'work on each other in a co-functionality which is subject to an incessant dynamism'.[38] When the sonic object opens to the plane of immanence the sonic object fades. The distinction between the listener and the sound object, the listener and the hearer, and listening and vision vanish.

In conclusion, the desiring-machine as suggested by Stead, might be imagined as a listening that 'hears' the sound towards which it directs itself, allowing for the becoming of the listener, the becoming of sound, and the becoming of listening as a multimodal activity. Listening as immanence, in this sense, would open a space for the becoming of future ways of listening. Such a conception of immanent listening calls on us to attend to the multifarious manifestations of listening in all its textured specificity and, to borrow from Lorraine, 'to open ourselves up to responses that go beyond a repertoire of comfortably familiar, automatic reactions'.[39] Thinking listening in this way potentially affirms what listening is as well as unfolding what it could become.

Notes

1 For example, recent research suggests that listening is not just confined to the ear but is experienced in other parts of the body as well. See Steph Ceraso, '(Re)Educating the Senses: Multimodal Listening, Bodily Learning, and the Composition of Sonic Experiences', *College English* 77/3 (2014), 102 23.

2 Ceraso highlights a significant issue raised by the idea of difference, saying that the 'deeply entrenched association between ears and the act of listening' (102) does not capture all that is involved in experiencing the sonic event. She says that it is 'possible to feel sound in one's stomach, throat and legs, and other areas of the body' (102), and that what is needed is a concept of 'multimodal listening' to expand how we think about and experience listening as a 'full bodied act' (103). She cites the well-known

example of deaf percussionist, Dame Evelyn Glennie, demonstrating how, in this case, multimodal listening not only changes the way in which we might view deafness but that understanding multiple sensory modes – such as sight, sound and touch – would expand and deepen the ways in which we might encounter multimodality in our scholarship and teaching. See Ceraso, '(Re)Educating the Senses', 102–23.

3   Gilles Deleuze and Félix Guattari, *A Thousand Plateaus: Capitalism and Schizophrenia*, trans. Brian Massumi (Minneapolis and London: University of Minnesota Press, 1987), 249.

4   Simon O'Sullivan, *Art Encounters: Deleuze and Guattari's Thought beyond Representation* (Houndmills, Basingstoke: Palgrave Macmillan, 2006), 100.

5   O'Sullivan, *Art Encounters*, 100.

6   Gilles Deleuze, *Difference and Repetition*, trans. Paul Patton (New York: Columbia University Press, 1994), 212.

7   O'Sullivan, *Art Encounters*, 103.

8   Deleuze, *Difference and Repetition*, 211.

9   Deleuze, *Difference and Repetition*, 212.

10 Deleuze, *Difference and Repetition*, 139.

11 O'Sullivan, *Art Encounters*, 1.

12 Timothy S. Murphy, 'What I Hear is Thinking Too: The Deleuze Tribute Recordings', in *Deleuze and Music*, ed. Ian Buchanan and Marcel Swiboda (Edinburgh: Edinburgh University Press, 2004), 159–75.

13 Gilles Deleuze and Félix Guattari, *What is Philosophy?*, trans. Hugh Tomlinson and Graham Burchell (New York: Columbia University Press, 1994[1991]), 37.

14 Some additions to the field include: Eric F. Clarke, *Ways of Listening: An Ecological Approach to the Perception of Musical Meaning* (New York: Oxford University Press, 2005); Salomé Voeglin, *Listening to Noise and Silence: Towards a Philosophy of Sound Art* (New York: Continuum, 2010); Joanna Demers, *Listening Through the Noise: The Aesthetics of Experimental Electronic Music* (Oxford: Oxford University Press, 2010); Jonathan Sterne, *The Sound Studies Reader* (London and New York: Routledge, 2012); and Anahid Kassabian, *Ubiquitous Listening: Affect, Attention, and Distributed Subjectivity* (Berkeley, Los Angeles and London: University of California Press, 2013).

15 Jonathon Sterne, 'Hearing, Listening, Deafness' in *The Sound Studies Reader*, 19.

16 Michel Chion, 'The Three Modes of Listening', in *The Sound Studies Reader*, ed. Jonathan Sterne (London and New York: Routledge, 2012), 48–53.

17 Chion, 'The Three Modes of Listening', 50.

18 Pierre Schaeffer in Leigh Landy, *Understanding the Art of Sound Organization* (Cambridge, MA: MIT Press, 2007), 35; also cited in Linda Kouvaras, *Loading the Silence: Australian Sound Art in the Post-Digital Age* (Farnham, UK and Burlington, VT: Ashgate, 2013), 26.

19 Schaeffer in Landy, *Understanding the Art of Sound Organization*, 26.

20 Salomé Voeglin, *Listening to Noise and Silence*, 35; quoted in Kouvaras, *Loading the Silence*, 26, n. 24.

21 Joe Hughes, *Philosophy After Deleuze* (London and New York: Bloomsbury, 2012), 54.

22 Hughes, *Philosophy After Deleuze*, 55.

23 Bronwyn Davies, *Listening to Children: Being and Becoming* (London and New York: Routledge, 2014), xi.

24 Davies, *Listening to Children*, xi.

25 Jean-Luc Nancy, *Listening*, trans. C. Mandell (New York: Fordham University Press, 2007).

26 Sterne, *The Sound Studies Reader*, 9.

27 According to Kouvaras, the term 'acousmatic' is rooted in Husserlian phenomenology which, in turn, has its origins in Pythagorean philosophy. The idea is that Pythagoras would speak, hidden behind a curtain, so that his listeners would not be distracted by extraneous things such as facial expressions or bodily gestures. Kouvaras says that the term was reintroduced in 1955 by Jérôme Peignot to suggest 'distance which separates

178 *Sally Macarthur*

sounds from their origin', that is, 'an audio-only presentation of sound common to electro-acoustic music'. See Kouvaras, *Loading the Silence*, n. 22, 25–6.

28 Deleuze, *Difference and Repetition*, 163.

29 Kassabian, *Ubiquitous Listening*, xi.

30 Kassabian, *Ubiquitous Listening*, xii.

31 Theodor Adorno, *Introduction to the Sociology of Music* (New York and London: Continuum, 1988), 4: cited in Kassabian, *Ubiquitous Listening*, xii.

32 Kassabian, *Ubiquitous Listening*, 6.

33 Kassabian, *Ubiquitous Listening*, xxi–xxii.

34 Kassabian, *Ubiquitous Listening*, xxi–xxii.

35 Kassabian, *Ubiquitous Listening*, 17.

36 Véronique Bergen, 'Politics as the Orientation of Every Assemblage', trans. Jeremy Gilbert, *New Formations* 68/2 (2009), 34.

37 For Karen Barad, the concept 'intra-action' '*signifies the mutual constitution of entangled agencies*. That is, in contrast to the usual "inter-action", which assumes that there are separate individual agencies that precede their interaction, the notion of intra-action recognizes that distinct agencies do not precede, but rather emerge through, their intra-action. It is important to note that "distinct" agencies are only distinct in a relational, not an absolute, sense, that is, *agencies are only distinct in relation to their mutual entanglement; they don't exist as individual elements.*' Karen Barad, *Meeting the Universe Halfway: Quantum Physics and the Entanglement of Matter and Meaning* (Durham, NC: Duke University Press, 2007), 33 [italics in the original].

38 Bergen, 'Politics as the Orientation', 36.

39 Tamsin Lorraine, *Deleuze and Guattari's Immanent Ethics: Theory, Subjectivity, and Duration* (New York: State University of New York Press, 2011), 1.

14 Seeing the sense

Imagining a new approach to acousmatic music and listening

Michelle Stead

Jonathon Crary argues that the dominance of vision in Western culture is a problem that is often assumed and adopted uncritically.[1] Rather than accept this problem as fact, he urges us to understand that this dominance is a problem that has emerged through complex power relations as a construct.[2] Contemporary musicological discourse accepts vision's privileged status as being evidenced by the musical score and, following Crary, this chapter argues that this, too, is a problem that has gone largely unquestioned.[3] Subsequently, a visual bias poses real implications for musics which are not written down (such as acousmatic music) and for the listener more broadly. Acousmatic music (music heard solely through loudspeakers) relies upon a *lack* of visual information and therefore does not fit neatly into an epistemological framework that cites vision as the dominant way of knowing. Thus, I argue that the portrayal of vision as the dominant way of knowing is disconcerting and potentially damaging, particularly for a discipline such as music that takes sound as its foundation. By drawing on the concept of difference as posited by Deleuze and Guattari,[4] a space is opened up whereby listeners are free to engage with the music without the limits of opticality.

Bull and Back preface their book with the assertion that our culture and language promotes sight as the source of knowledge.[5] However, even in 2003, when their book was published, this idea was not a new one. The privileged status of vision within the context of the history of Western art music has been scrutinised in the last three decades by musicologists. They have argued that the preoccupation with the visual is exemplified in music discourse by the elevated status of the musical score.[6] The score acts both as a visual representation of the composition and instruction booklet for the performer. More importantly, however, it is held as both the container of, and the key to, unlocking the composer's intentions.[7] Supported by music analysis, the written score is considered to be the ultimate authority over and above any audible realisation of the work.[8] To quote Richard Taruskin, 'the score produced by such exacting toil is now regarded (or if the composer is great enough, venerated) as a definitive text embodying the "work", of which performances can only be imperfect representations'.[9] The rise of the score is also inexorably linked to the rise of the individual as a self-governing and sovereign subject.[10]

180 *Michelle Stead*

Along with the instigation of commodity capitalism, printing played a part in the objectification of music as an artefact and, importantly, an artefact that was imprinted with the name of the composer and therefore rendered visible to history. Taruskin, following Foucault, warns that the act of naming is both a mechanism of power and a symptom of the grand narrative.[11] It took Barthes nearly a century after the Romantics to demonstrate that the authority of the composer-as-author is not natural but rather an effect of capitalism — a construct.[12] For Foucault, however, the function of the author is predominantly an attempt to unify and solidify a narrative that demonstrates personal progress and development of the work of the author/composer-genius.[13] The irony of this idea was not lost on Foucault and he fought to eschew any kind of positioning of his work (and his person) in this way. In an often cited account he says, 'do not ask who I am and do not ask me to remain the same'.[14] Thus, Foucault sees each new work produced by the author as different and unrelated to previous works.[15]

The act of writing music for the purpose of communicating musical ideas from composer to performer is also an act of power and, as Taruskin explains, reinforces the elevated status of the composer, thereby rendering the status of the performer to slave.[16] Furthermore, 'naming' validates the work as historical documentary fact and therefore functions as an exclusionary measure in order to maintain disciplinary boundaries.[17] Works considered for inclusion within the canon have to undergo a complex process, which means that the works will be, to quote Mills, 'circulated throughout society, reproduced in books, they will appear in school curricula and they will be commented on, described and evaluated by others in books and articles',[18] thus confirming and perpetuating the idea that the work was in fact a masterwork and that the composer a genius. Moreover, if these ideas are kept in circulation long enough, they contain enough institutional influence to be taken as natural common-sense knowledge.[19] The greatness of Beethoven, for example, is an opinion, not a fact. Yet his perceived greatness is accepted as factual, common-sense knowledge in an uncritical manner — a manner of which musicologists such as McClary were sceptical and subsequently deconstructed.[20] Upholding disciplinary boundaries is a complex process that is also enforced by the score. Discursively produced, the score therefore has the power to regulate the focus of the listener by structuring the listening experience and instructing listeners on how they should listen.[21] Listeners are therefore produced through the different mechanisms and manifestations of power by way of the institution and this occurs throughout music education. In this sense, the image of the musician (as a composer, a performer, analyst, etc.) is one that is shadowed by the image of the 'expert' listener produced through discourses such as music theory.

'Music theory' is a body of pedagogical discourse, which is intended to guide music students in developing the skills necessary for musical literacy, skills which Karpinski organises into ear-training and sight-singing.[22] As a body of discourse which is entrenched in academic music studies across the West, McCreless explains that music theory has been set the formidable task of teaching what are widely considered essential skills.[23] However, McCreless confesses that these skills are often taught in a fashion that has less in common with late twentieth- and

Seeing the sense   181

twenty-first-century scholarship than they do with the scholarship of the eighteenth and nineteenth centuries.[24]

One ear-training book promises that 'Beethoven's musical perception enabled him to write after losing his hearing. Your perception will allow you to transcribe or compose music without an instrument.'[25] This reference to Beethoven is interesting insomuch as Beethoven is the archetypal Romantic musical figure and he is upheld as embodying these nineteenth-century traits that reinforce the status of the individual composer as the creative-author-genius. More significantly, Beethoven was the exemplar of this music theory-in-action, in particular, the focus on being able to imagine the tones and timbres of music without actually being able to 'hear' them. His deafness meant that he was forced to draw on these skills, which have since come to be considered essential and common-sense skills for all 'good' musicians. This model therefore implicitly suggests that even profound deafness can be overcome, provided one is well disciplined in the doctrine of music theory.

It is Crary's argument, then, that since the nineteenth century, the subject has been discursively constructed in terms of a capability of 'paying attention'.[26] In other words, Crary argues that the problem of a 'lack of attention' is symptomatic of the greater social and cultural conditions of the second half of the nineteenth century rather than a natural fact or idea.[27] He demonstrates how, during the Romantic period, the very idea of 'paying attention' became a new object of study and similarly how a 'lack of attention' became a new problem, one which has been carried into present-day.[28]

Crary cites the reforms made by Wagner at the Bayreuth opera hall whereby an existing opera house was transformed specifically for the performance of Wagner's work.[29] The opera theatre was the first of its kind to implement elements which are taken today as standards in both opera and the theatre more broadly. These include a frontal view of the stage for the audience, and a lighting system that made the theatre itself extremely dark while keeping the stage illuminated.[30] To these alterations, Wagner also made a significant change in the location of the orchestra: rather than being on stage, it was moved below the stage and hidden from view in what Taruskin calls a 'mystic abyss'.[31] Crary suggests that the invisibility of the orchestra mystified the music because its source was unidentifiable.[32] Thus, the autonomy of the audience was somewhat removed by channelling the gaze of the audience and fixing attention solely on the spectacle of performance.[33]

This focus on channelling the attention of the audience is also recognised in acousmatic listening. Wishart explains that acousmatic listening means that the sound should be appreciated 'independent of, and detached from, a knowledge or appreciation of its source'.[34] The term acousmatic, from which we get acousmatic music, stems from the Greek word *akusmatikoi* and is commonly associated with Pythagoras.[35] It is alleged that Pythagoras delivered talks from behind a curtain in order to remove visual distraction and to channel the attention of his students.[36] In a similar fashion, acousmatic music is listened to through loudspeakers and without any performers present.[37] This results in what Luke Windsor refers to as an 'impoverished' state of listening because of the lack of visual connection

182   *Michelle Stead*

between the performers, their gestures and the production of sound.[38] Although this is debated, it is generally held that this environment, due to its 'impoverishment' of the spectacle of performance, is conducive to a concentrated level of listening, thus heightening the sensory, auditory experience for the listener.[39] The aim of acousmatic listening, then, is to ignore the origins of the sound source so that the sound can be considered in isolation of its context.[40] This means that the isolation of the sound coupled with the fact that it is mediated through the loudspeaker constitutes what Crary defines as a detachment from a broader area for the purpose of emphasising a reduced number of stimuli.[41] In this way, listeners of acousmatic music are shaped in terms of their capacity for 'paying attention'. It is a state of listening that has proven difficult for listeners to accept and achieve. Thus, it is not unusual for most first-time listeners of any twentieth-century music to feel, in the very least, a little bit lost.[42] As Taruskin suggests, 'it is the listening process that has proved durably problematical'.[43] Despite the fact that listening models suited specifically to acousmatic music do exist, the ubiquity of the more traditional approaches to music theory and aural training remain potent.[44]

Acousmatic music shares a close relationship with the advent of technologies such as the gramophone and tape recorder. For example, Pierre Schaeffer compared the role of the tape recorder in acousmatic music to Pythagoras' curtain, which emphasises the concentrated listening facilitated by 'creating not only new phenomena to be studied (by manipulations in the studio), but also, and above all, new conditions for observation'.[45] Acousmatic music does not depend on writing at all. Composition is usually undertaken in the studio, the loudspeaker replaces the performer, and a score is not needed to record or reproduce the piece given it already exists as a recorded artefact. In this way the recordability of music, as Taruskin explains, 'achieves what written texts achieve — namely, the fixing of the unique artwork — even better than written texts can do, and it does so without the use of texts'.[46] Traditionally, the score functions in a literary way both in the sense that it is something that is 'written', 'read' and 'understood'. Music history begins with what we know about music, and what we know about early music is only through what was written down. Therefore, the relationship of music and the visual written 'text' has, for centuries, been a complex one. Anything which is scored for acousmatic music is likened by Taruskin to a picture or a painting.[47] In this analogy, the score loses its predominantly literary relation to the work and is represented in a manner that cannot be 'read' in the same way as a literary text simply for the fact that there is no common language for the 'writing'. Learning to be literate in music, then, is only useful if one is interested in music that is notated (or written).

Historically, the score is also tasked with providing instructions for the performer and given there are no performers in acousmatic music, this relationship becomes redundant.[48] Because acousmatic works are exclusively created for the loudspeaker, their 'performances' are bereft of human performers and, more significantly, lacking in the pomp and spectacle associated with the performance of other kinds of music. Being present for a rock concert or an orchestral concert is as much about the music as it is about the experience of being present for its display. This raises important questions for how we might listen to acousmatic music which does not rely on the written score in the same way as other kinds of Western music. Given the veracity and ubiquity of music theory which, in turn, perpetuates a predominantly visual approach to music, it is difficult to envisage how and where acousmatic music might be included.

Yet, Crary makes the point that vision has too often been posed as an apologetic problem and that to proclaim the authority of vision is erroneous because what usually constitutes a domain of the visual is more often than not an effect of complex power relations.[49] In other words, Crary is suggesting that the perceived hegemony of vision is *constructed*. The very idea of attentiveness (which seems to be a requirement in acousmatic music) is concerned with subjectivity and ties in with the concept of 'the gaze'. The gaze, derived from Lacanian psychoanalysis, is concerned with the way a subject is perceived through the eyes of the viewer.[50] Attention, as Crary highlights, is therefore a mechanism for power insomuch as it leaves the observer open to coercion.[51] Spectacular culture, he argues, relies upon strategies where individuals are isolated, separated and inhabit time as disempowered.[52] These power relations functioned to make the subject productive during the nineteenth century through increasing its capacity to pay attention thus increasing the utility of the body.[53] Clearly these ideas draw on Foucault's *Discipline and Punish* where he explains that during this time a 'mechanics of power' was emerging that determined how bodies were controlled and made docile.[54]

Similarly, then, 'spectacular culture', as Crary calls it, is about reducing the subject's attentive field for the sake of docility. The emphasis on concentrated listening through the discourse of acousmatic music is essentially, a 'problem of attention' constructed through an epistemological framework that cites a hegemony of vision. In this way, attention imitates 'real' experience but it also compensates for it.[55] This suggests that there is something to be compensated for – a desire for the real which can never be fully reconciled by the subject and thus can only be qualified as a 'lack'.

A visual discursive framework means that knowledge can only operate within the norms offered for this paradigm. The ontological nature of the recording has a fundamentally different presence from that of the written score and the musical performance primarily because it is not acting as a representation of anything else – in other words, there is no object to represent.[56] If music is constructed according to the hegemony of vision (through its alignment with 'literacy') then it starts to become clear that acousmatic music does not always fulfil the visual, literate criterion. Furthermore, in channelling the listener's attention to the sound through the loudspeaker, the relationship to the spectacle of performance is severed.

The Freudian conception of desire is Oedipal and fundamentally relies upon a relationship which ensures that subjects define themselves according to 'lack'. Therefore, one of the aims of Deleuze and Guattari's *Anti-Oedipus* is to demonstrate that this model of desire is restrictive primarily because of its negative and unproductive relationship with 'lack'.[57] They write that, 'in point of fact, if desire is the lack of the real object, its very nature as a real entity depends upon an "essence of lack" that produces the fantasized object'.[58] They explain that psychoanalysis treats desire as a production of fantasies which can never be actualised and must therefore always result in lack.[59] This way, life can only be conceived of as an insufficient ontology or a life that is unable to 'be'.[60] Similarly, if we conceive of acousmatic music through a framework which relies upon opticality, the music can only ever be understood as 'lacking', thus leaving the subject always desiring 'the object' of the music and, because acousmatic music has no object, this lack is unable to be resolved. This form of desire assumes that vision acts independently of the other senses. If we accept Crary's view, however, that the perceived visual bias is one that is fabricated from nineteenth-century social and cultural discourses then acousmatic music is free to exist outside a model of what Deleuze and Guattari would categorise as a negative desire.

Moreover, if the dominance of opticality is constructed, it is also fluid and open to re-assembly. Desire, for Deleuze and Guattari, is positive (rather than negative) and is reconceived as a 'desiring-machine'. The desiring-machine is a continuous flow of force which is productive simply because it is the production of production itself and only functions when it stops functioning.[61] As Hulse explains, doing difference in this way is 'profoundly elusive to rational thought'.[62] In order to make connections there has to be radical deterritorialisation and while a connection is in place there is inevitably the creation of a territory. To quote Deleuze and Guattari, 'deterritorialisation must be thought of as a perfectly positive power that has degrees and thresholds (epsitrata), is always relative, and has reterritorialisation as its flipside or complement'.[63] In this way an epistemological framework that claims the dominance of vision is limiting in that it only enables a listener to engage with the music on terms which territorialises the experience of the listener so that she/he is shut off from the possibilities of what the music might offer beyond a visual element.

In the eyes of Deleuze, the Western philosophical tradition fails to *do* difference and I argue, similarly, that the Western musical tradition is guilty of this offence.[64] Rather than 'lacking' a relation to the written score or the spectacle, a desiring-machine opens up a space in which it becomes possible to imagine all different kinds of experiences of listening to acousmatic music that do not begin with the visual way of knowing. Listening is something we *do* as an embodied process and it is not something that is able to be detached from our other sensory experiences.[65] Therefore, it does not make sense to approach music from solely an optical perspective that would continue to perpetuate norms and standards which can only ever limit the potential of music. The dominance of vision, to return to Crary's argument, is a constructed problem and it is a problem that fails to engage with the complexities and nuances of the ways in which we come to know our world and, significantly, the ways in which we come to listen to music. Thus the desiring-machine makes it possible to imagine a space where listeners could engage with acousmatic music rhizomatically by drawing on multiple sensations existing outside the limiting visual discursive framework.

Rather than treating listening as something we *do*, I will conclude by reflecting on what happens if we think about listening as a concept. A concept, according to

Seeing the sense   185

Deleuze and Guattari, acts as 'a condition for the exercise of thought'.[66] Concepts are an act of creation and take shape only in accordance with other concepts and with problems.[67] The concept of listening, then, can be understood as being tied to the problem of sound, and it will take different forms according to each iteration of the problem – it is thus fluid. By thinking about listening as a fluid concept that is always in relation to other concepts and problems, questions to do with the very nature of listening come to the foreground. This chapter, for instance, demonstrates what listening 'looks' like if it is viewed from the perspective of a visual framework. By thinking about listening as a concept in relation to other kinds of concepts, it is very possible (and even practical) to begin to consider modalities which do not presuppose opticality. As I have shown, the hegemony of vision is not as rigid as it might first appear and only once we identify these constructed structures are we able to imagine listening as a flow that moves along a plane. In so doing, we dislodge it from the constrictive frameworks in which it is traditionally understood, thereby opening the listener up to new ways of experiencing acousmatic music.

Notes

1   Jonathan Crary, *Suspensions of Perception: Attention, Spectacle and Modern Culture*. An October Book (Cambridge, MA and London: the MIT Press, 2001).
2   Crary, *Suspensions of Perception*, 3.
3   The following authors have made similar observations to those of Crary: Andrew Dell'Antonio, ed., *Beyond Structural Listening? Postmodern Modes of Hearing* (Berkeley: University of California Press, 2004); Susan McClary, *Feminine Endings: Music, Gender, and Sexuality* (Minneapolis: University of Minnesota Press, 1991); and Richard D. Leppert and Susan McClary, eds, *Music and Society: The Politics of Composition, Performance, and Reception* (Cambridge: Cambridge University Press, 1987).
4   According to Hickey-Moody and Malins, 'difference is, first and foremost, and internal – rather than a relational or external – process'. See Anna Hickey-Moody and Peta Malins, eds., *Deleuzian Encounters: Studies in Contemporary Social Issues* (Houndmills, Bassingstoke: Palgrave Macmillan, 2007), 5.
5   Michael Bull and Les Back, eds., *The Auditory Culture Reader* (Oxford and New York: Berg, 2003), 1.
6   See McClary, *Feminine Endings*; Nicholas Cook, *Music: A Very Short Introduction* (Oxford and New York: Oxford University Press, 1988); and Rose Rosengard Subotnik, 'Toward a Deconstruction of Structural Listening: A Critique of Schoenberg, Adorno, and Stravinsky', in *Deconstructive Variations: Music and Reason in Western Society* (Minneapolis: University of Minnesota Press, 1996), 148–76.
7   Dell'Antonio, *Beyond Structural Listening?*, 3.
8   Dell'Antonio, *Beyond Structural Listening?*, 3.
9   Richard Taruskin, *Music in the Nineteenth Century* (New York: Oxford University Press, 2010), 10.
10   See Geoff Danaher, Tony Schirato, and Jen Webb, *Understanding Foucault* (London and Thousand Oaks, CA: Sage Publications, 2000), 20.
11   Taruskin, *Music in the Nineteenth Century*, xix.
12   Roland Barthes, 'The Death of the Author', in *Image, Music, Text*, trans. Stephen Heath (New York and London: Hill and Wang; Fontana, 1977), 142–8.
13   Michel Foucault, 'What is an Author?' in ed. Paul Rabinow, *The Foucault Reader* (Harmondsworth: Penguin, 1986), 101–20.

14 Michel Foucault, *The Archaeology of Knowledge*, trans. A.M. Sheridan Smith (Oxon: Routledge, 2011), 19.

15 Foucault. 'What is an Author?', 101–20.

16 Richard Taruskin, *Music in the Late Twentieth Century* (Oxford and New York: Oxford University Press, 2005), 195.

17 Sara Mills, *Michel Foucault* (Oxon and New York: Routledge, 2003), 60.

18 Mills, *Michel Foucault*, 74.

19 Mills, Sara, *Discourse* (Abingdon, Oxon: Routledge, 2004), 55.

20 See Susan McClary, 'The Blasphemy of Talking Politics During Bach Year', in *Music and Society*. 13–62. And Susan McClary, 'Terminal Prestige: The Case of Avant-Garde Music Composition', in *Keeping Score: Music, Disciplinarity, Culture*, ed. David Schwarz, Anahid Kassabian, and Lawrence Siegel (Charlottesville: University Press of Virginia, 1997), 54–74.

21 Dell'Antonio. *Beyond Structural Listening?*, 3.

22 Gary S. Karpinski, *Manual for Ear Training and Sight Singing* (New York: Norton, 2007), xi.

23 Patrick McCreless, 'Rethinking Contemporary Music Theory', in *Keeping Score*, 13.

24 Schwarz. Kassabian, and Siegel, *Keeping Score*, 14.

25 Ron Gorow, *Hearing and Writing Music: Professional Training for Today's Musician* (Studio City, California: September Publication, 2006), 9.

26 Crary, *Suspensions of Perception*, 1.

27 Crary, *Suspensions of Perception*, 17.

28 Crary, *Suspensions of Perception*, 17.

29 Crary, *Suspensions of Perception*, 251.

30 Crary, *Suspensions of Perception*, 251.

31 Taruskin. *Music in the Nineteenth Century*, 499.

32 Crary, *Suspensions of Perception*, 251.

33 Crary, *Suspensions of Perception*, 253.

34 Trevor Wishart, ed., *On Sonic Art* (The Netherlands: Harwood Academic Publishers, 1996), 67.

35 Simon Emmerson and Denis Smalley, 'Electro-acoustic music', *Grove Music Online* (Oxford: Oxford University Press), accessed 4 February 2014, http://www.oxfordmusiconline.com/subscriber/article/grove/music/08695.

36 Pierre Schaeffer, 'Acousmatics', in *Audio Culture: Readings in Modern Music*, ed. Christoph Cox and Daniel Warner (New York; London: Continuum, 2004), 76–81.

37 Michel Chion, *Guide To Sound Objects: Pierre Schaeffer and Musical Research*, trans. J. Dack and C. North (Leicester: EARS De Montfort University, 2009[1983]), 11–33, accessed 8 October 2015, http://ears.pierrecouprie.fr/IMG/pdf/Chion-guide/GuidePreface.pdf.

38 Luke Windsor, 'A Perceptual Approach to the Description and Analysis of Acousmatic Music'. PhD thesis, accessed 24 April 2013, http://www.zainea.com/Acousmatic.htm.

39 See Chion, *Guide To Sound Objects*, 11–33.; Eric F. Clarke, 'The Impact of Recording on Listening', *Twentieth-Century Music* 4/1 (2007): 47–70; Windsor, 'A Perceptual Approach'.

40 Wishart, *On Sonic Art*, 67.

41 Crary, *Suspensions of Perception*, 1.

42 This problem has been extensively discussed in electroacoustic music discourse. See Leigh Landy, *What's The Matter with Today's Experimental Music?: Organized Sound Too Rarely Heard* (New York: Routledge, 1991); and Robert Weale, 'Discovering How Accessible Electroacoustic Music Can Be: The Intention/Reception Project', *Organised Sound* 11/2 (2006): 189–200.

43 Taruskin. *Music in the Early Twentieth Century*, 163.

44 Perhaps the most comprehensive of these is the model developed by Pierre Schaeffer. For an account of this see Pierre Schaeffer, *In Search of a Concrete Music*, trans. Christine North and John Dack (Berkely, CA: University of California Press, 2012[1952]).

45 Chion, *Guide To Sound Objects*, 12.

46 Taruskin, *Music in the Late Twentieth Century*, 481.

47 Taruskin, *Music in the Late Twentieth Century*, 210.

48 Taruskin, *Music in the Late Twentieth Century*, 190.

49 Crary, *Suspensions of Perception*, 3.

50 'The gaze' is a concept typically associated with Jacques Lacan. Theorists such as Laura Mulvey and Michel Foucault have also developed these ideas. See Laura Mulvey, *Visual and Other Pleasures* (Houndmills, Basingstoke, Hampshire: Macmillan, 1989); and Michel Foucault, *Discipline and Punish: The Birth of the Prison* (New York: Vintage Books, 1995).

51 Crary, *Suspensions of Perception*, 5.

52 Crary, *Suspensions of Perception*, 3.

53 Crary, *Suspensions of Perception*, 4.

54 Foucault, *Discipline and Punish*, 138.

55 Crary, *Suspensions of Perception*, 361.

56 Brian Hulse and Nick Nesbitt, eds., *Sounding the Virtual: Gilles Deleuze and the Theory and Philosophy of Music* (Farnham, UK and Burlington, VT: Ashgate, 2010), 69.

57 Gilles Deleuze and Félix Guattari, *Anti-Oedipus: Capitalism and Schizophrenia* (London: Athlone, 1984).

58 Deleuze and Guattari, *Anti-Oedipus*, 25.

59 Deleuze and Guattari, *Anti-Oedipus*, 25.

60 Deleuze and Guattari, *Anti-Oedipus*, 26.

61 Deleuze and Guattari, *Anti-Oedipus*, 26.

62 Hulse and Nesbitt, eds., *Sounding the Virtual*, 23.

63 Gilles Deleuze and Félix Guattari, *A Thousand Plateaus: Capitalism and Schizophrenia*, trans. Brian Massumi (Minnesota and London: University of Minnesota Press, 1988), 60.

64 Brian Hulse, 'Thinking Musical Difference: Music Theory as Minor Science', in *Sounding the Virtual*, 23.

65 Fred Dretske, 'Seeing, Believing and Knowing', in *Perception*, ed. Robert Schwartz (Malden, Oxford, Melbourne and Berlin: Blackwell Publishing, 2004), 269.

66 Gilles Deleuze and Félix Guattari, *What is Philosophy?*, trans. Hugh Tomlinson and Graham Burchell (New York: Columbia University Press, 1994[1991]), 4.

67 Deleuze and Guattari, *What is Philosophy?*, 16.

15 Listening to ethnographic Holocaust musical testimony through the 'ears' of Jean-Luc Nancy

Joseph Toltz

> What truly betrays music and diverts or perverts the movement of its modern history is the extent to which it is indexed to a mode of signification and not to a mode of sensibility. (Jean-Luc Nancy)[1]

For the past 17 years I have been researching music and memory in Jewish Holocaust survivor testimonies, and the role of music in survivors' lives in the present day. In this chapter, I will use a critical approach based on listening to revisit the material of my original research, drawing on a model proposed by the French philosopher, Jean-Luc Nancy.[2] According to Nancy, the habituated practices of listening in philosophy are not really acts of listening but are, instead, acts of hearing for understanding: we hear (rather than listen) to understand. We hear to emphasise the meaning of what is said rather than to think about how listening in and of itself which comes to us by way of the sonorous is capable of generating new ways of hearing. Bronwyn Davies goes further to suggest that what we usually think of as listening is hierarchically constituted: 'we listen in order to fit what we hear into what we already know'.[3] The inference is that what we already know is more important than what we do not know yet.

I will suggest that Nancy's work, like that of Davies, posits a non-hierarchical, emergent listening. Whereas Davies is interested in how listeners emerge through the process of listening – both as listeners and as those who are listened to – Nancy's philosophical meditation ponders on the relationship of sound to the human body. He argues that as a phenomenon of the human body, sound, more than vision, envelops and enters the body in ways that cannot be ignored. Because sound engulfs all of our beings, it produces powerful effects long after its sounding ends, living on in the memory. I will suggest that this idea is demonstrated in my work on Holocaust survivor testimonies: survivors recall the music from their time in the camps and ghettos as if it is being heard for the first time. It resounds as a powerful memory in their lives in the present day.

Nancy's work is interested in how listening differs from hearing and from seeing. He questions whether it is possible to hear and understand at the same time. His meditation explores a deeper sense of what is entailed in listening, suggesting that it is a sensibility that is produced by the connections between our whole beings and the sounding phenomena resounding inside and outside our beings. Listening might begin with what is already known but it also opens up the possibility of the unknown. Thinking about listening in this way prompted me to revisit my research and to consider the musical testimonies I had collected as sonorous material. I bring this mode of sensibility to my work, imagining that the site of listening is an act of care within the scholarly space.

I will begin with a brief account of the normative modes of listening to the musical experience in the context of Holocaust studies. These dominant narratives have used music to serve as archival documentary, to garnish the historical narrative, and to perform the work of 'reconstruction' in order to 'understand' the 'truth' of experience. These are top-down modes of listening which emphasise hearing as understanding, privileging the researcher rather than allowing the voices of the participants to be 'heard' and listened to as emergent with the voice of the researcher. I will then propose that Nancy's mode of listening generates an emergent sonorous space in the re-reading of my earlier research. In so doing, I will demonstrate that when listening is conceived as emergent and resonant it becomes a mode of sensibility.

Music in the Holocaust: The limits of signifying complicity and resistance

In order to understand the normative modes of signification that music has been assigned in Holocaust testimony, I will begin by addressing the place of testimony itself. Individual survivor testimony did not receive public imprimatur until the 1961 trial of Adolf Eichmann. Deborah Lipstadt argues that one of most the significant historical developments of this trial was the first substantial inclusion of Holocaust survivor testimony.[4] After the conclusion of the Second World War and the completion of the Nuremberg Trials, almost an entire generation of individual voices of survivors were finally heard publicly in a juridical setting. Around the same time, the first literary testimonies to capture the imagination of the public emerged in English translation: Primo Levi's *If this is a Man* and Elie Wiesel's *Night*.[5] In their original languages, neither of these works were successful,[6] and nor did they find publishers willing to distribute them beyond a small print run. The prominence, however, of the Eichmann trial initiated a much larger public awareness, translation, and eventually an enthusiastic reading audience. Together with Jean Amery and the poet Paul Celan, Levi and Wiesel test what Leigh Gilmore has referred to as the limit of representation in which the 'compulsory inflation of the self to stand for others' muddies notions of clarity between a singular and shared perspective.[7] In Levi's narrative, the banality of the camp band playing the popular song *Rosamunde*[8] provides a momentary point of amusement on arrival in Auschwitz, before the writer returns to his relentlessly dispassionate description of the grey anti-life of camp existence.[9] In an even pithier fashion, Wiesel describes the musical accompaniment for the workers in and out of Monowitz, a forced labour satellite camp of Auschwitz.[10] For each of these authors, music is a descriptive tool of narrative, rather than a testimony in its own right: a mockery of a beloved art-form, perverted by the Nazi death camp system.

190   *Joseph Toltz*

Paul Celan is more condemnatory of the complicity of music in this place. In the *Todesfuge* of 1948 he notes that music plays a role darker than that of accompaniment:

> He calls play sweeter for death; Death is a Master from Germany
> He calls stroke the violins darker then you will rise as smoke into the air
> Then you will have a grave in the clouds where one has room to stretch.[11]

In reading this one hears a stark resonance with what Elaine Martin refers to as the aporetic tension at the heart of the thought of Theodor Adorno: the obligation to represent the Holocaust, and the impossibility of an adequate representation.[12] Here are Adorno's own words of that terrible musical moment:

> If thought is not measured by the extremity that eludes the concept, it is from the outset in the nature of the musical accompaniment, with which the SS drowned out the screams of its victims.[13]

The despair of the poet is not just for the murderous tragedy of the Holocaust itself but also for the retrospective implications it has on the meaning of German culture. Adorno pronounces that, '[w]ord hasn't yet got around that culture, in the traditional sense of the word, is dead',[14] finally to conclude that:

> Auschwitz has demonstrated irrefutably that culture has failed. That it could happen in the midst of the philosophical traditions, the arts and the enlightening sciences says more than just that these failed to take hold of and change the people. All culture after Auschwitz, including its urgent critique, is rubbish.[15]

At this aporetic moment, Adorno has nowhere to turn. The cultural past has failed miserably. He has already rejected popular forms with contempt, taking Siegfried Kracauer's notion of the distraction industry to its end limit. For Adorno, an aesthetic of irreconcilability was the only tenable solution. Only art that had the inbuilt potential to fail to reconcile the particular and the universal was worth pursuing. Moreover, this art had to aspire to negotiate between freedom and social order, and to provide an implicit critique of the conditions leading to its own production, thereby undermining itself in the process. As Terry Eagleton explains:

> every work of art pretends to be the totality it can never become; there is never any achieved mediation of particular and universal, mimetic and relational, but always a diremption [separation/disjunction] between them which the work will cover up as best it can.[16]

The placement of music at the complicit centre of the Nazi enterprise leaves no room for the discussion of musical experiences of Holocaust survivors, and no space for the resonance of musical testimony.

Listening to ethnographic Holocaust musical testimony   191

The other prime mode of signification can be found in the redemptive discourse of 'spiritual resistance'.[17] We begin again with Elie Wiesel, whose initial encounter with music in the camps is countered by a moment of reprieve experienced on a death march back into Germany. The character Eliezer reunites with his friend Juliek, a violinist from Warsaw, who manages to smuggle his instrument on the march. Here we read the first documented account in testimony of an act of free musical expression, one of the earliest instances in testimonial literature introducing a notion of spiritual resistance:

> To this day, whenever I hear the Beethoven played my eyes close and out of the dark rises the sad, pale face of my Polish friend, as he said farewell on his violin to an audience of dying men.[18]

By the 1970s, spiritual resistance was an entrenched construct, driving interest in new music-specific testimonies,[19] research into musical activities in Terezín, and eventually the exploration of everyday musical life in the Łódź Ghetto by Gila Flam in 1992.[20] Flam declared that it was her mission to determine the meaning of the songs in terms of their symbolic and aesthetic values as attributed by survivors. In so doing, she propagated a redemptive discourse. It would take another 13 years for this construct to be challenged by Gilbert who pointed out that the sentimental, mythologising rhetoric surrounding the redemptive reading of musical activity in the Holocaust had the potential to silence opposing voices.[21] By limiting the discourse to that of an honorific, memorialising status, this mode of signification simplified the accounts of human existence in the camps and ghettos.[22] Gilbert, however, whose work accessed primary historical sources such as Yiddish song collections and the testimony of musical activities from that time, argued for the reintroduction of complexity into the musical narrative, stating that:

> Musical activities in many camps and ghettos were prolific and diverse, and afforded the victims temporary diversion, entertainment, and opportunities to process what was happening to them.[23]

Although the impact of Gilbert's theoretical critique cannot be overestimated, her survey barely touched the surface of the body of historical musical material. Immediately after the war, Jewish historical commissions were established in Germany, Poland, the USSR and Hungary. These set out to collect thousands of written testimonies in the newly liberated East. Recordings of songs and poetry from camps and ghettos, such as the songbooks of Szmerke Kaczerginski, complemented the Yiddish accounts of life in occupied Europe.[24] At the same time, the Latvian-born American psychologist, David Boder, captured the first audio recordings of survivor testimony.[25] Kaczerginski's songbooks remained untouched by researchers until Gilbert's work, and Boder's musical recordings are only just now being examined in detail. Modern responses to this musical material has seen Klezmer renditions of the music in Flam's book,[26] and a controversial reconstruction of the performances of Verdi's Requiem in the Terezín Ghetto, a project

192   *Joseph Toltz*

known as *Defiant Requiem*. Using Nancy's model, I will now turn my attention to the music, focusing on the interpretations of musical memory in the recreation and reconstruction of this material.

Nancy and listening

Nancy's *Listening* begins with a confrontational question to philosophy. He asks whether philosophy is capable of listening (*écouter*) and suggests that it already superimposes an order of understanding (*entendre*) on that which is under examination.[27] Nancy uses the concept of sense (*sens*) to contrast the visual and the conceptual, and to argue that the sonorous is the excess of the visual and of form. He is interested in the differences thrown up by the senses, and the ways in which we perceive the senses in relation to meaning.[28] He suggests that the philosopher perceives the world through the ear. In this view, the ear is immersive: it is through the practice of listening that one is formed. My interview with Kitia Altman was held on a wet autumn day in 2008. For three hours I sat, entranced by her narrative that begins as a comfortable, middle-class existence in Będzin, Poland, moves through the traumas of five years in camps and ghettos, and culminates in a story about her time trapped in a slave-labour munitions factory underground in which she witnessed a Roma girl singing a popular melody called *Mamatschi, kauf mir ein Pferchen*. Despite claiming that she is tone deaf, having no musical ability or interest, Altman sang an excerpt to me. Her rendition of the song gave such bodily resonance to that experience, drawing me into that world and allowing me a space as witness to her story.

For Nancy, the body is like an echo chamber. It responds to the forces of its interior and exterior. As an echo chamber, it resounds freely. When listening takes over the whole of our being, it opens a world in which sonority rather than the message becomes important. There is a feeling of secrecy and privacy embedded in the practice of listening: to listen is 'literally to stretch the ear'.[29] Nancy suggests that there is a special relationship between the ear and sense, and to hear is to understand the sense. Listening must be delineated from the other senses. We thus strain towards a possible meaning that is not immediately accessible or apparent.[30] We listen to speech in order to understand. We listen to silence in order to hear what arises from it. We listen to music as background or foreground, and it produces a sense of listening that is of the whole, resonant body. To be listening thus is to be on the edge of meaning as if the sound to which one listens musically is emergent, not as an acoustic phenomenon, but as a resonant meaning in whose sense is found only in resonance. Nancy refers to this as reference (*renvoi*) by which he means a totality of referrals, from signs to things, to states of things, qualities, and from subject to another subject.[31] Sound also operates in a state of referral, for to sound is 'to vibrate in itself or by itself. It is not only, for the sonorous body, to emit a sound, but it is also to stretch out, to carry itself and be resolved into vibrations that both return to itself and place it outside itself.'[32] Meaning and sound thus share the space of a referral. When one listens, one looks for something that is identified by a resonance from self to self, in itself, for itself, and outside itself. And to be listening is to strain towards or to be in an approach to the self, not the singular self, nor the self of the other, but to the form, structure and movement of an infinite referral.[33]

In Nancy's view, the presence of sound is always within the return and the encounter. It is a place *as* relation to self. Sound resounds in the sonorous place. The sonorous place is where a subject becomes a subject because of who it is as a subject. Perhaps the survivor, inured to a world of brutality, bereft of control, may hear or create sound in the same manner: to realise or reassert their own selves?

Through a reading of Gérard Granel, Nancy then suggests that sound is not a phenomenon, as it does not stem from a logic of manifestation. Instead, it is an evocation, a summoning presence to itself, 'an impulsion'.[34] Nancy then introduces the notion of silence as an arrangement of resonance, rather than a privation. He says that the subject of listening, the subject who is listening, or the one subject to listening, are all places of resonance in which infinite tensions exist and rebound. Resonance thus opens itself up to the self. It becomes the resonant body and its vibrations become a being. The ear stretches and is stretched by meaning (*sens*). From this he deduces that musical listening is, in itself, the listening of self, arranged according to the profundity of the resonant chamber, the body. Listening is thus ahead of signification. It is in a state of return for which the end of the return is not given. Music played is music sounded, but resonance gives sense to it. In order to exist, however, music must play on sonorous bodies. Music thus silences and interprets sounds, and produces the body that sounds and senses its own resonance. So, within a text there is a musicality, a resonance that listens to itself, finds itself by this listening, and deviates from itself at the same time in order to resound.

Listening in aporetic moments

The year 1998 marked my first moment in the formal journey of survivor interviewing. At that time, I had completed my Hospital chaplaincy training, and was on my way to become Cantor at Temple Emanuel, a non-Orthodox Synagogue in Sydney. Through pastoral work and personal friendships, I encountered musical life in concentration camps via Ida Ferson, a Polish survivor and music lover. Ferson entrusted me with a set of unedited facsimile manuscripts of music given to her by the survivor, pianist and sister of composer Gideon Klein, Eliška (Lisa) Kleinová. All the works had been composed in Terezín. Meanwhile, the curators of a special exhibition on Terezín at the Sydney Jewish Museum commissioned my vocal quintet to perform a work composed in the Ghetto. We performed the highly chromatic, dissonant setting of a Friedrich Hölderlin poem (translated into Czech), *Madrigal* (1943), by Gideon Klein.[35] The translation reads as follows:

> The agreeable things of this world were mine to enjoy.
> How long gone are the hours of my youth.
> April, May and July are distant!
> I'm nothing anymore, yet listlessly I live on.[36]

194 *Joseph Toltz*

At the exhibition launch, a Terezín survivor approached me, identifying himself as Jerry (Jaroslav) Rind, a survivor of Terezín, Auschwitz and Gleiwitz, and a fifth-generation Jew from the small town of Sudoměřice in southern Bohemia. He asked why I had programmed such a discordant, unfamiliar, unknown work as Klein's *Madrigal*. My first aporetic moment was about to occur. Taken aback by his question, I explained that I had been asked to perform music that had been written in the camp. Rind spoke about the children's opera *Brundibár*, a work that contained for him many personal associations. He also spoke of other cultural activities that ghetto dwellers flocked to see   operas, cabaret, theatre, chamber music and choral presentations. This encounter caused me to listen, to consider listening in a different manner, and it changed the course of my research, extending it to include the cultural activities in Terezín. It captured what Adelaida Reyes refers to as the 'expressive culture' in which '"inside jokes" [are] intelligible only to those who have an insider's knowledge of the culture. It is the kind of meaning that music conveys, over and above the meaning made accessible by the discovery of the internal logic that makes the music coherent.'[37]

In addition to my interviews with Czech survivors, I accessed the experience of Yiddish speakers in Melbourne. Attentive 'listening' to this material proved fruitful: in 2011, during a fellowship at the US Holocaust Museum, I examined the musical recordings of David Boder.[38] One of the songs embedded in Boder's testimonies was absent from the annals of Holocaust histories and songbooks. Originating from Buchenwald, it was sung to Boder by a 19 year old, Israel Unikowski. Listening to the recording awakened a strange familiarity. I re-examined my own interview materials from 2007 and found a handwritten text of the same song, given to me by another survivor, Joe Szwarcberg. The song transmits in free verse-form a prosaic vision of the bleak existence in Buchenwald, while the simple, waltz-like chorus engenders the possibility of group participation. It is one of the most powerful moments in Unikowski's interview with Boder. In 2011 I travelled to Melbourne to interview Unikowski, now known as Jack. I played his song to him but he could not recall having heard it and wondered how he could have blocked this particular part of his memory. Unikowski demonstrated his own lucidity and memory retention by reciting in Yiddish (by heart) the entire text of Moshe Shulshtayn's poem 'We are the Shoes'. Once again, an aporetic moment allowed the space for listening, resulting in an extended dialogue between survivor and witness regarding the worth and function of musical memory, and the value of everyday songs from ghettos and camps.

Writing about listening, Georgina Born demands that we focus on the relations between the musical object and the listening subject. She says that the latter demands an analysis of the social and historical conditions, and the mediation of listening. It also asks us to pay attention to the changing forms of subjectivity brought to music.[39] Musical testimony as a form of listening opens up a new model of subjectivity through the resonance that it brings to the musical experience. Emmanuel Levinas asked us to reconceive of what it means to be a self, to have subjectivity, to consider oneself an active agent. Accordingly, he suggests that if we have subjectivity and agency by virtue of a dialogic relationship with others, then we are not opposed.[40] Kelly Oliver suggests that, instead, we are responsible for our abilities to respond, just as we are responsible to open ourselves to the responses that constitute us as subjects.[41] In first formulating the notion of musical testimony, I became preoccupied with an ethical hermeneutic dialogue of practice in the listening encounter with survivors.[42] I designated my subject the idea of its 'musical testimony', to give credence and voice to that aspect of testimonial memory that had been the province of only the most expert of musical witnesses. I wanted to show that audience or amateur participation, and incidental musical activities are as much a part of musical life in society as are the formal concerts or recorded music listening experiences. The text I was contemplating was survivor testimony of musical experience. At that time I defined this as Other in multivalent ways: it was essentially and assertively Other from my own experience as a person who was two generations removed from the actual events; it was Other in that it was a musical experience not of my own; and it was Other in that it was situated within, perhaps, the most Other of experience of the twentieth century, namely, that of the Holocaust. The failure of the Nazi mission to eradicate the Jewish Other echoes the Levinasian assertion that the destruction of the Other is unattainable. Approaching this Other experience (that of the Holocaust survivor) required a form of ongoing dialogue which enriched, corrected, modified and drew the Other into a collaborative approach that continued to inform aspects of the text produced and continued to refine the accounts that were presented. Applying this model of Self and Other constantly reinforced the approach taken by me as interviewer, and my subjects as interviewees. An intrinsic ethics was arrived at which resisted notions of 'empathic understanding'. Rather I aspired only to reach a sense of contemplation through dialogue, that is, through welcoming the Other by Me (the Self) into such an interaction, and vice-versa.

Revisiting this construct through my reading of Nancy, I see that I had previously been guilty of attempting to impose a mode of signification on my experience. Listening once again to my interviews, I come to the realisation that listening *is* the immediacy: in listening, I create an attentive space where the musical memories of Holocaust survivors are allowed to resound. In listening to my study in this manner, I approach my material in order to be on the edge of meaning, and to find in the material its inherent resonance. As I listen to my survivors speak of musical experience, coloured by many years of memory and further experience, I listen to look for a relationship within the self, for a sense of access and a continual passing and coming. This places me as not 'Other' but as simultaneously outside and inside. In this sense, listening to the sonorous presence, made up of an extraordinarily complex set of returns, is listened to from both the side of reception and that of emission. In absorbing this experience of listening, my ear is stretched according to the meaning generated, but also to what is happening prior to signification. This music is encapsulated in sonorous bodies of those who care to share their experiences in this fashion and, in so sharing, making their own bodies resonate. Writing about these experiences in this fashion is challenging. However, what emerges is a non-neutral sense of these experiences with their own musicality. In turn, this produces a resonance that listens to itself, and finds, deviates and resounds in the retelling.

Notes

1 Jean-Luc Nancy, *Listening*, trans. C. Mandel (New York: Fordham University Press, 2007), 57.
2 Nancy, *Listening*.
3 Bronwyn Davies, *Listening to Children: Being and Becoming* (London and New York: Routledge, 2014), 21.
4 See Deborah E. Lipstadt, *The Eichmann Trial* (New York: Nextbook/Schocken, 2011).
5 See Primo Levi, *Se Questo È Un Uomo* (Torino: F. de Silva, 1947); and Elie Wiesel, *Un Di Velt Hot Geshvign* (Buenos Aires: Tsentral-farband fun poylische yidn in Argentine, 1956).
6 Levi originally published *If This is a Man* in Italian in 1947 (see n. 5 above). The first English translation appeared in 1959.
7 Leigh Gilmore, *The Limits of Autobiography: Trauma and Testimony* (Ithaca, NY: Cornell University Press, 2001), 4.
8 Not to be confused with Schubert's incidental music D.797, this tune is known in English-speaking countries as the *Beer Barrel Polka*. The original song, *Škoda Lásky*, is Czech in origin. It belongs in the repertoire known as *schlager* (*šlagr*) sentimental ballads with catchy, popular tunes.
9 Levi, *If This Is a Man*, 20.
10 Elie Wiesel, *Night; Dawn; [and]. the Accident: Three Tales*, trans. Stella Rodway, Frances Frenaye, and Anne Borchardt (London: Robson Books Ltd, 1974), 57.
11 Paul Celan 'Todesfuge', in *German Poetry in Transition, 1945–1990* ed. and trans. Charlotte Melin (Hanover, New Haven: University Press of New England, 1999), 85–7.
12 Elaine Martin, 'Art after Auschwitz: Adorno Revisited', in *New Essays on the Frankfurt School of Critical Theory*, ed. Alfred J. Drake (Newcastle upon Tyne, UK: Cambridge Scholars, 2009).
13 Adorno translated and cited by Elaine Martin in 'Art after Auschwitz', 199; see the original German text in Theodor W. Adorno, *Negative Dialektik: Jargon Der Eigentlichkeit* (Frankfurt am Main: Suhrkamp, 1966), 358.
14 Adorno translated and cited by Elaine Martin in 'Art after Auschwitz', 200; see the original German text in Theodor W. Adorno, *Kritik: Kleine Schriften Zur Gesellschaft* (Frankfurt am Main: Suhrkamp, 1971), 23.
15 Adorno translated and cited by Martin, 'Art after Auschwitz', 200.
16 Terry Eagleton, *The Ideology of the Aesthetic* (Oxford, UK: Blackwell, 1990), 353.
17 According to Pnina Rosenberg, Miriam Novitch (survivor of the Vittel internment camp and first curator of the Ghetto Fighters' House) first coined the term 'spiritual resistance' in the 1950s. See Pnina Rosenberg, 'Art of the Holocaust as Spiritual Resistance: The Ghetto Fighters' House Collection', Block Museum of Art, Northwestern University, accessed 15 March 2015, http://lastexpression.northwestern.edu/essays/rosenberg.pdf.
18 Wiesel, *Night; Dawn; [and]. the Accident*, 101.
19 See Fania Fénelon and Marcelle Routier, *Sursis Pour L'orchestre* (Paris: Stock, 1976); Szymon Laks, *Music of Another World*, trans. C.A. Kisiel (Evanston: Northwestern University Press, 1989); Anita Lasker-Wallfisch, *Inherit the Truth, 1939–1945: The Documented Experiences of a Survivor of Auschwitz and Belsen* (London: Giles de la Mare, 1996); and Melissa Müller and Reinhard Piechocki, *A Garden of Eden in Hell: The Life of Alice Herz-Sommer* (London: Pan Books, 2006).
20 Gila Flam, *Singing for Survival: Songs of the Lodz Ghetto, 1940–1945* (Urbana and Chicago: University of Illinois Press, 1992).
21 Shirli Gilbert, *Music in the Holocaust: Confronting Life in the Nazi Ghettos and Camps* (Oxford: Oxford University Press, 2005).
22 Gilbert, *Music in the Holocaust*, 11.
23 Gilbert, *Music in the Holocaust*, 17.

24 See Szmerke Kaczerginski, *Dos Gezang Fun Vilner Geto* (Paris: Farband fun di vilner in frankraykh, 1947) and *Undzer Gezang* (Centralny Komitet żydów Polskich: Wydzią Kultury i Propagandy, 1947); and Szmerke Kaczerginski, Michl Gelbart, and H. Leivick, *Lider Fun Di Getos Un Lagern* (New York: Tsiko, 1948).

25 The testimonies have been streamed online with transcripts and translations available at, accessed 10 December 2014, http://www.voices.iit.edu. The most comprehensive account of Boder's testimonies is given in Alan Rosen, *The Wonder of Their Voices: The 1946 Holocaust Interviews of David Boder* (New York: Oxford University Press, 2010). Rosen's work discusses the songs embedded in five or six testimonies but it does not address the recorded song sessions.

26 See 'Brave Old World' (Musical group), *Dus Gezang Fin Geto Lodzh* (Ludwigsburg, Germany: Winter & Winter, 2004), CD, Red House Records CD 134.

27 Nancy, *Listening*, 5–6.

28 Nancy, *Listening*, 3.

29 Nancy, *Listening*, 5.

30 Nancy, *Listening*, 7.

31 Nancy, *Listening*, 7.

32 Nancy, *Listening*, 8.

33 Nancy, *Listening*, 9.

34 Nancy, *Listening*, 20.

35 Gideon Klein, 'Two Madrigals' (1942, 1943), ed. David Bloch (Berlin: Boosey & Hawkes, 2003).

36 Original text of the setting: 'Co příjemného dává svět/jsem měl, ach, ano. Let mladých radost je, ó, žel, jak dávno za mnou. Duben a máj a červen můj jsou kdepak! Už nejsem nic, už tady žiju nerad'. Emil A. Saudek made the translation from German to Czech. Facsimile score obtained from the collection of E. Kleinová, 1981.

37 Adelaida Reyes, 'What Do Ethnomusicologists Do? An Old Question for a New Century', *Ethnomusicology* 53/1 (2009), 14.

38 See n. 26 above.

39 Georgina Born, 'Listening, Mediation, Event: Anthropological and Sociological Perspectives', *Journal of the Royal Musical Association* 135/1 (2010): 79–89.

40 Emmanuel Levinas, *Totality and Infinity: an Essay on Exteriority* (Pittsburgh: Duquesne University Press, 1969).

41 Kelly Oliver, *Witnessing: Beyond Recognition* (Minneapolis, MN: University of Minnesota Press, 2001), 18–19.

42 I have taken this idea from Gary Tomlinson, *Music in Renaissance Magic: Toward a Historiography of Others* (Chicago: University of Chicago Press, 1993).

Part V
Deleuzian ontologies

16 Musical becomings

Judy Lochhead

Questions about the ontology of music tend to be addressed formally under the banner of philosophy, as the long bibliography on that topic attests.[1] But ontological debates arise frequently and intensely in other informal contexts. For instance, if I were to ask someone waiting in line to hear a performance of *Götterdämmerung* at Bayreuth if David Ocker's 7-minute digital rendition of Wagner's *Ring Cycle* is a performance of that four-opera work, the answer would most certainly engage issues of musical ontology.[2] Such ontological debates operate not only in classical but also in jazz and popular domains. For instance, the responses on YouTube to the posting of John Oswald's 'Dab', a sample-based collage of Michael Jackson's 'Bad', range from 'horrible' to 'amazing'.[3] Not far from the surface of these disparate responses is the ontological question: What *is* music? Another anecdote from my own teaching experience raises yet another dimension to issues of musical ontology. I often teach music of the 1950s and 1960s to undergraduate non-majors, and typically my syllabus includes John Cage's *4'33"* and Elliott Carter's Double Concerto for Harpsichord and Piano.[4] Students tend to be mildly amused by Cage's work, especially when they listen to a recorded performance by Frank Zappa, but Carter's Double Concerto often outrages them.[5] The outrage arises both from their personal sense of musical propriety (typically but not always: it should be tonal, have a backbeat, and last about 4 minutes) and from their realisation that a cultural economy exists that provides monetary compensation to Carter. These differing kinds of responses engage some fundamental questions about musical ontology. On one hand, Cage did not intend any particular sounding occurrences in *4'33"*. Rather, his intention is to delimit a temporal span of silence during which listeners may or may not choose to hear ambient sounds as music. For my students, this lack of intention for the work's particular sound seems to absolve Cage from responsibility, and their response seems to be: as a musical work, *4'33"* is playful experiment about listener response. But the reaction of outrage to Carter's Double Concerto entails recognition of Carter's intention – his sound design is deliberate. My students' reaction requires acknowledgement both of an aesthetic world that differs radically from the one they inhabit and of an aesthetic economy that rewards composers such as Carter. This two-faceted acknowledgement may or may not re-shape students' aesthetic tastes, but it does illuminate ontological difference.

202   *Judy Lockhead*

Because it exists in time as sounding and entails performance, music has and continues to be a vexed topic for formal discussions of its ontology. My examples of informal ontological debate highlight particular issues that arise in the twenty-first century in Western cultures: performance in the context of new digital technologies, digital sampling and the work concept, and aesthetic valuation in a pluralistic musical world. This chapter proposes some Deleuzian ontological pathways that illuminate both the vexations of music's ontology and the particular issues that arise in informal debates. Hainge's chapter in Part V addresses music's ontology from the Deleuzian perspective of its sonic materiality within a relational ontology that ascribes agency to musical sound.[6] In the following, I build both a conceptual prequel and sequel to Hainge's chapter in order to affirm that a materialist focus on sonic materiality opens up some new pathways for addressing not only formal but also informal ontological debates, including those generated by new technologies.

The materialist perspective of Hainge's ontology of music resonates with recent scholarship in what has been called speculative realism and the new materialism, all of which are flowerings of Deleuzian ontologies.[7] This material focus of Deleuze's philosophy is bound up specifically with his philosophy of difference and becoming. My task here is not to give a full exposition of Deleuze's philosophy   there are many excellent and clarifying introductions.[8] Rather, I focus on the intertwining of material, becoming and difference in relation to thinking in and about music.

Deleuze's philosophy focuses on thinking as a way of grappling with the world, which he understands not as pre-existent order but rather as a chaotic potential for all orderings in the world. Deleuze conceives this chaotic potential as the virtual, which is actualised in particular events of experience. For Deleuze, the chaotic potential of the virtual generates the real events of experience through differential relations. That is, the interactions of differing things produce a new, unique event. Deleuze's philosophy of difference then is focused not on matters of identity, on how things resemble one another, but on how they differ. As Smith and Protevi point out: 'Deleuze wants to provide an account of the genesis of *real* experience, that is, the experience of this concretely existing individual here and now'.[9] To take account of the genesis of this-event-now, the philosopher   like the scientist and the artist   turns to the materials of the world in all their differing.

Music poses a challenge to this material turn because its sounding may entail relations between all or some of these points on a complex network: creators, performers, performances, listeners, work, acoustic spaces, loud-speakers, earphones, ambient noise, and so on. But the relational ontology Hainge articulates for music in his chapter proves fruitful for taking account of this multiplicity. The relational ontology allows for the operation of multiple points of a network and can take account of differences in the intensive characters of musical experiences. And in particular, it allows for a non-anthropomorphic operation of musical sounding itself. For instance, if asked what *is* the opening sound of Stravinsky's *Rite of Spring*, a musician of an idealist philosophical perspective might say 'it is a pitch class C', identifying the sound in terms of a pitch essence.[10] On the other hand, a Deleuzian musician might say 'A couple of years ago, I heard a performance of the *Rite of Spring* in Los Angeles's Disney Hall and Loren Glickman played that ethereal high C, which had an eerily pinched sound that virtually transported me back to ancient Russia.'[11] This detailed description answers the ontological question by specifying performance, performer, sound quality, pitch and effect, and it highlights the this-event-now differentiated by who, how, when and what. In other words, the Deleuzian answer addresses the 'what *is*' the opening sound of Stravinsky's *Rite* in terms of a materialist account of the complex network of factors that through their interactions produce musical experiences of various sorts.

This focus on a multiplicity of material factors recognises the agency not only of humans but also of inanimate things involved in the production of sonic experience. For instance, imagine that you are listening to a CD recording of the opening of the *Rite of Spring* while sitting in your living room. Myriad factors interact to produce 'the opening bassoon solo' event, including the wood of the bassoonist's reed, the sound engineering of the digital file, the material features of the loud-speakers, the size of your living room, your mood and so on. All of these factors have agency in affecting the event, and a materialist approach takes account of these factors as real. This Deleuzian emphasis on the material recognises both the contingency of what music *is* and gives agency to non-human factors of music. Hainge's chapter worries the consequences of giving full agency to inanimate objects to produce music apart from any human artistic intention, but at the same time his relational ontology assumes non-anthropomorphic perspectives that allow him to give agency to a 'wounded CD' in the production of music.

Within this materialist perspective of Deleuze's philosophy, difference arises prior to the identity of events of the world. It is conceived, as Smith and Protevi point out, not 'as an empirical relation between two terms which each has a prior identity of its own ("x is different from y")'. Rather, the priority is inverted: identity 'is produced by a prior relation between differentials (dx rather than not-x)'.[12] Identities emerge from difference as ways of thinking the world – thinking either through philosophy, the arts or science. Or in other words, identities are emergent ways of thinking the world, such emergence characterised by Deleuze as becoming. While ontological questions have historically focused on being in terms of a static essence of identity, Deleuze reframes these questions around becoming as a differential and temporal process. In an aesthetic context, the question becomes not what the essence of an artwork *is* – what it means – but rather how does it work. In other words, how do the materials of an artwork produce its effects and how do these effects emerge over time. As Elizabeth Grosz writes: 'Becoming is the operation of self – differentiation, the elaboration of a difference within a thing, a quality or a system that emerges or actualizes only in duration. Duration is the "field" in which difference lives and plays itself out.'[13] Becoming emphasises the role of thinking in the Deleuzian sense of that term and the production of the new through the interactive and contingent temporal processes of material interactions.

The ontological focus on becoming in Deleuzian philosophy has ramifications for approaching music. Hainge's relational ontology approaches the formal

204   *Judy Lochhead*

questions of musical ontology, recognising the complex interactions of production (creation and performance) and reception (listening). Through the complex and contingent interactions of creation, performance, listening and a plethora of material factors *music* emerges from sound as an event of the world. Deleuze's philosophy of becoming illuminates such formal issues of music's ontology as Hainge demonstrates, and it also sheds light on the informal ontological debates discussed at the beginning of this chapter.

The ontological question for Ocker's micro-interpretation of Wagner's *Ring Cycle* revolves around whether this may be understood as valid performance of the work. The question arises because a new technology — digital manipulation of the playback speed of a recording — has radically transformed approximately 15 hours of recorded performance into seven minutes of sound.[14] The question for Oswald's 'Dab' also arises because of a new technology, the advent of digital sampling to construct a new work from sound files of an existing musical work. In this case, the comments of YouTube listeners are aesthetic evaluations — 'horrible' or 'amazing' — that verge on the question of whether the sampling and collaging of 'Dab' can qualify *as* music. For instance, one listener writes: 'WTF is up with the comments? how is this any good? I'm genuinely trying to understand here ... [sic]'.[15] Even an explicit attempt to comprehend 'Dab' is unsuccessful, or in other words the comment suggests that this listener cannot hear 'Dab' *as* music. From the Deleuzian perspective of becoming, these questions of the viability of Ocker's performance and of the status of Oswald's 'Dab' as music arise because of the introduction of something new — here digital sound technologies — which transforms the expectations of aesthetic reception and artistic production, to use Hainge's terms.

Such aesthetic expectations figure in the informal ontological questions of my students' responses to Cage's and Carter's music. In Deleuzian terms such expectations operate as frames for experience, and they act through processes of territorialisation. As Christa Albrecht-Crane writes: 'territorialisation functions through processes that organize and systematize social space and language production. These processes impose a certain kind of order and categorization on the world that become "fixed" in conceptual structure.'[16] Hearing a particular sonic event *as* music operates within such a territorial frame that is socially, historically and culturally contingent. On occasion the functioning of that territorial frame for hearing may itself become aurally apparent to listeners. For instance this is apparent in my students' response when they realise that Carter, in particular, creates music within another aesthetic frame that is shared and affirmed by others who support the aesthetic economy in which he creates music. In this instance, my students are forced to consider Carter's Double Concerto *as* music because I, as an authority figure, have told them it is. Since Carter clearly intends for the Double Concerto to have the sounds they hear, my students' outrage seems to emanate from an awareness that other territorial frames for aesthetic experience operate. In Deleuzian terms, this dismantling or dislodging of a territorial frame plays a role in processes of deterritorialisation. This process, as Albrecht-Crane points out, is not 'destructive'; rather, 'it is active, productive and affirmative ... [and] Deleuze emphasizes that deterritorialisation makes new thinking possible'.[17] And because new thinking emerges from deterritorialisation, the new leads to the formation of new habits of thinking in reterritorialisation. In the Deleuzian ontology of becoming, territorialisation, deterritorialisation and reterritorialisation are ongoing processes of thinking the world in the concepts of philosophy, the formula of science or the sensations of arts.

Difference, materiality and becoming stand at the heart of the ontological questions that flow from Deleuzian philosophy. These concepts open up fruitful pathways into thinking about music because they set out ways to approach music as participatory activity. The questions that concepts of difference, materiality and becoming generate for thinking about music entail a turn to music as sonic event by means of which listeners, and creators and performers think the world. The insistence on difference leads us to recognise the territorial frames that produce particular aesthetic responses, drawing attention to such issues as race, gender, technology, socio-economic conditions, and so on. The insistence on materiality leads us to realise a non-anthropomorphic ontology that recognises the agency of non-animate factors of musical sound. And the insistence on becoming leads us to recognise musical works as dynamic events arising from complex network of interactions between the materials of sounding, listening, creating and performing. The Deleuzian turn toward difference, materiality and becoming lead us not to some ideal essence of music, but rather lead us to questions of how music produces the sensations in sounding that 'render non-sonorous forces sonorous'.[18]

Notes

1 For a good general introduction to the philosophy of music, see: Theodore Gracyk and Andrew Kania, *The Routledge Companion to Philosophy and Music* (Abingdon and New York: Routledge, 2011). See also: Andrew Kania, 'The Philosophy of Music', in *The Stanford Encyclopedia of Philosophy* (Spring 2014 ed.), ed. Edward N. Zalta, accessed 15 February 2015, http://plato.stanford.edu/archives/spr2014/entries/music/. On thinking the ontology of music as 'ontologies' see: Philip Bohlman, 'Ontologies of Music", in *Rethinking Music* ed. Nicholas Cook and Mark Everist (Oxford and New York: Oxford University Press, 2001), 17–34.

2 Interested listeners may hear this digital version at Ocker's website, accessed 19 January 2015, http://davidocker.com/MMFiles/Wagner-The-Ring-Cycle-complete-in-7-minutes_128x–faster.html. Ocker writes further about his inspiration for the project, about the technical details, and about precedents with other technologies at, accessed 19 January 2015, http://mixedmeters.com/2010/05/listen-to-wagners-entire-ring-cycle-in.html.

3 John Oswald, 'Dab' from *Plunderphonics*, posted on YouTube, accessed 19 January 2015, https://www.youtube.com/watch?v=8xIWLG–F0Ag.

4 John Cage, *4'33"*, *Tacet, any instrument or combination of instruments* (New York: C.F. Peters, 1960) and Elliott Carter, *Double Concerto for Harpsichord and Piano with Two Chamber Orchestras* (New York: Associated Music Publishers, 1964).

5 Frank Zappa, *4'33"*, on *A Chance Operation: The John Cage Tribute* (Westbury, NY: Koch International Classics (3-7238-2 Y6x2), 1993), CD.

6 Hainge problematises a fully materialist approach (deriving from the perspective of speculative realism) and takes up questions of intention.

7 As new fields of thought, the names of these strands of scholarship are fluid. For instance, speculative realism is associated with object-oriented philosophy, transcendental materialism, and many others. The new materialism is related to 'thing theory' developed by Bill Brown. Two instructive books on the topic are: Levi Bryant, Graham Harman, and Nick Srnicek, *The Speculative Turn: Continental Materialism and Realism* (Melbourne: re.press, 2011) and Bill Brown, *A Sense of Things: The Object Matter of American Literature* (Chicago: University of Chicago Press, 2003).

8 For a good general discussion and bibliography see: Daniel W. Smith and John Protevi, 'Gilles Deleuze', *The Stanford Encyclopedia of Philosophy* (Spring 2013 ed.), ed. Edward N. Zalta, accessed 15 March 2015, http://plato.stanford.edu/archives/spr2013/entries/deleuze/.

9 Smith and Protevi, 'Gilles Deleuze'.

10 Such idealist approaches to musical sound have recently been articulated in Dmitri Tymoczko, *A Geometry of Music: Harmony and Counterpoint in the Extended Common Practice* (New York: Oxford University Press, 2011).

11 Full disclosure: I do not know if Loren Glickman ever played the *Rite of Spring* at Disney Hall, but the interested reader can hear him playing on the Columbia recording with Stravinsky conducting: Igor Stravinsky, 'The Rite of Spring', on *Three Favorite Ballets*, cond. Igor Stravinsky (New York: Columbia Masterworks, MS3705, 1960), vinyl record. Glickman describes his experience of playing the piece with Stravinsky as conductor in an interview with Nora Post, see: Nora Post, 'The Many Careers of Bassoonist Loren Glickman: An Interview by Nora Post', *The Double Reed* 35/2 (2012): 39–55.

12 Smith and Protevi, 'Gilles Deleuze'.

13 Elizabeth Grosz, 'Bergson, Deleuze and the Becoming of Unbecoming', *parallax* 11/2 (2005), 4.

14 The sonic trace of Wagner's music in this performance is faint and depends on whether the listener is aware of the time-compression of the digital sound file.

15 Oswald, 'Dab'.

16 Christa Albrecht-Crane, 'Style, Stutter', in *Gilles Deleuze: Key Concepts*, ed. Charles J. Stivale, 2nd ed. (Durham, England: Acumen, 2011), 143.

17 Albrecht-Crane, 'Style, Stutter', 146.

18 Gilles Deleuze, *Francis Bacon: The Logic of Sensation*, trans. Daniel Smith (Minneapolis: University of Minnesota Press, 2004), 48.

17 Material music

Speculations on non-human agency in music

Greg Hainge

In this chapter, I consider some questions concerning the ontology of music and offer some speculations on the conditions under which 'music' might be said to emerge. Many have no uncertainty about what music *is*, yet debates about its essence still rage in certain circles. For example, Andy Hamilton claims that 'music is the art of tones', an assertion that leads him to suggest that works with 'unpitched or not discretely pitched' sounds should be called sound-art and not music.[1] For Hamilton, 'To allow that any sounds can be *incorporated into* music is not ... to say that any sounds can *constitute* music. ... [M]usic makes predominant use of tonal sounds and ... [should not be confused with] a non-musical sound-art.'[2]

Hamilton's position is not uncommon in the field of the philosophy of music. Roger Scruton, for instance, argues that musical expression is necessarily tied to meaning and that such meaning arises only in the context of musical tonality even if a conscious decision has been made to avoid the tonal system. He writes: 'The possibility remains that tonal music is the only music that will ever really mean anything to us, and that, if atonal music sometimes gains a hearing, it is because we can elicit within it a latent tonal order.'[3] However, nearly all such universalist statements made about the ontological status of music betray a predominantly Western cultural bias that undermines many of the claims made. Since I have critiqued such claims elsewhere,[4] in what follows I will turn instead to a brief overview of my own ontological taxonomy of music in order to consider a separate yet related question that is raised by Hamilton's comments above. I argue here that Hamilton's distinction between music and sound-art gestures towards a different question – namely towards the possibility of positioning as 'music' an installation or other sound-art event that does not require direct human intervention either to produce a sonic event or, even more troubling, to compose such an event. In order to consider this question of non-human agency in music, I need, first, however, to propose an alternative ontology of music that takes as its starting point a consideration of what is often considered to be the opposite of music: noise

Noise

In my recent work, I approach noise from an ontological point of view, a vantage that requires discarding 'common-sense' definitions which pose noise as a loud and/or disagreeable sound.[5] Such definitions depend on subjective judgements for which one person's music is another person's noise and vice versa. These judgements arise not only from differing musical tastes but also from the differing perspectives of those who hear, for example, the concert-goer vs. a resident of a property adjoining a music venue. In addressing the ontology of noise, I also reject the approach taken by some authors who, in examining noise as cultural expression, imbue it with a miraculous power of transubstantiation. In the very influential work of Jacques Attali, for example, noise operates somewhat like the concept of force in Alexandre Kojève's reading of Hegel a force that renders change and thus history possible. For Attali noise brings about change in the field of musical production by first resisting current orthodoxies and then becoming a reconfigured musical orthodoxy an orthodoxy which in turn is resisted by different forms of noise.[6] In contrast to these formulations of noise, I use certain elements of the concept of noise in communications theory, specifically the idea that noise is an interference arising in a communications channel through which a message passes from an emitter to a receiver. However, rather than figure noise as a third element external to the message transmitted and hence deleterious for its clean and proper transmission I posit that noise needs to be understood as an artefact of the communication system. Noise, then, becomes not so much an annoyance to be eradicated but rather a necessary part of the communications system, indeed, it can be thought of as the essence of the relation between the components of a communications system in operation.

In this conception, the ontology of noise is relational. Such a relational approach to ontology follows the philosophy of Gilles Deleuze and certain strands of recent philosophical schools of thought such as speculative realism, object-oriented ontology, actor network theory, and new materialism. In a relational ontology Being is generated not from within an autonomous entity but rather from the in-between of (partial) entities and the environment in which they are situated, in the space between the virtual and the actual via an expressive act that is constitutive of ontology. Arising as an artefact of communication or expression, noise necessarily talks to us of ontology when ontology is conceived of as being fundamentally expressive.

To examine the noise of any expression, then, is to examine the way that expression comes to be rather than to posit what it *is*. Such an ontological reformulation allows us to think about process rather than forms and to approach the ontology of music from a relational perspective as well. Such a relational approach to music allows us to avoid the subjective and cultural historical pitfalls that have plagued many prior approaches. All too often, ontological claims about music are made on matters of taste or aesthetic judgement. When approaching the ontology of music from the perspective of noise, however, which is to say from the perspective of an ontology conceptualised not from the outside but, rather, from within, a different picture of music emerges. Apprehended in this way, music can be described according to the following ontological taxonomy:

i Music is sound that is
ii structured,
iii eminently expressive since its only form is its expressed content, and hence
iv irreducible to a secondary function (such as representation),
v conditioned by an assemblage in the real world (and therefore not transcendent or ahistorical).[7]

Material music

This brief overview sets the stage for my primary concern here: does this ontological taxonomy of music enable us to qualify sounding expressions generated by non-human agentic forces as 'music'. With the terminology 'non-human agentic forces' I refer to a range of sounding phenomena such as the sounds of water fountains, Aeolian harps, musical readymades and field recordings. The relational ontological taxonomy I have sketched here allows us to ask if these sounding phenomena *are* music, a question made possible by the philosophical perspectives shaped by speculative realism, new materialism and various related movements.[8] All of these perspectives resist in slightly different ways anthropocentric philosophies of access in which knowledge of the world is necessarily produced via thought located within a human subject. Outside such anthropocentric bounds, in much recent philosophy other kinds of non-human forms, both animate and inanimate, are afforded an agentic force or capacity. As Diana Coole and Samantha Frost write:

> new materialists are rediscovering a materiality that materializes, evincing immanent modes of self-transformation that compel us to think of causation in far more complex terms; to recognize that phenomena are caught in a multitude of interlocking systems and forces and to consider anew the location and nature of capacities for agency.

Conceiving matter as possessing its own modes of self-transformation, self-organisation and directedness, and thus no longer as simply passive or inert, disturbs the conventional sense that agents are exclusively humans who possess the cognitive abilities, intentionality and freedom to make autonomous decisions and the corollary presumption that humans have the right or ability to master nature. Instead, the human species is being relocated within a natural environment whose material forces themselves manifest certain agentic capacities and in which the domain of unintended or unanticipated effects is considerably broadened. Matter is no longer imagined here as a massive, opaque plenitude but is recognised instead as indeterminate, constantly forming and reforming in unexpected ways. One could conclude, accordingly, that 'matter becomes' rather than that 'matter is'.[9]

210   *Greg Hainge*

If we accept the fundamental premise of new materialism, there is no reason to limit these ontological speculations to matter narrowly conceived. If ontology is conceived as expressive then it should be applicable to expressions including music. This question of non-human agency in music has been analysed in-depth by Stan Godlovitch in *Musical Performance: A Philosophical Study*, which contains chapters on 'Computers, readymades and artistic agency' and 'Experiments with musical agency'. Godlovitch defines music as 'an art of structuring sound for display in sound', and he privileges performance as a defining feature of music.[10] His goal in the book is 'to build sympathy for a performance-centred conception of music, the overall plan being to epitomize a tradition of music-making'.[11] This perspective requires the implicit disqualification of certain kinds of computer or technologically enhanced musical expression from the artistic realm of music. For instance, he writes: 'Recordings of performances ... are not performances. Recordings are just traces or records of performances, and no more performances in their own right than photos are the objects photographed.'[12] Godlovitch's reflections impact only a theory of performance and not the ontology of music, however, and his theory does not, consequently, require us to deny a recording of a musical performance the ontological status of music.

Such ontological issues are further complicated by musical expressions created not via the immediate agency of a human performer but via a kind of technological prosthesis. For Godlovitch, 'Performances are deliberate, intentionally caused sound sequences. ... The intention to perform and beliefs about the context are integral to performance.'[13] Performances, as the defining features of musical expression, are 'not mere occurrences, but actions undertaken by agents. As such, performance points both to its origin and purpose ... [in the] human being.'[14] Given Godlovitch's reliance on intentionality, technologically mediated expressions pose a problem and lead him to theorize an entirely new kind of art form.[15] He writes:

> Computer-assisted music, musical quasi-readymades, and experimental music challenge the centrality of immediate agency. For those with a stake in the traditions, it is worthwhile to expose these developments as neither threats nor alternatives to performance paradigms. Instead, at their best, they represent new enough ways of dealing with sound as to merit consideration as new artforms, much as photography and film have become.[16]

Godlovitch's focus on performance as a defining feature of music leads him to posit a new form of artistic expression which would not go by the name of music. A relational ontology, however, provides an alternative. The idea of a pure, human-centred intentionality able to exert complete mastery of a violin, for example, is unnecessarily anthropocentric since a violinist's actions are technologically conditioned and constrained by the materiality of the violin. To borrow the terminology of object-oriented philosophy, we might suggest that this is a case of the violin expressing its agentic capacity, or, to return to my ontological taxonomy of music, we might simply say that this is an instance of music being 'conditioned by an assemblage in the real world'. Whilst there are obvious differences between how violinists and laptop performers relate to and produce sounds with their instruments, in both instances performers make choices about the kinds and sequences of sounds that occur.[17] In the case of laptop performance, then, Godlovitch's paradigm of performance applies and there is no need to suppose that less traditional forms of music signal the appearance of ontologically distinct forms of art.

The use of generative algorithms to produce sound raises different issues since the human agent is involved only in the design of a sound-producing assemblage. In these cases, no human agency is involved in the choices and actions through which sound is produced in performance. Similarly, we might ask if the musical sounds produced by a suikinkutsu may be considered a musical performance in the same sense that a performance of Bach's *Six Suites for Unaccompanied Cello* is? The non-anthropocentric perspective of speculative realism would suggest that it can but I believe some caution is required.

Suikinkutsu

A suikinkutsu, a sounding Japanese garden ornament, consists of a pot with a hole in the bottom which is then buried upside down in the ground so that the hole sits at the top. Water drips through his hole into a pool of water in the buried pot, the sound of these drips resonating inside the acoustic chamber provided by the pot. The sounds emanating from a suikinkutsu present themselves as remarkably – even surprisingly – 'musical', and it is at times possible to believe that one is listening to a melodic line. Yet one cannot 'play' a suikinkutsu in the way one plays an instrument, and while human action is primarily responsible for releasing water into the vessel – often as part of a hand-washing ritual associated with a Japanese tea ceremony – the resulting sounds are produced by several factors: the original design, the resonant properties of the pot, the level of the water in the subterranean pool, chance operations related to the amount of water released into the structure and the path that the water takes, the arrangement of rocks, stones or plants around the top of the suikinkutsu and gravity.

It would appear, then, that the sounds produced by a suikinkutsu conform to a relational ontology of music. The suikinkutsu produces sound that is organised or structured, expressive since its only form is its expressed content, irreducible to a secondary function such as representation and conditioned by a material assemblage in the real world. And yet I am uneasy with this speculation since when I originally drew up this taxonomy I had, without realising it, implicitly imagined that any 'musical' expression would be partially determined by the immediate agency of a human subject or subjects, no matter if that agency is hybrid, technologised or prosthetic. For someone with sympathy for the ontological formulations of speculative realism and a deep-seated conviction that ontology requires a relational conception, this seems like a strangely anthropocentric position. Nonetheless, my discomfort in extending the logic of relational ontology to encompass

212 *Greg Hainge*

non-human agents in the realm of music signals an important question in relation to music and also to non-human agency more generally.

In drawing up the ontological taxonomy of music presented earlier, I assumed that territorial birdsong would not count as music because it was reducible to a secondary function – the sonic delineation of a territory. Music, conceived as artistic expression, does not obey such pragmatic imperatives. It is, perhaps, the form of artistic expression that, more than any other, problematises any direct equivalence between its forms and the world in which they occur. Or, in other words, music does not 'represent' objects or phenomena in the real world in the same way as do paintings or photography, even if the music is imitative.[18] In the visual realm, the situation of territorial birdsong has a parallel in the plumage of a peacock. This colourful display has a very different agentic impetus from an artistic expression such as Gustave Courbet's *The Origin of the World*, even if both are loosely linked by a theme of procreation. Even if art can perform a secondary worldly function as perhaps political, ethical or social commentary, its primary *modus operandi* is to generate an interruption or spacing between the spectator/listener and the immersive flow of existence. This interruption or spacing produced by the work of art consists of a self-reflexive performative gesture of the work itself as art in a manner irreducible to any secondary function. When art is liberated from a subservient relation to the world, akin to that we find in philosophies of access in which the world is always in thrall to the perspective of a human subject, artworks take on a life – or agency – of their own. This point is made abundantly clear by Andrew Benjamin with respect to painting:

> Moving beyond the hold of exemplarity necessitates that it is the painting's work that figures. Work for the painting, because those moments in which what is displayed cannot be separated from its presence as the effect of painting, involves the painting's materiality. A materiality continually marked by an immaterial presence. Figures effected by the painting's work are – as a consequence – able to figure.[19]

Benjamin does not suggest here that painting is imbued with its own autonomous agency nor that this *work* of the work of art could take place in the absence of an originary human artistic sensibility. Rather, he asserts that the figurative potential of the work of art is a capacity released only via a relation that arises in the act of criticism.[20]

If artistic expression is always fundamentally, then, a performative gesture of its ontological status as art and if, what is more, the work of art is produced only through an act of criticism that serves primarily to effect the figuration of the work itself, art entertains a very peculiar relationship to the world insofar as it is doubly futile, a term I use without any negative inflection. Music is such an expression, in contradistinction to bird song for the reasons explained above, and if music is ultimately futile in the sense that it does not fulfil any pragmatic function then the term 'music' should refer only to expressions in which the agentic force of production is partially human – and only partially human since the human may only express itself via relations with other human or non-human expressive beings. This point has ramifications for all new materialist or speculative realist philosophies. While anti-anthropocentric philosophical approaches open the world to perspectives other than the human – if only to bring about a greater consciousness of the environmental havoc wreaked by an anthropocentric worldview – it does not follow that expressive forms specific to a certain kind of human agency can unproblematically be applied to other kinds of expressive agents. To do so, indeed, would be to re-inscribe the anthropomorphism that such philosophies seek to escape. In attributing such capacities to non-human forms we do not step out of the frame of the human to try and understand how the ontological deployments of other kinds of expressive being might operate on their own terms. This is perhaps an unavoidable quandary for thought produced via philosophies which are irrevocably related to the human realm, even when one argues, as does Deleuze, that thought can be produced in different modes via other kinds of assemblages.[21] Thus, while the new materialist philosophies raise important issues about non-human agency and relational ontologies, the application of agentic capacity and intentionality to certain categories of objects and forms might, in retrospect, reveal itself to be a wrong-footed distraction from an important philosophical debate.

And yet ...

Music brings into the fray a complex ontology involving different modes. If we take music as a fundamental ontological category, music comes to be in the world through two main modes or through two different kinds of assemblages in which the human agent's role is very different. These correspond to the moment of production, which includes the two potentially distinct events of composition and performance, and the moment of reception. Often these aspects of music are considered apart from each other since each foregrounds very different questions. In the past I have argued that the ontology of music arises exclusively in the expressive act itself, in the mode of production. Contrary to scholars such as Ridley,[22] I have claimed that the ontology of music does not arrive retrospectively, as music is related back to the world via the receptive or interpretive agency of the listener since this is a secondary ontological phase belonging to an assemblage different from that which gives rise to the ontology of music per se.[23] While still disagreeing with Ridley on this point, I do want to complicate my position. For in a fully relational ontology in which everything comes to be through expressive acts, the reception of music is, I wish to suggest, a constitutive aspect of the ontology of music – just as, in Benjamin's analysis seen above the work of figuration of painting is effected only through the act of criticism. To put it simply, the listener, whether actual, future or virtual, is an integral and vital part of music's ontology since it is through her that music is expressed in the world. A fully relational ontology cannot be understood simply in relation to the supposed centre or form that constitutes the core of that which is being defined but must also be understood via the relations that it entertains with the outside in which it is situated. This does not simply

214   *Greg Hainge*

mean that we have to be aware of the context in which everything comes to pass, the way in which being expresses itself in an environment; it implies, rather, that we need to account for the ways in which the expressive capacity of any Being is partially determined by its situation such that its agency is partially relinquished or constrained by its possible futures in the world.

In suggesting this, it becomes apparent that I have only tackled half of the question I posed initially: the possibility of non-human agents' capacity to produce music. What happens if we turn to the question of how sounds produced by non-human agents might be perceived by a listener not aware of how the sounds were generated? The earlier example of the suikinkutsu does not suffice for this question because the mechanics of this sound-producing assemblage are too readily identifiable. Rather, it is necessary to consider a situation in which the listener is unaware of the means of production generating the sounds. I thus turn to the digital realm, in which it is harder to intuit or deduce the mechanics of sound production because of the lack of analogue relations between physical activity and sonic event. Yasunao Tone's *Solo for Wounded CD* provides a good test case.[24]

Tone's work is made by 'wounding' a CD, that is by making micro abrasions on its surface and affixing perforated adhesive tape to it. When inserted into a playback machine this CD produces burst errors. The 'wounding' of the CD required for this to happen is a more subtle and complex operation than one might imagine. If the CD is wounded too much, the error-correction software of the player prevents the disk from playing; yet, if the errors are too subtle the software mutes the error.[25] Even though CD-wounding is then a deliberate process, the 'composer's' actions are not directly related to the controlled production of sound. Tone's role is more like that of an instrument-maker: he creates an object which will subsequently be used to produce sound. The difference between Tone's instrument and a violin, however, is that the actual production of sounds through the interactions of the wounded CD and the CD player is devoid of human agency or intentionality.[26] Furthermore, since each playback of the wounded CD produces different sonic results, especially if one uses different CD players, there is no way to foresee what sounds will occur. According to the criteria discussed earlier, then, the sonic event of *Solo for Wounded CD* is not music, no matter whether the work is 'performed' in a live setting as it was originally conceived or considered in the reified form of a recorded performance released as a non-wounded CD artefact.

Herein lies a problem. From the perspective of a listener, the disqualification of Tone's *Solo for Wounded CD* from the realm of music according to the previous criteria can occur only if that listener is aware of the means of production of the sonic content. There is no reason to suppose, however, that this will necessarily be so. Nor is there any reason to suppose that another glitch composer could not deliberately and intentionally assemble a piece that would sound like Tone's piece by using sampled CD glitches as the building blocks or by some other means. Some glitch artists use sampled glitches to create music with discernible melodies, rhythms, lines or organisational attributes bearing the trace of a more readily recognisable human-centred artistic sensibility.[27] But for other artists in the realm of digital music, it can be hard to intuit the presence of a guiding human hand since their works seem to reject the organisational principles according to which music has been predominantly structured in many and especially Western forms. In a comment posted on his blog 'Irreversible Noise' on 6 March 2013, Inigo Wilkins writes that 'contemporary musicians working in the non-standard phase space between periodic sine tones and non-periodic complex modulation (such as Haswell and Hecker, Mark Fell and many others) are capable of producing a radically inhuman and non-aesthetic music that mobilizes unpredictable complexity across many orders of magnitude'.[28] While Wilkins' comments might be thought to reinforce my suggestion that non-human agents cannot produce something called music – the blog post is titled 'Enemy of Music' – the important point for my argument is that the music he describes is produced as the result of compositional choices made by a human agent. Given this there is no reason to assume, according to my previous taxonomy, that these works are not music. And further, such music is not the enemy of music, nor 'inhuman', even if it sounds like the machinic music produced without human intervention we find on Tone's *Solo for Wounded CD*, nor non-aesthetic, even if the aesthetic choices differ radically from prior modes of aesthetic expression.

In saying this, however, I return to my original question, which had to do with musical production. What we need to consider is whether a piece crafted by a human agent could, to a listener uninformed about the genetic conditions of production, sound like a piece generated by a non-human agentic force or, conversely, whether a piece such as Tone's could be produced as the result of the human, conscious, aesthetic choices of a composer. Bearing in mind Wilkins's comments, the answer to this would seem to be yes, and given that, from the point of view of reception it is no longer possible to disqualify a piece such as Tone's *Solo for Wounded CD* from the category of music.

It might be suggested that in answer to the question 'Is Yasunao Tone's *Solo for Wounded CD* music?' we need to answer either yes or no depending on whether we are talking about the ontology of music at the point of production or the point of reception given that music is a complex ontological substance that is expressed in different modes. This hardly seems a satisfactory answer, however, and some might suggest that it is not an answer at all.

Instead, I propose that music can be said to come into being as the result of an aesthetic framing of sound regardless of whether this takes place at the point of production or reception. This is not to be interpreted as a corrective to the taxonomy proposed earlier but, rather, an addition that might help us think through the questions posed here in regards to non-human agency. In this framing Tone's *Solo for Wounded CD is* music since the sound produced results from a certain aesthetic and thus human disposition that seeks to produce and arrange sounds for a non-utilitarian end, even if direct agency over the actual sounds produced is surrendered. At the point of reception, meanwhile, if we add this qualification to the proposed taxonomy it is no longer necessary to know anything about the genetic conditions of production of a piece. The important thing is that the listener is inclined to an aesthetic disposition in which these sounds are perceived as

216 *Greg Hainge*

being arranged in such a way that they are apprehended not as the by-product of another primary process or phenomenon (such as nature) but rather as sounds intentionally arranged for non-utilitarian ends.

Notes

1 Andy Hamilton, *Aesthetics and Music* (New York and London: Continuum, 2007), 41–2.
2 Hamilton, *Aesthetics and Music*, 45. Emphasis in the original.
3 Roger Scruton, *The Aesthetics of Music* (Oxford: Oxford University Press, 1999), 296.
4 Greg Hainge, *Noise Matters: Towards an Ontology of Noise* (New York: Bloomsbury Academic, 2013), 247–9.
5 Greg Hainge, *Noise Matters*.
6 See Alexandre Kojève, *Introduction to the Reading of Hegel: Lectures on the Phenomenology of Spirit*, ed. Allan Bloom, trans. James Nichols (orig. French 1947; Ithaca: Cornell University Press, 1980) and Jacques Attali, *Noise: The Political Economy of Music*, trans. Brian Massumi (Minneapolis: University of Minnesota Press, 1985), 34.
7 Hainge, *Noise Matters*, 251.
8 Some of these related movements are: speculative materialism, object-oriented philosophy, transcendent materialism or neo-vitalism, transcendental nihilism, flat ontology, and so on.
9 Diana Coole and Samantha Frost, eds, *New Materialisms: Ontology, Agency and Politics* (Durham, NC: Duke University Press, 2010), 10.
10 Stan Godlovitch, *Musical Performance: A Philosophical Study* (London: Routledge, 1998), 2.
11 Godlovitch, *Musical Performance*, 11.
12 Godlovitch, *Musical Performance*, 14.
13 Godlovitch, *Musical Performance*, 16.
14 Godlovitch, *Musical Performance*, 15.
15 Another aspect of Godlovitch's argument which bears on but is not central to my argument here involves his desire to retain a Guild tradition for performance and the requirement for specific technical skills that can only be accrued through a long disciplining of the body.
16 Godlovitch, *Musical Performance*, 97.
17 As should be clear, the form of laptop performance referred to here does not include the playing of previously coded music or the launching of generative algorithms.
18 This notion of representation for painting and photography is problematic if one examines it from the perspective of speculative realism. This, however, is not the focus of the present discussion and must be left aside.
19 Andrew Benjamin, *Disclosing Spaces: On Painting* (Manchester: Clinamen Press, 2004), 46.
20 Benjamin, *Disclosing Spaces*, 3.
21 This is not a dismissal of Deleuze's approach for his point is slightly different. Deleuze does not imbue the technological assemblage of the cinema, for instance, with something akin to a human-centred concept of consciousness, capacity for thought or intentionality but, rather, to suggest that in the relation instigated between a human subject and the cinematic apparatus, a different kind of thought is produced that has the potential to extend philosophy beyond the bounds of that which is possible from solely within a human perspective.
22 See Aaron Ridley, *The Philosophy of Music: Themes and Variations* (Edinburgh: Edinburgh University Press, 2004), 10.
23 Hainge, *Noise Matters*, 251.
24 Yasunao Tone, *Solo for Wounded CD* (New York: Tzadik TZ 7212, 1997), CD.

25 See Yasuao Tone and Christian Marclay, 'Record, CD, Analog, Digital', in *Audio Culture: Readings in Modern Music*, ed. Christoph Cox and Daniel Warner (New York and London: Continuum, 2004), 341–2.

26 Another related instance involves the pianola. It is programmed and governed by human intentionality, but the production of performed sound does not require human agency. Godlovitch travails over the issues of the pianola. See, Godlovitch, *Musical Performance*, 16.

27 Oval is a good example of such an artist. Consider, for instance, *94 Diskont* (1994).

28 Inigo Wilkins, 'Enemy of Music', Blog entry, 6 March 2013, accessed 14 March 2013, http://irreversiblenoise.wordpress.com/2013/03/06/enemy–of–music/.

Bibliography

Adams, Stephen. 'The 2010 World New Music Days: Hear the World's Best New Music Festival on Your Radio.' In *Limelight: Music Arts, Culture*, edited by Diane Parks and Marija Beram. Australian Broadcasting Corporation. May 2010.

Adorno, Theodor W. *Negative Dialektik: Jargon Der Eigentlichkeit*. Frankfurt am Main: Suhrkamp, 1966.

———. *Kritik: Kleine Schriften Zur Gesellschaft*. Frankfurt am Main: Suhrkamp, 1971.

———. *Introduction to the Sociology of Music*, translated by E.G. Ashton. New York: Seabury Press, 1976.

———. *Introduction to the Sociology of Music*. New York and London: Continuum, 1988.

Al-Nakib, Mai. 'Assia Djebar's Musical Ekphrasis.' *Comparative Literature Studies* 42 (2005): 253–76.

Albrecht-Crane, Christa. 'Style, Stutter.' In *Gilles Deleuze: Key Concepts*, edited by Charles J. Stivale, 142–52. 2nd ed. Durham, England: Acumen, 2011.

Andriessen, Louis. *The Art of Stealing Time*, edited by Mirjam Zegers, translated by Clare Yates. Todmorden, UK: Arc Music, 2002.

Appleby, Rosalind. *Women of Note: The Rise of Australian Women Composers*. Fremantle: Fremantle Press, 2012.

Applegate, Celia. *Bach in Berlin: Nation and Culture in Mendelssohn's Revival of the St. Matthew Passion*. Ithaca, NY: Cornell University Press, 2005.

Applegate, Celia, and Pamela Potter. *Music and German National Identity*. Chicago: University of Chicago Press, 2002.

Atherton, Michael. 'At the Edge of What Comes Next: "Comprovised" Meaningfulness in Jiriyai, a New Work for Percussionist and Dancer.' In *Intercultural Music: Creation and Interpretation*, edited by Sally Macarthur, Bruce Crossman and Ronald Morelos, 83–9. Sydney: Australian Music Centre, 2007.

Attali, Jacques. *Noise: The Political Economy of Music*, translated by Brian Massumi. Minneapolis: University of Minnesota Press, 1985.

Augoyard, Jean-François, and Henry Torgue. *Sonic Experience: A Guide to Everyday Sounds*, translated by Andra McCartney and David Paquette. Montreal: McGill-Queen's University Press, 2005.

Australian Government. 'Australia in the Asian Century', 2012. Accessed 1 December 2014. http://asialink.unimelb.edu.au/media/media_releases/media_releases/Australia_in_the_Asian_century.

Austern, Linda. '"Alluring the Auditorie to Effeminacie": Music and the Idea of the Feminine in Early Modern England.' *Music and Letters* 74 (1993): 343–54.

220 Bibliography

Barad, Karen. *Meeting the Universe Halfway: Quantum Physics and the Entanglement of Matter and Meaning*. Durham, NC; London: Duke University Press, 2007.

Barber, Christie, Mio Bryce and Jason Davis. 'The Making of Killer Cuties.' In *Anime and Philosophy: Wide Eyed Wonder*, edited by Joseph Steiff and Tristan. D. Tamplin, 13–25. Chicago, IL: Open Court, 2010.

Barker, Kenneth, ed. *The NIV Study Bible: The New International Version*. Michigan: Zondervan, 1985.

Barnhart, Richard. 'The Inner World of the Brush.' *The Metropolitan Museum of Art Bulletin* 30/5 (1972): 230–41.

Barrett, Estelle. 'Foucault's "What Is an Author": Towards a Critical Discourse of Practice as Research.' In *Practice as Research: Approaches to Creative Arts Research*, edited by Estelle Barrett and Barbara Bolt, 135–46. London: I.B. Tauris, 2007.

———. 'Introduction.' In *Practice as Research: Approaches to Creative Arts Enquiry*, edited by Estelle Barrett and Barbara Bolt, 1–13. London: I.B. Tauris, 2007.

Barrett, Estelle, and Barbara Bolt, eds. *Practice as Research: Approaches to Creative Arts Enquiry*. London: I.B. Tauris, 2007.

———, eds. *Carnal Knowledge: Towards a 'New Materialism' Through the Arts*. London: I.B. Taurus, 2013.

———. 'Introduction.' In *Material Inventions: Applying Research in the Creative Arts*, edited by Estelle Barrett and Barbara Bolt, 1–21. London: I.B. Tauris, 2014.

Barthes, Roland. *S/Z*. Paris: Éditions du Seuil, 1973. Trans. Richard Miller. Oxford: Blackwell, 1990.

———. 'The Death of the Author.' In *Image, Music, Text*, translated by Stephen Heath, 142–8. New York and London: Hill and Wang; Fontana, 1977.

Bartleet, Brydie-Leigh, Dawn Bennett, Ruth Bridgstock, Paul Draper, Scott David Harrison and Huib Schippers. 'Preparing for portfolio careers in Australian music: Setting a research agenda.' *Australian Journal of Music Education* 1 (2012): 32–41.

Benjamin, Andrew. *Disclosing Spaces: On Painting*. Manchester: Clinamen Press, 2004.

Bennett, Dawn. 'What do Musicians Do for a Living?' Music Council of Australia website. Accessed 2 June 2014. http://www.musiccareer.com.au/index.php/What_do_Musicians_do_for_a_Living%3F.

Bennett, Jane. *Vibrant Matter: A Political Ecology of Things*. Durham, NC: Duke University Press, 2010.

Bergen, Véronique. 'Politics as the Orientation of Every Assemblage', translated by Jeremy Gilbert. *New Formations* 68/2 (2009): 34–41.

Bidima, Jean-Godefroy. 'Intensity, Music and Heterogenesis in Deleuze', translated by Michael Wiedorn. In *Sounding the Virtual: Gilles Deleuze and the Theory and Philosophy of Music*, edited by Brian Hulse and Nick Nesbitt, 145–58. Farnham, UK and Burlington, VT: Ashgate, 2010.

Biggs, Michael A.R. 'Learning from Experience: Approaches to the Experiential Component of Practice-Led Research.' In *Forskning, Reflektion, Utveckling*, edited by H. Karlsson, 6–21. Stockholm, Sweden: Vetenskapsrådet, 2004.

Bloom, Harold. *The Anxiety of Influence: A Theory of Poetry*. New York: Oxford, 1979.

Bogue, Ronald. *Deleuze on Music, Painting and the Arts*. New York and London: Routledge, 2003.

———. 'The Minor.' In *Gilles Deleuze: Key Concepts*, edited by Charles J. Stivale, 110–20. 2nd ed. Durham, England: Acumen, 2011.

Bohlman, Philip. 'Ontologies of Music.' In *Rethinking Music*, edited by Nicholas Cook and Mark Everist, 17–34. Oxford and New York: Oxford University Press, 2001.

Bolt, Barbara. 'Heidegger, Handlability, and Praxical Knowledge.' Paper presented at the Australian Council of University Art and Design Schools Conference, University of New South Wales, 25–27 September, 2013. Accessed 22 October 2014. http://acuads.com.au/wp-content/uploads/2014/12/bolt.pdf.

Boretz, Benjamin, Robert Morris and John Rahn, eds. 'A Thousand Plateaus.' *Perspectives of New Music* 46 (2008): 59–158.

Borgdorff, Henk. 'The Debate on Research in the Arts.' *Dutch Journal of Music Theory* 12/1 (2007): 1–17.

Born, Georgina. 'Listening, Mediation, Event: Anthropological and Sociological Perspectives.' *Journal of the Royal Musical Association* 135 (2010): 79–89.

Bost, Matthew and Ronald Walter Greene. 'Affirming Rhetorical Materialism: Enfolding the Virtual and the Actual.' *Western Journal of Communication* 75 (2011): 440–44 (doi:10.1080/10570314.2011.588902).

Boyd, Anne. 'Peter Sculthorpe's *Sun Music I*: An Analysis.' *Miscellanea Musicologica: Adelaide Studies in Musicology* 3 (1968): 3–20.

———. 'Listening to the Landscape.' Interview with Geoff Watt. *POL* (1977): 89.

———. 'Draft Biography.' Unpublished, 1983. Anne Boyd file, Australian Music Centre.

———. 'A Solitary Female Phoenix Reflects on Women in Music.' *Contemporary Music Review* 11 (1994): 39–43.

———. 'Dreaming Voices: Australia and Japan.' In *Intercultural Music: Creation and Interpretation*, edited by Sally Macarthur, Bruce Crossman and Ronaldo Morelos, 9–26. Sydney: Australian Music Centre, 2006.

———. 'Writing the Wrongs? A Composer Reflects.' *Sounds Australian: Igniting the Flame – Documentation & Discourse* 67 (2006): 18–23.

———. 'To *didj* or not to *didj*: Indigenous representation in Margaret Sutherland's *The Young Kabbarli* and Andrew Schultz's *Journey to Horseshoe Bend*.' In *Opera Indigene: Re/presenting First Nations and Indigenous Cultures*, edited by Pamela Karantonis and Dylan Robinson, 93–113. Farnham, UK and Burlington, VT: Ashgate, 2011.

Boyes, Georgina. *The Imagined Village: Culture, Ideology, and the English Folk Revival*. Manchester; New York: Manchester University Press, 1993.

Braidotti, Rosi. *Transpositions: On Nomadic Ethics*. Cambridge, UK and Malden, MA: Polity, 2006.

Brave Old World. *Dus Gezang Fin Geto Lodzh*. Ludwigsburg, Germany: Winter & Winter, 2004. Red House Records CD 134.

Bregman, Albert S. *Auditory Scene Analysis: The Perceptual Organization of Sound*. 2nd MIT Press paperback ed. Cambridge, MA: MIT Press, 1999.

Brophy, Philip. *100 Anime: BFI Screen Guides*. London: BFI Publishing, 2005.

Brown, Bill. *A Sense of Things: The Object Matter of American Literature*. Chicago: University of Chicago Press, 2003.

Brown, Lesley, ed. *The New Shorter Oxford English Dictionary: Volume 1*. Oxford: Clarendon Press, 1993.

Bruhn, Siglind. 'A Concert of Paintings: "Musical Ekphrasis" in the Twentieth Century.' *Poetics Today* 22 (2001): 551–605.

Bryant, Levi, Graham Harman, and Nick Srnicek. *The Speculative Turn: Continental Materialism and Realism*. Melbourne: re.press, 2011.

Buchanan, Ian, and Marcel Swiboda, eds. *Deleuze and Music*. Edinburgh: Edinburgh University Press, 2004.

Bull, Michael and Les Back, eds. *The Auditory Culture Reader*. Oxford and New York: Berg, 2003.

222 *Bibliography*

Burkholder, J. Peter. *Charles Ives: The Ideas Behind the Music*. New Haven: Yale University Press, 1985.

Cage, John. *4'33''. Tacet, any instrument or combination of instruments*. New York: C.F. Peters, 1960.

Campbell, Edward. *Music After Deleuze*. London: Bloomsbury, 2013.

Capon, Edmund. *I Blame Duchamp: My Life's Adventures in Art*. Camberwell, Victoria, Australia: Lantern, 2009.

Carfoot, Gavin. 'Deleuze and Music: A Creative Approach to the Study of Music.' Master of Music (Research) Thesis, University of Queensland, 2004.

Carroll, Lewis. *Alice's Adventures in Wonderland* and *Through The Looking-Glass And What Alice Found There*. London: Vintage Books, 2007 [first published in 1865 and 1871].

Carter, Elliott. *Double Concerto for Harpsichord and Piano with Two Chamber Orchestras*. New York: Associated Music Publishers, 1964.

Cavallaro, Dani. *Art in Anime: The Creative Quest as Theme and Metaphor*. Jefferson, NC: McFarland & Co, 2012.

Celan, Paul. '*Todesfuge*.' In *German Poetry in Transition, 1945–1990*, edited and translated by Charlotte Melin, 85–7. Hanover, New Haven: University Press of New England, 1999.

Ceraso, Steph. '(Re)Educating the Senses: Multimodal Listening, Bodily Learning, and the Composition of Sonic Experiences', *College English* 77/3 (2014): 102–23.

Chion, Michel. *Guide to Sound Objects: Pierre Schaeffer and Musical Research*. Leicester: EARS De Montfort University, 2009[1983]. Accessed 8 October 2015. http://ears.pierrecouprie.fr/IMG/pdf/Chion-guide/GuidePreface.pdf.

——— . 'The Three Modes of Listening.' In *The Sound Studies Reader*, edited by Jonathan Sterne, 48–53. London and New York: Routledge, 2012.

Clarke, Eric F. *Ways of Listening: An Ecological Approach to the Perception of Musical Meaning*. New York: Oxford University Press, 2005.

——— . 'The Impact of Recording on Listening.' *Twentieth-Century Music* 4/1 (2007): 47–70.

Clifton, Thomas. *Music as Heard: A Study in Applied Phenomenology*. New Haven: Yale University Press, 1983.

Cohen, S. Marc. 'Aristotle's Metaphsyics.' *The Stanford Encyclopedia of Philosophy* (Summer 2014 ed.), edited by Edward N. Zalta. Accessed 5 March 2014. http://plato.stanford.edu/archives/sum2014/entries/aristotle-metaphysics/.

Colebrook, Claire. 'Introduction.' In *Deleuze and Feminist Theory*, edited by Ian Buchanan and Claire Colebrook, 1–17. Edinburgh: Edinburgh University Press, 2000.

——— . *Gilles Deleuze*. London and New York: Routledge, 2002.

——— . *Understanding Deleuze*. Crows Nest, Sydney: Allen & Unwin, 2002.

——— . 'On the Very Possibility of Queer Theory.' In *Deleuze and Queer Theory*, edited by Chrysanthi Nigianni and Merl Storr, 11–23. Edinburgh: Edinburgh University Press, 2009.

Colebrook, Claire, and Ian Buchanan, eds. *Deleuze and Feminist Theory*. Edinburgh: Edinburgh University Press, 2000.

Cook, Nicholas. *Music: A Very Short Introduction*. Oxford and New York: Oxford University Press, 1988.

Coole, Diana, and Samantha Frost, eds. *New Materialism: Ontology, Agency, and Politics*. Durham, NC: Duke University Press, 2010.

Cox, Arnie. 'Hearing, Feeling, Grasping Gestures.' In *Music and Gesture*, edited by Anthony Gritten and Elaine King, 45–60. Aldershot: Ashgate, 2006.

Crary, Jonathan. *Suspensions of Perception: Attention, Spectacle and Modern Culture.* An October Book. Cambridge, MA and London: The MIT Press, 2001.

Crisp, Deborah. 'Elements of *Gagaku* in the Music of Anne Boyd.' Honours Thesis, University of Sydney, 1978.

Crossman, Bruce. *Gentleness-Suddenness*, Sydney: Filigree Films, 2014.

———. 'Spiritual Essences: Sounds of an Asian-Pacific Place, Personality and Spirit in *Double Resonances*.' In *Music of the Spirit: Asian-Pacific Musical Identity*, edited by Michael Atherton and Bruce Crossman, 20–32. Sydney, Australian Music Centre, 2008.

———. *In Gentleness and Suddenness*. Wollongong, NSW: Wirripang, 2010.

———. *Not Broken Bruised-Reed*. Wollongong, NSW: Wirripang, 2010.

Culler, Jonathan. 'Presupposition and Intertextuality.' *Modern Language Notes* 91/6 (1976): 1380–96.

Cunniff Gilson, Erinn. 'Responsive Becoming Ethics between Deleuze and Feminism.' In *Deleuze and Ethics*, edited by Nathan Jun and Daniel W. Smith, 63–88. Edinburgh: Edinburgh University Press, 2011.

Dack, John, and Christine North. 'Translating Pierre Schaeffer: Symbolism, Literature and Music.' In *Conference of the Elecrtoacoustic Music Studies Network*. Beijing, 2006. Accessed 8 October 2015. http://www.ems-network.org/IMG/EMS06-JDack.pdf.

Danaher, Geoff, Tony Schirato, and Jen Webb. *Understanding Foucault*. London; Thousand Oaks, CA: Sage Publications, 2000.

Davies, Bronwyn. *Listening to Children: Being and Becoming*. London and New York: Routledge, 2014.

De Man, Paul. 'Hypogram and Inscription: Michael Riffaterre's Poetics of Reading.' *Diacritics* 11/4 (1981): 17–35.

DeLanda, Manuel. *Intensive Science and Virtual Philosophy*. London: Continuum, 2009[2002].

———. 'Emergence, Causality and Realism.' In *The Speculative Turn: Continental Materialism and Realism*, edited by Levi Bryant, Nick Srnicek and Graham Harman, 381–92. Melbourne: re.press, 2011.

———.*Philosophy and Simulation: The Emergence of Synthetic Reason*. New York: Continuum, 2012.

Deleuze, Gilles. *Foucault*, translated by Sean Hand. Minneapolis: University of Minnesota Press, 1988.

———. 'Mediators.' In *Zone 6: Incorporations*, edited by Jonathan Crary and Sanford Kwinter, 280–95. New York: Urzone, 1992.

———. *The Fold: Leibniz and the Baroque*, foreword and translated by Tom Conley. Minneapolis: University of Minnesota Press, 1993.

———. *Difference and Repetition*, translated by Paul Patton. London: Athlone Press, 1994.

———. *Difference and Repetition*, translated by Paul Patton. New York: Columbia University Press, 1994.

———. *Francis Bacon: The Logic of Sensation*, translated by Daniel Smith. New York: Continuum, 2003[1981].

———. *Francis Bacon: The Logic of Sensation*, translated by Daniel Smith. Minneapolis: University of Minnesota Press, 2004.

———. *The Logic of Sense*, translated by Mark Lester with Charles J. Stivale and edited by Constantin V. Boundas. London: Continuum, 2004[1969].

———. 'How Do We Recognize Structuralism?', translated by Michael Taormina. In *Desert Islands and Other Texts, 1953–1974*, edited by David Lapoujade, 170–92. Semiotext(E) Foreign Agents Series. Cambridge, MA: Semiotext(e), 2004[1972].

224 *Bibliography*

Deleuze, Gilles, and Félix Guattari. *Anti-Oedipus: Capitalism and Schizophrenia.* London: Athlone, 1984.

———. *A Thousand Plateaus: Capitalism and Schizophrenia*, translated by Brian Massumi. Minneapolis and London: University of Minnesota Press, 1987.

———. *What is Philosophy?*, translated by Hugh Tomlinson and Graham Burchell. New York: Columbia University Press, 1994[1991].

———. *Kafka: Toward a Minor Literature*, translated by Dana Polan. Minneapolis: University of Minnesota Press, 2003[1986, French 1975].

Deleuze, Gilles, and Claire Parnet. *Dialogues*, translated by Hugh Tomlinson and Barbara Habberjam. New York: Columbia University Press, 1987.

Dell'Antonio, Andrew, ed. *Beyond Structural Listening? Postmodern Modes of Hearing.* Berkeley: University of California Press, 2004.

Demers, Joanna. *Listening Through the Noise: The Aesthetics of Experimental Electronic Music.* Oxford: Oxford University Press, 2010.

Dhomont, Francis. 'Schaeffer, Pierre.' *Grove Music Online. Oxford Music Online.* Oxford: Oxford University Press. Accessed 31 January 2015. http://www.oxfordmusiconline. com/subscriber/article/grove/music/24734.

Doel, Marcus A. 'Representation and Difference.' In *Taking-Place: Non-Representational Theories and Geography*, edited by Ben Anderson and Paul Harrison, 117–30. Farnham, UK and Burlington, VT: Ashgate, 2010.

Dolphijn, Rick, and Iris van der Tuin. *New Materialism: Interviews & Cartographies.* Ann Arbor: Open Humanities Press, 2012.

Dretske, Fred. 'Seeing, Believing and Knowing.' In *Perception*, edited by Robert Schwartz, 268–86. Malden, Oxford, Melbourne and Berlin: Blackwell Publishing, 2004.

The Drunken Emperor Orders His Brother's Execution. Paichangxi Repertoires of Cantonese Opera, Ko Shan Theatre, Kowloon, Hong Kong. 13–14 October 2010.

Eagleton, Terry. *The Ideology of the Aesthetic.* Oxford, UK: Blackwell, 1990.

Emmerson, Simon and Denis Smalley. 'Electro-acoustic music.' In *Grove Music Online.* Oxford: Oxford University Press. Accessed 4 February 2014. http://www.oxfordmusiconline. com/subscriber/article/grove/music/08695.

Everett, Yayoi Uno. 'Calligraphy and Musical Gestures in the Late Works of Chou Wen-Chung.' *Contemporary Music Review* 26/5 (2007): 569–84.

Feld, Steven. 'Aesthetics as Iconicity of Style, or "Lift-up-over Sounding": Getting into the Kaluli Groove.' *Yearbook for Traditional Music* 20 (1988): 74–113.

Fénelon, Fania and Marcelle Routier. *Sursis Pour L'orchestre.* Paris: Stock, 1976.

Fiske, John. *Television Culture.* London and New York: Routledge, 1987.

Flam, Gila. *Singing for Survival: Songs of the Lodz Ghetto, 1940–1945.* Urbana and Chicago: University of Illinois Press, 1992.

Foucault, Michel. *The Order of Things: An Archaeology of the Human Sciences.* New York: Vintage, 1973.

———. 'What is an Author?' In *The Foucault Reader*, edited by Paul Rabinow, 101–20. New York: Pantheon Books, 1984.

———. *Discipline and Punish: The Birth of the Prison.* New York: Vintage Books, 1995.

———. *The Archaeology of Knowledge*, translated by A.M. Sheridan Smith. Oxon: Routledge, 2011.

Franklin, Jim. 'Japanese Shakuhachi Honkyoku Tradition and its Reinterpretation into a Contemporary Composition Practice.' In *Music of the Spirit: Asian-Pacific Musical Identity*, edited by Michael Atherton and Bruce Crossman, 93–102. Sydney: Australian Music Centre, 2008.

Franklin, Peter. *Reclaiming Late Romantic Music: Singing Devils and Distant Sounds*. Berkeley and Los Angeles: University of California Press, 2014.

Garrop, Stacy. String Quartet no. 3, 'Gaia.' King of Prussia: Theodore Presser, 2010[2008].

———. String Quartet no. 3. On *In Eleanor's Words: Music of Stacy Garrop*. Biava Quartet. Cedille 90000 122, 2011. CD.

Gaver, William W. 'How Do We Hear in the World? Explorations in Ecological Acoustics.' *Ecological Psychology* 5/4 (1993): 285–313.

Gier, Christina Bindslev. 'Intertextuality in Music and Gender Ideology in Alban Berg's Modernist Aesthetics.' PhD dissertation, Duke University, 2003.

Gilbert, Shirli. *Music in the Holocaust: Confronting Life in the Nazi Ghettos and Camps*. Oxford: Oxford University Press, 2005.

Gilmore, Leigh. *The Limits of Autobiography: Trauma and Testimony*. Ithaca, NY: Cornell University Press, 2001.

Glieck, James. *Chaos Theory: Making a New Science*. New York: Viking, 1988[1987].

Godlovitch, Stan. *Musical Performance: A Philosophical Study*. London: Routledge, 1998.

Goehr, Lydia. 'How to Do More with Words. Two Views of (Musical) Ekphrasis.' *The British Journal of Aesthetics* 50 (2010): 389–410 (doi:10.1093/aesthj/ayq036).

Gorow, Ron. *Hearing and Writing Music: Professional Training for Today's Musician*. Studio City, California: September Publication, 2006.

Gough, Paul, 'Research in the ERA Era.' Paper presented at the Deputy Deans of Creative Arts Inaugural Conference, The Victorian College of the Arts, University of Melbourne. 1 October 2014. Accessed 4 March 2015. http://ddca.edu.au/wp-content/uploads/2014/10/Gough_DDCA-September-2014.pdf.

Gracyk, Theodore, and Andrew Kania. *The Routledge Companion to Philosophy and Music*. Abingdon and New York: Routledge, 2011.

de Grocheio, Johannes. *De musica*, translated by Albert Seay. Colorado Springs, CO: The Colorado College Music Press, 1974.

Grosz, Elizabeth. 'A Thousand Tiny Sexes: Feminism and Rhizomatics.' *Topoi* 12 (1993): 167–79. Accessed 5 May 2014. http://link.springer.com/article/10.1007%2FBF0082 1854#page-1.

———. 'Bergson, Deleuze and the Becoming of Unbecoming.' *Parallax* 11/2 (2005): 4–13.

———. *Chaos, Territory, Art: Deleuze and the Framing of Earth*. New York: Columbia University Press, 2008.

Guibert, Hervé. 'La Peinture enflame l'écriture', interview with Gilles Deleuze, *Le Mode*, 3 December 1981, 51.

Hainge, Greg. 'Is Pop Music?' In *Deleuze and Music*, edited by Ian Buchanan and Marcel Swiboda, 36–53. Edinburgh: Edinburgh University Press, 2004.

———. *Noise Matters: Towards an Ontology of Noise*. New York: Bloomsbury Academic, 2013.

Hamilton, Andy. *Aesthetics and Music*. New York and London: Continuum, 2007.

Hamm, Charles. '*Graceland* Revisited.' In *Putting Popular Music in Its Place*, edited by Charles Hamm, 299–304. Cambridge: Cambridge University Press, 1995.

Hanslick, Eduard. *Vom Musikalisch-Schönen: Ein Beitrag zur Revision der Ästhetik in der Tonkunst*. Leipzig: Rudolph Weigel, 1854.

Harker, Dave. *Fakesong: The Manufacture of British 'Folksong' 1700 to the Present Day*, Popular Music in Britain. Milton Keynes and Philadelphia: Open University Press, 1985.

Haraway, Donna, 'Situated Knowledges: The Science Question in Feminism and the Privilege of Partial Perspective.' *Feminist Studies* (1988): 575–99.

Harrison, Holly. *Frumious*. Sydney, unpublished, 2012.

226   *Bibliography*

Hatten, Robert S. 'The Place of Intertextuality in Music Studies.' *American Journal of Semiotics* 3/4 (1985): 69–82.

Heidegger, Martin. *Being and Time*, translated by John Macquarrie and Edward Robinson. Oxford: Blackwell, 2005.

Helmholtz, Hermann von. *On the Sensations of Tone as a Physiological Basis for the Theory of Music*, translated by Alexander John Ellis. 2nd English ed. New York: Dover Publications, 1954.

Henry, Ken. 'Australia in the Asian Century: Reflections on the Australian Government White Paper'. Speech delivered at the *Knowing Asia: Asian Studies in an Asian Century, 19th Biennial Conference of the Asian Studies Association*, Parramatta Campus, Western Sydney University, 12–13 July 2012. Accessed 1 December 2014. http://www.uws.edu.au/ics/events/past_events/asaa_conference/asaa_video_15.

Hickey-Moody, Anna, and Peta Malins. *Deleuzian Encounters: Studies in Contemporary Social Issues*. Houndmills, Basingstoke: Palgrave Macmillan, 2007.

Hinton, David. *The Four Chinese Classics: Tao Te Ching, Analects, Chuang Tzu, Mencius*. Berkeley: Counterpoint, 2013.

Ho, Edward. 'Aesthetic Considerations in Understanding Chinese Literati Musical Behavior.' *British Journal of Ethnomusicology* 6 (1997): 35–49.

Hoichiu, Tang. 'The Way of Ink Painting: The Origin and in Search of Zen.' In *Lui Shou-kwan: New Ink Painting*, edited by Tang Hoichiu, 12–15. Hong Kong: Leisure and Cultural Services Department, 2003.

Hu, Tze-yue G. *Frames of Anime: Culture and Image-Building*. Hong Kong: Hong Kong University Press, 2010.

Hughes, Joe. *Philosophy After Deleuze*. London and New York: Bloomsbury, 2012.

Hulse, Brian. 'Thinking Musical Difference: Music Theory as Minor Science.' In *Sounding the Virtual: Gilles Deleuze and the Theory and Philosophy of Music*, edited by Brian Hulse and Nick Nesbitt, 23–50. Farnham, UK and Burlington, VT: Ashgate, 2010.

———. 'Of Genre, System, and Process: Music Theory in a "Global Sonorous Space".' Accessed 15 March 2015. https://www.yumpu.com/user/operascore.com.

Hulse, Brian, and Nick Nesbitt, eds. *Sounding the Virtual: Gilles Deleuze and the Theory and Philosophy of Music*. Farnham, UK and Burlington, VT: Ashgate, 2010.

Husserl, Edmund. *Crisis of European Sciences and Transcendental Phenomenology*, translated by David Carr. Evanston: Northwestern University Press, 1970.

Hwang, Byung-ki. 'Philosophy and Aesthetics in Korea.' In *The Garland Encyclopedia of World Music: East Asia: China, Japan, and Korea*, edited by Robert Provine, J. Lawrence Witzleben and Yosihiko Tokumaru, 813–16. Vol. 7. New York: Routledge, 2001.

Johnson, Julian. *Webern and the Transformation of Nature*. Cambridge: Cambridge University Press, 1999.

Kaczerginski, Szmerke. *Dos Gezang Fun Vilner Geto*. Paris: Farband fun di vilner in frankraykh, 1947.

———. *Undzer Gezang*. Centralny Komitet żydów Polskich: Wydzią Kultury i Propagandy, 1947.

Kaczerginski, Szmerke, Michl Gelbart, and H. Leivick. *Lider Fun Di Getos Un Lagern*. New York: Tsiko, 1948.

Kane, Brian. *Sound Unseen*. New York: Oxford University Press, 2014.

Kania, Andrew. 'The Philosophy of Music.' In *The Stanford Encyclopedia of Philosophy* (Spring 2014 ed.), edited by Edward N. Zalta. Accessed 15 February 2015. http://plato.stanford.edu/archives/spr2014/entries/music/.

Karpinski, Gary S. *Manual for Ear Training and Sight Singing*. New York: Norton, 2007.

Kassabian, Anahid. *Ubiquitous Listening: Affect, Attention, and Distributed Subjectivity.* Berkeley, Los Angeles and London: University of California Press, 2013.

Kaufman, Eleanor. 'Levi-Strauss, Deleuze and the Joy of Abstraction.' *Criticism* 49 (2007): 447–58 (doi:10.1353/crt.0.0045).

Keil, Charles. 'Participatory Discrepancies and the Power of Music.' *Cultural Anthropology* 2/3 (1987): 275–83.

Keller, Hans. *Functional Analysis: The Unity of Contrasting Themes: Complete Edition of the Analytical Scores*, edited by Gerald W. Gruber. Frankfurt am Main: P. Lang, 2001.

Kerman, Joseph. *Contemplating Music: Challenges to Musicology.* Cambridge, MA: Harvard University Press, 1985.

Kilgannon, Corey. 'A Composer's Best Friend.' *The New York Times*, 10 May 2013. Accessed 15 December 2014. http://www.nytimes.com/2013/05/12/nyregion/lucy-mann-keeps-american-composers-spirits-alive.html.

Kim-Cohen, Seth. *In the Blink of an Ear: Towards a Non-Cochlear Sonic Art.* New York: Continuum, 2009.

Klein, Gideon. 'Two Madrigals' (1942, 1943), edited by David Bloch. Berlin: Boosey & Hawkes, 2003.

Klein, Michael L. *Intertextuality in Western Art Music.* Bloomington, Indiana: Indiana University Press, 2005.

Kojève, Alexandre. *Introduction to the Reading of Hegel: Lectures on the Phenomenology of Spirit*, edited by Allan Bloom, translated by James Nichols (orig. French 1947). Ithaca: Cornell University Press, 1980.

Korsyn, Kevin. 'Beyond Privileged Contexts: Intertextuality, Influence, and Dialogue.' In *Rethinking Music*, edited by Nicholas Cook and Mark Everist, 55–72. Oxford and New York: Oxford University Press, 1999.

Kouvaras, Linda. *Loading the Silence: Australian Sound Art in the Post-Digital Age.* Farnham, UK and Burlington, VT: Ashgate, 2013.

———. '"Effing the Ineffable": The Work of Susan McClary and Richard Leppert and (Part of) their Legacy.' *Musicology Australia* 36/1 (2014): 106–20. Accessed 14 February 2015. http://dx.doi.org/10.1080/08145857.2014.911059.

Kristeva, Julia. 'Problèmes de la structuration du texte.' *Tel Quel: Théorie d'ensemble*, 298–317. Paris: Éditions du Seuil, 1968.

———. *La Revolution du langue poétique.* Paris: Éditions du Seuil, 1974.

———. *Revolution in Poetic Language*, translated by Margaret Waller with introduction by Leon S. Roudiez. New York: Columbia University Press, 1984.

———. '"Nous Deux" or a (Hi)story of Intertextuality.' *Romanic Review* 93/1–2 (2002): 7–13.

Laks, Szymon. *Music of Another World*, translated by Chester A. Kisiel. Evanston: Northwestern University Press, 1989.

Lambert, Gregg. *The Non-Philosophy of Gilles Deleuze.* London: Continuum, 2002.

Landy, Leigh. *What's The Matter with Today's Experimental Music? Organized Sound Too Rarely Heard.* New York: Routledge, 1991.

———. *Understanding the Art of Sound Organization.* Cambridge, MA: MIT Press, 2007.

Lau, Frederick. 'Context, Agency and Chineseness: The Music of Law Wing Fai.' *Contemporary Music Review* 26/5 (2007): 585–603.

Lasker-Wallfisch, Anita. *Inherit the Truth, 1939–1945: The Documented Experiences of a Survivor of Auschwitz and Belsen.* London: Giles de la Mare, 1996.

Lecercle, Jean-Jacques. *Philosophy of Nonsense: The Intuitions of Victorian Nonsense Literature.* London and New York: Routledge, 1994.

228 *Bibliography*

Lee, Kang Sook. 'An Essay on Korean Modes.' *Asian Music* 9/2 (1978): 41–7.

Leppert, Richard. *Music and Image: Domesticity, Ideology, and Socio-Cultural Formation in Eighteenth-Century England*. Cambridge: Cambridge University Press, 1989.

Leppert Richard D., and Susan McClary, eds. *Music and Society: The Politics of Composition, Performance, and Reception*. Cambridge: Cambridge University Press, 1987.

Letts, Richard, Huib Schippers, and Helen Lancaster. *Submission to the Higher Education Base Funding Review*. Sydney: Music Council of Australia, 2011.

Levi, Primo. *Se Questo È Un Uomo*. Torino: F. de Silva, 1947.

Levinas, Emmanuel. *Totality and Infinity: An Essay on Exteriority*. Pittsburgh: Duquesne University Press, 1969.

Lipstadt, Deborah E. *The Eichmann Trial*. New York: Nextbook/Schocken, 2011.

Livesey, Graham. 'Assemblage.' In *The Deleuze Dictionary*, edited by Adrian Parr, 18–19. Edinburgh: Edinburgh University Press, 2005.

Lochhead, Judy. 'Lulu's Feminine Performance.' *Cambridge Companion to Berg*, edited by Anthony Pople, 227–44. Cambridge: Cambridge University Press, 1997.

———. 'Hearing *Lulu*.' In *Audible Traces*, edited by Elaine Barkin and Lydia Hamessley, 231–55. Zurich: Carciofoli Verlagshaus, 1999.

———. *Reconceiving Structure in Contemporary Music: New Tools in Music Theory and Analysis*. New York: Routledge, 2015.

Lopez, Alan. 'Deleuze With Carroll.' *Angelaki: Journal of Theoretical Humanities* 9 (2010): 101–20 (doi:10.1080/0969725042000307664).

Lorenz, Edward Norton. 'Deterministic Nonperiodic Flow.' *Journal of Atmospheric Science* 20 (1963): 130–41.

———. 'Predictability: Does the Flap of a Butterfly's Wings in Brazil Set off a Tornado in Texas?' Paper for the American Association for the Advancement of Science. December 1972.

Lorraine, Tamsin. *Deleuze and Guattari's Immanent Ethics: Theory, Subjectivity, and Duration*. New York: State University of New York Press, 2011.

Macarthur, Sally. 'Feminist Aesthetics in Music: Politics and Practices in Australia.' PhD Thesis, University of Sydney, 1997.

———. *Feminist Aesthetics in Music*. Westport, CT and London: Greenwood Press, 2001.

———. 'Women, Spirituality, Landscape: The Music of Anne Boyd, Sarah Hopkins and Moya Henderson.' In *The Soundscapes of Australia: Music, Place and Spirituality*, edited by Fiona Richards, 51–74. Aldershot: Ashgate, 2007.

———. *Towards a Twenty-First-Century Feminist Politics of Music*. Farnham, UK and Burlington, VT: Ashgate, 2010.

McClary, Susan. 'The Blasphemy of Talking Politics During Bach Year.' In *Music and Society: The Politics of Composition, Performance, and Reception*, edited by Richard Leppert and Susan McClary, 13–62. Cambridge: Cambridge University Press, 1987.

———. *Feminine Endings: Music, Gender, and Sexuality*. Minneapolis: University of Minnesota Press, 1991.

———. 'Terminal Prestige: The Case of Avant-Garde Music Composition.' In *Keeping Score: Music, Disciplinarity, Culture*, edited by David Schwarz, Anahid Kassabian, and Lawrence Siegel, 54–74. Charlottesville: University Press of Virginia Press, 1997.

———. *Modal Subjectivities: Self-Fashioning in the Italian Madrigal*. Berkeley and Los Angeles: University of California Press, 2004.

———. 'The World According to Taruskin.' *Music and Letters* 87/3 (2006): 408–15.

———. *Desire and Pleasure in Seventeenth-Century Music*. Berkeley and Los Angeles: University of California Press, 2012.

————. 'The Master Narrative and Me.' *Introduction to The Music History Classroom*, edited by James A.im Davis. Farnham, UK and Burlington, VT: Ashgate Publishing, 2012.

McCreless, Patrick. 'Rethinking Contemporary Music Theory.' In *Keeping Score: Music, Disciplinarity, Culture*, edited by David Schwarz, Anahid Kassabian, and Lawrence Siegel, 1–49. p. 13. Charlottesville: University Press of Virginia Press, 1997.

Maceda, José. 'A Concept of Time in a Music of Southeast Asia (A Preliminary Account).' *Ethnomusicology* 30/1 (1986): 11–53.

McLennan, David and Emma Macdonald. 'ANU reaffirms cuts to music.' *Canberra Times*, 16 June 2012. http://www.canberratimes.com.au/anu-reaffirms-cuts-to-music-20120615-20fuz.html.

McMahon, Melissa. 'Difference, repetition.' In *Gilles Deleuze: Key Concepts*, edited by Charles J. Stivale, 44–5. 2nd edition. Durham: Acumen, 2011.

McNeilly, Kevin. 'Ugly Beauty: John Zorn and the Politics of Postmodern Music.' *Postmodern Culture* 5/2 (1995). Accessed 1 June 2013. http://pmc.iath.virginia.edu/text-only/issue.195/mcneilly.195 (doi:10.1353/pmc.1995.0005).

Mari, Shimosako. 'Japan: Philosophy and Aesthetics.' In *The Garland Encyclopedia of World Music: East Asia: China, Japan, and Korea*, edited by Robert Provine, J. Lawrence Witzleben, and Yosihiko Tokumaru, 545–55. Vol. 7. New York: Routledge, 2001.

Mark, Lindy Li, trans. *Peony Pavilion: Young Lovers' Edition: A life-affirming legend of love and resurrection*. UCLA International Institute: Asia Institute. Accessed 31 May 2011. http://www.international.ucla.edu/china/mudanting/.

Martin, Elaine. 'Art after Auschwitz: Adorno Revisited.' In *New Essays on the Frankfurt School of Critical Theory*, edited by Alfred J. Drake, 193–209. Newcastle upon Tyne, UK: Cambridge Scholars, 2009.

Massumi, Brian. *A User's Guide to Capitalism and Schizophrenia: Deviations from Deleuze and Guattari*. Cambridge, MA: MIT Press, 1992.

Meintjes, Louise. 'Paul Simon's *Graceland*, South Africa, and the Mediation of Musical Meaning.' *Ethnomusicology* 34 (1990): 37–73.

Merleau-Ponty, Maurice. *Phenomenology of Perception*. Routledge Classics. London: Routledge, 2002[1945].

Message, Kylie. 'Territory.' In *The Deleuze Dictionary*, edited by Adrian Parr, 274–6. Edinburgh: Edinburgh University Press, 2005.

Middleton, Richard. 'Popular Music Analysis and Musicology: Bridging the Gap.' *Popular Music* 12/2 (1993): 177–90.

Mills, Sara. *Michel Foucault*. Oxon and New York: Routledge, 2003.

————. *Discourse*. Abingdon, Oxon: Routledge, 2004.

Moss, Merrilee. 'Puppets to Playwrights: Girls on Stage.' In *Australia for Women: Travel and Culture*, edited by Susan Hawthorne and Renate Klein, 142–8. Melbourne: Spinifex Press, 1994.

Müller, Melissa and Reinhard Piechocki. *A Garden of Eden in Hell: The Life of Alice Herz-Sommer*. London: Pan Books, 2006.

Mulvey, Laura. *Visual and Other Pleasures*. Houndmills, Basingstoke, Hampshire: Macmillan, 1989.

Murphy, Timothy S. 'What I Hear is Thinking Too: The Deleuze Tribute Recordings.' In *Deleuze and Music*, edited by Ian Buchanan and Marcel Swiboda, 159–75. Edinburgh: Edinburgh University Press, 2004.

Nancy, Jean-Luc. *Listening*, translated by Charlotte Mandell. New York: Fordham University Press, 2007.

230 Bibliography

Napier, Susan. *Anime from Akira to Princess Mononoke: Experiencing Contemporary Japanese Animation*. New York: Palgrave Macmillan, 2001.

Nuss, Steven. 'Hearing "Japanese", Hearing Takemitsu.' *Contemporary Music Review* 21/4 (2002): 35–71.

Ocker, David. 'Listen to Wagner's Entire Ring Cycle in 1 Second.' Accessed 19 January 2015. http://mixedmeters.com/2010/05/listen-to-wagners-entire-ring-cycle-in.html.

——. 'Wagner's Ring Cycle in Just 7 Minutes.' Accessed 19 January 2015. http://davidocker.com/MMFiles/Wagner-The-Ring-Cycle-complete-in-7-minutes_128x-faster.html.

O'Sullivan, Simon. 'Fold.' In *The Deluze Dictionary*, edited by Adrian Parr, 102–4. Edinburgh: Edinburgh University Press, 2005.

——. *Art Encounters: Deleuze and Guattari's Thought beyond Representation*. Houndmills, Basingstoke: Palgrave Macmillan, 2006.

Oliver, Kelly. *Witnessing: Beyond Recognition*. Minneapolis, MN: University of Minnesota Press, 2001.

Oswald, John. 'Dab' from *Plunderphonics*, posted on YouTube. Accessed 19 January 2015. https://www.youtube.com/watch?v=8xIWLG-F0Ag.

Oval, 94 Diskont (US: Thrill Jockey, 1996), CD and vinyl record.

Papp, Zilia. *Anime and its Roots in Early Japanese Monster Art*. Kent, UK: Global Oriental, 2010.

Pareles, Jon. 'Davy Graham, 68, Widely Influential British Guitarist: [Obituary (Obit)].' *New York Times*, 21 December, 2008, 42.

Parr, Adrian, ed. *The Deleuze Dictionary*. 2nd ed. Edinburgh: Edinburgh University Press, 2010.

Patton, Paul. *Deleuzian Concepts: Philosophy, Colonisation, Politics*. Stanford: Stanford University Press, 2010.

Post, Nora. 'The Many Careers of Bassoonist Loren Glickman: An Interview by Nora Post.' *The Double Reed* 35/2 (2012): 39–55.

Puterbaugh, John David. 'Between Location and Place: A View of Timbre through Auditory Models and Sonopoietic Space.' PhD dissertation, Princeton University, 1999.

Rajan, Tillotama. 'The Phenomenological Allegory: From Death and the Labyrinth to The Order of Things.' *Poetics Today* 19 (1998): 439–66.

Reich, Nancy B. *Clara Schumann: The Artist and the Woman*. Ithaca, NY: Cornell University Press, 2001.

Reyes, Adelaida. 'What Do Ethnomusicologists Do? An Old Question for a New Century.' *Ethnomusicology* 53/1 (2009): 1–17.

Ridley, Aaron. *The Philosophy of Music: Themes and Variations*. Edinburgh: Edinburgh University Press, 2004.

Riffaterre, Michael. *Semiotics of Poetry*. Bloomington, Indiana: Indiana University Press, 1978/London: Methuen, 1980.

——. 'Syllepsis.' *Critical Inquiry* 6/4 (1980): 625–38.

——. 'Fear of Theory.' *New Literary History* 21/4 (1990): 921–38.

——. *Fictional Truth*. Baltimore and London: Johns Hopkins University Press, 1996.

Roeder, John. 'The Craft of Hybrid Composition: Meter, Tonality, and Grouping in Michael Torke's "Adjustable Wrench."' *Perspectives of New Music* 41/22 (2003): 122–58.

Roffe, Jonathan. 'The Revolutionary Dividual.' In *Deleuzian Encounters: Studies in Contemporary Social Issues*, edited by Anna Hickey-Moody and Peta Malins, 40–49. Houndmills, Basingstoke: Palgrave Macmillan, 2007.

Rosen, Alan. *The Wonder of Their Voices: The 1946 Holocaust Interviews of David Boder*. New York: Oxford University Press, 2010.

Rosenberg, Pnina. 'Art of the Holocaust as Spiritual Resistance: The Ghetto Fighters' House Collection.' Block Museum of Art, Northwestern University. Accessed 15 March 2015. http://lastexpression.northwestern.edu/essays/rosenberg.pdf.

Saariaho, Kaija. *Prés.* On *Private Gardens*. Annsi Karttunen, cello. Ondine, 906–2, 1997. CD.

———. *Prés* for Cello and Electronics. London: Chester Music, 2004[1992].

Said, Edward. *Orientalism*. London: Penguin, 2003.

Samson, Jim. 'Analysis in Context.' In *Rethinking Music*, edited by Nicholas Cook and Mark Everist, 35–54. Oxford and New York: Oxford University Press, 1999/2001.

Saslaw, Janna K. 'Forces, Containers, and Paths: The Role of Body-Derived image Schemas in the Conceptualization of Music.' *Journal of Music Theory* 40/2 (1996): 217–43.

Schaeffer, Pierre. *Traité Des Objets Musicaux: Essai Interdisciplines*. 2nd ed. Paris: Éditions du Seuil, 1966.

———. 'Acousmatics.' In *Audio Culture: Readings in Modern Music*, edited by Christoph Cox and Daniel Warner, 76–81. New York and London: Continuum, 2004.

———. *In Search of a Concrete Music*, translated by Christine North and John Dack. California Studies in 20th-Century Music. Berkeley, CA: University of California Press, 2012[1952].

Schaeffer, Pierre, and Pierre Henry. *L'œuvre Musicale*. INA-GRM 6027/6029. 1998. CD.

Schenker, Heinrich. *Free Composition (Der freie Satz)*, translated and edited by Ernst Oster. Vienna: Universal Edition, 1935; New York: Longman, 1979.

Schippers, Huib. 'Blame it on the Germans! A cross-cultural invitation to revisit the foundation of training professional musicians.' In *Preparing Musicians, Making New Sound Worlds*, edited by Orlando Musumeci, 199–208. Barcelona: ISME/ESMUC, 2004.

Schoenberg, Arnold. 'Postlude', *Genesis* Suite. Werner Janssen and Nat Shilkret, 1945; re-released France: Pristine Audio PASC306, 2011. CD.

———. 'Prelude', *Genesis* Suite. US: Capital Records, 1950; reissued EMI, 2001. CD.

———. 'Prelude', *Genesis* Suite. Naxos, 2005. CD.

Scruton, Roger. *The Aesthetics of Music*. Oxford: Oxford University Press, 1999.

S.G.S. Review of Pristine Audio PASC 306, March 2012, accessed 3 March 2015, http://www.classicalcdreview.com/306.html.

Shaw, Caroline. *Partita for 8 Voices* (2009–2011). *Roomful of Teeth*. Brooklyn, NY: New Amsterdam Records, 2012. CD.

Shaw, Jennifer. 'Arnold Schoenberg and the Intertextuality of Composing and Performing.' *Context* 31 (2006): 109–21.

Shigihara, Laura. 'Choose your Seeds', 2009. http://laurashigihara.bandcamp.com/track/choose-your-seeds-in-game. Authorised digital file.

———. 'Choose your Seeds', piano/violin sheet music, arranged Sebastian Wolff, 2009. http://sebastianwolff.info/download/plants-vs-zombies/PvZ-Choose_Your_Seeds.pdf

———. 'Grasswalk', 2009. http://laurashigihara.bandcamp.com/track/grasswalk. Authorised digital file.

———. 'Grasswalk', piano sheet music, arranged Sebastian Wolff, 2009. http://sebastianwolff.info/download/plants-vs-zombies/PvZ-Grasswalk.pdf

Shimosako, Mari. 'Japan: Philosophy and Aesthetics.' In *The Garland Encyclopedia of World Music: East Asia: China, Japan, and Korea*, edited by Robert Provine, Yosihiko Tokumaru and J. Lawrence Witzleben: 545–55. New York: Routledge, 2001.

Skinner, Graeme. *Peter Sculthorpe: The Making of an Australian Composer*. Sydney: University of New South Wales Press, 2007.

Small, Christopher. *Music of the Common Tongue: Survival and Celebration in African American Music*. Hanover, NH: Wesleyan University Press, 1987.

232   *Bibliography*

———. *Music, Society, Education*, with a new Foreword by Robert Walser. Middletown, CT: Wesleyan University Press, 1997.

———. *Musicking: The Meanings of Performing and Listening*. Middletown, CT: Wesleyan University Press, 1998.

Smith, Daniel W. *Essays on Deleuze*. Edinburgh: Edinburgh University Press, 2012.

Smith, Daniel, and John Protevi. 'Gilles Deleuze.' *The Stanford Encyclopedia of Philosophy* (Spring 2013 ed.), edited by Edward N. Zalta. Accessed 15 March 2015. http://plato.stanford.edu/archives/spr2013/entries/deleuze/.

Smith, Hazel, and Roger T. Dean, eds. *Practice-led Research, Research-led Practice in the Creative Arts*. Edinburgh: Edinburgh University Press, 2009.

Smith, Paul. *Kawaii Suite*. In *Childhood in Music*, piano Antonietta Loffredo. Wollongong, NSW: Wirripang, 2011. CD.

Smith, Ronald Bruce, and Tristan Murail. 'An Interview with Tristan Murail.' *Computer Music Journal* 24/1 (2000): 11–19.

Sotheran, Joy. 'Concepts as Organising Elements in Selected Works of Anne Boyd.' Master of Music thesis, University of New South Wales, 1992.

Stagoll, Cliff. 'Difference.' In *The Deleuze Dictionary*, edited by Adrian Parr, 72–3. Edinburgh: Edinburgh University Press, 2005.

———. 'Event.' In *The Deleuze Dictionary*, edited by Adrian Parr, 87. Edinburgh: Edinburgh University Press, 2005.

Steele, Christopher J., Jennifer A. Bailey, Robert J. Zatorre, and Virginia B. Penhune. 'Early Musical Training and White-Matter Plasticity in the Corpus Callosum: Evidence for a Sensitive Period.' *Journal of Neuroscience* 33 (2013): 1282–90 (doi:10.1523/JNEUROSCI.3578–12.2013).

Sterne, Jonathan, ed. *The Sound Studies Reader*. London and New York: Routledge, 2012.

———. 'Hearing, Listening, Deafness.' In *The Sound Studies Reader*, edited by Jonathan Sterne, 19–21. London and New York: Routledge, 2012.

Stewart, Susan. *Nonsense: Aspects of Intertextuality in Folklore and Literature*. Baltimore: Johns Hopkins University Press, 1989.

Straus, Joseph N. 'The "Anxiety of Influence" in Twentieth-Century Music.' *The Journal of Musicology* 9/4 (1991): 430–47.

Stravinsky, Igor. 'The Rite of Spring.' On *Three Favorite Ballets*, cond. Igor Stravinsky. Columbia Masterworks MS3705, 1960. Vinyl record.

Strogatz, Steven H. *Nonlinear Dynamics and Chaos: With Applications to Physics, Biology, Chemistry, and Engineering*. Boulder, CO: Westview Press, 2001.

Stuckenschmidt, Hans Heinz. *Schoenberg: His Life, World and Work*, translated by Humphrey Searle. New York: Schirmer, 1977.

Subotnik, Rose Rosengard. *Deconstructive Variations: Music and Reason in Western Society*. Minneapolis: University of Minnesota Press, 1996.

Suzuki, Daisetz Taitaro. *Zen and Japanese Culture*. Princeton: Princeton University Press, 2010.

Szendy, Peter. *Listen: A History of Our Ears*. New York: Fordham University Press, 2008.

Tang, Hoichiu. 'The Way of Ink Painting: The Origin and in Search of Zen.' In *Lui Shou-kwan: New Ink Painting*, edited by Tang Hoichiu, 12–15. Hong Kong: Leisure and Cultural Services Department, 2003.

Taruskin, Richard. *Music in the Late Twentieth Century*. Oxford and New York: Oxford University Press, 2005.

———. *Oxford History of Western Music*. Oxford: Oxford University Press, 2005.

———. *Music in the Nineteenth Century*. New York: Oxford University Press, 2010.

Thomson, Virgil. 'Why Composers Write How.' In *Virgil Thomson: A Reader: Selected Writings, 1924–1984*, edited by Richard Kostelanetz, 22–46. New York: Routledge, 2002.

Tibbs, Kathryn. 'East and West in the Music of Anne Boyd.' Honours thesis, University of Sydney, 1989.

Tinctoris, Johannes. *Liber de arte contrapuncti* (1477), translated by Albert Seay. Rome: American Institute of Musicology, 1961.

Tomlinson, Gary. *Music in Renaissance Magic: Toward a Historiography of Others*. Chicago: University of Chicago Press, 1993.

Tobin, Joseph. *Pikachu's Global Adventure: The Rise and Fall of Pokémon*. Durham, NC: Duke University Press, 2004.

Tone, Yasunao. *Solo for Wounded*. New York: Tzadik TZ 7212, 1997. CD.

Tone, Yasunao and Christian Marclay. 'Record, CD, Analog, Digital.' In *Audio Culture: Readings in Modern Music*, edited by Christoph Cox and Daniel Warner, 341–47. New York and London: Continuum, 2004.

Tregear, Peter J. *Enlightenment or Entitlement? Rethinking Tertiary Music Education*. Platform Papers. Quarterly Essays on The Performing Arts 38. Strawberry Fields, NSW: Currency Press, 2014.

Tymoczko, Dmitri. *A Geometry of Music: Harmony and Counterpoint in the Extended Common Practice*. New York: Oxford University Press, 2011.

Voeglin, Salomé. *Listening to Noise and Silence: Towards a Philosophy of Sound Art*. New York: Continuum, 2010.

Walser, Robert. 'Eruptions: Heavy Metal Appropriations of Classical Virtuosity.' *Popular Music* 2 (1992): 263–308.

————, ed. *The Christopher Small Reader*. Middletown, CT: Wesleyan University Press, forthcoming.

Weale, Robert, 'Discovering How Accessible Electroacoustic Music Can Be: The Intention/Reception Project.' *Organised Sound* 11/2 (2006): 189–200.

Weber, William. 'Consequences of Canon: Institutionalization of Enmity between Contemporary and Classical Music, c. 1910.' *Common Knowledge* 9 (2003): 78–99.

————. *The Great Transformation of Musical Taste: Concert Programming from Haydn to Brahms*. Cambridge: Cambridge University Press, 2008.

Website of The Australian Council of Deans and Directors of Creative Arts. Accessed 4 March 2015. http://ddca.edu.au/.

Weiss, Piero and Richard Taruskin, eds. *Music in the Western World*. New York: Schirmer, 1984.

Wen-Chung, Chou. 'The Aesthetic Principles of Chinese Music: A Personal Quest.' *Canzona* 7/4 (1986): 74–8.

————. '*Wenren* and Culture.' In *Locating East Asia in Western Art Music*, edited by Yayoi Uno Everett and Frederick Lau, 208–20. Middletown, CT: Wesleyan University Press, 2004.

Wessel, David L. 'Timbre Space as a Musical Control Structure.' *Computer Music Journal* 3/2 (1979): 45–52.

White-Schwoch, Travis, Kali Woodruff Carr, Samira Anderson, Dana L. Strait, and Nina Kraus. 'Older Adults Benefit from Music Training Early in Life: Biological Evidence for Long-Term Training-Driven Plasticity.' *Journal of Neuroscience* 33/45 (2013): 17667–74 (doi:10.1523/JNEUROSCI.2560–13).

Whitesell, Lloyd. 'Men with a Past: Music and the "Anxiety of Influence."' *19th-Century Music* 18/2 (1994): 152–67.

Wiesel, Elie. *Un Di Velt Hot Geshvign*. Buenos Aires: Tsentral-farband fun poylische yidn in Argentine, 1956.

234 *Bibliography*

———. *Night; Dawn; [and], the Accident: Three Tales*, translated by Stella Rodway, Frances Frenaye, and Anne Borchardt. London: Robson Books, 1974.

Wilkins, Inigo. 'Enemy of Music.' Blog entry, 6 March 2013. Accessed 14 March 2013. http://irreversiblenoise.wordpress.com/2013/03/06/enemy-of-music/.

Williams, James. *Gilles Deleuze's 'Difference and Repetition': A Critical Introduction and Guide*. Edinburgh: Edinburgh University Press, 2003.

———. 'Identity.' In *The Deleuze Dictionary*, edited by Adrian Parr, 124–5. Edinburgh: Edinburgh University Press, 2005.

———. *Gilles Deleuze's 'Logic of Sense': A Critical Introduction and Guide*. Edinburgh: Edinburgh University Press, 2008.

Williams, Joseph. 'Londonderry Air Jo Williams.' *YouTube* video 3:15. Accessed 15 July 2014. https://www.youtube.com/watch?v=fznYNygYAIk.

———. 'Sakura Jo Williams.' *YouTube* video 5:58. Accessed 15 July 2014. https://www.youtube.com/watch?v=5bs3pvkEb7Q&feature=youtu.be.

Williams, Rita. 'Asian Influences are Integral to the Music of Anne Boyd.' Honours thesis, University of Sydney, 1996.

Windsor, Luke. 'A Perceptual Approach to the Description and Analysis of Acousmatic Music.' PhD thesis. London: City University 1995. Accessed 24 April 2013. http://www.zainea.com/Acousmatic.htm.

Wise, Macgregor J. 'Assemblage.' In *Gilles Deleuze: Key Concepts*, edited by Charles J. Stivale, 77–87. Chesham, UK: Acumen, 2005.

Wishart, Trevor, ed. *On Sonic Art*. The Netherlands: Harwood Academic Publishers, 1996.

Wolff, Christoph. *Johann Sebastian Bach: The Learned Musician*. New York: W.W. Norton, 2001.

———. *Mozart at the Gateway to His Fortune: Serving the Emperor, 1788–1791*. New York: W.W. Norton, 2012.

Woodward, Ashley. 'Deleuze and Suicide.' In *Deleuzian Encounters: Studies in Contemporary Social Issues*, edited by Anna Hickey-Moody and Peta Malins, 62–76. Houndmills, Basingstoke: Palgrave Macmillan, 2007.

Xianzu, Tang. *The Peony Pavilion: Mudan ting*, translated by Cyril Birch. 2nd ed. Bloomington: Indiana University Press, 2002.

Xin, Yang. 'Approaches to Chinese Painting: Part 1.' In *Three Thousand Years of Chinese Painting*, edited by Richard Barnhart, Yang Xin, Nie Chongzheng, James Cahill, Lang Shaojun, and Wu Hung. 1–4. New Haven: Yale University Press, 2002.

Young, Rob. *Electric Eden: Unearthing Britain's Visionary Music*. London: Faber and Faber, 2010.

Zappa, Frank. '4'33".' On *A Chance Operation: The John Cage Tribute*. Koch International Classics 3-7238-2 Y6x2, 1993. CD.

Zbibkowski, Lawrence. *Conceptualizing Music. Cognitive Structure, Theory, and Analysis*. New York: Oxford University Press, 2002.

Zeller, Beatriz. 'On Translation and Authorship.' *Meta: Journal des Traducteurs* 45 (2000): 134–9 (doi:10.7202/004640ar).

Zepke, Stephen. 'Becoming a Citizen of the World: Deleuze Between Allan Kaprow and Adrian Piper.' In *Deleuze and Performance*, edited by Laura Cull, 109–25. Edinburgh: Edinburgh University Press, 2009.

Index

abstraction and listening 109–10
academic music machine 3–4, 17–23
acousmatic listening 179–86
acousmatic music 106; and vision 12
actual dimension 103
Adjustable Wrench (Torke) 154, 156
Adorno, Theodor 190
Aeon time 95
agential realism 11
'aition' concept 49
Albrecht-Crane, Christa 204
Al-Nakib, Ali 145
Andriessen, Louis 150
anime impacting music 120, 139–47
anthropomorphism 202–5, 213
applied aesthetics 117–22
Aristotle 102–3
art and logic of sensation 118–19
art-becoming 121
art criticism 72, 74–75
art-thinking 118, 121–2
Asian-Pacific: influence on composition 125–35; and materialities of sound 131–3
As I Crossed a Bridge of Dreams (Boyd, 1975) 97
assemblage 3–4, 5, 12, 19–21, 51, 53, 60; creative-theoretical 47; territorial 4
Atlman, Kitia 192
Attali, Jacques 208
Augoyard, Jean-François 103
Austern, Linda 28
Australia 30; influence on music 125–6; landscape influencing music 91–92, 96
Australian Council of Deans and Directors of Creative Arts (DDCA) 46
Austro-German music, superiority of 17
author-function 47, 49
auto-connoisseurship 49

Babbitt, Milton 29
Bach, Johann Sebastian 26–28
Bacon, Francis 59, 65, 72, 118
Bakhtin, Mikhail 37
Barad, Karen 10, 11, 48
Barrett, Estelle 49
becoming 3, 22–23, 59, 121–2, 203–5
becoming-landscape-becoming-music 97
becoming-minor 59, 67, 68
becoming-woman 59, 64–67, 90–91
Beethoven, Ludwig van 181
Benjamin, Andrew 212
Bennett, Jane 121
block organisation of time as musical portmanteau 161–5
Boder, David 191, 194
body: in continuous sense of change 63; dynamic nature of 94; and sound 188
body of sensations 7, 65, 66
body without organs 7
Bolt, Barbara 49
Borgdorff, Henk 122
Born, Georgina 194
Boyd, Anne 6, 61, 90–99; associated with Australian landscape 91–92, 96; associated with South East Asian music 92–93, 96; changing aesthetic of her music 96; identified as female composer 93–94; music as multiplicity of relations 98–99; plane of immanence and 94–98; as a solitary figure 91–92
break lines 61
Brophy, Philip 141
Bruhn, Siglind 140
Burkholder, Peter 150

236 *Index*

calligraphy, Japanese 127–8, 133
Cantonese opera 127, 133
Capon, Edmund 127
Carfoot, Gavin 9
Carolina Chisel Show, The 61, 62
Carroll, Lewis 149
Carter, Elliott 201
causality 10
causal listening 173
Celan, Paul 190
change affected by producing
    knowledge 64–67
chaos 73–74 118
chaos theory 64
chaotic mappings 72–88
character strands 76–82
Chion, Michel 108, 173
chordal portmanteaus 158
Chronos time 95
classical music, supremacy of 26–31
Colebrook, Claire 9, 60, 62, 90–91
collective assemblage of enunciation
    6, 17, 20–22, 47–49, 53, 62, 90,
    93, 96–98
colour's impact on music 133–4
complicity signified by music in the
    Holocaust 189–92
composer: elevated status of 180; as a
    woman 60, 62, 64, 67, 90, 93–94
composer-identity 60, 62
composition influenced by the Asian
    Pacific 125–35
comprehending and listening 109–10
Confucius 127
conservatorium assemblage 62;
    deterritorialisation of 20–21
Coole, Diana 209
corporeal realm vs physical realm 95
Crary, Jonathan 179, 183
Creation (Haydn) 41
creation, power of 9
creative arts as a form of research 46–54
creative-theoretical assemblage 47, 51–54
creativity 11, 19, 47, 49–51; and spirit 129
cross-cultural border crossings 128
Crossman, Bruce 120
Crossman, Wallace 127, 134
Culler, Jonathan 38
cutting edges of deterritorialisation 47

dao 129
Davies, Bronwyn 6, 188
Dean, Roger T. 49–50, 128

DeLanda, Manuel 10, 64
Deleuze, Gilles 1–3, 7–9, 19–20, 23,
    47–48, 51, 67, 91, 93–94, 208; art-
    thinking 65, 72–74, 118; relation and
    effect 102–3
Deleuzian concept of territory 19
Deleuzian ontologies 10–11, 201–16
De Man, Paul 37
descriptive mapping 75–76
desiring-machine 175–6, 184
deterritorialisation 47–48, 53, 66–67,
    204–5; of conservatorium assemblage
    20–21; and intertextuality 21; for
    tertiary music institutions 21
deyi 128
dichotomies in rhythm 150–1
difference 202, 205; managing 10, 202
difference feminism 62, 63
difference-in-itself 93–94
direction and elation movement in
    'Gaia' 82, 85–87
discursive space 37–38
dividual 5–6, 60
dividual assemblage 60–64

Eagleton, Terry 190
effect as a special relation 103
egalitarian feminism 63
Eichmann, Adolf 189
ekphrasis 140, 145
ekstasis in 'Gaia' 82, 84–88
electronics strand 76–82
emergence 10
emergent listening 174, 188
evental time 94–95, 98
everyday listening 108
exchange between two art medias 145–6

facture 105
feminism 61, 65, 90; approach to
    compositional identity 59–64; politics in
    music 61–64
Flam, Gila 191
'fold' idea of Deleuze 2, 146–7
folk-baroque 52–53
Foucault, Michel 2, 49, 127, 180
Franklin, Jim 129, 130
Frost, Samantha 209
Frumious (Harrison, 2012) 149–66

'Gaia,' fifth movement (Garrop, 2008)
    82–88
Gaia motive 82–84

Index   237

game music 41–42
Garrop, Stacy 6, 12, 82
German music, supremacy of 25, 27–28
gestures strand 76–82
Gilbert, Shirli 191
glisses 76–82
Godlovitch, Stan 210
Graceland (Simon) 30
Graham, Davy 51–52
Grainger, Percy 126
Granel, Gérard 193
Grisey, Gérard 126
Grocheio, Johannes de 30
groove and rhythm 154–7, 159
Grosz, Elizabeth 73, 91, 118, 203
Guanzhong, Wu 127
Guattari, Félix 1, 3, 8, 19–20, 23, 47–48, 67, 72, 74, 91, 93–94

Hamilton, Andy 207
handlability 47, 49
Hanslick, Euard 28
haptic hearing 119
Harrison, Holly 120
hearing 174; for understanding 188
Ho, Edward 127, 129
Hoichiu, Tang 128
Holocaust and role of music 188–95
homogeneity in music academia 17
human reciprocity between non-human beings 7–8
hybridity of composition 125–6

identity 5–6, 10, 12, 203; as an hierarchy 92–93; as becoming 5, 6; categories 5; as a composer 60, 62; knowable 6; relation of 102; unknowable 6; of women in music 60–64, 91–94
immanence 8–9, 10; in creative arts research 46–54; of theory and practice 51–54
immanent listening 8–9, 171–85
infinite fold 2
In Gentleness and Suddenness (Crossman, 2003) 130, 133–4
'inside-the-note' 130
institutional assemblage 60, 61
intertextuality 5, 11, 19, 21; of listening, performing and teaching 36–44
interval-colour 131–3
intra-actions 11, 50, 64, 66
intra-activity of theory and practice 10, 48–49, 51, 117

iterative cyclic web of research 47, 49–50
Ives, Charles 150

Japanese calligraphy 127–8, 133
Jewish Holocaust survivors and role of music 188–95
juxtapositions in music 149–50

Kaczerginski, Szmerke 191
Karttunen, Anssi 76, 77
Kassabian, Anahid 175
kawaii aesthetics 120, 139–47; and power 142–4
Kawaii Suite (Smith) 139, 143–4
Klein, Gideon 193
knowable identity 6
knowledge production 47; affecting change 64–67
Kristeva, Julia 2, 37–39, 43

landscape impacting music 96–97
lateral thinking 127–8
law of normativity 91
Leppert, Richard 28
Levinas, Emmanuel 194
Levi, Primo 189
life as an infinity of folds 2
lines of flight 48
Lipstadt, Deborah 189
listening 171, 174–6, 192–5; acousmatic 179–86; causal 173; emergent 174, 188; everyday 108; immanent 8–9, 171–6; multiplicity of 173; musical 108; ordinary and specialist 108–11; reduced 106, 108, 173; reflective 174–5; re-imagining of 12; and representation 171–2; semantic 173
listening subject and musical object 7, 109–10, 192–4
living colours aesthetic of musical sound 120, 125–35
logic of sensation 65, 66, 72, 75; and art 118–19
'Londonderry Air' (*Sillage*, 2015) 52
Lorenz, Edmund 64

ma and musical structure 125, 126, 129–31, 133
Macarthur, Sally 30
machine 3
machinic assemblage 3, 17, 20, 47–51, 52–53
Madrigal (Klein, 1943) 193

238 Index

majoritarian practices 5
Martin, Elaine 190
materialities of sounding 7–8, 117–66, 203, 205, 209–11
material thinking 121
McClary-machine 20, 23
McMahon, Melissa 10
Mediations on a Chinese Character (Boyd, 1996) 96
mediators 51–54
Mendelssohn, Felix 27
Merleau-Ponty, Maurice 66
Middleton, Richard 154
mind of the artist 125–6, 128
minoritarian: music 59, 67, 68; tendencies 4–5, 23
'Mokona' (Smith, 2011) 143–4
molar lines 4, 22, 48, 52, 61, 91
molecular lines 22, 48
Mozart, Wolfgang Amadeus 27
multiplicity 6, 60
Murail, Tristan 126
Murakami, Takashi 141
music: criticism 72–75; as a discrete category 18–19; fear of in England 28; as a form of research 19; impacting landscape 96–97; material 209–11; non-human agency in 207–16; as relations 104; role in Jewish Holocaust survivors' lives 188–95; as sensation 73–75; visual rendition of 175; and the written text 179–86
music academia, homogeneity in 17
musical design as musical portmanteau 160–1
musical ekphrasis 140, 145
musical listening 108
musical object 104, 105; and listening subject 7, 109–10, 192–4
musical ontology. *See* ontology
musical portmanteaus 149–66; block organisation of time 161–5; musical design 160–1; rhythm 150–8; sonority juxtapositions 158–60
musical silence 120
musical sound 104–5
musical testimony 188–95
musical training 21–22
music education 36–37
musicianly 104
music institution, transformation of 22
musicking 5, 11, 17, 18, 26
music science 27

music studies, increasing inclusivity of 25–33
music theory 180–1
music-thinking 118–19
Musikwissenschaft 27
musique concrète 104

Nancy, Jean-Luc 2, 174, 188; and listening 192–3
negative desire 183–4
new, production of 7
noise 208–9; distinguished from sound 106–7
noise strand 76–82
non-human agency in music 207–16
non-human beings' reciprocity between human 7–8
nonsense as a genre 149–50, 166
Not Broken Bruised Reed (Crossman, 2009) 131–3
Nuss, Stephen 127

objectivity and listening 109–10
Oliver, Kelly 194
online learning 21
ontology 10–11, 12, 201–16; of difference 11, 202
ordinary listening 108–11

Peony Pavilion: Mudan ting, The (Xianzu) 133
perceiving and listening 109–10
perceptual activity of listener 173–4
performance as feature of music 210–11
permanence 107
phenomena 11
philosophy, defined 72
physical realm vs corporeal realm 95
pitch and timbre 107
pitch areas 76–82
plane of composition 8–9
plane of consistency 8–9
plane of immanence 8–9, 173; and Anne Boyd 94–98
plane of representation 93, 172
plane of transcendence 8–9
Plants vs. Zombies (video game) 41
political feminism 61–64
portmanteau 120, 149, 166
power and *kawaii* aesthetics 142–4
practice-led research 22, 47–54
Prelude to the *Genesis* movie (Schoenberg) 39–41

Près, Movement 1, for cello and electronics (Saariaho, 1992) 76–82
principle of non-contradiction 103

qi 129, 134

reception of music 213–14
reduced listening 106, 108, 173
reflective listening 174–5
reflective thinking 48–51
re-imagining of listening 12
relation of identity 102
relation of opposition 102
relations as connections 102–3
representational modes of thinking 6
representation of woman composers 91–94
research 46–54; practice-led 22
resistance signified by music in the Holocaust 191–2
resonance 131–2; and silence 193
reterritorialisation 205
Reyes, Adelaida 194
rhythm as musical portmanteau 150–8
Riffaterre, Michael 37, 39, 43
Roeder, John 154
Ryohei, Miyata 127

Saariaho, Kaija 6, 12, 76
'Sakura' (*Sillage*, 2015) 53
Samson, Jim 36
Schaeffer, Pierre 6, 12, 68, 102–12, 173, 182; interdisciplinary method of research 104–5; listening model 108–11; sound effects 106–7; structuralism of 111–12
Schoenberg, Arnold 25, 39–41
Schulthorpe, Peter 92, 93, 126
Schumann, Clara 27, 62
Schumann, Robert 27
score, musical 179
Scruton, Roger 31, 207
semantic listening 173
sensation 73–75
Serafin Canticles (Boyd, 2008) 96
Shigihara, Laura 41–42
Shilkret, Nat 40
Shou-Kwan, Lui 127, 128
sight as source of knowledge 179
silence as resonance 193
Sillage (album) 51–52
Simon, Paul 30
situated knowledge 49
Small, Christopher 5, 17, 26

Smith, Daniel 7, 72, 122
Smith, Hazel 49–50, 128
Smith, Paul 120
Solo for Wounded CD (Tone, 1997) 203, 214–15
sonic colour 126
sonic effect 103, 105, 107
sonic object 173–4
sonority juxtapositions as musical portmanteau 158–60
sonorous material/sonority 9, 85–86, 107, 109, 120, 128, 131, 149, 192–3
sound 192–3; distinguished from noise 106–7
sound-art 207
sound-block 151–4
sound effects 106–7
sounding materialities 7–8, 12, 131–3
sound object 68, 107
sound sensation 119
specialist listening 108–11
spectacular culture 183
spirit 129; and mind in music composition 125–6
spiritual resistance of music in the Holocaust 191–2
stasis and equilibrium moment in 'Gaia' 82–87
Stewart, Susan 149, 166
structuralism of Pierre Schaeffer 111–12
subjectivity and listening 109–10
suikinkutsu producing music 211–13

Taizan, Kawamuru 130
Taruskin, Richard 179, 182
territorial assemblages in music institutions 4
territorialisation 47–48, 204–5; mechanisms 17; of woman composer 91
theory and practice in creative arts research 46–54
thing-power 121
thinking as the Other 127
thinking Chinese 127
Thomson, Virgil 31
threshold 19, 39–40
timbre 105; altered 131–3; and pitch 107
time signatures, shifting 151–4
time, two-directional concept of 95–96
Tinctoris, Johannes 32
Tone, Yasunao 203, 214
Torke, Michael 154, 156

240   *Index*

transcendence 8–9
transcendental 9

ungrammaticalities 39
Uninkowski, Israel 194
unknowable identity 6
unspoken word 125, 128

virtual, actualization of 172
virtual dimension 103
virtual whole of being 2
vision: and acousmatic music 12; and
    hearing 174
visual deterritorialised into musical 140,
    145–6

Walser, Robert 32
Wen-Chung, Chou 128, 129

Western art music 17–18
Whitehead, Gillian 61
Wiesel, Elie 189, 191
Wilkins, Inigo 215
Williams, James 5, 8
Wolff, Christoph 27
women, becomings of 59, 64–67, 90–91
women composers 60, 62, 64, 67, 90,
    93–94
Woolf, Virginia 31

Xin, Yang 128

Young, Ian 37
yun 134
yurui 141

Zorn, John 150